Lecture Notes in
Computer Science

Lecture Notes in Computer Science

Vol. 296: R. Janßen (Ed.), Trends in Computer Algebra. Proceedings, 1987. V, 197 pages. 1988.

Vol. 297: E.N. Houstis, T.S. Papatheodorou, C.D. Polychronopoulos (Eds.), Supercomputing. Proceedings, 1987. X, 1093 pages. 1988.

Vol. 298: M. Main, A. Melton, M. Mislove, D. Schmidt (Eds.), Mathematical Foundations of Programming Language Semantics. Proceedings, 1987. VIII, 637 pages. 1988.

Vol. 299: M. Dauchet, M. Nivat (Eds.), CAAP '88. Proceedings, 1988. VI, 304 pages. 1988.

Vol. 300: H. Ganzinger (Ed.), ESOP '88. Proceedings, 1988. VI, 381 pages. 1988.

Vol. 301: J. Kittler (Ed.), Pattern Recognition. Proceedings, 1988. VII, 668 pages. 1988.

Vol. 302: D.M. Yellin, Attribute Grammar Inversion and Source-to-source Translation. VIII, 176 pages. 1988.

Vol. 303: J.W. Schmidt, S. Ceri, M. Missikoff (Eds.), Advances in Database Technology – EDBT '88. X, 620 pages. 1988.

Vol. 304: W.L. Price, D. Chaum (Eds.), Advances in Cryptology – EUROCRYPT '87. Proceedings, 1987. VII, 314 pages. 1988.

Vol. 305: J. Biskup, J. Demetrovics, J. Paredaens, B. Thalheim (Eds.), MFDBS 87. Proceedings, 1987. V, 247 pages. 1988.

Vol. 306: M. Boscarol, L. Carlucci Aiello, G. Levi (Eds.), Foundations of Logic and Functional Programming. Proceedings, 1986. V, 218 pages. 1988.

Vol. 307: Th. Beth, M. Clausen (Eds.), Applicable Algebra, Error-Correcting Codes, Combinatorics and Computer Algebra. Proceedings, 1986. VI, 215 pages. 1988.

Vol. 308: S. Kaplan, J.-P. Jouannaud (Eds.), Conditional Term Rewriting Systems. Proceedings, 1987. VI, 278 pages. 1988.

Vol. 309: J. Nehmer (Ed.), Experiences with Distributed Systems. Proceedings, 1987. VI, 292 pages. 1988.

Vol. 310: E. Lusk, R. Overbeek (Eds.), 9th International Conference on Automated Deduction. Proceedings, 1988. X, 775 pages. 1988.

Vol. 311: G. Cohen, P. Godlewski (Eds.), Coding Theory and Applications 1986. Proceedings, 1986. XIV, 196 pages. 1988.

Vol. 312: J. van Leeuwen (Ed.), Distributed Algorithms 1987. Proceedings, 1987. VII, 430 pages. 1988.

Vol. 313: B. Bouchon, L. Saitta, R.R. Yager (Eds.), Uncertainty and Intelligent Systems. IPMU '88. Proceedings, 1988. VIII, 408 pages. 1988.

Vol. 314: H. Göttler, H.J. Schneider (Eds.), Graph-Theoretic Concepts in Computer Science. Proceedings, 1987. VI, 254 pages. 1988.

Vol. 315: K. Furukawa, H. Tanaka, T. Fujisaki (Eds.), Logic Programming '87. Proceedings, 1987. VI, 327 pages. 1988.

Vol. 316: C. Choffrut (Ed.), Automata Networks. Proceedings, 1986. VII, 125 pages. 1988.

Vol. 317: T. Lepistö, A. Salomaa (Eds.), Automata, Languages and Programming. Proceedings, 1988. XI, 741 pages. 1988.

Vol. 318: R. Karlsson, A. Lingas (Eds.), SWAT 88. Proceedings, 1988. VI, 262 pages. 1988.

Vol. 319: J.H. Reif (Ed.), VLSI Algorithms and Architectures – AWOC 88. Proceedings, 1988. X, 476 pages. 1988.

Vol. 320: A. Blaser (Ed.), Natural Language at the Computer. Proceedings, 1988. III, 176 pages. 1988.

Vol. 321: J. Zwiers, Compositionality, Concurrency and Partial Correctness. VI, 272 pages. 1989.

Vol. 322: S. Gjessing, K. Nygaard (Eds.), ECOOP '88. European Conference on Object-Oriented Programming. Proceedings, 1988. VI, 410 pages. 1988.

Vol. 323: P. Deransart, M. Jourdan, B. Lorho, Attribute Grammars. IX, 232 pages. 1988.

Vol. 324: M.P. Chytil, L. Janiga, V. Koubek (Eds.), Mathematical Foundations of Computer Science 1988. Proceedings. IX, 562 pages. 1988.

Vol. 325: G. Brassard, Modern Cryptology. VI, 107 pages. 1988.

Vol. 326: M. Gyssens, J. Paredaens, D. Van Gucht (Eds.), ICDT '88. 2nd International Conference on Database Theory. Proceedings, 1988. VI, 409 pages. 1988.

Vol. 327: G.A. Ford (Ed.), Software Engineering Education. Proceedings, 1988. V, 207 pages. 1988.

Vol. 328: R. Bloomfield, L. Marshall, R. Jones (Eds.), VDM '88. VDM – The Way Ahead. Proceedings, 1988. IX, 499 pages. 1988.

Vol. 329: E. Börger, H. Kleine Büning, M.M. Richter (Eds.), CSL '87. 1st Workshop on Computer Science Logic. Proceedings, 1987. VI, 346 pages. 1988.

Vol. 330: C.G. Günther (Ed.), Advances in Cryptology – EUROCRYPT '88. Proceedings, 1988. XI, 473 pages. 1988.

Vol. 331: M. Joseph (Ed.), Formal Techniques in Real-Time and Fault-Tolerant Systems. Proceedings, 1988. VI, 229 pages. 1988.

Vol. 332: D. Sannella, A. Tarlecki (Eds.), Recent Trends in Data Type Specification. V, 259 pages. 1988.

Vol. 333: H. Noltemeier (Ed.), Computational Geometry and its Applications. Proceedings, 1988. VI, 252 pages. 1988.

Vol. 334: K.R. Dittrich (Ed.), Advances in Object-Oriented Database Systems. Proceedings, 1988. VII, 373 pages. 1988.

Vol. 335: F.A. Vogt (Ed.), CONCURRENCY 88. Proceedings, 1988. VI, 401 pages. 1988.

Vol. 336: B.R. Donald, Error Detection and Recovery in Robotics. XXIV, 314 pages. 1989.

Vol. 337: O. Günther, Efficient Structures for Geometric Data Management. XI, 135 pages. 1988.

Vol. 338: K.V. Nori, S. Kumar (Eds.), Foundations of Software Technology and Theoretical Computer Science. Proceedings, 1988. IX, 520 pages. 1988.

Vol. 339: M. Rafanelli, J.C. Klensin, P. Svensson (Eds.), Statistical and Scientific Database Management. Proceedings, 1988. IX, 454 pages. 1989.

Vol. 340: G. Rozenberg (Ed.), Advances in Petri Nets 1988. VI, 439 pages. 1988.

Vol. 341: S. Bittanti (Ed.), Software Reliability Modelling and Identification. VII, 209 pages. 1988.

Vol. 342: G. Wolf, T. Legendi, U. Schendel (Eds.), Parcella '88. Proceedings, 1988. 380 pages. 1989.

Vol. 343: J. Grabowski, P. Lescanne, W. Wechler (Eds.), Algebraic and Logic Programming. Proceedings, 1988. 278 pages. 1988.

Vol. 344: J. van Leeuwen, Graph-Theoretic Concepts in Computer Science. Proceedings, 1988. VII, 459 pages. 1989.

Vol. 345: R.T. Nossum (Ed.), Advanced Topics in Artificial Intelligence. VII, 233 pages. 1988 (Subseries LNAI).

Vol. 346: M. Reinfrank, J. de Kleer, M.L. Ginsberg, E. Sandewall (Eds.), Non-Monotonic Reasoning. Proceedings, 1988. XIV, 237 pages. 1989 (Subseries LNAI).

Vol. 347: K. Morik (Ed.), Knowledge Representation and Organization in Machine Learning. XV, 319 pages. 1989 (Subseries LNAI).

Vol. 348: P. Deransart, B. Lorho, J. Maluszyński (Eds.), Programming Languages Implementation and Logic Programming. Proceedings, 1988. VI, 299 pages. 1989.

Vol. 349: B. Monien, R. Cori (Eds.), STACS 89. Proceedings, 1989. VIII, 544 pages. 1989.

Vol. 350: A. Törn, A. Žilinskas, Global Optimization. X, 255 pages. 1989.

Vol. 351: J. Díaz, F. Orejas (Eds.), TAPSOFT '89. Volume 1. Proceedings, 1989. X, 383 pages. 1989.

Lecture Notes in Computer Science

Edited by G. Goos and J. Hartmanis

409

A. Buchmann   O. Günther
T.R. Smith   Y.-F. Wang (Eds.)

Design and Implementation of Large Spatial Databases

First Symposium SSD '89
Santa Barbara, California, July 17/18, 1989
Proceedings

Springer-Verlag

Editors

Alejandro P. Buchmann
GTE Laboratories, Inc.
40 Sylvan Road, Waltham, MA 02254, USA

Oliver Günther
Forschungsinstitut für anwendungsorientierte Wissensverarbeitung (FAW)
Universität Ulm
Postfach 2060, D-7900 Ulm, FRG

Terence R. Smith
Yuan-Fang Wang
Department of Computer Science, University of California
Santa Barbara, CA 93106, USA

CR Subject Classification (1987): A.0, E.1–2, E.5, F.2.2, H.2.1–2, H.2.8, I.2.1, I.3.5

ISBN 3-540-52208-5 Springer-Verlag Berlin Heidelberg New York
ISBN 0-387-52208-5 Springer-Verlag New York Berlin Heidelberg

© Springer-Verlag Berlin Heidelberg 1990
Printed in Germany

Printing and binding: Druckhaus Beltz, Hemsbach/Bergstr.

Dedicated to the Memory of

Markku Tamminen

1945 - 1989

Preface

This book contains the proceedings of the First Symposium on the Design and Implementation of Large Spatial Databases (SSD '89), which was held with about 175 participants at Santa Barbara, California, on July 17 and 18, 1989.

The great interest in this symposium seems to be representative of the growing interest in spatial data management in general. There are numerous spatial applications in geography, computer vision, robotics, computer-aided manufacturing, and environmental information systems, and these applications require more powerful data management tools than the ones available today.

Research in spatial data management requires expertise in these application areas *and* in various fields within computer science, such as database management, data structures and algorithms, computational geometry, solid modeling, and computer vision. Experts from the application areas have to cooperate with computer scientists in a highly interdisciplinary field to obtain systems that are both practical and at the cutting edge of today's computer science.

It is our hope that this symposium also served as an opportunity to bring together people from these various disciplines and to establish closer connections between these fields.

We would like to thank NASA, the Environmental Protection Agency, the Oak Ridge National Laboratory, and the U.S. Geological Survey for their generous support. Thanks also to ACM, the IEEE Computer Society, and to Springer-Verlag for their cooperation. The National Center for Geographic Information and Analysis here at Santa Barbara has been supportive of this project from the beginning. Thanks to the members of the program committee for returning their reviews promptly under great time pressure. And thanks to Sandi Glendinning for taking care of our local arrangements.

Santa Barbara, November 1989   The Editors

General Chair:

Oliver Günther, FAW-AI Laboratory, University of Ulm, FRG

Program Chair:

Alejandro Buchmann, GTE Laboratories Inc., Waltham, Massachusetts, USA

Symposium Committee:

Renato Barrera, University of Maine, USA

Stavros Christodoulakis, University of Waterloo, Canada

Umesh Dayal, Digital Equipment Corporation, Cambridge, Massachusetts, USA

Hans-Dieter Ehrich, University of Braunschweig, FRG

John Estes, NASA and University of California, Santa Barbara, USA

Christos Faloutsos, University of Maryland, USA

Andrew Frank, University of Maine, USA

Sylvia Osborn, University of Western Ontario, Canada

Ralf H. Güting, University of Dortmund, FRG

Klaus Hinrichs, University of Siegen, FRG

Alfons Kemper, University of Karlsruhe, FRG

Hans-Peter Kriegel, University of Bremen, FRG

Raymond Lorie, IBM Almaden Research Center, California, USA

Frank Manola, GTE Laboratories Inc., Waltham, Massachusetts, USA

Jack Orenstein, Object Design, Inc., Burlington, Massachusetts, USA

Hans-J. Schek, ETH Zürich, Switzerland

Timos Sellis, University of Maryland, USA

Terence Smith, University of California, Santa Barbara, USA

Markku Tamminen, Helsinki University of Technology, Finland

Yuan-F. Wang, University of California, Santa Barbara, USA

Eugene Wong, University of California, Berkeley, USA

Contents

Data Structures

Invited Talk:
7 ± 2 Criteria for Assessing and Comparing Spatial Data Structures
J. Nievergelt, ETH Zürich, Switzerland 3

The Fieldtree: A Data Structure for Geographic Information Systems
A. U. Frank, R. Barrera, University of Maine, USA. 29

A Full Resolution Elevation Representation Requiring Three
Bits per Pixel
C. A. Shaffer, Virginia Polytechnic Institute, USA 45

System and Performance Issues

The DASDBS GEO-Kernel: Concepts, Experiences, and the
Second Step
A. Wolf, ETH Zürich, Switzerland 67

Performance Comparison of Point and Spatial Access Methods
*H.-P. Kriegel, M. Schiwietz, R. Schneider, B. Seeger,
University of Bremen, FRG* 89

Strategies for Optimizing the Use of Redundancy in Spatial Databases
J. A. Orenstein, Object Design, Inc., Cambridge, Massachusetts, USA 115

Geographic Applications

Invited Talk:
Tiling Large Geographical Databases
M. F. Goodchild, University of California, Santa Barbara, USA 137

Extending a Database to Support the Handling of Environmental
Measurement Data
L. Neugebauer, University of Stuttgart, FRG 147

Thematic Map Modeling
M. Scholl, A. Voisard, INRIA, Chesnay, France 167

Quadtrees

Invited Talk:
Hierarchical Spatial Data Structures
H. Samet, University of Maryland, USA 193

Distributed Quadtree Processing
C. H. Chien, T. Kanade, Carnegie-Mellon University, Pittsburgh, USA . . . 213

Node Distribution in a PR Quadtree
C.-H. Ang, H. Samet, University of Maryland, USA 233

Modeling and Data Structures

An Object-Oriented Approach to the Design of Geographic
Information Systems
P. van Oosterom, J. van den Bos, University of Leiden, The Netherlands . . 255

A Topological Data Model for Spatial Databases
M. J. Egenhofer, A. U. Frank, J. P. Jackson, University of Maine, USA ... 271

A Well-Behaved File Structure for the Storage of Spatial Objects
M. W. Freeston, European Computer-Industry Research Center,
Munich, FRG 287

Spatial Reasoning

Invited Talk:
The Design of Pictorial Databases Based upon the Theory
of Symbolic Projections
S.-K. Chang, E. Jungert, Y. Li, University of Pittsburgh, USA 303

Reasoning on Space with Object-Centered Knowledge Representations
L. Buisson, Laboratoire Artemis/Imag, Grenoble, France 325

Qualitative Spatial Reasoning: A Semi-Quantitative Approach
Using Fuzzy Logic
S. Dutta, University of California, Berkeley, USA 345

Data Structures

7 ± 2 criteria for assessing and comparing spatial data structures

Jurg Nievergelt
ETH Zurich and UNC at Chapel Hill

Abstract

Spatial data structures have evolved under the influence of several forces: 1) Database technology, with its emphasis on modeling and logical organization; 2) the long history of data structures developed in response to requirements from other applications; and 3) the recent rapid progress in computational geometry, which has identified typical queries and access patterns to spatial data. Rather than attempting a comprehensive survey of many spatial data structures recently developed, we aim to identify the key issues that have created them, their common characteristics, the requirements they have to meet, and the criteria for assessing how well these requirements are met. As a guideline for tackling these general goals, we begin with a brief history and recall how past requirements from other applications have shaped the development of data structures. Starting from the very early days, five major types of applications generated most of the known data structures. But the requirements of these applications do not include one that is basic to spatial data: That objects are embedded in Euclidian space, and access is mostly determined by location in space.

We present six specifically geometric requirements spatial data structures must address. Sections 3, 4, 5 discuss the mostly static aspects of how space is organized, and how objects are represented and embedded in space. Sections 6, 7, 8 consider the dynamic aspects of how objects are processed. We differentiate three types of processing, of increasing complexity, that call for different solutions: common geometric transformations such as translation and rotation; proximity search, and traversal of the object by different types of algorithms. Together with the general requirement of effective implementability, we propose these seven criteria as a profile for assessing spatial data structures. This survey leads us to two main conclusions: 1) That the current emphasis on comparative search trees is perhaps unduly influenced by the great success balanced trees enjoyed as a solution to the requirements of older applications that rely on single-key access, and 2) that spatial data structures are increasingly of the 'metric' type based on radix partitions of space.

Affiliation of author: Jurg Nievergelt (jn@inf.ethz.ch, jn@cs.unc.edu)
Informatik, ETH, CH-8092 Zurich, Switzerland and
Dept.Computer Sci., Univ. of North Carolina, Chapel Hill, NC 27514, USA

Contents

1   The problem
1.1 The conventional data base approach to "non-standard" data
1.2 Geometric modeling separated from storage considerations
1.3 Structures for spatial data bases
2   The development of data structures: Requirements drive design
2.1 Scientific computation: Static data sets
2.2 Batch processing of commercial data: Single key access to dynamic sets
2.3 Interactive transaction processing: Multikey access to dynamic sets
2.4 Knowledge representation: Associative recall in random nets
2.5 Spatial data management: Proximity access to objects embedded in space
3   Representation of space
3.1 Space partitioning and cell addressing
3.2 Radix trees in various dimensions: quadtrees, oct-trees, r^d-trees. Grid File
3.3 Space partitions induced by comparative search trees. Load balancing
3.4 Constrained space partitions: BSP trees, Octet
4   Representing a useful class of objects
4.1 Geometric modeling: CSG, boundary and sweep representations
4.2 Hierarchical approximations
4.3 Object specification by means of parameters
5   A scheme for embedding objects in space
5.1 Anchors: representative points or vectors
5.2 Mark inhabited space
5.3 Transformation to parameter space
6   Support for geometric transformations
7   Proximity search: simplify complex objects to access disk sparingly
8   Support data access patterns of typical geometric algorithms
9   Implementation: Reconcile conceptual simplicity and efficiency

1 The problem

1.1 The conventional data base approach to "non-standard" data

Data base technology developed over the past two decades in response to the needs of commercial data processing, characterized by large, record-oriented, fairly homogeneous data sets, mostly retrieved in response to relatively simple queries: Point queries that ask for the presence or absence of a particular record, interval or range queries that ask for all records whose attribute values lie within given lower and upper bounds. But today, data base research and practice are increasingly concerned with other applications, such as real-time control, hypertext and multimedia. Collectively lumped into the amorphous pool of "non-standard" applications, they confront data base research with new requirements that stretch conventional technology to its limits, and beyond. Among these new applications, none is more important or imposes more stringent new requirements than the management of spatial data, as used in graphics, computer-aided design (CAD), and geographical data bases.

Spatial data lends itself naturally to geometric computation, a topic that has progressed very rapidly in recent years. Thus it is understandable that data base software has yet to take into account the specific requirements and results of geometric computation. Geometric objects are lumped into the amorphous pool of non-standard data, often ignoring any specific properties they might have. But in fact geometric problems possess a great deal of structure to be exploited by efficient algorithms and data structures. This is due primarily to the fact that geometric objects are embedded in space, and are typically accessed through their position in space (as opposed to access by means of identifiers or other non-spatial attributes). Let us begin with a plausible example of how geometry is often introduced as an afterthought to other properties.

1.2 Geometric modeling separated from storage considerations

In this early stage of development of geometric data base technology, we cannot afford to focus on modeling to the exclusion of implementation aspects. *In graphics and CAD the real issue is efficiency*: 1/10-th of a second is the limit of human time resolution, and a designer works at maximal efficiency when "trivial" requests are displayed "instantaneously". This allows a couple of disk accesses only, which means that geometric and other spatial attributes must be part of the retrieval mechanism if common geometric queries (intersection, inclusion, point queries) are to be handled efficiently.

The sharp distinction between the *logical view* presented to the user and the *physical aspects* that the implementor sees has been possible in conventional data base applications because data structures that allow efficient handling of point sets are well understood. The same distinction is premature for geometric data bases: in interactive applications such as CAD efficiency is today's bottleneck, and until we understand geometric storage techniques better we may not be able to afford the luxury of studying geometric modeling divorced from physical storage. Consider the frequent example where a spatial object is represented (or approximated) as the union of a set of disjoint tetrahedra. If the latter are stored in a relational data base by using the *boundary representation (BR)* approach, a tetrahedron t is given by its faces, a face f by its bounding edges, an edge e by its endpoints p and q. Four relations *tetrahedra*, *faces*, *edges* and *points* might have the following tuple structure:

- *tetrahedra* : a pair (t_i, f_k) identifies a tetrahedron t_i and one of its faces f_k.
- *faces* : a pair (f_k, e_j) identifies a face f_k and one of its edges e_j.
- *edges* : a triple (e_j, p_m, p_n) identifies an edge e_j and its two points p_m and p_n.
- *points* : a tuple (p_n, x, y, z) identifies a point and its coordinates x, y, z.

This representation smashes as simple an object as a tetrahedron into parts spread over different relations and therefore over the storage medium. The question whether a tetrahedron t intersects a given line L is answered by intersecting each of its faces f_k with L. If the tuple (t_i, f_k) in the relation *tetrahedra* contains the equation of the corresponding plane, the intersection point of the plane and the line L can be computed without accessing other relations. But in order to determine whether this intersection point lies inside or outside the face f_k requires accessing tuples of *edges* and *points*, i.e. accessing different blocks of storage, resulting in many more disk accesses than the geometric problem requires.

Efficiency requires, at least, retrieving as a unit all the data that defines a basic volume element such as a tetrahedron. In addition, we can use geometric properties to design representations that answer certain proximity queries more efficiently, for example by representing an primitive object by a suitable chosen set of parameters. A tetrahedron can be defined by 12 parameters in many useful ways: 4 vertices of 3 coordinates each, or 4 faces, each of whose equations has 3 coefficients; or as the minimal containing sphere (4 parameters) and 4 vertices that lie on the surface of the sphere, each one given by 2 spherical coordinates. The 4–parameter sphere serves as a simple container to provide a negative answer to many intersection queries more efficiently than the 12–parameter tetrahedron can. If we represent a more complex polyhedron as a union of tetrahedra, the latter can often be ordered so as to support efficient processing (for example through hierarchical decomposition in the case of a convex solid). The point of these examples is that, if geometric objects are merely considered to be logical entities, we fail to take advantage of the rich structure of geometry, with grievous consequences for efficiency.

1.3 Structures for spatial data bases

In recognition of the fact that modeling is only the peripheral part of spatial data management, and physical storage is the key to efficiency, many data structures, old and new, have been studied in conjunction with computational geometry and CAD: [EL 80] is a comprehensive bibliography, [Me 84], [Gun 88], and [Sa 89] are survey books. The majority of these are variations and combinations of a few themes: Mostly, multidimensional trees based on comparative search, used to organize different types of objects such as points, intervals, segments, or rectangles. A smaller number of structures, such as quad trees and oct-trees, is based on hierarchical radix partitions of space.

Recent years have seen intense efforts in studying spatial data structures, and many new have been developed (for example [Gut 84], [SRF 87], [SK 88], [HSW 89]). Rather than attempting a comprehensive survey of many spatial data structures recently developed, I aim to identify the key issues that have created them, their common characteristics, the requirements they have to meet, and the criteria for assessing how well these requirements are met. As a guideline for tackling this more general endeavor, let us begin with a brief history and recall how past requirements from other applications have shaped the development of data structures. Starting from the very early days, the following sections summarize five types of applications whose specific requirements led to most of the known data structures. This survey leads us to two main conclusions: 1) That the current emphasis on comparative search trees is perhaps unduly influenced by the great success balanced trees enjoyed as a solution to the requirements of older applications that rely on single-key access, and 2) that spatial data structures are increasingly of the 'metric' type based on radix partitions of space.

2 The development of data structures: Requirements drive design

2.1 Scientific computation: Static data sets

Numerical computation in science and engineering mostly leads to linear algebra and hence matrix computations. Matrices are static data sets: The values change, but the shape and size of a matrix rarely does - this is true even for most sparse matrices, such as band matrices, where the propagation of nonzero elements is bounded. Arrays were Goldstine and von Neumann's answer to the requirement of random access, as described in their venerable 1947 report "Planning and coding of problems for an electronic computing instrument". FORTRAN '54 supported arrays and sequential files, but no other data structures, with statements such as DIMENSION, READ TAPE, REWIND, and BACKSPACE.

Table look-up was also solved early through hashing. The software pioneers of the first decade did not look beyond address computation because memories were so small that any structure that "wastes" space on pointers was considered a luxury. Memories of a few K words restricted them to using only the very simplest of data structures, and the limited class of problems dealt with let them get away with it. The discipline of data structures had not yet been born.

2.2 Batch processing of commercial data: Single key access to dynamic sets

This application led to the most prolific phase in the development of data structures, comprehensively presented in Knuth's pioneering books on "The Art of Computer Programming" [K 68, 73]. Commercial data processing brought an entirely different set of requirements for managing data typically organized according to a single key, the 'primary key'. When updating an ordered master file with unordered transaction files, sorting and merging algorithms determine data access patterns. The emergence of disk drives extended the challenge of data structure design to secondary storage devices. Bridging the 'memory-speed gap' became the dominant practical problem. Central memory and disk both look like random access devices, but they differ in the order of magnitude of two key parameters:

	Memory	Disk	Ratio
Access time (seconds):	10^{-6}	$10^{-2} - 10^{-1}$	$10^4 - 10^5$
Size of transfer unit (bits):	$10 - 10^2$	10^4	$10^3 - 10^2$

Whereas technology, time– and space–parameters have changed a lot, the ratios have hardly changed. This speed gap of 4 orders of magnitude makes the number of disk accesses the most relevant performance parameter of data structures. Many data structures make effective use of central memory, but disk forces us to be more selective; in particular, to avoid following pointer chains that cross disk block boundaries. The game in designing data structures suitable for disk has two main rules: the easy one is to use a small amount of central memory effectively to describe the current allocation of data on disk, for rapid retrieval; the hard one is to ensure that this scheme adapts gracefully to the ever-changing content of the file.

Index-sequential access methods (ISAM) order records according to a single key so that a small directory, preferably kept in central memory, ideally directs any point query to the correct data bucket where the corresponding record is stored, if it is present at all. But the task of maintaining this single-disk-access performance in a dynamic file, under insertions and deletions, is far from trivial. The first widely used idea splits storage into two areas, a primary and an overflow area. It suffers from several defects, by now well-known: 1) Once the primary area has been allocated, it is not easily extended, even if there is space on disk, as an extension may force data to be moved between many buckets. 2) Insertions or deletions of real data are usually biased (non-uniformly distributed and dependent), so some primary buckets will become the heads of long overflow chains, and others may become sparsely populated. The former degrades access time, the latter storage utilization. Many studies have reached the conclusion that ISAM with overflow works effectively only as long as the amount of data in the overflow area is below about 20%. With the high rate of change typical of transaction processing, this bound is reached quickly, causing frequent reorganization of the entire file.

Balanced trees of any kind [e.g. AL 62, BM 72, and many others] provided a brilliant solution to the problem of 'maintaining large ordered indexes' without degradation: Frequent small rebalancing operations that work in logarithmic time eliminate the need for periodic reorganization of the entire file. Trees based on comparative search derive their strength from the ease of modifying list structures in central memory. They have been so successful that we tend to apply and generalize them beyond their natural limitations. In addition to concerns about the suitability of comparative search trees for multikey access, discussed in the next section, these limitations include [Ni 81]:
1) The number of disk accesses grows with the height of the tree. The fan-out from a node, or from a page containing many nodes, varies significantly (from dozens to hundreds) depending on page size, on page occupancy, and on the space required to store a key. For files containing 10^6 records, the tree may well have more than 2 or 3 levels, making the goal of "instantaneous" retrieval impossible.
2) Concurrency. Every node in a tree is the sole entry point to the entire subtree rooted at that node, and thus a bottleneck for concurrent processes that pass through it, even if they access different leaves (physical storage units). Early papers (e.g. [BS 77, KL 80) showed that concurrent access to trees implemented as lists requires elaborate protocols to insure integrity of the data.

2.3 Interactive transaction processing: Multikey access to dynamic sets

Whereas single-key access may suffice for batch processing, transaction processing, as used in a reservations or banking system, calls for for multikey access (by name, date, location, ..). The simplest ideas were tried first. Inverted files try to salvage single-key structures by ordering data according to a 'primary key', and 'inverting' the resulting file with respect to all other keys, called 'secondary'. Whereas the primary directory is compact as in ISAM, the secondary directories are voluminous: Typically, each one has an entry for every record. Just updating the directories makes insertions and deletions time-consuming.

Comparative search trees enhanced ISAM by eliminating the need for overflow chains, so it was natural to generalize them to multikey access and improve on inverted files. This is easy enough, as first shown by k-d trees [Be 75]. But the resulting multi-key structures are neither as elegant nor as efficient as in the single-key case. The main hindrance is that no total order can be imposed on multidimensional space without destroying some proximity relationships. As a consequence, the simple rebalancing operations that work for single-key trees fail, and rebalancing algorithms must resort to more complicated and less efficient techniques, such as general dynamization [Wi 78, Ov 81].

Variations and improvements on multidimensional comparative search trees continue to appear [e.g. LS 89]. Their main virtue, acceptable worst case bounds, comes from the fact that they partition the actual data to be stored into (nearly) equal parts. The other side of this coin is that data is partitioned *regardless of where in space it is located.* Thus the resulting space partitions exhibit no regularity, in marked contrast to radix partitions that organize space into cells of predetermined size and location.

2.4 Knowledge representation: Associative recall in random nets

There is a class of applications where data is most naturally thought of as a graph, or network, with nodes corresponding to entities and arcs to relationships among these. Library catalogs in information retrieval, hypertexts with their many links, semantic nets in artificial intelligence are examples. The characteristic access pattern is 'browsing': A probe into the net followed by a walk to adjacent nodes. Typically, a node is not accessed because of any inherent characteristic, but because it is associated with (linked to) a node currently being visited. The requirements posed by this type of problem triggered the development of list processing techniques and list processing languages.

These graphs look arbitrary, and the access patterns look like random walks - neither exhibit any regular structure to be exploited. The general list structures designed for these applications have not evolved much since list processing was created, at least not when compared to the other data structures discussed. The resulting lack of sophisticated data structures for processing data collections linked as arbitrary graphs reminds us that efficient algorithms and data structures are always tailored to specific properties to be exploited. The next application shows such a special case.

2.5 Spatial data management:
Proximity access to objects embedded in space

Three key characteristisc distinguish spatial data management from the other four applications described:

1) Data represents objects embedded in some d-dimensional Euclidian space $\mathbb{R}^d$.
2) These objects are mostly accessed through their location in space, in response to a proximity query such as intersection or containment in some query region.
3) A typical spatial object has a significantly more complex structure than a 'record' in the other applications mentioned.

Although other applications share some of these characteristics to a small extent, in no other do they play a comparably important role. Let us highlight the contrast with the example of a collection of records, each with two attributes, 'social security number' and 'year of birth'.

1) Although it may be convenient to consider such a record to be a point in a 2-d attribute space, this is not a Euclidian space; the distance between two such points, for example, or even the distance between two SSNs, is unlikely to be meaningful.
2) Partial match and orthogonal range queries are common in data processing applications, but more complex query regions are rare. In contrast, arbitrarily complex query regions are common in geometric computation (e.g. intersection of objects, or ray tracing).
3) Although a record in commercial data processing may contain a lot of data, for search purposes it is just a point. A typical spatial object, on the other hand, is a polyhedron of arbitrary complexity, and we face the additional problem of reducing it to predefined primitives, such as points, edges, triangles, tetrahedra.

3 Representation of space

3.1 Space partitioning and cell addressing

The first point to be made about spatial data structures sounds so trite that it is often overlooked: *The main task of a spatial data structure is to represent space.* The way empty space is organized and represented has important consequences for the representation and storage of objects, much as the choice of a coordinate system has important consequences for the manipulation of geometric formulas. A representation of space suitable for data storage and management has two main components:

1. A scheme for partitioning the entire space into cells.
2. A two-way mapping that relates regions of space to the cells that inhabit them.

The space partition serves as a skeleton for organizing objects located in space, and leads to a characteristic two-step procedure for accessing objects: Given a region of space, first find the cells that intersect the region (cell addressing), then find the objects that inhabit those cells (data access).

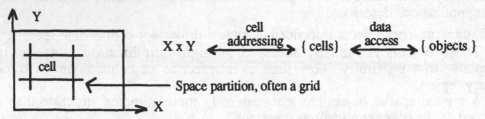

Posing the issue of space representation in this generality makes some useful observations obvious:
- For efficient addressing, cells must have a simple shape, usually boxes.
- The simplest space partitions are orthogonal grids.
- We want to control the size of cells, most easily done by means of hierarchical grids.

These desiderata lead directly to radix trees, the archetypal hierarchical space partitions, discussed in the next section. But first, consider an inverted file as an example of a data structure that was not designed for spatial access. Like any data structure, it partitions space by the way it allocates data to buckets. If x is the primary key, and y a secondary key, space is cut up into slices orthogonal to the x-axis, thus revealing that it is really a 1-d data structure. Inverted files support queries with specified x-values efficiently, but not with y.

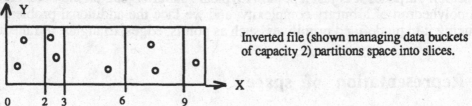

Inverted file (shown managing data buckets of capacity 2) partitions space into slices.

We now turn our attention to hierarchical space partitions, which come in two major classes: radix trees and comparative-search trees.

3.2 Radix trees in various dimensions: quadtrees, oct-trees, r^d-trees. Grid file

All general-purpose schemes for partitioning space into regions must permit refinement, and thus are naturally hierarchical. Radix trees, more exactlyt r^d-trees, apply to arbitrary dimension d and radix r > 1 and generate the most easily computed refinable space partitions. The picture below shows the space partition generated by a quad tree (the case d=2, r=2), and three ways of addressing its cells.

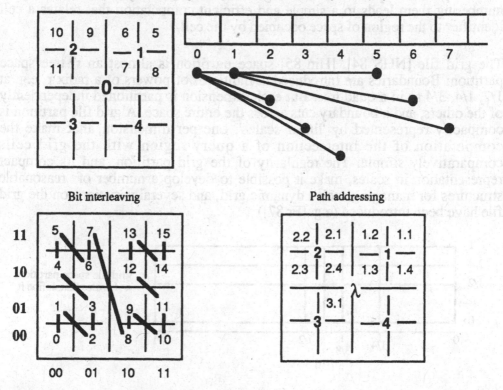

1) **Breadth-first addressing** leads to the simplest address computation based on formulas that make tree traversal very efficient: the node at address (index) i has children at addresses 4i+1, 4i+2, 4i+3, 4i+4; conversely, the node at address j has its parent at (j-1) div 4. The analogous breadth-first storage of a binary tree (d=1, r=2) is well known as the key idea that makes heap sort efficient and elegant.

2) **Bit interleaving** or z-order, is another way to treat all dimensions (axes) equally. The (linear) address of a cell at coordinates (x, y), for example, is obtained by writing x and y as binary integers: x = x1 x0, y =y1 y0, and constructing the address a as the binary integer a = x1 y1 x0 y0.

3) **Path addressing** assigns a string over the alphabet { 1, .., r } to each cell. The null string λ to the entire space, strings of length 1 to the quadrants at depth 1, strings of length 2 to the subquadrants at depth 2, etc. When these strings are ordered lexicographically we obtain breadth-first addressing.

The point of listing these addressing schemes is not to argue about minor advantages or disadvantages, but to show that r^d-trees partition space in such a r^d-trees partition space in such a regular manner that any reasonable way of numbering them leads to a simple and efficient computation that relates a cell identifier to the region of space occupied by the cell.

The grid file [NHS 84], [Hin 85] space partition is almost an r^d-tree space partition: Boundaries are introduced at multiples of powers of a radix r, e.g. at 1/2, 1/4, 3/4 as in a quad tree. But each dimension is partitioned independently of the others, and a boundary cuts across the entire space. A grid file partition is compactly represented by 'linear scales', one per dimension, that make the computation of the intersection of a query region with the grid cells comparatively simple. The regularity of the grid partition, and its compact representation in scales, make it possible to develop a number of reasonable structures for managing such a dynamic grid, and several variations on the grid file have been introduced (e.g. [Fr 87])

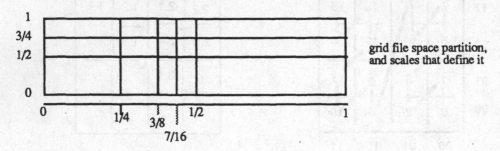

grid file space partition, and scales that define it

3.3 Space partitions induced by comparative search trees. Load balancing

In contrast to the regularity of the r^d-tree space partition, those based on comparative search generate less regular partitions. Drawing a boundary so as to balance the load among the left and right subtrees works much better for 1-d data than for multi-dimensional space. The result is shown in the figure below:

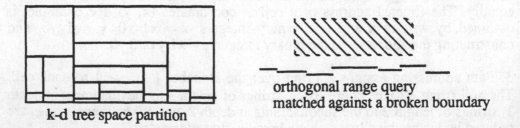

k-d tree space partition

orthogonal range query matched against a broken boundary

Among the disadvantages:
- Crafty but complicated rebalancing techniques, called 'general dynamization'

are necessary. These are less effective than the logarithmic rebalancing algorithms (such as those for height- or weight-balanced trees) that work in totally ordered domains, but not w.r.t. the partial order natural in multidimensional spaces.

- Ill-suited for concurrent access - the root of a tree represented as a list structure is a bottleneck through which all processes must travel as they access data. (Notice that this objection need not hold for radix trees, as these permit access by means of address computation).

- A multitude of small boundaries (e.g. along the bottom of the figure) complicates the computation of queries as simple as orthogonal range queries.

3.4 Constrained space partitions: BSP trees, Octet

The space partitions presented so far have some structure that is independent of the objects that populate the space. Radix partitions, in particular, have a fixed 'skeleton', and the set of objects merely determines the degree of refinement. Space partitions for comparative search trees are more data-dependent, but there is some choice in placing boundaries. In some applications, such as computer graphics or finite element computations, we want space partitions that are determined by the objects to be represented. For these, the distinction between 'organizing space' and 'representing objects' gets blurred.

Binary space partition trees [FKN 80] were introduced to speed up image generation of objects in situations where the world model changes less frequently than the viewpoint of the observer. Consider an object consisting of many polygons in space. We select a suitable polygon (e.g. one whose plane f cuts only a few other polygons), and make it the root of a binary tree. Recursively, one of its subtrees partitions the half-space f^+ in front of f, the other the half-space f^- behind f. Polygons that stick out into both f^+ and f^- get cut into two. The following figure shows a 2-d example.

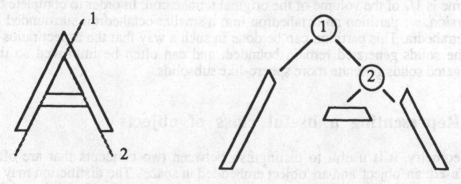

BSP tree partitions the letter A into quadrilaterals

We are working on Octet, a space partition scheme designed for mesh generation for 3-d finite element analysis. We typically have a static collection of objects, or, equivalently, one large complex object. The space inside the object must be partitioned into cells that meet stringent conditions: (1) simple polyhedra, such as tetrahedra or hexahedra (distorted boxes), (2) with a good fit to the boundary of the objects, (3) that avoid excessively acute angles and excessive elongation, (4) that can be refined in such a way that condition (3) holds again for all subcells generated. Oct-trees do a great job on 1), 3) and 4), but not on 2) - even simple surfaces such as planes force the oct tree to its level of resolution unless they are orthogonal to an axis.

Octet partitions arbitrary 3-d regions of space hierarchically into tetrahedra and octahedra in such a way that aspect ratios of all cells (their elongation) is bounded. Consider a good and a bad way of tessellating the plane into triangles.

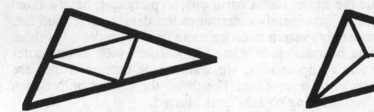

At left, the outer traingle is refined into 4 triangles of similar shape.
At right, into 3 increasingly elongated triangles.

The problem gets harder in 3-d space. It is clear how to refine a tetrahedron into 4 tetrahedra by introducing a new vertex in the middle, but that generates elongated tetrahedra that quickly become useless. The refinement analogous to the picture at left goes as follows. From each of the original vertices, cut off 4 tetrahedra that are all similar to the original: all linear extensions are halved, for a volume of 1/8 of the original. That leaves an octahedron at the core, whose volume is 1/2 of the volume of the original tetrahedron. In order to complete the recursion, we partition an octahedron into a smaller octahedron surrounded by 12 tetrahedra. This partition can be done in such a way that the aspect ratios of all the solids generated remain bounded, and can often be improved so that elongated solids generate more sphere-like subsolids.

4 Representing a useful class of objects

In geometry, it is useful to distinguish between two concepts that are often confused: an 'object' and an 'object embedded in space'. The distinction may be unnecessary if objects never move, but we are concerned with the increasing number of interactive applications of geometric computation where the data configuration is highly dynamic. All the representations we discuss allow us to make a clean distinction except one. In the technique that we call 'mark inhabited space', an object is represented, or at least approximated, by marking all the space cells it occupies. This is the traditional use of quad trees in image processing, for example, which supports only the concept 'object embedded in space' but lacks the notion of a 'generic object' independent of its location. Thus we do not consider this a true *object representation* technique. We discuss it in 5.2 as a scheme for *embedding* objects in space.

4.1 Geometric modeling:
CSG, boundary and sweep representations

Computer science has developed a great variety of object representations. Wireframe and surface patch models, the early workhorses of computer graphics, were the precursors of boundary representation (BR). BR, constructive solid geometry (CSG), and sweep representations are most widely used in solid modeling. [Man 88] contains a recent survey that describes several others. These representations have the advantage that they can model any type of spatial objects. But they were designed primarily for processing in central memory, not for their suitability for retrieval from disk in response to geometric queries.

A representation for complex objects necessarily contains two distinct types of data:
- The primitive data items from which complex objects are built (points, line segments, surface patches, volume elements, ..).
- The relationships between these items (e.g., who touches whom, who belongs to whom).

Conventional object representations intermingle all this data, which serves a good purpose when drawing an object on the screen: Traversing the relationship structure one encounters the definition of all primitives, and can draw them as one goes along. But this intermingling can have a negative effect on retrieval performance, as I will argue in the next section.

These two types of data (primitive items and relationships) usually have rather distinct characteristics that suggest they should be treated separately. Many engineering applications use only a small number of different **types** of primitives from which they build complex structures with a rich, irregular network of relationships. For these cases we advocate a representation that separates primitives from relationships in the following manner.

Primitives. Each type of primitive is characterized by a number of parameters: circles and spheres by their radius, intervals by their lengths, triangles by their shape and size. Thus an instance of each type is fully defined by giving the values of each of its parameters, and can be considered to be a point in its parameter space. Points are the simplest objects to store and retrieve, and many data structures do a creditable job in managing large collections of points. Geometric proximity queries start by identifying primitives that meet the query condition, and only access the relationship data as needed.

The **relationships** between the primitives are represented as a graph tied to the embedding space through the primitives.

4.2 Hierarchical approximations

Computational geometry has developed some object representations that are highly effective in particular circumstances. Hierarchical representations approximate a convex object by piling layers of simple primitives on top of each other, as the following example illustrates. We inscribe a triangle as a level-0 approximation to a given polygon. This triangle is surrounded by a layer of level-1 triangles that are also inscribed in the target polygon. The approximation improves with each additional layer. The structure of these approximations is a tree, and if care has been taken to grow a balanced tree, some operations on an target object of size n can be done in time O(log n).

Hierarchical approximation
of a convex 9-gon as a 3-level tree
of triangles. The root is in black,
its children in dark grey,
grandchildren in light grey.

4.3 Object specification by means of parameters

In some applications, for example VLSI design, the data consists of a large number of very simple primitives, such as aligned rectangles in the plane (i.e. with sides parallel to the axes). In many more engineering applications, for example technical drawing, all objects are constructed from relatively few types of simple primitives, such as points, line segments, arcs, triangles, rectangles, or the 3-d counterparts of such typical primitives. Under these circumstances it is natural and often efficient to split the representation of a complex object into two parts: A graph or network that specifies the relationships among the primitives, and, for each type of primitive, an unstructured set of all the instances of the primitives.

Each instance of a primitive is given by as many parameters as are necessary to specify it within its type. Continuing the example of the class of aligned rectangles in the plane, we observe that each rectangle is determined by its center (cx, cy) and the length of each side, dx and dy. We consider the *size parameters* dx and dy to represent the object, and the *location parameters* cx and cy to specify the embedding of the object in the space. The representation of simple objects in terms of parameters becomes interesting when we consider how the metric in the object space gets transformed into parameter space - we continue this topic in section 5.3.

5 A scheme for embedding objects in space

The question of how objects are represented can be asked, and partly answered, independently of how space is organized. But obviously, representation of space and of objects must be compatible, and their interrelationship is **the** key issue in designing SDSs. The problem is to ensure that the relationship between 1) regions of space, and 2) objects that inhabit these regions, can be computed efficiently **in both directions:** S → O, space-to-objects; and O → S, objects-to-space. Consider how the following schemes for embedding objects in space fare in this respect.

5.1 Anchors: representative points or vectors

Every object has some prominent point, such as the center of gravity, or the lower left corner, that can be used to anchor an object in space. Many practical objects also have a prominent axis, such as a symmetry axis, that is conveniently used to orient the object. Such a representative point or vector is an **anchor**: if all the parameters of the anchor are specified, the object is located (anchored) in space.

CSG, boundary and sweep representations often use coordinates relative to an anchor. Relative coordinates have the great advantage that common transformations, translations and rotations,become efficient $O(1)$ operations: transforming the anchor transforms the whole object.

Both functions S → O (given a region, e.g. a cell, retrieve the objects in it) and O → S (given an object, what cells does it intersect) can be implemented efficiently if the objects satisfy constraints, as is often the case in practice. If we know a bound r on the size of all objects, for example, the sphere of radius r centered at the anchoring point is a container that often eliminates the need to examine objects in detail. If there are only a few distinct types of objects, anchoring becomes similar to the parameter specification approach of 5.3

5.2 Mark inhabited space

The most straightforward embedding is based on the idea that each object leaves its mark (name, identifier, pointer to itself) in every space cell that it occupies. This is the technique traditionally used with radix trees, illustrated by the segment tree and quad tree below. Some of its properties include:

- Potentially high redundancy; an object may require a lot of pointers to itself.
- S → O: as efficient as is practically possible;
- O → S: not as efficient as one might hope for: Many an object (e.g. a rectangle) has a simple description, but a radix tree forces us to break up the region it occupies.

The picture below shows the 1-d space [0, 8) hierarchically partitioned into cells by a binary tree (r = 2) of depth t = 3 One interval at level 0, 2 at level 1, 4 at level 2, 8 = 2^t at level t = 3. This scheme is called 'buddy or twin system' in systems programming, 'segment tree' in computational geometry, and, for various radices r, is the basis for most systems of measurement.

Segment tree stores interval A = [2, 5] by marking 2 cells of the space partition.

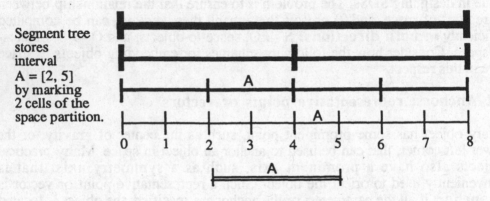

The following picture of a digitized quadrant of a circle stored in a quad tree (d = 2, r = 2) shows not only the underlying space partitions, but also the correspondence between space cells and nodes in the tree.

A quarter circle digitized on a 16 * 16 grid, and its representation as a 4-level quad tree

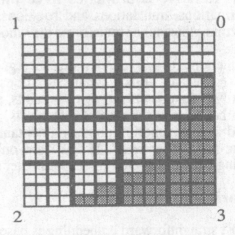

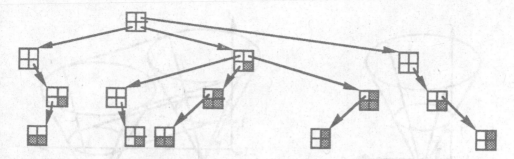

When used in image processing, the tree typically serves both as a directory and as actual storage. In other applications the tree is just a directory, with a leaf of the tree holding not just a black/white bit, but a pointer to all the data associated with the corresponding space cell. Notice that this technique has no way of capturing the concept of a quarter circle independent of its location - if the object is moved ever so slightly, its representation changes completely.

5.3 Transformation to parameter space

Given a parameter space assigned to a class of objects as in section 4.3, we construct the cartesian product with a space of *location parameters* to obtain a higher-dimensional space that tells us everything about a collection of objects of this type located in space [NH 85]. As an example, consider a collection of circles in the plane. Each instance of a circle is specified by its radius, the size parameter r, and by its center, given by two location parameters cx and cy. Thus the collection of circles to be stored is transformed into a set of points in the parameter space with axes cx, cy, r shown in the two figures below.

Under this transformation, common proximity queries in object space turn into region queries to retrieve points in parameter space. Continuing with the example of the circles, it is straightforward to verify that the point query 'retrieve all circles that cover the point q' gets transformed into the region query 'retrieve all points in parameter space that lie in the search cone shown in the figure at left'. A region query in the object space of circles, such as 'retrieve all circles that intersect (or contain) the line L' is a union of point queries and gets transformed into the reqion query which is the union of search cones, namely 'retrieve all points in parameter space that lie in the search region shown in the figure at right'.

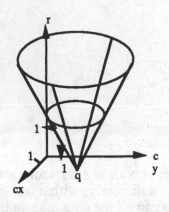

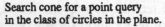

Search cone for a point query
in the class of circles in the plane.

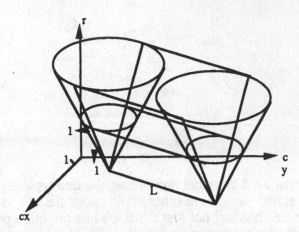

Search region for an intersection query with a line L

Transformation to parameter space reduces object retrieval to point retrieval in a parameter space that is typically of higher dimensionality than the original object space. And it generates region queries of a large variety of shapes. The grid file was designed to evaluate complex region queries with a minimum of disk accesses. The data buckets that may contain points in the search region are identified on the basis of a small amount of directory information (the 'scales') that is kept in central memory. Thus a search region of complex shape affects the computation time, but not the number of disk accesses - the latter are determined primarily by the size of the answer.

6 Support for geometric transformations

Geometry is the study of object-properties that remain invariant under some group of geometric transformations. Thus a general purpose spatial data structure must be judged according to the efficiency with which the most common transformations can be performed, in particular linear transformations such as translation, rotation, scaling, and stretching.

The efficiency of the two most frequently used transformations, translation and rotation, depends primarily on the scheme chosen for embedding objects in space. All embeddings based on the principle 'mark inhabited space' fare poorly in this respect. But the other embeddings we discussed all have the potential of transforming an object of arbitrary complexity as an O(1) operation. The common geometric models used in CAD, by using relative coordinates, make it possible to embed objects using the anchoring technique. Parameter space representations also make it possible to separate the six location and orientation parameters from the size parameters.

The efficiency of scaling and stretching depends primarily on the object-representation scheme, but in general no scheme can do better than O(n), the inherent complexity of the object.

7 Proximity search: simplify complex objects to access disk sparingly

The most basic query a spatial data structure must be designed to answer efficiently is of the type 'retrieve the object(s) at or near point p = (x, y, ..)'. This *point-proximity search* is the prototype on which more complex proximity queries are based (region queries, intersection, containment, etc.).

The main idea that serves to speed up proximity search is to make the *processing effort independent of the complexity n of the objects involved.* Although this ideal cannot be achieved in general, it can often be approximated fairly well, in at least two ways:

1) Certain objects of complexity n can be represented exactly in terms of a structure that permits proximity search in time o(n). Example: The hierarchical representation of a convex polygon or polyhedron (see section 4.2) serves to answer the point-in-object query in time O(log n). Although this search time does depend on the complexity n of the object, for practical values of n the difference between logarithmic time and constant time may not tell.

2) Approximation of a complex object by a simpler one is a more generally applicable idea. The two most prominent kinds of approximations are containers and kernels. Both serve to replace costly proximity searches by cheaper ones. Containers are used when we expect most searches to fail, kernels when we expect them to succeed.
- By enclosing the object in a simple container such as a bounding box or a circumscribed sphere we achieve the saving that when the low-cost search for the container fails, we know that the expensive search for the actual object must also fail. Only when the container search succeeds we must follow up with a search for the object.
- By inscribing a simple kernel, such as a sphere or tetrahedron, inside an object we achieve the analogous effect. Successful kernel searches give a definite answer, only failed kernel searches must be followed by the costlier object search.

Different classes of objects require different types of containers or kernels if the approximation is to be effective. For example, aligned objects with sides parallel to the coordinate axes call for box-shaped approximations, whereas rounded object are better approximated by spheres or ellipsoids. A data structure that permits rapid answers to the point-proximity query for standard containers or kernels such as aligned boxes, tetrahedra, and spheres provides a basis for the efficient implementation of proximity search for a more general class of objects also.

Among all the geometric operations performed on a collection of objects stored on disk, proximity search is the most critical in terms of its potential for saving or wasting disk accesses. Disk accesses are not the bottleneck of most other operations: These rely on proximity search to identify the objects they must process, read them off disk, then spend considerable time processing this data. Proximity search is the main filter that takes a quick look at many objects, in the hope of discarding most of them. Simple approximations to complex objects may make it possible to keep the containers (only) of most objects in central memory, and be highly selective in accessing entire objects.

8 Support data access patterns of typical geometric algorithms

Having discussed separately the two most important special cases of object processing, namely transformation and proximity search, we now attempt to characterize the requirements imposed by arbitrary algorithms that may be used to process objects. Fortunately, the majority of the practical geometric algorithms we are aware of fall naturally into three classes only:
- Sweeping the plane with a line, or sweeping 3-d space with a plane.
- Boundary traversal
- Recursive data partitioning in divide-and-conquer algorithms.
Each of these types of algorithms generates distinct data access patterns.

Sweep algorithms ask for the data sorted in lexicographic order: by increasing x, for equal x by increasing y, etc. This is by far the easiest data access pattern to implement efficiently. Indeed, the initial step of sorting the data dominates the work in practically all plane-sweep algorithms: Most of them run in time $O(n \log n)$, the time complexity of sorting, and some of them run in linear time $O(n)$ on data that is already sorted. Data access in sweep algorithms satisfies a locality principle both in object space and in address space: In object space, because we move from one event (typically a point) to the next event to the right; in address space, because lexicographically sorted data is easily mapped *monotonically* into a linear address space.

Boundary traversal algorithms start at some point of a boundary line or surface and march from a vertex to an adjacent vertex selected according to local conditions. Computing the intersection of two surfaces serves as an example:

Once any intersection point has been found, one follows the intersection line. Data access in boundary traversal satisfies a locality principle in object space, but usually not in address space: when data is allocated, we have no way of knowing which one among several neighboring vertices will be visited next. Thus most geometric neighbors reside far apart in address space. This is no problem as long as all the data resides in memory, but is likely to cause many page faults when data is processed off disk.

Recursive data partitioning typically generates the most irregular data access patterns. A recursive computation may hop around its data at 'random', but even when it can be sequenced to exhibit locality in object space, not much locality in address space is gained. This is simply because of the ever-present problem that proximity in multi-dimensional space gets lots under a mapping to 1-d address space.

A systematic experimental investigation of how well different spatial data strucures support these access patterns would be useful, but we are unaware of any.

9 Implementation:
Reconcile conceptual simplicity and efficiency

Geometric computation and data bases, the two main forces that affect the development of spatial data structures, evolved independently, emphasizing goals that are often incompatible. Computational geometry focused on sophisticated algorithms tailored to a particular problem, using intricate data structures to obtain asymptotic optimality. Data bases, on the other hand, emphasized very general architectures that can model anything by breaking complex structures into constituent pieces and using the decomposition relationships as access paths, with a resulting loss of direct access.

Neither of these two extreme points serve as a good model for implementations. Practical software requires a *careful balance* between conceptual simplicity, which leads to understandable programs, and sophisticated algorithms and data structures, which lead to efficiency. If a data structure is implemented in a stand-alone test program, this point may not be of great importance. But when it is used as a component in a complex data management system, this point can hardly be overemphasized. The data structures mentioned have proven their value as systems components, and we urge designers of new ones to attach as great an importance to this aspect of implementability as to any of the other criteria.

Acknowledgement. I am grateful to Klaus Hinrichs for helpful comments. This work was supported in part by the National Science Foundation under grant DCR 8518796.

References

[AL 62]   G. M. Adelson-Velskii, Y. M. Landis: An algorithm for the organization of information (in Russian), Dokl. Akad. Nauk SSSR, Vol 146, 263-266, 1962.

[BM 72]   R. Bayer, E. M. McCreight: Organization and maintenance of large ordered indexes, Acta Informatica, Vol 1, 173-189, 1972.

[BS 77]   R. Bayer, M. Schkolnick: Concurrency of operations on B-trees, Acta Informatica, Vol 9, 1-21, 1977 .

[Be 75]   J. L. Bentley: Multidimensional binary search trees used for associative searching, Comm. ACM, 18, No 9, 509-517, Sep 1975.

[EL 80]   H. Edelsbrunner, J. van Leeuwen: Multidimensional algorithms and data structures (bibliography), Bulletin of the EATCS, 1980.

[Fr 87]   M. W. Freeston: The Bang file: a new kind of grid file, Proc. ACM SIGMOD Conf. 1987.

[FKN 80] H. Fuchs, Z.M. Kedem, B.F. Naylor: On visible surface generation by priority tree structures, Computer Graphics (Proc. SIGGRAPH '80), Vol 14, 3, 123-133, 1980.

[Gun 88] O. Gunther: Efficient structures for geometric data management, Lecture Notes in Computer Science, 337, Springer 1988.

[Gut 84] A. Guttman: R-trees: a dynamic index structure for spatial searching, Proc. ACM SIGMOD Conf. on Management of Data, 47-57, 1984.

[HSW 89] A. Henrich, H-W. Six, P. Widmayer: The LSD tree: spatial access to multidimensional point- and non-point-objects, Proc. VLDB, Amsterdam, 1989.

[Hin 85] K. Hinrichs: *Implementation of the grid file: design concepts and experience*, BIT 25 (1985), 569 - 592.

[K 68,73] D. E. Knuth: "The Art of Computer Programming", Addison-Wesley. Vol 1 "Fundamental Algorithms", 1968; Vol 3 "Sorting and Searching", 1973.

[KL 80]   H. T. Kung, P. L. Lehman: Concurrent manipulation of binary search trees, ACM TODS, Vol 5, No 3, 354-382, Sep 1980.

[LS 89]   D. Lomet, B. Salzberg: The hB-tree: A robust multiattribute search structure, Proc. 5-th Int. Conf. on Data Engineering, Feb 1989.

[Man 88]   M. Mantyla: An introduction to solid modeling, Computer Science Press, Rockville, MD, 1988.

[Me 84]   K. Mehlhorn: Data structures and algorithms, Vol 3, Multi-dimensional search and computational geometry, Springer, 1984.

[Ni 81]   J. Nievergelt: Trees as data and file structures. In CAAP '81, Proc. 6th Coll on Trees in Algebra and Progamming, (E. Astesiano and C. Bohm, eds.), Lecture Notes in Comp Sci 112, 35-45, Springer 1981.

[NHS 84]   J. Nievergelt, H. Hinterberger, K. C. Sevcik: *The grid file: an adaptable, symmetric multikey file structure*, ACM Trans. on Database Systems 9, 1, 38 - 71, 1984.

[NH 85]   J. Nievergelt, K. Hinrichs: Storage and access structures for geometric data bases, Proc. Kyoto 85 Intern. Conf. on Foundations of Data Structures (eds. Ghosh et al.), 441-455, Plenum Press, NY 1987.

[Ov 81]   M. H. Overmars: Dynamization of order decomposable set problems, J. Algorithms, Vol 2, 245-260, 1981.

[PS 85]   F. Preparata, M. Shamos: Computational Geometry, Springer-Verlag, 1985.

[Sa 89]   H. Samet: The design and analysis of spatial data structures, and Applications of spatial data structures, Addison Wesley, 1989

[SK 88]   B. Seeger, H-P. Kriegel: Techniques for design and implementation of efficient spatial access methods, 360-371, Proc. 14-th VLDB, 1988.

[SRF 87]   T. Sellis, N. Roussopoulos, C. Faloutsos: The R^+-tree: A dynamic index for multidimensional objects, 507-518, Proc. VLDB, 1987.

[Wi 78]   D. E. Willard: Balanced forests of h-d trees as a dynamic data structure, Harvard Report, 1978.

The Fieldtree: A Data Structure for Geographic Information Systems[*]

Andrew U. Frank

Renato Barrera

National Center for Geographic Information and Analysis

and

Department of Surveying Engineering

University of Maine

Orono, ME 04469, USA

FRANK@MECAN1.bitnet

RENATO@MECAN1.bitnet

Abstract

Efficient access methods, such as indices, are indispensable for the quick answer to database queries. In spatial databases the selection of an appropriate access method is particularly critical since different types of queries pose distinct requirements and no known data structure outperforms all others for all types of queries. Thus, spatial access methods must be designed for excelling in a particular kind of inquiry while performing reasonably in the other ones. This article describes the Fieldtree, a data structure that provides one of such access methods. The Fieldtree has been designed for GIS and similar applications, where range queries are predominant and spatial nesting and overlaping of objects are common. Besides their hierarchical organization of space, Fieldtrees are characterized by three other features: (i) they subdivide space regularly, (ii) spatial objects are never fragmented, and (iii) semantic information can be used to assign the location of a certain object in the tree. Besides describing the Fieldtree this work presents analytical results on several implementations of those variants, and compares them to published results on the Rtree and the R^+tree.

1 Introduction

Spatial databases deal with the description of the geometry and other attributes of objects in space. Present technology provides a persistent storage media (hard disk) with a linear address space, partitioned into pages. We will call *original* space to the one that contains the locus of the spatial entities.

---
[*]This research was partially funded by grants from NSF under No. IST 86-09123 and Digital Equipment Corporation (Principal Investigator: Andrew U. Frank). The support from NSF for the NCGIA under grant number SES 88-10917 is gratefully acknowledged.

The purpose of spatial access methods is to provide a mapping from regions in original space to sets of pages in *disk* space. To be efficient, that mapping should have two characteristics: (i) use disk space efficiently and (ii) require the least possible amount of disk accesses.

Spatial databases are used in several fields: CAD-CAM, GIS, VLSI design, image processing, etc. Spatial access methods are also used in non-spatial databases for the implementation of multikey indices, of joins in relational databases [Kitsuregawa 1989], etc.

This paper is organized as follows: The next section presents several existing spatial access methods that provide a foundation for section 3, in which the Fieldtree is described. Section 4 presents two implementations of the Fieldtree and the following section discusses the operations upon the trees. Section 6 presents analytical results for different implementations of the Fieldtree, and finally, we conclude with some comments.

2 Access Methods for Spatial Objects

A spatial access method should provide a mapping from a (multidimensional) original space to a (unidimensional) disk space. Ideally this mapping should preserve vicinities, i.e., should map neighboring objects in original space into neighboring disk pages. This is unfortunately impossible, since any bijective mapping from the $2\text{-}d$ plane to a line is discontinuous.

There are mappings, such as Morton keys [Samet 1984] or z-order [Orenstein 1986], that preserve some vicinities. The selection of an adequate mapping is complicated further by the fact that pages can hold a limited amount data; if the capacity of one of them is exhausted, a mechanism (such as splitting or chaining) for passing data to other pages should be provided, thus interfering with the desire of preserving vicinity relationships. Moreover, a good spatial access method ought to take into account the dynamic characteristics of data.

This section will deal with the types of spatial queries, with a method to simplify the solution to those inquiries, and with a taxonomy of spatial access methods.

2.1 Types of Spatial Queries

General-purpose DBMS's usually provide two types of access methods: the *primary* one that fetchs a record when given a unique identifier, and the *secondary* ones, retrieving sets of records that obey a specific predicate. The methods that provide the fastest primary access are ill-suited for secondary access; secondary access methods are not efficient enough for primary access.

In a similar fashion, spatial queries can be divided into two categories: (i) *point* queries, that return objects containing that point, and (ii) *range* queries that deal with objects fulfilling a given relationship with respect to a window $\mathbf{W}$ in original space. That relationship can be one of: (i) intersection (all objects with points in common with $\mathbf{W}$), (ii) inclusion (all objects that contain $\mathbf{W}$), (iii) containment (all objects wholly inside $\mathbf{W}$).

In agreement with the access methods used in general-purpose DBMS's, no known spatial access method performs optimally for all applications. Hence, we conclude that they should be designed for an outstanding performance under the most frequent conditions and a reasonably good one during the rest of the time. This implies that spatial access methods should be selected depending on the application area and that a spatial DBMS may provide more than one.

2.2 Simplifying the Description of Shape

Geometric information can be decomposed into two constituents: (i) position and (ii) shape. It is straightforward to include position into an indexing schema, but the expenses involved in utilizing a thorough description of the shape outweigh the advantages.

Thus, the simplification of the shape of an objects is very convenient for the design of efficient algorithms. That simplification is exclusively provided for the spatial index; the exact description of the shape should continue to be stored into the database. The most common simplification is based upon the tight enclosure of the object inside a simple figure; that figure will be later used by the access method as the object's spatial surrogate. The selection of a suitable figure involves two criteria: (i) a simple description, and (ii) good fit of the spatial objects to be considered. The most common ones are rectangles [Guttman 1984], circles [Hinrichs 1985] or a convex bodies [Günther 1989].

Circumscription with a simple figure has two advantages: (i) it reduces the storage needed for the access method and (ii) it simplifies and accelerates the processing of locational queries. It might, however, include references to objects that do not satisfy the desired spatial predicate.

Enclosing the objects within simple figures leads to the concepts of *transformed* spaces of higher dimension. A rectangle, for example, is completely characterized by the position of two diagonally opposed vertices, each described by two coordinates. Hence, any rectangle can be represented by four numbers, and thus, rectangles can be considered as a *point* in a four dimensional spaces. The coordinate selection for that four-dimensional space is not unique. Figure 1 illustrates three of those selections. Fig. 1a) shows a set of line segments, and figures 1b), 1c) 1d) display three coordinate selections, that use respectively: i) The coordinates of two opposed vertices ii) The coordinates of one vertex together with the extents of the rectangle along the ordinate and the abscissa axis iii) The coordinates of the centroid, together with the half-extents of the rectangle along the ordinate and abscissa axis.

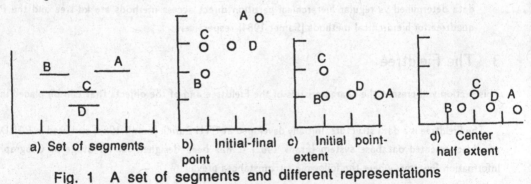

a) Set of segments b) Initial-final point c) Initial point-extent d) Center half extent

Fig. 1 A set of segments and different representations

2.3 Types of Spatial Retrieval Methods

A brief review of existing spatial retrieval methods will be given, as a preamble to the presentation of the Fieldtree with the intention of relating its characteristics to those of other methods.

Spatial retrieval methods can be classified in several categories, according to:

Type of geometric data (point vs. region)

A spatial access provides a map from a multidimensional original space to *disk* space. The access method is simpler if all spatial information refers to isolated points, since each can be assigned to a unique position in disk. Ambiguity may arise, however, while dealing with region data, because the mapping of an object from original to disk space can yield several disk addresses. That causes a need for methods specially tailored to a particular type of geometric data.

Handling of objects (non-fragmenting vs. fragmenting)

A spatial access method provides a map from the object spatial characteristics to a page in disk; if objects have non-zero dimensions, a fraction of them might be mapped into more than one page. Two alternatives follow: either (i) divide the object (at least conceptually) so each fragment is assigned to a unique page and increase memory size , or (ii) mantain the integrity of the objects and perform extra disk accesses. The R^+tree [Sellis 1987] is an example of the first alternative, while the Rtree [Guttman 1984] exemplifies the second one.

Retrieval method (direct vs. hierarchical)

This classification takes into account the implementation of the mapping between original and disk spaces and subdivides access methods into two categories: *direct* methods (such as the grid file [Nievergelt 1984]), that implement this mapping as a function, and *hierarchical* methods (such as the PR quadtree [Samet 1984]) that navigate through a data structure to obtain the desired disk address.

Space subdivison (regular vs. data determined)

Both direct and hierarchical methods consider subdivisions of space. That subdivision can be done in either of two fashions: (i) in a regular one, or (ii) according to the object's geometry and a criterion of minizing space usage and maximizing the speed of operations. Examples of data determined vs regular hierarchical partition direct access methods are kd-tree and the PR quadtree for hierarchical methods [Samet 1984] respectively

3 The Fieldtree

This section will present the characteristics of the Fieldtree and of the objects that can be placed into it.

The Fieldtree is a data structure, initially developed at ETH Zurich [Frank 1983] and used in PANDA, an object-oriented database system [Frank 1982] It has been designed for its usage in Geographic Information Systems, where the following circumstances prevail:

- Point, line and area objects are coexistent.
- Spatial nesting and partition of objects is common
- Range queries are frequent
- Spatial coverage among objects induce a lattice rather than a hierarchy.

3.1 Characterization of the Fieldtree

The Fieldtree provides a spatial access method that is:

- Region-oriented, works in the original space.
- Non-fragmenting.
- Hierarchical in nature.
- Based upon regular decomposition.

3.1.1 Original Space-Region Oriented

The Fieldtree is a hierarchical organization of (not necessarily disjoint) regions, called fields, each one associated to a disk page. If a disk page contains the data of an object, then the field associated to that page must cover the spatial extent component of the object. Organization in fields insures that many of the neigborhood relationships among objects are preserved in disk space.

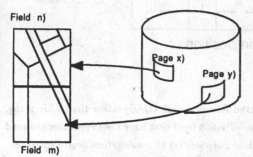

Fig. 2 Relationship between fields in original space and pages in disk space

A minimal bounding rectangle, as those introduced in Section 2.2, is associated to each object to facilitate geometric manipulation of data.

3.1.2 Non-Fragmenting

All of the data of an object is stored in a page associated with the field that covers the spatial component of the object. Fields are not necessarily mutually disjoint. If an object can be stored in several existing fields, additional rules are provided to allocate it to the one most suited to its type and size.

3.1.3 Regular Decomposition

Space is decomposed into squares, each one of them being a field. Similarly to a quadtree, there can exist several *levels* of decomposition; the squares at a certain level are regularly spaced and have the same extent, and the extents of the fields is typically halved from one level to the next. Two facts must be stressed:

i) Fields of a certain level need not be mutually disjoint (i.e, they form a cover, athough not necessarily a partition)

ii) A given level of decomposition nees not refine previous levels, i.e., a given field need not be exactly described as a union of fields at following levels.

Figure 3 shows two regular decompositions of space: (i) a partition and (ii) a covering. Dotted lines represent the boundaries of the so-called "median subfield", that is, the subfield spanned by the medians of the centroids of the fields.

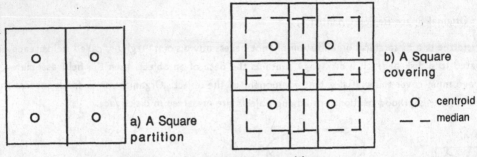

a) A Square partition

b) A Square covering

O   centrpid

_ _   median

FIG 3   Two   regular decompositions

3.1.4   Hierarchical organization

Fields at different levels of decomposition form a Directed Acyclic Graph (DAG) rather than a hierarchy. The descendants of a field F are all those at the next subdivision level that have their centroids spanned by the median subfield of F. That hierarchy serves a dual purpose: (i) as a navigation device for access to data, (ii) and as a pathway for data migration when fields become filled.

Since successive levels of decomposition need not refine each other, we are free to specify the relative displacement among the centroids of different levels of decomposition. The criterion for that relative displacement is one that avoids the placement of objects into fields far bigger than their size. Fig. 4.b) 4.d) show two different one-dimensional equivalents of the Fieldtree; the trees' fields are shown in 4.a), 4.c); those of 4.a) form a partition and the ones of 4.b) a cover. Section 4 will present two variations of the Fieldtree: one involving partitions and the other covers.

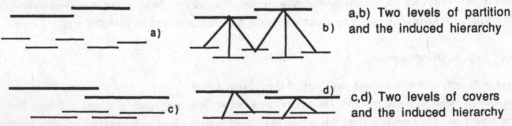

a)

b)

c)

d)

a,b) Two levels of partition and the induced hierarchy

c,d) Two levels of covers and the induced hierarchy

Fig. 4 Hierarchies induced   by partitions and coverings (1 dimension)

3.2   Optimization of Object Allocation

Two topics will be treated here: how to use semantic information to facilitate the retrieval and creation operations of objects, and how to handle overflow after an insertion.

3.2.1 Semantic Information

Queries in a database specify *a priori* the object types to be retrieved, as shown in the following query posed in a spatial SQL dialect [Egenhofer 1988a] that asks for the name of all cities in Maine and that utilizes the object types *city* and *state*:

```
SELECT  city.name
FROM    city, state
WHERE   state.name = "Maine" AND
        city.geometry INSIDE state.geometry
```

The approximate size of cities is much bigger than the one of many other entities (e.g., farms), and will be necessarily placed in the levels of the Fieldtree where fields cover larger areas. If that information is not available to the DBMS, an exhaustive and unnecessary search in the lower levels of the Fieldtree would be performed. It seems reasonable to attach to each type an 'importance' attribute that indicates the minimum size of a field where it can be placed, and thus limit the levels of the tree to be searched for objects of this type.

3.2.2 Overflow Management

The insertion of a new object into the database involves locating the proper field of the tree, using information both on the object data type and its size. Since a field has associated a certain data capacity, if that capacity has already been reached, the inclusion of an extra object causes the creation of one (or more) descendants of the field; all the objects from the original field that fit in the new field (or fields) will be transferred to their new location. If no object can migrate, the field disk storage is extended with an overflow page.

4 Variants of the Fieldtree

This section presents two versions of the Fieldtree. Some results on the behavior of those variants are presented in Section 6, and a more detailed presentation of those results can be found in [Barrera 1989].

4.1 The Partition Fieldtree

In this variant, in similarity to the PR quad-tree [Samet 1984], the fields constitute a partition of the space. In opposition to the PR tree, the centroids of the fields at the different levels of subdivision are not symmetrically placed. If objects are to be stored unfragmented, the symmetric placement of the centroids in the PR tree causes those objects that intersect edges of the Fieldtree to be stored at nodes of unnecessary large extent (Fig 5). This problem has been circumvented by some authors [Abel 1984] [Orenstein 1989] by allowing some controlled fragmentation in those cases. One of the design goals of the fieldtree was to avoid fragmentation.

The partition Fieldtree avoids this problem by shifting the positions of the centroids of one level with respect to those of the previous one. A relative displacement of one half the extent of a field in both coordinates guarantees that an object can be stored at most two levels above the lowest possible one

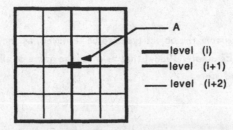

**Fig 5 Small objects might be positioned
at large nodes in a quadtree**

(based on its size only). Even if all objects are of the same size, their x-y position will determine in which of those three levels a particular object is placed and hence, the size of the receiving field. Fig. 6 shows the relative arrangement of fields at different levels.

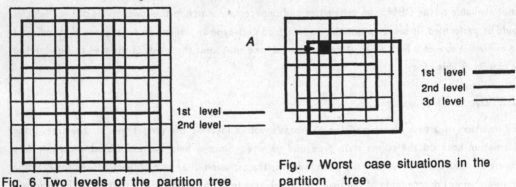

Fig. 6 Two levels of the partition tree

Fig. 7 Worst case situations in the partition tree

Some peculiarities of the partition Fieldtree are:

- Fields at different levels cannot have collinear edges.
- A field can have up to nine descendants. Althoug field form a DAG, then do not constitute a tree in the strict sense of the word. Depending on their position, fields can have a maximum of 1, 2 or 4 ancestors.
- Objects are intended to be placed into the field that fits them best. The worst fit involves placing an object in a field 2^3 times its size; that situation is illustrated by the black square of Fig. 7
- An object may be forced to descend two levels when a field splits (e.g, when it is placed in a position such as the one marked with an A in Fig. 7)

Even if the partition Fieldtree forms really a DAG, it can be implemented using that structure by selecting a spanning tree and treating the descendants of a field as *direct* and *indirect* children, as suggested by Banerjee et al. [Banerjee 1988]. A possible selection of the spanning tree for the one dimensional case is shown in Fig. 8. The use of a spanning tree has several advantages: it enables the adoption of a Morton-type key for each field, thus allowing a physical implementation as a linear array [Abel 1984]. It also provides a method for page clustering.

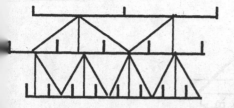

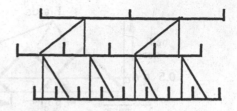

a) The Partition DAG   b) A spanning tree

Fig. 8 A DAG for a 1-d partition fieldtree and its spanning tree

4.2 The Cover Fieldtree

Similar to the PR quad-tree [Samet 1984] this tree keeps the centroids of the different space division levels symmetrically aligned. In opposition to it, fields generate a cover, not a partition: if d_c is the distance along the coordinate axis between two consecutive centroids, adjacent fields overlap $p \times d_c$ units along that axis (see fig. 10). Hierarchical regular covers of space have been used also in computer vision [Burt 1981].

Fig. 9a) shows the arrangement of the fields at a given partition levels, Fig. 9.b) the arrangement of the centroids of two consecutive partitions.

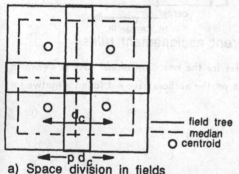

— field tree
-- median
O centroid

a) Space division in fields

b) Positioning of centroids at different levels

O level (i)
O level (i+1)

FIG 9 FIELDS IN THE COVER FIELD TREE

When $p < 1$:

- Each field has one main subfield, four subfields that it shares with either of its four *direct* neighbors along the coordinate axis, and four subfields that it shares with two direct neigbhors and one neighbor along a diagonal.
- A field can have up to 4 descendants and only one ancestor.
- Edges of different fields at different levels never coincide.

An overlap $p > 0$ between consecutive fields enables the storage of any object of size pd_c inside a field (see Fig. 10). Unlike the partition Fieldtree, it needs not resort to several tree levels to store a set of objects of identical size; moreover, only immediate descendants need to be considered when a field is split.

A consequence for overlapping fields is that objects can be placed in more than one field at a certain level of the tree. Thus, assignment rules must be provided. Some possible rules are:

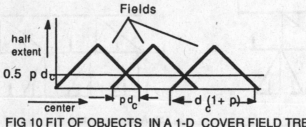

FIG 10 FIT OF OBJECTS IN A 1-D COVER FIELD TREE

Closest Centroid Assign to the field whose centroid is closest to that of the object's rectangle

Closest Corner   Assign to the field whose SW (or SE, etc.) corner is closest to the corresponding corner of the object's rectangle

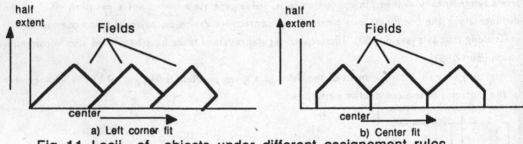

a) Left corner fit   b) Center fit

Fig 11 Locii of objects under different assignement rules

The coverage of fields under different assignment rules for the one dimensional case is shown in Fig. 11, using transformed (center, half-extent) space. As yet the authors have not found a motive for preferring among different rules.

5 Operations on Fieldtrees

Having considered the structure of the Fieldtree, its storage and retrieval algorithms will now be discussed. Afterwards, an overview of the different program modules will be presented.

5.1 Storage Algorithm

Each object is always stored into the smallest possible field, i.e., an existing field that fulfills the rules:

Fit: The object lies completely within the boundaries of the field

Importance: The field extension is large enough for the importance of the object. The importance is determined by the type of the object.

This leads to a (simplified) version of the algorithm:

1. Descend the tree while a smaller field exists that obeys both the fit and the importance rules.
2. Store the object into that smallest field.

The previous algorithm version will never make the tree grow; to do so, rules for creating new fields must be added:

- If the tree is empty, create the first and largest field; this field is the root of the tree.
- If the page on which to store the object has reached its capacity, reorganize the corresponding field

Reorganization is a mechanism intended at distributing the contents of one field that is overfilled over other (smaller) fields; if a field becomes saturated, one or more of its descendants must be created for the reception of all the data they can hold according to the fit and importance rules. Reorganization takes care both of the creation of a minimum of descendants and of the transference of a maximum of data; if no descendant can relieve a field of its excessive burden, an overflow page would be provided. Since overflow pages preserve the logical organization of a Fieldtree, a *lazy* reorganization can be included. That procedure always uses overflow pages and marks the fields as a candidates for a thorough off-line reorganization. Two courses of action can be taken during reorganization: either i) create all the descendant pages, or ii) follow a greedy strategy and create only the one descendant field that relieves the outfilled field most.

5.2   Retrieval

The recursive algorithm for retrieval has the following structure:

1. Initialize; start with the root of the Fieldtree.
2. Test a field (recursive)

While testing a field, if the field under consideration touches (or includes, is contained, etc.) the query window and obeys the importance rules then:

- The objects of the field must be included in the answer and
- All its existing subfields must be tested

6   Performance of the Fieldtree

This section presents in brief analytical results for the partition and the cover variants of the Fieldtree. A more detailed description of those results can be found in [Barrera 1989].

For each of those variants, two methods of implementing the hierarchy of the fieldtree are considered:

i) Including pointers inside the fields. This implementation will be referred to as the *pointer* one.
ii) Providing the fields with a Morton code, and using a B^+ tree to store pairs of (*field code, disk address*). This implementation will be referred to as the *multiway* one.

These results are compared to those obtained for the Rtree and the R^+tree by Faloutsos et al. [1987] Similarly to those authors:

- Objects are supposed to reside in a one dimensional space, inside the interval $[0.0, 1.0]$.
- Both point and range queries are considered.
- The analysis considers objects belonging to either one or two populations. Objects within a population have a fixed size and are uniformly distributed through space.

The same terminology of [Falcutsos 1987] will be used, namely:

C Maximum number of data items in a data leaf.

n Total number of data items.

σ Size of a data item.

f Fan-out of the tree (R^+tree, Rtree or B^+tree, depending on the context).

6.1 Comparisons, one population case

This subsection presents analytical results for point location and range queries. The performance in both cases is measured by the number of page accesses needed.

Taken from [Faloutsos 1987], a case with a population of $100,000$ objects, a fan-out factor f of 50 and a field capacity C of 50 objects was considered. All results are given for different values of the paremater $\sigma n/C$, that renders the fraction of the objects that overlap the edges of an R^+tree.

6.1.1 Point location Queries

Fig. 12 compares the performance of the partition and the cover Fieldtree to that of the R^+tree and the Rtree. Only the multiway implementation of the Fieldtree appears in this figure, since for this particular case is superior to that of the pointer implementation. Two extra cases are analyzed for the partition Fieldtree: one that passes the objects that overflow a field to the field's ancestor and one that utilizes overflow buckets.

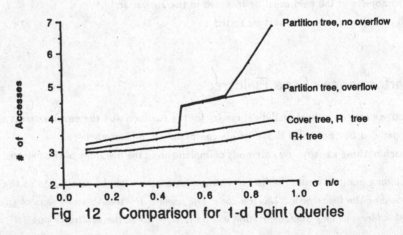

Fig 12   Comparison for 1-d Point Queries

From Fig. 12, it can be concluded that for the one-dimensional, one population case:

- The Cover Fieldtree and the Rtree perform identically.
- The Cover Fieldtree outperforms both variants of the partition Fieldtree. The variant of the partition Fieldtree that provides overflow records outperforms its alternate variant.

Further results in [Barrera 1989] show that, for point location queries, the superiority of the cover variant over the partition variant is preserved for the two-dimensional case.

6.1.2 Range Queries

Fig. 13 shows the average number of pages needed to access C objects in a range query as a function of the size of the query window. Three sets of graphs are provided, corresponding to values of $\sigma n/C$ of 0.1, 0.3 and 0.5. The parameter $\sigma n/C$ is a measure of the overlap of objects: a value of 0 corresponds to no overlap; a value of 1 completely disrupts the behavior of a 1-dimensional R^+tree.

That figure shows that:

- For the one population Fieldtree case, implementation by multiway trees outperforms that of pointers interior to the fields.
- Rtrees and Cover Fieldtrees that use multiway indexes again behave identically. They outperform all other variants.
- R^+trees are outperformed by partition Fieldtrees for high values of $\sigma n/C$

6.2 Results for two populations: Rtree vs. Cover Fieldtree

Faloutsos [1987] considers the case of a 1 dimensional Rtree with two populations of objects. The number and the extension of the objects in each population are called (σ_1, n_1), (σ_2, n_2). That reference also proves that in the case of two populations of objects one of them dominates, i.e., all formulas are the same as if they were from a single population with the dominant characteristics.

In the cover Fieldtree two situations can happen:

1. The importance of both types of objects is the same and, thus, their items are placed in the same level of the Fieldtree, and, as in [Faloutsos 1987], one of the populations dominates.
2. The importance of both types of objects is different and they are placed in the different levels of the Fieldtree.

Situation (2) is particularly attractive for range queries since then both populations become independent; no coupling at all occurs for the case of a pointer implementation of the hierarchy, and very little in the case of a an implementation by multiway trees. In this later case, the coupling can be greatly diminished if the positional keys of the objects are ordered "by levels", i.e., keys of fields a given level of the Fieldtree preceding all those corresponding to descendant levels.

As an example of that let us consider the following case: suppose that C and f are the same as above, and the existance of two populations such that:

$$n_2 = 16n_1 \quad . \quad n_1 + n_2 = 10^5$$

$$\sigma_1 = 16 * \sigma_2 \quad . \quad \sigma_1 n_1/C = 0.2$$

$$importance_1 > importance_2$$

The results of that example are illustrated in Fig. 14. In it, a case where the cover Fieldtree shows its superiority for range queries is demonstrated; it also shows that the superiority of a multiway implementation over a pointer one becomes less marked for mixed populations. Examples can be found, specially in the two dimensional case, where that superiority disappears.

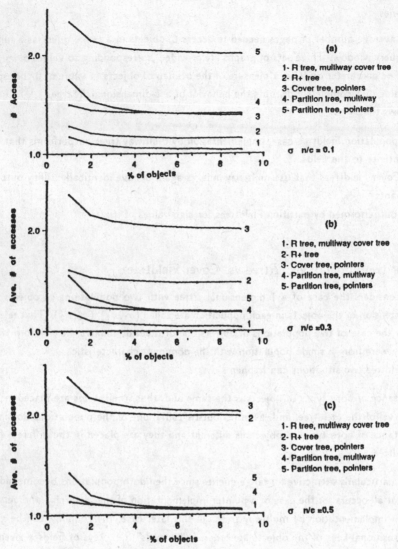

Fig 13 Comparison of Range Query Performance

7 Conclusions

The spatial access method presented here has the capability of clustering spatial objects according to their type; this feature is specially helpful in making the solution time of a query independant of the contents of the database, while still using a single spatial access mechanism. In opposition to the R^+ tree its performance does not degrade indefinitely as the object overlap increases. It differs from the R tree in the possibility of elliminating the *population dominance* effect. It is thus especially well suited for cases where data sets with many different types of spatial objects are stored, and queries refer to objects from a particular data collection.

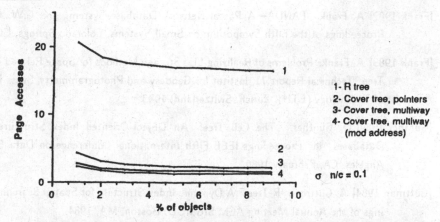

Fig 14 Average Number of Page Accesses, "C" objects

8 Acknowledgements

The authors wish to thank Max Egenhofer and Douglas Hudson for their discussions and their suggestions to improve this paper, and Jeff Jackson for his help in the preparation of the graphs.

References

[Abel 1984] D. Abel and J. Smith. A Data Structure and Query Algorithm Based on a Linear Key for a Database of Areal Entities. The Australian Computer Journal, 16(4), November 1984.

[Banerjee 1988] J. Banerjee et al. Clustering a DAG for CAD Databases. IEEE Transactions on Software Engineering, 14(11), November 1988.

[Barrera 1989] R. Barrera and A. Frank. Analysis and Comparison of the Performance of the Fieldtree. Technical Report, Department of Surveying Engineering, University of Maine, Orono, ME, March 1989.

[Burt 1981] P. Burt et al. Segmentation and Estimation of Image Region Properties through Cooperative Hierarchical Computation. IEEE Transactions on Systems, Man, and Cybernetics, 11(12), December 1981.

[Egenhofer 1988a] M. Egenhofer. A Spatial SQL Dialect. Technical Report, Department of Surveying Engineering, University of Maine, Orono, ME, September 1988. submitted for publication.

[Egenhofer 1988b] M. Egenhofer and A. Frank. Towards a Spatial Query Language: User Interface Considerations. In: D. DeWitt and F. Bancilhon, editors, 14th International Conference on Very Large Data Bases, Los Angeles, CA, August 1988.

[Faloutsos 1987] Faloutsos et al. Analysis of Object-Oriented Spatial Access Methods. In: Proceedings of SIGMOD Conference, May 1987.

[Frank 1982] A. Frank. PANDA—A Pascal Network Database System. In: G.W. Gorsline, editor, Proceedings of the Fifth Symposium on Small Systems, Colorado Springs, CO, 1982.

[Frank 1983] A. Frank. Problems of Realizing LIS: Storage Methods for Space Related Data: The Field Tree. Technical Report 71, Institut for Geodesy and Photogrammetry, Swiss Federal Institute of Technology (ETH), Zurich, Switzerland, 1983.

[Günther 1989] O. Günther. The Cell Tree: An Object-Oriented Index Structure for Geometric Databases. In: Proceedings IEEE Fifth International Conference on Data Engineering, Los Angeles, CA, February 1989.

[Guttman 1984] A. Guttman. R-Trees: A Dynamic Index Structure for Spatial Searching. In: Proceedings of the Annual Meeting ACM SIGMOD, Boston, MA, 1984.

[Hinrichs 1985] K. Hinrichs. The GRid File System: Implementation and Case Studies of Applications (in German). PhD thesis, Swiss Federal Institute of Technology, Zurich, Switzerland, 1985.

[Kitsuregawa 1989] M. Kitsuregawa et al. Join Strategies on KD-tree Indexed Relations. In: Proceedings Fifth International Conference on Data Engineering, Los Angeles, CA, February 1989.

[Nievergelt 1984] J. Nievergelt et al. The GRID FILE: An Adaptable, Symmetric Multi-Key File Structure. ACM Transactions on Database Systems, 9(1), March 1984.

[Orenstein 1986] J. Orenstein. Spatial Query Processing in an Object-Oriented Database System. ACM-SIGMOD, International Conference on Management of Data, 15(2), 1986.

[Orenstein 1989] J. Orenstein. Redundancy in Spatial Databases. ACM-SIGMOD, International Conference on Management of Data, 1989.

[Samet 1984] H. Samet. The Quadtree and Related Hierarchical Data Structures. ACM Computing Surveys, 16(2), June 1984.

[Sellis 1987] T. Sellis et al. The R+-Tree: A Dynamic Index for Multi-Dimensional Objects. In: P. Stocker and W. Kent, editors, 13th VLDB conference, Brighton, England, September 1987.

A FULL RESOLUTION ELEVATION REPRESENTATION REQUIRING THREE BITS PER PIXEL

Clifford A. Shaffer

Department of Computer Science
Virginia Polytechnic Institute and State University
Blacksburg, Virginia 24061

ABSTRACT

A quadtree-like representation for storing gridded elevation data is described. The data structure is a pyramid with each node containing two bits of data. The root of the pyramid has associated with it the minimum elevation for the corresponding grid and the maximum variance (the difference between the minimum and maximum values). The elevation value at any pixel is calculated by traversing a path from the root to the pixel, refining the local elevation value during the decent by interpreting the two bit codes stored with each node along the path. Since the total number of nodes in the pyramid is 4/3 the number of pixels required for the bottom level of the pyramid, the amortized storage cost is less than 3 bits per pixel, regardless of vertical resolution. This scheme is most appropriate for efficient secondary storage archival, such as on a CD-ROM. It allows efficient retrieval of complete elevation data from any sub-region, at multiple scales, within the entire elevation database. This is a lossless encoding when the difference between sibling pixels is not "too great".

1. INTRODUCTION

The need for high quality topographic data combined with the difficulties encountered when processing such large volumes of data have resulted in many competing representations. One method is to store a collection of benchmark points with associated elevation values. The value for locations not explicitly stored is derived by interpolating the values of nearby *a priori* data points. This approach is time consuming since the nearby data points must be located, and the interpolation performed. The reliability of

This work was partially supported by General Dynamics and by the Virginia Center for Innovative Technology.

such an interpolation is also questionable (consider for example, the results of fractal geometry [Mand82]). Finally, the storage requirements include space for the coordinates of the data points since they may not be at specified intervals. One popular variation on the benchmark point approach is the Triangulated Irregular Network [Peuk78].

Another approach to storing elevation data is as a grid with an elevation value at every cell. Stereographic gestalt mapping techniques make this an attractive approach since grid data is easily captured from areal photographs [Kell77]. This method typically requires 8 or 16 bits of data at every grid cell (depending on the range and resolution of the elevation values). For large areas of the earth at any reasonable resolution, this approach requires a great deal of storage.

The quadtree [Same84] and its many variants has successfully supported a number of cartographic applications. The quadtree data structure provides a spatial index to locate spatial data objects efficiently. For example, see [Shaf86] for a description of a prototype GIS that supports thematic regions, points, and linear feature data. Many related approaches have also been applied to computer cartography and computer graphics applications requiring spatial indexing. For example, EXCELL [Tamm81], image pyramids [Anto86, Shaf87], and others. For the remainder of this section, I will loosely use the term "quadtree" to refer to all such spatial indexing methods.

The quadtree approach attempts to save both space and time over simple grid approaches by either aggregating homogeneous regions (as does the simple region quadtree), or by spatially organizing a collection of data objects (as does the PM quadtree for lines [Same85b]). Such approaches have not been successful in the past for representing elevation data since such data does not fall into either category. Elevation data may be viewed as a surface whose z value varies over the x and y dimensions. Unless the vertical resolution is extremely coarse in relation to the horizontal resolution, neighboring pixels in the corresponding grid are not homogeneous. Thus the region quadtree approach will not be space efficient since there are no homogeneous blocks to aggregate. [Cebr85] suggests that while the quadtree will not compress homogeneous blocks, the elevation grid should still be arranged in Morton order [Mort66] since it would than be more compatible with quadtree-based GIS.

Another approach to applying a quadtree representation to topographic data is to derive a relatively small collection of spatial data objects from the data to be stored by means of a spatial index. One approach is to generate a collection of surface patches to approximate the topographic surface [Mart82]. [Chen86, Leif87] apply the quadtree representation to this technique.

The benchmark point method of storing elevation data may be more amenable to spatial indexing methods since the data points could be indexed with a PR quadtree [Same84] or a grid file [Niev84]. However, while the spatial index makes it easier to locate data points near to a query point, the interpolation problems remain. In addition, if the number of data points is high in relation to the number of grid cells at the desired resolution, than the additional storage required to support the spatial indexing method may well be greater than that required by simply interpolating the data points over the grid and storing the grid. Note that the grid requires no storage overhead beyond the data value at each grid cell. If the number of data points is greater than about 10% of the grid cells, the grid will probably be more efficient in space and time than the aforementioned quadtree methods.

We present an alternative approach to representing elevation data, termed the *elevation pyramid*. The elevation pyramid uses an image pyramid structure [Tani75] to allow aggregation of the elevation data at higher levels in the pyramid. This aggregation allows full resolution elevation data to be stored at an amortized cost of less than 3 bits per grid cell. It is a generalization of the DEPTH coding scheme of Dutton [Dutt83], though our approach to coding methods is quite different.

2. DATA AMORTIZATION

Trees are often used to aggregate computation costs when processing the data stored in the tree. For example, if every leaf node in a tree must be visited, it is inefficient to travel from the root to each leaf node of the tree in turn. Instead, a tree traversal is performed where each node of the tree is visited once. Since the total number of nodes in the tree is $O(N)$ where N is the number of leaf nodes, the total cost of a traversal is $O(N)$, not $O(N \log N)$ or worse as would be required if each leaf were processed separately. The cost of traversing the path from the root to any leaf node is amortized over the entire traversal. An example of such amortization of the computation in a quadtree is the neighbor passing traversal algorithm of [Same85a]. Here, the neighbors of the child of a quadtree node Q are recognized to be children of Q and its neighbors. Thus, the neighbor-finding computation can be amortized over the traversal of the tree.

While amortization of computation by tree methods is commonly practiced, amortization of the data to save storage is less common. One well known approach is the *trie* [Fred60, Aho83], which can be used to store dictionaries in a space efficient manner. For example, assuming a 26-letter alphabet, the trie can be represented as a 26-way tree with each branch labeled by a corresponding letter. All words starting with 'a' would be placed in the 'a' branch of the tree; those starting with 'b' in the 'b' branch, etc. At the second level of the tree, words are further separated by their second letter, and so on. To locate a word in the trie, the path from the root to the desired word is followed, collecting the letters during the process. The total amount of storage required is related to the number of differences between words, not to the total number of characters in the words.

The trie data structure not only compresses the number of characters that must be stored, but also organizes one-dimensional data for efficient retrieval. When storing elevation data, we must be concerned with three dimensions: the location in 2-D space and its elevation value. Both the grid, and hierarchical spatial data structures such as the quadtree, index space with the location of cells or nodes implicitly contained in their structure. Objects whose data values are correlated to their positions are amenable to data aggregation.

An idealized (though impractical) example of such an aggregation would be the location of quadtree blocks. Morton codes [Mort66, Garg82] have been used extensively as an addressing technique to support the linear quadtree (i.e., a quadtree representation that stores only leaf nodes along with a description of their size and location). One way to derive the Morton code is by interleaving the bits of the x and y coordinates for a pixel. An alternative characterization is as a description of the path from the root to the pixel. The NW branch has a 2 bit code, say, 00. The NE branch has code 01, and so on. The address for a pixel is the concatenation of the codes for each branch in the path. If it were desirable to explicitly store the Morton code address for each node, one could store the complete address of size $2 * n$ (for a $2^n \times 2^n$ image) with each node. A more space efficient approach is to store with each node the 2 bit code representing the branch from the node's father. The complete address is generated by concatenating the codés during the descent. The addresses of neighboring nodes are perfectly correlated, and perfectly inheritable from the parent. A simple inductive proof on k-ary trees shows that the total number of nodes in a quadtree is $\frac{4}{3}L$ where L is the number of leaf nodes in the tree. Thus, this technique would require only $\frac{8}{3}$ bits per node.

Of course, there is no reason to store Morton code addresses with the nodes in a tree structure since they can be computed from the tree structure during traversal. In fact, the most significant application of Morton codes in quadtree representations is to eliminate the tree structure itself. However, other types of data are such that nearby nodes have correlated data values. The concept of aggregating the related portions of the data in the common ancestor nodes can be used in these cases. One significant example of such data is elevation.

The method developed in this paper is related to the technique of progressive transmission for images [Sloa79, Know80, Hill83, Hard84]. Progressive transmission contains elements of both computation and data amortization. These methods store in a variable some form of "average" value for the image, and utilize a tree structure to store "differences" indicating how the refinement takes place as one proceeds through the tree. These methods allow for transmission of images with no loss of information, no increase in storage requirements, and yet at the same time allowing ever-improving versions of the image to be transmitted. In addition, homogeneous regions of such images need not be redundantly transmitted at finer resolution. Progressive transmission allows the receiver to cut the transmission prematurely if the full resolution image is not desired. Note that these methods do not utilize data aggregation for storage compression. The application of lossless image transmission does not encourage the storage saving method described in this paper since adjacent image pixel values are not sufficiently well correlated.

3. THE ELEVATION PYRAMID

This section describes our representation for elevation, termed the *elevation pyramid*. This representation reduces the storage requirements of the grid method for storing elevation data to less than 3 bits per grid cell. It does this by taking advantage of the correlation of the data values for pixels within any region of the grid.

The pyramid structure [Tani75] is derived from a $2^n \times 2^n$ grid. The pyramid can be viewed as a stack of arrays which stores at the bottom level the entire image of size $2^n \times 2^n$. At the next level, each disjoint 2×2 pixel block is represented by a single cell, with the entire image at this level represented by $2^{n-1} \times 2^{n-1}$ cells. This process continues until the nth level, which contains a single cell. Thus, the pyramid is equivalent to a complete quadtree, i.e., one in which all internal nodes have four children and all leaf nodes are at the lowest level of resolution. However, the pyramid representation requires no pointers since the memory location of the children, sibling, and parent nodes can be derived from the memory location of the current node (much like traditional storage techniques for the *heap* data structure [Aho83]). We define the bottom level to be level 0, and the root to be level n.

The basic elevation pyramid represents an elevation map as follows. Associated with the pyramid is the minimum value of all pixels in the image, and the difference (or variance) between the minimum and maximum values. We define two global variables, ALLMIN and ALLVAR. ALLMIN stores the minimum value within the image. ALLVAR is the greatest power of 2 less than or equal to the difference between the minimum value of in the image and the maximum value. As the pyramid is traversed, local copies of these variables will be refined until the pixel level is reached, at which point the actual value for that pixel is determined.

Each internal node of the pyramid is 8 bits long, divided into 4 fields of 2 bits each. Strictly speaking, these four fields represent the codes for the children of that internal node; however, implementation is more efficient if these values are grouped together to form a single byte value. Leaf nodes (i.e., level 0 in the pyramid) thus do not require any storage. Since the complete pyramid contains $\frac{1}{3}N$ internal nodes where N is the number of pixels, with each internal node requiring 8 bits, the total amount of storage is $\frac{8}{3}$ bits/pixel.

Each 2-bit field represents the required modification to the minimum and variance values for the current node to generate the corresponding values for the child associated with that field. In our initial coding scheme, the first bit indicates modification to the minimum elevation for that subtree, while the second bit indicates modification to the maximum variance for that subtree. Specifically, the two bits can be defined by the following operations on variables M and V, which will then be passed to the child node for future operations:

Code 00 - $M_{new} := M_{old}; V_{new} := V_{old}/2;$
Code 01 - $M_{new} := M_{old}; V_{new} := V_{old};$
Code 10 - $M_{new} := M_{old} + V_{old}/2; V_{new} := V_{old}/2;$
Code 11 - $M_{new} := M_{old} + V_{old}; V_{new} := V_{old};$

Determining the value of a pixel begins with the root of the tree, where M is initialized to ALLMIN, and V is initialized to ALLVAR. As the pyramid is traversed from the root to the desired pixel, the appropriate two-bit field is processed and the variables updated. When a pixel is reached, the stored value for that pixel is in M. Algorithm 1 shows Pascal-like pseudocode for the decoding operation using this coding method. Figure 1 shows a sample elevation grid and the corresponding elevation pyramid. Pointers are drawn between nodes in these figures purely to aid in viewing the picture. An actual implementation would store the nodes as a list in memory.

Construction of the coded elevation pyramid is easily performed. We assume that the original elevation array is available during the coding process. This elevation data is stored into the base of a temporary pyramid which is capable of storing the minimum value and variance for each node in the pyramid. Two passes are then made over the temporary pyramid. The first pass sets at each internal node of the temporary pyramid the minimum value and variance for its sub-pyramid. This is performed by a simple post-order traversal of the pyramid. The second phase generates (and outputs) the encoded form of the final pyramid. ALLMIN and ALLVAR are set based on the minimum value and variance of the root. For each internal node of the pyramid, the minimum and variance values of each child are examined. The function MAKECHILDCODE compares these values to the current value of M and V to generate the proper code. As a side effect, MAKECHILDCODE sets the minimum and variance values of the child node in the intermediate pyramid to the values computed from the codes traversed thus far, making these values available when MAKECHILDCODE is executed on the child. One advantage of this approach is that the algorithm we present can easily be converted to operate as a breadth-first traversal. The PASCAL pseudo-code for the second pass in this process is shown in Algorithm 2.

4. VARIANTS ON THE ELEVATION PYRAMID

Ideally, the elevation pyramid would provide a completely faithful representation of the original elevation data. The term "faithful" is used instead of "accurate" considering that the source of elevation data is often suspect. A potentially significant problem with the coding scheme described in the previous section is that rapidly changing elevation values cannot be faithfully represented, as shown in Figure 2. Note in this figure that 5 pixels (whose values are circled) were incorrectly labeled. In each case the computed value is one less than the true value. Figure 3 reverses the pixel elevation values of Figure 2 in order to demonstrate that the minimum elevation representation does not give anomalous affects when the minimum value varies rapidly. Figure 3 yields similar results to Figure 2.

We see that the elevation pyramid tends to smooth out rapid changes in elevation. The significance of this problem would depend on the relationship between horizontal and vertical resolution. If the original elevation data is not extremely accurate, minor degradation in the representation may not be of concern. However, greater faithfulness can be achieved through various modifications to the basic coding algorithm.

Note that the code generation function of Algorithm 2 has been very carefully constructed. Changes in this function can lead to significant changes in the quality of the codes produced. For example, the variance value can be the greatest power of 2 *less than or equal to* the true variance, as opposed to the greatest power of 2 *less than* the true variance. Otherwise, a variance of 1 would always be reduced to 0, yielding incorrect values. Another feature of the function MAKECHILDCODE is that it first checks and, if possible, modifies the minimum value for the child without regard to the child's variance. In the case of code 11, this could lead to rapid increases of the minimum value while maintaining the variance even when the true variance for that area is rather low. However, it is reasonable to expect that in general, if the minimum value is changing rapidly, the variance will remain high. Likewise, code 10 allows a moderate increase in the minimum value, but forces a decrease in the variance regardless of the true state. One might be concerned that an area with a slightly higher minimum value but a high variance might be incorrectly coded since the variance is artificially reduced at the expense of an increase in the minimum value. However, this is not normally a problem since small increases in the minimum value can only occur when the variance is already low enough to allow them (since the least increase is $V/2$). Modifications to the code generating function, or the definition of the codes themselves, would form one class of variants to our algorithm.

Another class of variants on our basic coding scheme results from storing and modifying values other than the local minimum and variance. For example, the average elevation value for the subtree and the variance could be stored, with a suitable modification being to add or subtract the current variance at each branch in the tree. We do not speculate further on such variants.

A third class of variants results from modifying the definition of the codes based on the current level in the pyramid. Defining the lowest level to be 0, the next as 1, etc., we can modify the codes based on level to take advantage of peculiarities at the bottom two levels. In particular, we note that modification to the variance at the bottom level is not significant, except for its affect when added to the minimum. A better coding for the bottom level would be to increase the range of effect for the variance. Thus, an improved coding for the bottom level would be as follows.

Code 00 - $M_{new} := M_{old}$;
Code 01 - $M_{new} := M_{old} + V_{old}/2$;
Code 10 - $M_{new} := M_{old} + V_{old}$;
Code 11 - $M_{new} := M_{old} + 3V_{old}/2$;

Further, we expect that the bottom level will require lower variance than higher levels. Thus, we prefer to modify the code for level 1 as follows.

Code 00 - $M_{new} := M_{old}$; $V_{new} := V_{old}/2$;
Code 01 - $M_{new} := M_{old}$; $V_{new} := V_{old}$;
Code 10 - $M_{new} := M_{old} + V_{old}/2$; $V_{new} := V_{old}/2$;
Code 11 - $M_{new} := M_{old} + V_{old}$; $V_{new} := V_{old}/2$;

Note that this version changes the meaning of only code value 11 from the original, decreasing the variance. This works especially well in conjunction with the described modification for level 0 which allows more flexibility for smaller variances. Figure 4 shows the elevation grid for Figure 2 as it would be coded using these modified functions. In this example, only the lower right pixel varied too quickly for the coding scheme to faithfully reproduce. Algorithm 3 presents the modified MAKECHILDCODE function.

A fourth class of variants has to do with the number of bits stored at each node of the pyramid. Storing more bits would allow for a greater number of codes. This in turn would allow for more flexibility in representing images with high local variance. In fact, we can view the 2 bit per pixel elevation pyramid as being at one extreme of a continuum of representations whose other end would store complete elevation data at every node, as in the traditional image pyramid [Tani75]. A space-efficient modification that is worthy of future examination is to store an extra 2 bits for internal nodes of the pyramid. Since $\frac{3}{4}$ of the nodes are at the bottom level, this would raise the amortized storage requirements only from $\frac{8}{3}$ to $\frac{10}{3}$ bits/pixel.

A fifth class of variants is based on use of a bintree pyramid instead of a quadtree pyramid [Tamm84]. A bintree pyramid would store at level 1 a $2^n \times 2^{n-1}$ array with each cell corresponding to 2 cells at level 0; level 1 would be a $2^{n-1} \times 2^{n-1}$ array; and so on. Since the bintree pyramid has as many internal nodes as leaf nodes, the storage requirements will be 4 bits/pixel. However, the bintree provides additional control over the elevation and variance values, allowing more accurate representation. This is because each internal node of the quadtree is equivalent to three internal nodes in the bintree, arranged in a triangle. The result is that for each internal node along a path in the quadtree, there will be two equivalent nodes in the bintree. This allows for more opportunity to correctly modify the values. Another alternative is to use a bintree, but store only 1 bit/node instead of two. Odd levels would store, e.g., V bits, even levels would store M bits (thereby making the final modification be to the pixel's minimum value). This would require only 2 bits/pixel total storage. The relative abilities of these variants to faithfully represent elevation data as compared to the 2 bit/node quadtree method await further investigation.

A final consideration is the order of storage for nodes in the pyramid. Heaps [Aho83] are traditionally stored in breadth-first order. It may be the case that for large, disk-based images, that a depth-first storage order is preferable to minimize disk accesses during traversal.

5. ARCHIVAL STORAGE, RETRIEVAL, AND TRANSMISSION

The primary motivation for the elevation pyramid technique is not so much to store elevation data for direct manipulation, but rather for large scale archival with relatively fast retrieval. Using the elevation pyramid, large portions of the earth's surface could be stored on disk or CD-ROM. In this application, the user would like to retrieve portions of the database for further processing. Such retrieval must be done quickly, so long term archival methods are not desirable if they slow the retrieval process. The region to be represented may not be a simple square region of land, but may include significant portions of ocean or lake. We suggest that a quadtree be used to represent the entire map, perhaps using a scheme to account for the spherical shape of the earth as reported in [Mark87]. This upper-level quadtree would be used primarily to distinguish ocean from land. At a certain level in the tree, those nodes that do not represent entirely water would store a pointer to an elevation pyramid. Additional savings can be obtained by storing a single node in the quadtree in lieu of any large flat area, not just the ocean. Such a representation would allow for the efficient representation of elevation for large portions of the earth's surface.

Given an elevation pyramid encoding, it may be desirable to extract a smaller region, possibly at some intermediate scale. For example, given an elevation pyramid archived at size 8K $\times$ 8K at 1:100,000 resolution, the user may desire a 512×512 subtree. This is easily obtained by traversing from the root of the pyramid to the appropriate internal node representing the root of the subtree containing the desired region, and generating only the complete elevation data for that subtree. If arbitrarily positioned regions are desired, windowing techniques such as described in [Shaf89] are appropriate. Images at double scale, quadruple scale, etc. are easily obtained by stopping before reaching the bottom of the pyramid. Scales that are not powers of two above the base scale can also be obtained, but would require resizing and interpolating.

The motivation for the progressive transmission techniques mentioned at the end of Section 2 are to support efficient transmission of images. This was facilitated both by compact storage, and by the ability to generate ever improving resolution for the image. The elevation pyramid can be used for progressive transmission of elevation data in the same sense. The upper levels of the pyramid can be transmitted first, followed by lower levels, providing ever improving resolution.

6. STORAGE REQUIREMENTS

It should be clear that the elevation pyramid provides enormous space savings for topographic data as compared to the standard grid method when the topography data has high resolution, e.g., 8-16 bits/pixel. Region quadtrees and related data structures must expect to require even more storage to represent elevation data since they require additional overhead with no benefit from aggregation of data. One might expect, however, that the region quadtree would perform better for contour maps, such as the one shown in Figure 5. This image shows the 100 foot contour levels from part of a USGS quadrangle depicting the Russian river region in northern California. This map is about as simple a set of topographic data as would ever likely be used.

Surprisingly, the elevation pyramid compares quite favorably to the quadtree even for this simple image. The original image is 400 × 450 pixels, yielding an image array of 360 kbytes if each pixel requires 16 bits. Since there are only 11 contour levels in this particular image, we could compress this to 4 bits/pixel, requiring 80 kbytes. The elevation pyramid would require about 350,000 nodes at 2 bits/node. This gives a total of 87 kbytes of storage, regardless of the vertical resolution. The quadtree for this image requires about 25,000 leaf nodes. As an example of an actual quadtree GIS implementation, the **QUILT** system [Shaf86], which uses a linear quadtree [Garg82] organized by a B-tree for efficient access requires 8 bytes/node, spread onto a disk file requiring a total of about 270 kbytes. However, this implementation does not provide great storage savings over the array; its goal it to provide efficient manipulation of maps.

A storage optimizing linear quadtree implementation might forego the B-tree in favor of a simple linear list. The data portion of the linear quadtree node could be reduced to 2 bytes, requiring a total of 6 bytes/node. This yields a total requirement of 144 kbytes. Even better space performance could be obtained by a DF-expression [Kawa80] representation for the quadtree. This structure could store full resolution nodes requiring only 2 bytes/node, but would store 4/3 the total number of leaf nodes (about 25,000). Thus the total storage requirements would be 67 kbytes. Using only 4 bits/node would reduce the requirements to only 17 kbytes. This is much better than the most compact array or the elevation pyramid. However, this relies on (1) a very sparse quadtree; (2) low vertical resolution; and (3) sacrifices random access to the quadtree nodes.

The main points to be observed are that the elevation pyramid is easily manipulated (i.e., windows and point queries can easily be performed), has high vertical resolution, and still compares favorably in storage requirements to the array or quadtree under all but the most favorable conditions for those latter structures.

7. CONCLUSIONS AND FUTURE WORK

The elevation pyramid allows for full gridded elevation data to be stored in a manner that requires less than 3 bits/pixel. It's storage and time requirements should compare quite favorably to traditional non-grid methods for storing elevation data. Many variants on the basic scheme are possible, and a few are described. No doubt, better refinements will be discovered in the future. Extension of the elevation pyramid to 3 dimensions (for example, to store 3-D densities) are straightforward.

Our plans for the immediate future are to test the elevation pyramid algorithms on wide range of elevation data to determine the amount of information loss in typical images. We will implement and compare several of the variants described. Finally, we will develop characterizations for the types of images that can be encoded without loss of information for the most promising variants.

8. ACKNOWLEDGEMENTS

I would like to thank Dave Boldery for implementing the algorithms described in this paper, and for double-checking and correcting my calculations.

9. REFERENCES

1. [Aho83] A.V. Aho, J.E. Hopcroft, and J.D. Ullman, *Data Structures and Algorithms*, Addison Wesley, Reading MA, 1960.

2. [Anto86] R. Antony and P.J. Emmerman, Spatial reasoning and knowledge representation, in *Geographic Information Systems in Government*, vol. 2, B.K. Opitz, Ed., A. Deepak Publishing, Hampton, VA, 795-813.

3. [Cebr85] J.A. Cebrian, J.E. Mower, and D.M. Mark, Analysis and display and digital elevation models within a quadtree-based geographic information system, *Proceedings, Auto-Carto 7*, Washington, D.C., 1985, 55-65.

4. [Chen86] Z.T. Chen and W.R. Tobler, Quadtree representations of digital terrain, *Proceedings of Auto-Carto London*, Vol. 1, London, September 1986, 475-484.

5. [Dutt83] G.H. Dutton, Efficient encoding of gridded surfaces, in *Spatial algorithms for processing land data with a microcomputer*, Cambridge MA: Lincoln Institute for Land Policy Monograph Series, 1983.

6. [Fred60] E. Fredkin, Trie memory, *Communications of the ACM 3*, 9(September 1960), 490-499.

7. [Garg82] I. Gargantini, An effective way to represent quadtrees, *Communications of the ACM 25*, 12(December 1982), 905-910.

8. [Hard84] D.M. Hardas and S.N. Srihari, Progressive refinement of 3-D images using coded binary trees: Algorithms and architecture, *IEEE Transactions on Pattern Analysis and Machine Intelligence 6*, 6(November 1984), 748-757.

9. [Hill83] F.S. Hill, Jr., W. Sheldon, Jr., and F. Gao, Interactive image query system using progressive transmission, Computer Graphics 17, 3(July 1983), 323-330.

10. [Kawa80] E. Kawaguchi and T. Endo, On a method of binary picture representation and its application to data compression, *IEEE Transactions on Pattern Analysis and Machine Intelligence 2*, 1(January 1980), 27-35.

11. [Kell77] R.E. Kelly, E.P.H. McConnell, and S.J. Mildenberger, The Gestalt photomapping system, *Photogramm. Engng Rem. Sens. 43*, (11), 1407-1417.

12. [Know80] K. Knowlton, Progressive transmission of grey-scale and binary pictures by simple, efficient, and lossless encoding schemes, *Proceedings of the IEEE 68*, 7(July 1980), 885-896.

13. [Leif87] L.A. Leifer and D.M Mark, Recursive approximation of topographic data using quadtrees and orthogonal polynomials, *Proceedings of Auto-Carto 8*, Baltimore, MD, 1987, 650-659.

14. [Mand82] B.B. Mandelbrot, *The Fractal Geometry of Nature*, Freeman, New York, 1982.

15. [Mark85] D.M. Mark and J.P. Lauzon, Approaches for quadtree-based geographic information systems at continental or global scales, *Proceedings of Auto-Carto 7*, Washington, D.C., 1985, 355-364.

16. [Mort66] G.M. Morton, A computer oriented geodetic data base and a new technique in file sequencing, IBM Canada, 1966.

17. [Niev84] J. Nievergelt, H. Hinterberger, and K.C. Sevcik, The grid file: an adaptable, symmetric multikey file structure, *ACM Transactions on Database Systems 9*, 1(March 1984), 38-71.

18. [Peuk78] T.K. Peuker, R.J. Fowler, J.J. Little, and D.M. Mark, The triangulated irregular network, in *Proceedings of the DTM Symposium, American Society of Photogrammetry - American Congress on Survey and Mapping*, St. Louis, MO, 1978, 24-31.

19. [Same84] - H. Samet, The quadtree and related hierarchical data structures, *ACM Computing Surveys 16*, 2(June 1984), 187-260.

20. [Same85a] H. Samet, A top-down quadtree traversal algorithm, *IEEE Transactions on Pattern Analysis and Machine Intelligence 7*, 1 (January 1985), 94-98.

21. [Same85b] H. Samet and R.E. Webber, Storing a collection of polygons using quadtrees, *ACM Transactions on Graphics 4*, 3(July 1985), 182-222.

22. [Shaf87a] - C.A. Shaffer, H. Samet, and R.C. Nelson, **QUILT**: a geographic information system based on quadtrees, University of Maryland TR 1885, July 1987.

23. [Shaf87b] C.A. Shaffer and H. Samet, An in-core hierarchical data structure organization for a geographic database, Computer Science TR 1886, University of Maryland, College Park, MD, July 1987.

24. [Shaf89] C.A. Shaffer and H. Samet, Set operations for unaligned linear quadtrees, to appear in *Computer Vision, Graphics, and Image Processing*, also Department of Computer Science TR 88-31, Virginia Polytechnic Institute and State University, Blacksburg, VA, September 1988.

25. [Sloa79] K.R. Sloan and S.L. Tanimoto, Progressive refinement of raster images, *IEEE Transactions on Computers 28*, 11(November 1979), 871-874.

26. [Tamm81] M. Tamminen, The EXCELL method for efficient geometric access to data, *Acta Polytechnica Scandinavia*, Mathematics and Computer Science Series No. 34, Helsinki, 1981.

27. [Tamm84c] - M. Tamminen, Encoding trees, *Computer Vision, Graphics, and Image Processing 28*, 1(October 1984), 44-57.

28. [Tani75] S. Tanimoto and T. Pavlidis, A hierarchical data structure for picture processing, *Computer Graphics and Image Processing 4*, 2(1975), 104-119.

10. APPENDIX

---

function DECODE(*root* : ↑ PYR; *x, y* : integer) : ELEVATION;
  { Generate the elevation value at point (x, y) in the pyramid with root pointer *root*
  and size $2^n \times 2^n$. ALLMIN and ALLVAR is the minimum and total variance for
  the entire pyramid. While *root* and *currnode* are indicated as pointers to pyramid
  nodes, in practice they would likely be indexes into an array implementing the
  pyramid. }
var
  currnode : ↑ PYR;
  m, v, currx, curry, currlev, half : integer;
begin
  currnode := *root*; *m* := ALLMIN; *v* := ALLVAR;
  currx := 0; *curry* := 0; *currlev* := *n*;
  repeat
    currlev := *currlev* − 1; *half* := $2^{currlev}$;
    if *x* >= *currx*+ *half* **then**
      if *y* >= *curry*+ *half* **then**
        begin *child* := SW; *currx* := *currx*+ *half*; *curry* := *curry*+ *half* **end**
      else begin *child* := NW; *currx* := *currx*+ *half* **end**
    else if *y* >= *curry*+ *half* **then**
      begin *child* := SE; *curry* := *curry*+ *half* **end**
    else *child* := NE;
    case *currnode.value[child]* **of**
      '00': *v* := *v*/2;
      '01': ;
      '10': **begin** *v* := *v*/2; *m* := *m* + *v* **end**;
      '11': *m* := *m* + *v*
    end{ Case }
    currnode := CHILDOF(*currnode*, *child*);
  until *currlev* = 0;
  return (*m*)
end;

Algorithm 1. Decoding algorithm.

---

procedure PASS2(*root* : ↑ NODE; *n* : integer);
  { Second pass of pyramid construction. Produces the pyramid in depth-first order. *root* is the root of a subtree in the intermediate pyramid containing minimum and variance values for each node. }
var
  q : integer;
begin
  for *q* in { NW, NE, SW, SE } **do**
    OUTPUT(MAKECHILDCODE(*root.min*, *root.var*, *root.child*[*q*].*min*,
                 root.child[*q*].*var*));
  if *n* <> 1 **do**
    for *q* in { NW, NE, SW, SE } **do** PASS2(*root.child*[q], *n* − 1)
end; { PASS2 }

function MAKECHILDCODE(*currmin*, *currvar* : integer;
                var *childmin*, *childvar* : integer) : CODE
  { Create the child's code. In the process, set the child's computed estimage of minimum and variance values into the pyramid for future use. }
var *code* : CODE;
begin
  if ((*currmin* + *currvar*) <= *childmin*) **then**
    begin *code* := '11'; *childmin* := *currmin* + *currvar*; *childvar* := *currvar***end**
  else if ((*currmin* + *currvar*/2) <= *childmin*) **then begin**
    code := '10'; *childmin* := *currmin* + *currvar*/2; *childvar* := *currvar*/2 **end**
  else if (*currvar* <= *childvar*) **then**
    begin *code* := '01'; *childmin* := *currmin*; *childvar* := *currvar* **end**
  else
    begin *code* := '00'; *childmin* := *currmin*; *childvar* := *currvar*/2 **end**
end; { MAKECHILDECODE }

Algorithm 2. Encoding algorithm: second pass.

```
function MAKECHILDCODE(currmin, currvar : integer;
      var childmin, childvar : integer): CODE; { Modified child code generator. }
var code : CODEVAL;
begin
   if level <> 0 then { not bottom level }
      if ((currmin + currvar) <= childmin) then
         begin code := '11'; childmin := currmin + currvar;
            if level <> 1 then childvar := currvar else childvar := currvar/2
         end
      else if ((currmin + currvar/2) <= childmin) then
         begin
            code := '10'; childmin := currmin + currvar/2; childvar := currvar/2 end
      else if (currvar <= childvar) then
         begin code := '01'; childmin := currmin; childvar := currvar end
      else begin code := '00'; childmin := currmin; childvar := currvar/2 end
   else { bottom level }
      if ((currmin + 3 * currvar/2) <= childmin then code := '11'
      else if ((currmin + currvar) = childmin then code := '10'
      else if ((currmin + currvar/2) = childmin then code := '01'
      else code := '00';
end; { MAKECHILDECODE }
```

Algorithm 3. Modified encoding algorithm with special codes at bottom two levels of the pyramid.

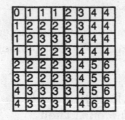

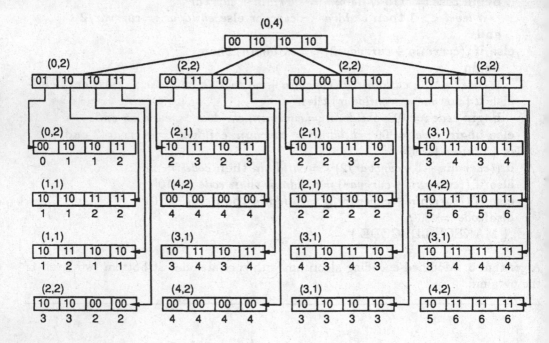

Figure 1.   An elevation grid and its elevation pyramid using standard coding.

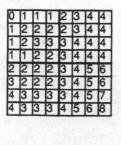

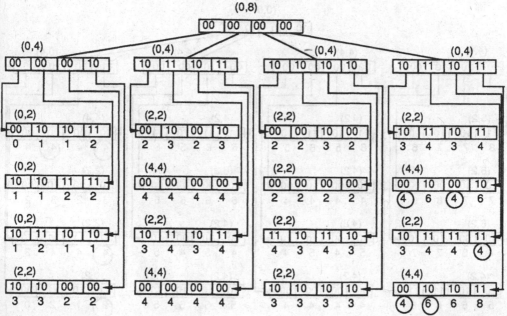

Figure 2. Elevation grid and pyramid using standard coding for an elevation grid whose values rise too rapidly for the pyramid to faithfully represent all grid values. Incorrectly valued pixels are circled.

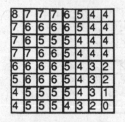

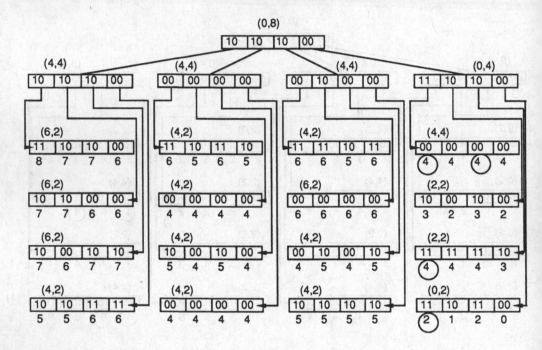

Figure 3. Elevation grid and pyramid for the same grid as in Figure 2, except that all values v have been replaced by 8 - v. Incorrectly labeled values in the pyramid are circled.

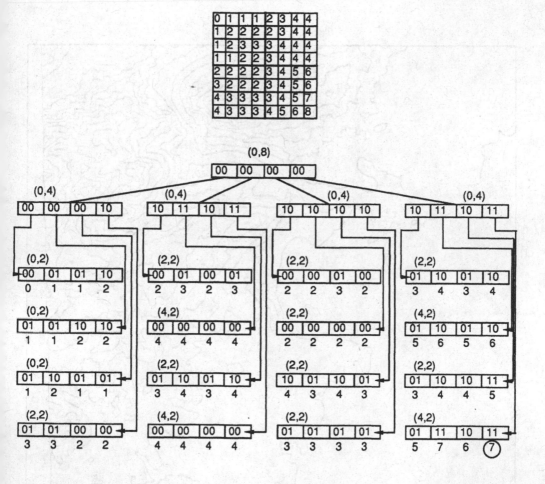

Figure 4. The elevation grid of Figure 2 and its elevation pyramid derived using the level-modified coding rules. Pixels incorrectly labeled by the pyramid are circled.

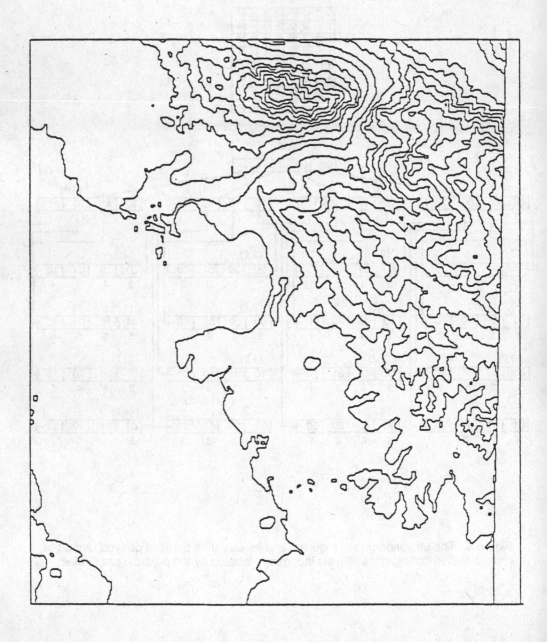

Figure 5. A simple elevation map.

System and Performance Issues

The DASDBS GEO-Kernel,
Concepts, Experiences, and the Second Step

Andreas Wolf
ETH Zürich
Computer Science Department

Abstract:

The DASDBS GEO-Kernel, a member of the DASDBS family, has been developed as an extension of the DASDBS kernel system, especially configurated for the management and manipulation of geoscientific data. It is a combined approach using a new powerful data model for the description of storage structures and a set-oriented user interface with an Object Buffer and extensibility to achieve a closer connection to the application programs. First evaluations that have been made will be presented here. They resulted in a deeper knowledge of the real requirements of geoscientific applications. A partial redesign of the DASDBS GEO-Kernel resulting from this experiences will be presented here too. It enhances the capabilities of the application oriented Object Buffer and the external type interfaces for very large data items.

1. History and Motivation

The DASDBS[1] project was started by H.-J. Schek in 1983 at the Technical University of Darmstadt as a research project for non-standard database systems [DOP*85]. Its main goals can be summarized as

- kernel architecture to support different application classes with one storage system
- data model for storage structures to support complex objects
- set oriented interfaces inside the system and to the application programs to reduce interface crossings
- support for large structured and unstructured data items
- good software engineering to allow development with a large group of people including students with small subtasks

This ideas led to an overall architecture called the DASDBS family:

---

[1] DArmStadt DataBase System

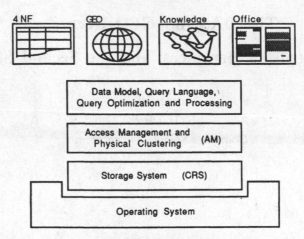

Fig. 1: The DASDBS family

The basic system part the *Complex Record System* (CRS), the application independent storage system for hierarchically structured data. It is designed to build an efficient storage manager with a high level user interface to reduce the algorithmic complexity for the higher system levels. Its complex records are mapped to an "ideal operating system interface", a set-oriented, transaction based page-I/O interface.

On top of this storage system the *Access Manager* (AM) provides different methods for mapping application objects to those of the CRS *(Clustering)* and for additional access paths *(Indexing)*. The AM allows to embed new types in the database system via a configuration interface. Such *Externally Defined Types* (EDT) [WSSH88] are introduced via predicates and procedures that are defined for them. Clustering and access strategies can be embedded too, to allow the use of dedicated algorithms designed for externally defined types.

The two components together, CRS and AM, constitute the DASDBS application oriented kernel and can possibly be used as a stand alone base for expert application programmers and developers of dedicated application interfaces.

The system must be completed by an application specific query processor which can be derived from a kind of generic query processor with an extensible and configurable data model. It includes an extensible optimizer, e.g. a rule based system, to handle the varying parts of the model together with the fixed ones. It also provides a query language adequate for the specific application class.

Although our current implementations in the DASDBS family deal with all the four different application fields, sketched in the picture above, this paper will focus only on the geoscientific front-end.

Throughout the last years, a large effort in research and implementation has been in the area of geoscientific information processing [SW86,HSWW86]. Two research projects, 'Digital Geoscientific Maps' [NLfB88] and 'GEO Database Systems'[2], led us to an almost complete implementation of the so called GEO-Kernel. Its main goal is to support the storage and retrieval of spatial information, like geometries of rivers, towns, meadows,

[2]Both projects are funded by the German Research Association (DFG)

and fields, together with numerical and alphanumerical informations according to this geometric data in a dedicated database kernel. We provide spatial search (e.g. select the area of interest out of a map) together with object based retrieval (e.g. give all information about the town 'Washington').

During the last years several other projects started to evaluate new architectural models. Extensibility concepts have been worked out e.g. in GENESIS [BBG*86], Starburst [SCF*86], POSTGRES [SR86], Probe [DS86], and EXODUS [CDF*] where the first one especially focussed on the aspect of generating a complete dedicated system from a kind of component library. More remarks on the similarities and differences between our approach and these projects are added at the end.

In this paper we review our design, and report on implementation experiences and our first performance evaluations from the two geo-data management projects. We will especially take a closer look on the EDT implementation and integration and their use together with the spatial access and clustering techniques. We also draw some conclusions and indicate new design alternatives for a second implementation.

2. The First Implementation

We have implemented our system following a bottom up strategy. This has the disadvantage of getting system parts that may work quite well but offer a bad user interface. The advantage is the chance to optimize deeper levels of the system during the implementation of the upper ones, a kind of evolutionary development for the different layers.

2.1 The Complex Record System

This main component of all future members of the DASDBS family has been designed in two parts. The *Stable Memory Manager* (SMM) provides us with an abstract interface to an (optimal, future) operating system. It allows a fast access to sets of pages, optimized with chained I/O [Wei89]. A basic transaction mechanism for the higher layers guarantees atomicity, persistency, and isolation for sequences of SMM actions, the so called *SMM Transactions*. The implementation uses the Cache-Save technique [EB84] which guarantees optimal I/O performance especially with chained I/O.

The *Complex Record Manager* (CRM) implements NF^2-relations with a subset of the NF^2-relational algebra, completely defined in [Scho88], the set of so called *single pass processible* operations. It is designed to handle those types of queries that can be processed within a single scan through the affected page set. NF^2 tuples are clustered by the CRM: long tuples exclusively occupy a set of pages (a 'cluster', their 'local address space'), only short tuples share pages. Structural information is clustered separately within the local address space of a tuple to provide for selecting the necessary pages of the cluster for I/Os [DPS86]. Parts within an NF^2 tuple are referenced via hierarchical TIDs (HITIDs) [DPS86], a variant of the classical TID scheme, which makes references relative to the cluster. Thus we keep addresses stable against local and global reorganisations.

The interface of the Complex Record System (CRS) is algebraic and thus set oriented. *Object Buffers* (OB) are used for the management of sets of input and result tuples. They are a consequent follow-on of the portals approach described in [SR84]. The Object Buffer is designed and implemented as an abstract data type to allow a free choice of its internal representation. We decided to use one similar to the external storage organisation, i.e. a page oriented internal structure, exclusive page sets for tuples, and the same locally defined HITIDs for references between the tuples components. The decision was made to allow the CRS as the only module in the system to by-pass the procedural interface and to do a direct copy from page frames to the Object Buffer to minimize interpretation overhead. However because of the parallel bottom-up development of the system in its current stage, the CRS uses the standard user interface to the OBs and does not exploit its knowledge of the special internal structure.

The Object Buffer interface consists of two major parts: one for the navigation through the tuple set via a cursor which is moved by *next* and *prior* within one level and *down* and *up* to move through the NF²-hierarchy. The second group of operations is used for the manipulation of objects: to *create* and *delete* (sub-)tuples and to *insert*, *delete*, and *change* bytestring attributes.

2.2 The GEO Access Manager

The Access Manager encapsulates the management of different data organisation methods (*storage methods*) and index techniques (*access methods*). It has almost the same interface as the CRS, extended with procedures for physical design control. Most importantly, it is the first layer handling different attribute types. An example for the capabilities of the AM retrieval interface can be seen in appendix 1, part of an example program using the AM is given in appendix 2.

The introduction of types at this system layer is directly coupled with the purpose and implementation of storage and access methods. These are designed as an optimized path to data with respect to a well defined set of predicates on attributes. Examples are B+-trees, built to support equality, less/greater than, and intervals, hash structures for equality or similarity (e.g. soundex), and Grid-File for spatial neighbourship, intersection, and inclusion tests. Obviously, the algorithms of those methods require the existence of some predicates and procedures as part of the implementation, like less_than, modified equality operators e.g. sounds_like, or intersection test. Therefore the introduction of predicates and operations - which is introduction of types - requires access methods for efficiency, on the other hand, the latter require the former for their implementation. The dependence is two-fold.

The tasks of the Access Manager can be subdivided into those dedicated algorithms based on the semantics of the application and many common management functions (see fig. 2). The common functions include algorithms for the analysis and modification of queries, e.g. to detect predicates supported by access methods, to transform user predicates into supported ones, or to add maintenance qeuries for secondary access structures. They manage the address sets resulting from access method calls, integrate them into the original query, and apply this modified query to the storage methods containing the affected data. They also handle *meta information* about the stored relations, their storage structure, available indices, and statistics like estimated retrieval cost. Even though the system is prepared for these functions necessary for (non-algebraic) query optimization, only a few of them are currently implemented.

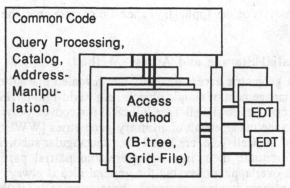

Fig. 2: The Access Manager

The second part of the AM deals with the *extension* with specific data organization and access algorithms. They can be integrated via a well defined interface to allow a free configuration of the system, depending on the needs of the application class to support. The interface supports general methods with flexible parameter lists to *create* and *drop* indices, operations to *insert, retrieve*, and *delete* sets of <key,{value}> or <key,{address}> tuples. In addition to those standard routines, index implementations have to offer an interface for statistical information to allow the optimizer to calculate the cost of a potential index operation. The optimizer also uses some additional method descriptions like allowed key types and supported predicates.

Both system parts require access to the implementation of predicates and procedures of the application specific types, as an integrated part of the access methods algorithms and to postprocess results. Data organisation techniques and indices only exist for some simple predicates to guaranty generality. Only very few storage structures exist to support predicates like point in polygon directly (e.g. external plane sweep structures [BG87]), but they do not allow other query types. Therefore in general, the more specific predicates have to be transformed into inexact primitive ones and the exact predicate is tested later on the resulting (small) set of candidates. A spatial search with a polygonial search area, for example, is converted into a test against a rectangular window which is quite simple and well supported by several methods e.g. Grid-File or R-Tree. Afterwards the result is postprocessed in the common system part by applying the exact *polygon versus polygon* check. (An analogous procedure in text retrieval is a signature test.)

In the same way, storage and access methods are imported via a defined interface, types in the AM are only plugged in procedure implementations and not build-in code. This allows for free extension of the AM with any type necessary to support an application and, moreover, it allows an application to do this extension by introducing a type to the AM that is implemented *in the application program*.

A schematic view in figure 2 shows the two-way extensibility of the system, externally defined user types (EDT), to introduce semantics of the applications, and access methods to support the new predicates and procedures serving in two functions: in the classical way as indices and more advanced as storage methods to organize data directly.

Even though the main parts of the AM are developed and implemented as an application independent universal module, many aspects of the architecture and design have been influenced by the analysis of the application specific components, the GEO storage and access methods.

2.3 Extensible Spatial Storage and Access Methods

Our investigation in geometric access methods has revealed that all of the well-known techniques for the management of simple objects, e.g. Grid-File [NHS84] for points, R-Tree [Gutt84] for rectangles, and Cell-Tree [Gue89] for convex polygonial objects, can be easily extended to the management of arbitrary geometries [WWH88]. Most of them, with the exception of the Cell-Tree, are based on a rectangular subdivision of space into cells. We can differentiate them into complete and partial partitioning methods, overlapping and non-overlapping ones, but the general idea is always the same. Objects (which are points in most implementations) belong to cells, if they are inside the rectangular area represented by the cell.

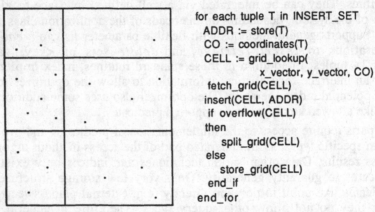

```
for each tuple T in INSERT_SET
    ADDR := store(T)
    CO := coordinates(T)
    CELL := grid_lookup(
                    x_vector, y_vector, CO)
    fetch_grid(CELL)
    insert(CELL, ADDR)
    if overflow(CELL)
    then
        split_grid(CELL)
    else
        store_grid(CELL)
    end_if
end_for
```

Fig. 3: Point-Grid-File storing addresses

As an example, the principal structure of (the classical implementation of) the Grid-File insert algorithm is sketched in figure 3. It allows to store the addresses of points in a dynamically refined partitioning of space that is complete, non-hierarchic, non-overlapping, and non-equidistant.

This simple mechanism can be applied to more complex geometries as well. Only the inclusion test, which is geometry type-specific and often more complicated than in the point case, has to be performed instead of the simple coordinate test for point geometries. When reduced to a test on the minimum circumscribing rectangle (bounding box) instead of the correct geometry test, the *grid_lookup* routine at least will work without any changes, although now returning multiple cells as result of one call. These observations, to be made in every access method, lead directly to an advanced usage of those well known techniques.

When handling more complex objects, a new problem has to be solved, because the relation between objects and subparts of space (cells) is no longer simple. Points belong to only one cell, whereas lines or areas may belong to multiple ones. If we want both, the original algorithms and the non-redundant storage, we have to cut objects in a way, such that subparts are related to only one cell. Therefore additional operations for *clipping* and *composing* geometries have necessarily to be implemented for each geometry type. In figure 4 you will find the slightly modified Grid-File algorithm that handles extended geometries. The major changes are handling of CELL_SETs instead of single CELLs, because of the complex geometries, and calling the geometry-type specific algorithms for computing the bounding box and the clip function to compute the cell-specific subparts of the geometries.

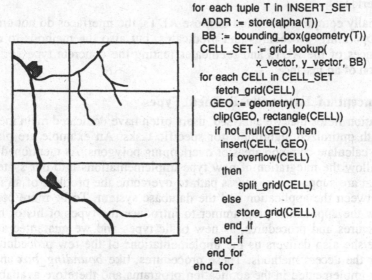

```
for each tuple T in INSERT_SET
    ADDR := store(alpha(T))
    BB := bounding_box(geometry(T))
    CELL_SET := grid_lookup(
                x_vector, y_vector, BB)
    for each CELL in CELL_SET
        fetch_grid(CELL)
        GEO := geometry(T)
        clip(GEO, rectangle(CELL))
        if not_null(GEO) then
            insert(CELL, GEO)
            if overflow(CELL)
            then
                split_grid(CELL)
            else
                store_grid(CELL)
            end_if
        end_if
    end_for
end_for
```

Fig. 4: Area-grid-File storing complete geometries

An important result of our research is that any geometry type, regardless of its structure, can be handled by those slightly modified spatial access methods. Additionally, any such method can be used as storage method too. All we need is the implementation of the mentioned operations. The methods become **extensible**. In the above algorithm we can emphasize this fact by changing the geometry-type specific calls to *bounding_box* and *clip* and *not_null* into

    bounding_box(geometry_type(geometry(T),geometry(T))
    clip(geometry_type(GEO),GEO,rectangle(CELL))
    not_null(geometry_type(GEO),GEO)

A detailed analysis of other techniques, e.g. hierarchical partitionings of space like quadtree related algorithms, shows, that this method can easily be applied to them too. There are only a few techniques that need different operations on the geometric types. One of the most important, the R-Tree, is a technique already developed for one class of non point geometries namely rectangles. It is obvious, that this algorithm can work with arbitrary geometries if just a subset of the above mentioned procedures is available, the *bounding_box* calculation. Another exception is the Cell-tree, a hierarchical partitioning of space into convex-polygonial subspaces. Its algorithm, designed to handle convex polygons, can be made extensible by providing a **clip** versus a convex polygonial area and the reverse **compose**. Although the operations are different in this case, the general method remains the same.

This observation can be generalized to all kinds of access methods for different application fields. Classes of access methods like the above class of rectangular search supporting spatial methods, but also for example signature access methods for text retrieval [eg. CS89], define a set of procedures that have to be supported by a geometric (or text) type, that is, they define an *Abstract Data Type (ADT)*. The methods will work well with any concrete representation of this geometry-ADT (text-ADT), e.g. polygon-lines, splines, circles, polygon-areas, and with any subtype supplying at least this minimum interface.

To get a formally complete definition of those ADTs, the interfaces do not only have to include the 'operating' procedures and predicates, but also the methods to create and destroy instances of the ADTs and predicates testing the concrete type i.e. the actual implementation of an instance.

2.4 The Concept of Externally Defined Types

In the application fields that we analysed, users often have dedicated main memory data structures with optimized algorithms for specific tasks. An example are plane-sweep algorithms to calculate common areas of overlapping polygons. As mentioned in the last section, we allow the integration of new type implementations into our system as new base types that are supported by access path to overcome the problem of an *impedance mismatch* between the application and the database system. To be more concrete, we want to allow the application programmer to introduce the types of his or her choice, i.e. data structures and procedures, as new basic types and we guarantee access path support, if he/she also delivers us the implementations of the few procedures that are necessary for the access methods. These procedures, like *bounding_box* and *clip*, are often already implemented in the application programs and therefore available without any additional work. Anyway, this forces us to find an extension mechanism allowing storage and retrieval of arbitrary data structures, defined in an arbitrary application language, and calling the corresponding operations, predicates and procedures from within the database system.

So we need an interface between the application program type representation and a database representation. We restrict the discussion here to the case that user defined objects are basic atomic types with respect to the data model of the kernel although the principal idea can be used in other cases too.

This interface has to be crossed at two different places in the system. One is the standard host-language interface which is always necessary when an application uses an embedded query language. In contrast to the known host language coupling supporting the exchange of values of *base types* like integer, real, or character string through special variables, we want to allow any *constructed type*, record, array, or even a pointer structure, to be transferred as one value of a user defined base type. Therefore we need a transformation of structured types to our database system's internal type, the linear bytestring representing the base type. This technique in principle has to be applied even in todays simple basic-type interfaces, but it is trivial because those types are already represented as strings. Only the more complex structures need an explicit conversion routine for both directions. We therefore have to detect in which cases the routines

IN :   User type   ->   Database type
OUT :   Database type   ->   User type

are trivial and in which they really need a transformation.

But there is a second place in the system, where the two worlds, the application with its specific type system in its specific programming environment and the database system with its implementation environment, have to fit together: the AM. Here the interpretation of types has to be done via calls to the procedures implementing the predicates and operations on the user's data structures. These procedures, implemented by the user in the application program environment, require their input in the application's type system. Therefore, the database system, with the only knowledge of its base type bytestring has to convert the data before calling the user's procedures. The mechanism is identical to the one at the programming interface. The complete processing model of our database system with the externally defined types can be seen in figure 5.

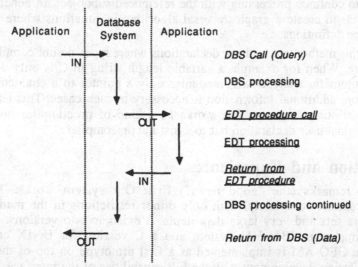

Fig. 5: Type conversions during DBMS processing

Since the IN and OUT conversion routines have to produce a valid representation of a value of a specific type, that will be used by the corresponding programming environment later on, they are extremely sensitive with respect to type correctness because they by-pass the standard language and compiler specific checks. Inside one program environment the assignment and processing operations are guaranteed to produce only valid instances and they are guaranteed to work correct on valid instances. The OUT procedure has to convert a string representation into a structured one and to move it to a variable of a different environment without using the standard assignment operation. It is therefore responsible to produce a value that looks like one produced by the compiler according to value ranges (e.g. only positive values), representation (e.g. encoding of numbers, adresses, etc.), and alignment (e.g. word boundaries for floats). Although IN and OUT are simple 'type casts' in the easy cases, it is a critical task to implement and integrate them and it should not be the responsibility of the application programmers.

Rather, our solution is to avoid any manual development of IN/OUT functions by generating the procedures automatically from the application programmers data structure definition. An EDT preprocessor analyses the type declarations and the procedure definitions in an application program or a special type implementation module. It creates and compiles the IN/OUT routines and prepares and establishes the links between the database system as the type user and the procedures implementing the types operations.

Our investigations have shown that this automatic generation of IN/OUT routines is possible in most languages in most cases. It is a task similar to the type analysis of a compiler. The difference is in declarations using pointers: here compilers only have to notice a variable, normally containing an address. A data structure analysis for the development of a conversion function, however, has to recognise that pointers refer to other parts of the structure, i.e. a conversion algorithm has to follow the pointer structure and to continue processing with the referenced subobject. In general, the EDT preprocessor has to create a graph traversal algorithm in situations where pointers are included in type definitions.

The limits of this method are in those declarations where types do not completely define a data structure. When for example a variable length string in C is only defined via a pointer, the automatic analysis will recognise only a pointer to a character and not a string. Therefore additional information is necessary in such cases. This leads us to an additional description language that works as a kind of precompiler option, not to replace the original user declaration but to assist the precompiler.

3. Evaluation and Experiences

The positive remarks (the "good news") first: Our system works. The CRS is implemented almost completely, with only minor restrictions in the manipulation of very large data sets and very large data items. It exists in two versions. A PASCAL version running in an IBM-VM system and a C version for UNIX environments [DBKSI]. The GEO-AM is implemented as a first prototype on top of the C version, allowing application development with the full capabilities of the interface. The internal algorithms are partially simulated, resulting in some performance lacks. Several access methods like Grid-File, R-Tree and Quad-Tree have been implemented and work with different GEO-EDTs. The first demo applications implemented are running quite well, a demo has been given on ACM SIGMOD '88, Chicago, and other research groups start to implement applications using the GEO-Kernel [Neu89].

To be honest, it has to be stated that this prototype has some problems. Besides the typical bugs in a new system (a problem that will be solved more or less in an intensive testing phase in the next month) we are not satisfied with the current performance of the system. Even though the applications are not terrifically slow, we do not reach the speed we have expected.

In this section we summarize the most important results of our first evaluation and analysis. The bottlenecks we found are discussed, the differences between the true requirements of our geoscientific test applications and our assumptions are described, and finally it is mentioned briefly what we learned about software engineering.

3.1 The Object Buffer

The Object Buffer (OB) appears in three different functions. It is the transfer unit between layers, a work unit inside our system, and the transfer unit between the set oriented kernel and the tuple and attribute oriented application world. The interface we chose, is a (sub-) tuple by (sub-)tuple and attribute by attribute interface using procedures like next/prior to move one step inside a level, up/down, to move one level in the hierarchy, and get/put to change one attribute at a time. Together with creation and deletion of attributes and tuples and some service functions we have 21 interface procedures. These very simple procedures have two advantages. They make the implementation very easy, and they are easy to understand for a user. The result is, that the OB had only a few bugs and the implementors of the CRM, the first users of the OB, had no problems using it.

Somehow opposit to this simplicity is the usability for more complex tasks. The effect of the traversal procedures of the OB, *up*, *down*, *next*, and *prior*, is pretty similar to dereferencing a pointer in a pointer chain. In the same way, the effect of attribute access via *get* and *put* is similar to accessing an array element via an index. Therefore, using the OB is similar to using pointer structures and arrays in a programming language, easy to understand and to use in simple cases. As an example, scanning the second atomic attribute of a set of tuples is shown in both ways in the following example

```
reset(OB_ID, Returncode);                          OB_PTR = OB[OB_ID].first;
while (Returncode<>End_of_OB)                       while (OB_PTR <> NIL)
{                                                   {
   get_attribute(OB_ID,2,value_buffer,Returncode);     val = OB_PTR -> attributes[2];
   next_tuple(OB_ID,Returncode)                         OB_PTR = OB_PTR -> next
}                                                   }
```

It is obvious, that a complex task like unnesting a subrelation of level 4 of a nested relation is as easy to understand, but much more complex to implement, because it requires at least 4 nested loops with actions on two different levels in source and target OB. The resulting program consists of OB-procedure calls at more then 80 percent.

In the early project stages the main effort has been to simplify the data transfer between the page layer and the structured object layers and the transfer between layers. Therefore the design of the internal structures has been chosen equivalent to the external tuple representation on the database pages. This allows for an optimized data transfer: internally data can be copied page by page and data structures need not be interpreted, in the cases where no projection changes the tuples structure, i.e. in insertions and some retrieval queries. On the other hand this internal OB-structure lacks performance when using the standard interface. Table 1 gives an impression on the CPU-times and the number of procedure calls needed for two sample programs using OB's. The programs both create and fill an Object Buffer, perform one scan reading every attribute once, and destroy the OB afterwards. The schemes used were:

FLAT(A1, A2, A3, A4 : char(4); A5 : char(200)),   2000 Tuple

NEST(A1, A2, A3, A4 : char(4); R1(A11, A12, A13, A14, A15: char(4)),

1000 Tuple, 10000 Subtuple

Procedures	Flat Relation		Nested Relation	
Tuple Size	216 Byte/Tuple		216 Byte/Tuple	
OB Size	~ 500 KByte		~ 560 KByte	
	#calls	time	#calls	time
generation	1	0.03	1	0.02
insertion	12000	14.68	66000	111.16
scan	12000	5.01	66000	43.80
deletion	1	1.00	1	0.54

Table 1. CPU-Times (seconds total) for sample OB-procedures

We see that the manipulation of complex structures costs much more than the manipulation of large, simply structured objects in terms of CPU-time and memory, and that the system itself is very expensive in terms of CPU-time.

3.2 Externally Defined Types

Our current system includes different implementations of geometric data types. Completely integrated are line and area representations via polygons implemented in C as variable length arrays of two-dimensional points. Developed and implemented, but not completely integrated, is a quadtree representation of two-dimensional areas. Both run together with the routines of the AM. The CRS has been extended with the new base-types point and rectangle, the basis for the implementation of spatial storage and access methods. The types are used in a demo application based on two different realistic data sets. One is a digitised map of Germany, containing cities, rivers, streets, railways, forests and conurbations. The second is a three dimensional thematic map containing results of geologic drillings with information about stratifications and faults.

The IN and OUT procedures for these types are trivial, because their representations belong to the class of data structures that are already allocated as linear strings by C compilers. A simple type cast yields the correct type in either world. Despite that, data has to be copied at least twice in the current implementation, before the AM can apply the external operations to it, once to move them from the page frames to the OB and a second time from the OB to a variable used in the procedures. The results of the procedures have to be copied too, back into the OB and in the application program into the target variable. Copying steps could be avoided, if the procedures could have a direct access to the page frames in the buffer pool or at least to the OB attributes for their read-only parameters.

One restriction has not been overcome yet, the problem of very long values, because the possibility to use long fields is not available until now. EDTs are always transformed to standard atomic attributes, leading to an upper limit of the EDTs length between 1 and 64 kByte depending on the users choice of the databases page size.

3.3 Externally Defined Storage and Access Methods

Our first implementation of storage and access methods started with stand-alone versions, proving the concepts of extensible methods with the duplicate functionality of clustering and indexing. We started using an existing implementation of Grid-File and a detailed description of a R-Tree development. Parallel to that we implemented our own versions to evaluate the usability of the extended functionality of our kernel system. The implementation of the modified Grid-File, a version with 2 directory levels, based on the CRS is completely integrated in the AM and is able to use the different geometric types implemented. R-Tree is running stand alone using the CRS and will be integrated into the AM soon.

The Grid-File has already been used in demo applications as a geometric index and the first evaluation results have been collected [Doe88]. Tables 2 and 3 present the first results with different database sizes and different sizes of randomly located query windows. The data sets used are parcels, simple polygones with 4 to 8 edges, which are relatively simple objects. Different databases have been created by replicating the base data set multiple times. The index is based on the circumscribing rectangles of the objects. In case of rectangles overlapping cell boundaries, multiple references have been stored.

#tuples	#references	#buckets	fill	#2nd level dirs	fill
2529	3626	151	54%	4	45%
7025	10683	432	55%	25	59%
22761	35465	1429	56%	25	65%
101141	161236	6285	58%	122	61%

Table 2. Data of generated Grid-Files

query size	db_2529	db_7025	db_22761	db_101141	result cand.
2 x 2	0.33	0.25	0.24	0.27	1
10 x 1000	0.33	0.33	0.37	0.47	7
100 x 10000	0.85	0.82	0.99	1.63	40
2000 x 2000	1.85	1.20	1.42	2.59	70

Table 3. Query evaluation times (seconds)

The detailed analysis has shown, that the implementation works very efficient for small query windows. A significant increase in CPU-time with the growth of the query result set has been detected as caused by an inefficient use of the OB by the chosen Grid-Files data structures and can be avoided.

The increase of the clipping factor, in the index expressed in the replication factor (#references/#tuples), is a little bit worrying. It is a measure for insert and retrieval cost because of the necessary EDT-procedure calls. If the cost for the EDT-clip-procedure gets significant when more complex geometries are managed, an improved clipping strategy, a slight modification of Grid-File may be necessary. Certainly, this data related costs for clip and compose will become part of the optimizing parameters in addition to the structure and algorithm related ones.

3.4 Application Development

In the application development field we have two sources of informations. We ourselves implemented several demo applications, some using the CRS directly, some using the

AM. The other feedback comes from those groups in other universities currently implementing their systems on top of DASDBS. This is mainly the group of H.-D. Ehrich at TU Braunschweig, developing and implementing a language and a query processing front end for geoscientific applications.

In the field of geometric data processing, our example implementations have shown, that the usage of the AM is easy and the resulting performance is acceptable. The retrieval interface is powerful enough so that many queries can be handled with only one AM call. Very helpful is the fact, that the management of storage and secondary access is completely hidden from the user.

The feedback of the external research group is positive too. It is obvious, that 'external' users have some more problems. Especially with a prototype system, there are two critical fields that make the use more difficult, errors and the missing or poor documentation. This was also true for the first version of our system and an intensive dialog with the users led to a large improvement in both areas. Apart from that, the users made experiences similar to those of the students implementing our own applications. The interfaces are easy to understand and especially the AMs powerful retrieval capabilities helped to increase implementation speed.

The systems performance is not satisfying the users. It is comparable to standard systems 'mis'used for non-standard applications. This is not very bad for the first prototype, but it is the main point to change.

3.5 Software Engineering - Theory and Praxis

The motivation for some of our decisions in program development style was, as mentioned, that our system is implemented by a few Ph.D. and more than a dozen master students. This required not only well defined, but also save interfaces. They rely on calling by value, to be sure to protect original data, but causing many copying actions. Most of the components are based on abstract data type concepts, using complete procedural access, fully hiding the implementation of the data structures. This allows flexibility in the choice of implementations and early interface definitions but it results in enormous path length. Most of the modules do intensive parameter checking to guarantee early error detection and to help testing upper system layers. The cost is a high testing overhead when modules are proven to be correct.

Remembering the main goals of software engineering, the methods worked well. We had less problems with module integration then one would expect in our heterogenous development environment. Testing has been made easy and the usage of subcomponents was simple and easy to understand. The internal interfaces support system development in the same good quality as the externals do for application development.

What has been left aside is the performance aspect. The straight forward implementation according to well known software engineering techniques guaranteed a fast development of the system but not the development of a fast system. Many of the ideas, like information hiding, call by value etc., are necessary design rules but, as our system pointed out, never implementation hints. A future implementation has to take care of this and to spend more time in development of implementation rules and control for the implementors. Software engineering has to be a rule of program behaviour and not of program implementation. So, as an example call by value means: >Don't change the values of this reference!< and not: >Let's make a copy to guarantee unchanged variables.<.

4. The Second Step

As pointed out in the last chapter, we started a partial reimplementation of our kernel system. Its major goal is a significant increase in system performance and some extensions in the systems functionality. Remembering our experiences with the implementation of the current system we decided to do the reimplementation ourselves, with only a few members of our group and without a participation of masters students.

4.1 A New Object Buffer

The motivation for a new implementation of the OB can easily be found. The principal module structure is shown in figure 6. It is a result of a first design and development step more than 5 years ago. The implementation has been done by 6 students using PASCAL. An almost one-to-one conversion to C led to our current Object Buffer.

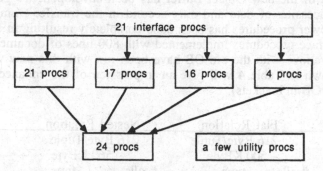

Fig. 6: Module structure and size of the Object Buffer

The lower 6 modules together have 6300 lines of well structured, documented code, i.e. less than half of it are true statement lines. With more than 90 procedures, this is about 30 to 35 statements per procedure, one third of them for parameter checks and error handling. The 21 top level procedures consist of 5500 lines of code, i.e. some 2500 statements, 20 percent parameter checks, and more than half of the remaining lines are calls to the deeper procedure levels. An intensive profiling of retrieval operations (insertions into the Object Buffer) showed that 90 percent of processing time of the Object Buffer was spent in those deeper procedures.

The result is, that all of the short subprocedures have to be eliminated. Using the 'low level features' of C, we will reduce the amount of code e.g. for type conversions using 'good' PASCAL with the use of casting, and the number of procedure calls with the use of macros. This will reduce the internal path length in the Object Buffer from currently three or four to one in most cases. It will shorten the code and the runtime overhead for procedure calls and stack management. An important improvement will be the widely reduced parameter checking, because the less strict encapsulation will allow the usage of the knowledge, that values have to be correct due to former tests.

Our goal is to get rid of the deepest procedure level, and a reduction of the intermediate level to about a dozen procedures. This should reduce code to at most 500 lines for these two layers. The speed-up cannot be estimated exactly in the moment, but we hope to reach a factor of 10 or more. Additional changes in the top layer of the Object Buffer Manager should increase this.

The third refinement step, not directly in the Object Buffer management, but strongly related to it, has been already mentioned shortly. The internal data structures have been chosen equivalent to the tuple layout on database pages, to allow the CRM to transfer data between the Object Buffer and the database buffer in larger units than attribute by attribute. In a database insert for example, the Object Buffer pages can be copied to disk almost without any changes by either copying them in one block transfer into buffer frames or by transfering the control over the pages directly from the Object Buffer manager to the database buffer manager without any copying at all. This will reduce the amount of interpretation of structural information of the NF^2-data significantly. In principle, the same mechanism can be applied in case of a retrieval. However, the retrieval algorithm is more sophisticated, because it has to detect, what transfer unit is applicable (projections may prohibit 'overlaying' the page buffer or page transfers) and the best in the specific case: page transfer, sub-structure transfer, or attribute transfer.

A first prototype of the new Object Buffer has been developed. It's goal was at first efficiency in processing of data and only second in the transfer from/to pages. The deletion of the lower procedures has been done completely resulting in a small module with the 21 interface procedures implemented with 800 lines of documented code. The two tests shown above with the old OB have been run with this new version and the early results shown in Table 4 will give an impression of the enhanced performance (times of the old OB in brackets).

Procedures	Flat Relation		Nested Relation	
Tuple Size	216 Byte/Tuple		216 Byte/Tuple	
OB Size	~ 500 KByte		~ 560 KByte	
	#calls	time	#calls	time
generation	1	0.00 (0.03)	1	0.01 (0.02)
insertion	12000	2.80 (14.68)	66000	7.02 (111.16)
scan	12000	1.90 (5.01)	66000	3.02 (43.80)
deletion	1	1.19 (1.00)	1	8.38 (0.54)

Table 4. CPU-Times (seconds) for sample OB-procedures

The problem with this new implementation is that the data structure has been changed and the equivalence with the external representation is only partially left. Therefore the third refinement step, the direct transfer between pages and the Object Buffer can only be implemented partially.

4.2 Extending the EDT Concept

The extension of our Access Manager with application specific geometry types has shown, that the EDT concept is an applicable method. Although we currently have no automatic IN/OUT generator (a first version for Modula-2 is currently in the design phase) we had no problems, because the standard geometries we had to handle only needed the most primitive IN/OUT: type casting. We have no doubts that the more complex cases, structures with pointers, will work too. With respect to the observations in other system parts that interpretation of administrative data and copying of data is the critical bottleneck in our system, the limits of our straight-forward implementation of the extensibility concept can be seen quite easily. The methods must fail for very large data and for very complex pointer structures.

To solve the problem of very large pointer structures, e.g. graphs with ten thousands of nodes, we have only vague ideas. It is true that a traversal to linearise them, even if programmed optimal with linear cost, is very expensive and only applicable if the algorithms programmed on that graph are significantly less expensive than those on the linearisation. One idea is to directly manipulate parts of the program heap where such dynamic variables are located. Our knowledge of runtime systems of programming languages seems to suggest this, but there is a large step left to a working algorithm.

The problem with very large unstructured data in the range of megabytes and more, e.g. raster images, can only principally be solved with the simple overlay IN/OUT methods. The standard database system operations require, that every atomic element, a complete atomic attribute or a subpart of a long field has to fit on a database page. These pages have a standard layout, found in many other systems: a page header with page related administrative data, a trailer with a slot list, containing entry related data, and between them, in the free space, data items and structural information of the data tuples. When transferring long field data like a raster image from the application program to pages, our current implementation will have to split the field into several subparts that have to be moved seperately into the different pages data spaces.

A more efficient solution would be to overlay the application programm's data space with page frames, i.e. to give the Object Buffer, or the database buffer, temporary control over the applications data area, to build a virtual page set to work on. This would avoid any copying of data.

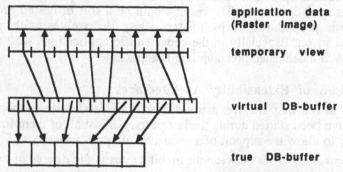

Fig. 7: Direct manipulation of very large user objects

This method requires, that pure data pages without any internal structure like header and trailer can be written into the database. The current implementation of the structure managing components of our system, the CRM and the OBM would allow this technique with only slight modifications. A larger piece of work has to be done in the SMM, especially in the recovery component. The current implementation of logging uses page headers to write information like transaction ids and commit flags together with the data pages onto the log. This allows easy log management, because the atomicity of page-writes to the log guarantees synchronisation between data and administrative information. Pages without headers and trailers need a different mechanism with two seperated log files, one for the user data and one for the SMMs administrational data, that have to be synchronized by a special protocol.

4.3 Precompiling versus Interpretation

Immense interpretation overhead is a problem especially in the CRM. This module is designed to support a variety of dedicated storage structures for special types of attributes. It is planned to support fixed length atoms (no length fields), fixed length subrelations (subtuple arrays instead of pointer arrays), and long fields (multiple pages instead of one fragment). The current implementation handles this flexibility by interpreting a catalog information partially stored within the CRM and partially delivered together with the query. This means an interpretation for every tuple and every subtuple (of a tuple) and so on. For each atom access, multiple interpretation steps have taken place and several procedure calls via alternative selections (switch/case statements) have been processed.

A comparable situation can be found in the system parts handling EDTs and externally defined storage and acces methods. The type of an attribute, index, or cluster is detected from a catalog and interpreted every time an external routine has to be called.

This interpretation is not necessary because the meta information encoded in the interpreted fields does not change during the processing of a query, in some cases not even between several queries. Therefore it is possible to do one precompilation step of the query, replacing all the interpreted information by the addresses of the routines that will perform the specific tasks. In the resulting query tree only the NF^2-structure related information has to be interpreted, all other type specific data is compiled and only a procedure call has to be made.

A consequent follow up of this method, the additional compiling of the structure into procedure calls is in discussion. The result would be a sort of nested procedure call, a CRM call with procedures as parameters, they themselves with procedures as parameters and so on. Especially in the geoscientific applications with slow changing requirements such a dedicated precompiling is applicable.

4.4 Comparison of Extensibility Architectures

As mentioned in the first chapter, many different approaches to support non-standard applications have been started during the last years. Almost all of them focus on the idea of extensibility to allow the support of a wide area of applications.

One of the major differences between the architectures is the *degree of extensibility*, the question, which parts of the architecture are fix, which exchangable, and which extensible. Related to this is the way *how the resulting system is created*.

Without doubt, the idea of making existing B-tree indexes in conventional databases generic and available for those new types for which total ordering is defined, is due to Stonebraker [SRG83,Ston86]. We have applied and generalized this observation for geometric data types using generic Grid-Files and R-Trees.

The introduction of clearly defined interfaces in order e.g. to exchange a Grid-File index by an R-Tree is also advocated in the STARBURST Project. However their "attachements" can be more general and may include user written concurrency control and recovery while we require the index component to be written on top of the CRS (or at least on the SMM) in order to utilize the transaction management provided there.

The idea of generating DBMS code is pursued in GENESIS and EXODUS to a great extent. In our current project we restrict code generation to a few critical places such as the generation of IN/OUT conversion functions.

The utilization of standard approximations of a user's geometric type within a DBMS has been investigated in the PROBE project to a large extent [MOD87]. We use the less precise approximations imposed by e.g. a Grid-File and call the "real" EDT geometry functions more often. A symbiosis of both approaches seams sensible by the introduction of cost factors for the EDT functions envolved.

5. Conclusion and Further Developments

The DASDBS GEO-Kernel is a working system. The first applications using realistic data have proven the concepts of Externally Defined Types and Externally Defined Access and Storage Methods. The experiences and evaluations of the GEO-Kernel users have shown bottlenecks in the current implementation. Based on this informations we have done a partial redesign of the system that will be implemented in the next month.

Together with the changes motivated by performance lacks, we implement some enhancements in the functionality especially in handling large unstructured objects.

The IN/OUT generator is currently under development for the language Modula-2. It is able to handle any type of data structure completely defined through the type declarations. A later version will be extended by the additional declaration features to handle all kinds of structure definitions.

Additional geometric and standard access methods will be analysed and integrated into the access manager. Especially the geometric methods have to be tested for the usability for clustering.

An important step will be the development of the geometric query optimization and processing layer. Some of the topics that we started to work on in this area are the mapping of complex predicates to simpler ones (e.g. rectangle based retrieval) and the introduction of approximations. Especially the derivation of approximations from the partitioning created in an access method will be part of the future research

Acknowledgement

DASDBS and the GEO-Kernel are the work of a team so I would like to thank all those members of the Darmstadt Database Research Group that took part in the development and implementation of the system for the discussions. Especially I want to thank Dagmar Horn, who implemented large parts of the AM, Walter Waterfeld supporting me with measurement data about access methods, and Gisbert Dröge, Marc Scholl, and Hans-Jörg Schek for carefully reading the paper and the intensive discussions on this work.

Literature:

BBG*86 Batory, D.S., Barnett, J.R., Garza, J.F., Smith, K.P., Tsukuda, K., Twichell, B.C., Wise, T.E., GENESIS: A Reconfigurable Database Management System, UT TR-86-07, University of Texas, Austin, 1986

BG87 Blankenagel, G., Güting, R. H., Internal and External Algorithms for the Points-in-Regions Problem - the INSIDE Join of Geo-Relational Algebra, Research Report 228, Department of Comp. Science, University of Dortmund, 1987

CS89 Chang, W. W., Schek, H.-J., A Signature Access Method for the Starburst Database System, in Proc. 1989 VLDB Conf., Amsterdam, 1989

CDF*86 Carey, M., DeWitt, D., Frank, D., Graefe, G., Muralikrishna, M., Richardson, J.E., Shekita, E.J., The Architecture of the EXODUS Extensible Database System, in [OO86]

DPS86 Deppisch, U., Paul, H.-B., Schek, H.-J., A Storage System for Complex Objects, in Proc. Int. Workshop on Object Oriented Database Systems, Pacific Grove, 1986

Doe89 Doerpinghaus, F., Implementation of a Spatial Access Method using the Grid-File Method, master thesis, TH Darmstadt, 1989, in german

DOP*85 Deppisch, U., Obermeit, V., Paul, H.-B., Schek, H.-J., Scholl, M.-H., Weikum, G., The storage Component of a Database Kernel System, TR DVS1-1985-T1, TU Darmstadt, 1985

DS86 Dayal, U., Schmidt, J.M., PROBE: A Knowledge-Orientad Database Management System, in Brodie and Mylopoulos (eds.), On Knowledge Base Management Systems: Integrating Artificial Intelligence and Database Technologies, Springer Verlag, 1986

EB84 Elhard, K., Bayer, R., A Database Cache for High Performanvˋce and Fast Restart in Database Systems,in ACM Trans. on Database Systems 9,4 (Dec. 1984)

Gue89 Guenther, O., Bilmes, J., The Implementation of the Cell Tree: Design Alternatives and Performance Evaluations, in [BTW89]

Gutt84 Guttman, A., R-Trees: A Dynamic Index Structure for Spatial Search, Proc. of the ACM SIGMOD Conf.

HSWW86 Horn, D., Schek, H.-J., Waterfeld, W., Wolf, A., Spatial Access Paths and Physical Clustering in a Low-Level GEO-Database System, held at the COGEODATA Conf., Dinkelsbühl, 1986, appeared in NLfB88

MOD87 Manola, F., Orenstein, J., Dayal, U., Geographic Information Processing in the PROBE Database System, Proc. 8th Int. Symp. on Automation in Cartogrphy, Baltimore, 1987

NHS84 Nievergelt, J., Hinterberger, H., Sevcik, K.C., The Grid-File: An Adaptable, Symmetric Multikey File Structure, ACM Trans. on Database Systems, Vol. 9, No. 1

Neu89 Lohmann, F., Neumann, K., Ehrich, H.-D., Design of a Database Prototype for Geoscientific Applications, in [BTW89], in german

Neu88 Neumann, K., A Geoscientific Database Language with User Definable Data Types, Ph.D. Thesis, TU Braunschweig, 1988, in german

NLfB88 Niedersächsisches Landesamt für Bodenforschung (ed.), Construction of Geoscientific Maps Derived from Databases (Proc. of an Intern. Colloquium), Geologisches Jahrbuch, Sonderband, Hannover 1988

SCF*86 Schwarz, P., Chang, W., Freytag, J.C., Lohman, G., McPherson, J., Mohan, C., Pirahesh, H., Extensibility in the Starburst Database System, in [OO86]

SR84 Stonebraker, M., Rowe, L.A., Database Portals - A New Application Program Interface, Proc. 1984 VLDB Conf., Singapore, 1984

SR86 Stonebraker, M., Rowe, L.A., The Design of POSTGRES, Proc. ACM SIGMOD Conf., 1986

SRG83 Stonebraker, M., Rubenstein, B., Guttmen, A., Application of abstract data types and abstract indices to CAD data bases, Proc. Database Week ACM SIGMOD, 1983

Ston86 Stonebraker, M., Inclusion of New Types in Relational Database Systems, Proc. 2nd Int. Conf. on Database Engineering, Los Angeles, 1986

Sche78 Schek, H.-J., The Reference String Indexing Method, in Proc. of the ECI Conference

Scho88 Scholl, M., The Nested Relational Model - Efficient Support for a Relational Database Interface, Ph.D. Thesis, TH Darmstadt, 1988, in German

SS88	Schek, H.-J., Scholl, M., Two Roles of Nested Relations, in Abiteboul, S., Fischer, P. C., Schek, H.-J.,(ed.), Nested Relations and Complex Objects, Springer LNCS 361
SW86	Schek, H.-J., Waterfeld, W., A Databese Kernel System for Geoscientific Applications, in Proc. of the 2nd Int. Symp. on Spatial Data Handling, Seattle, 1986
Wei89	Weikum, G., Set Oriented Disk Accesss to Large Complex Objects, Proc. of the 5th Int. Conf. on Data Engineering, Los Angeles, 1989
WSSH88	Wilms, P.F., Schwarz, P.M., Schek, H.-J., Haas, L.M., Incorporating Data Types in an Extensible Database Architecture, in Proc. of the 3rd Int. Conf. on Data and Knowledge Bases, Jerusalem, June 1988
WWH88	Waterfeld, W., Wolf, A., Horn, D., How to make Spatial Access Methods Extensible, in Proc. of the 3rd Int. Symp. on Spatial Data Handling, Sydney, August 1988
BTW87	Schek, H.-J., Schlageter, G., (ed.), Datenbanksysteme in Büro, Technik und Wissenschaft, Conference Procedings, Darmstadt, 1987
BTW89	Härder, T., (ed.), Datenbanksysteme in Büro, Technik und Wissenschaft, Conference Procedings, Zürich, 1989
DBKSI	DatenBank Kernsystem Insotec, Software product, Insotec Consult, München
OO86	Dayal, U., (ed.), Proc. 1986 Int. Workshop on Object-oriented Database Systems, Asilomar, 1986

Appendix 1

A sample Access-Manager Retrieval

Sample Schema:
```
Map( Map-Id : char[8],
        Towns( Name : char[20], Inhabitants : integer, ....., T_Geometry : polygon_area),
        Rivers( Name : char[20], ....., R_Geometry : polygon_line),
        Streets( Identifier : char[20], Category : char[8], ....., S_Geometry : polygon_line)
    )
```

Sample query:
Give me all highways in a certain rectangular area.

Transformed textual version:
From those maps, containing any street that matches my selection,
    give me only those streets,
        that are categorised as 'highway' and
        whose geometry intersects my search window,
    but give me only those parts of the streets geometry,
        that is inside the window.

Query-tree Structure:
```
Map: project, select
    atom_project: <empty>
    atom_select: <empty>
    subrelations:
        Towns: no flags
            atom_project: <empty>
            atom_select: <empty>
        Rivers: no flags
            atom_project: <empty>
            atom_select: <empty>
        Streets: not_null, project, select
            atom_project: clip(S_Geometry, window)
            atom_select:   equal(Category, 'highway') and
                             intersect(S_Geometry, Window)
```

Appendix 2

Usage of the GEO kernel

As an example, the query of appendix 1 is processed and the result displayed.

Assumptions
- The geo-type *polygon_line* is defined by the user together with the IN/OUT procedures.
- A procedure *display* exists, that is able to display line in the *polygon_line* representation.
- The Query-Tree described in appendix 1 is already created with its root pointer *qt*.

Code example

```
retcode = am_retrieve_tup( ta_id, rel_id, NO_ADDRESS,addresses, qt, result,  scan);
       /*   this retrieves the tupels of relation rel_id specified by qt
            into result. No tuple addresses are known from past calls indicated
            by the NO_ADDRESS flag and an empty addresses buffer.
            If the result buffer is to small, retrieve can be continued via scan */

if (retcode != am_ok)  error_handle;

ret = ct_ntp( result, number_of_tuples );
if (retcode != ct_ok) error_handle;

for (i=1, i<=number_of_tuples, i++)
{   ret = ct_dwn( result, 1 );
    if (retcode != ct_ok) error_handle;
    /* there is only one subrelation, so step down into the first */

    ret = ct_nst( result, number_of_subtuples );
    if (retcode != ct_ok) error_handle;

    for (j=1, j<=number_of_subtuples, j++)
    {
        ret = ct_polygon_line_gat( result, 1, &poly_line_var);
        if (retcode != ct_ok) error_handle;
        /*  reads the value of the geometry-attribute into
            a variable of type poly_line */

        display( poly_line_var );

        destroy_polygon_line( &poly_line_var );

        ret = ct_nxt( result );
        if (retcode != ct_ok) error_handle;
        /*  switches to the next geometry to process */
    }
    /* last subtuple processed, therefore go to next tuple */

    ret = ct_up( result );
    if (retcode != ct_ok) error_handle;
    /* first go back to tuple level */

    ret = ct_nxt( result );
    if (retcode != ct_ok) error_handle;
    /* then go to next tuple */
}
```

Performance Comparison of
Point and Spatial Access Methods *

Hans-Peter Kriegel, Michael Schiwietz
Ralf Schneider, Bernhard Seeger
Praktische Informatik, University of Bremen, D-2800 Bremen 33, West Germany

Abstract

In the past few years a large number of multidimensional point access methods, also called multiattribute index structures, has been suggested, all of them claiming good performance. Since no performance comparison of these structures under arbitrary (strongly correlated nonuniform, short "ugly") data distributions and under various types of queries has been performed, database researchers and designers were hesitant to use any of these new point access methods. As shown in a recent paper, such point access methods are not only important in traditional database applications. In new applications such as CAD/CIM and geographic or environmental information systems, access methods for spatial objects are needed. As recently shown such access methods are based on point access methods in terms of functionality and performance. Our performance comparison naturally consists of two parts. In part I we will compare multidimensional point access methods, whereas in part II spatial access methods for rectangles will be compared. In part I we present a survey and classification of existing point access methods. Then we carefully select the following four methods for implementation and performance comparison under seven different data files (distributions) and various types of queries: the 2-level grid file, the BANG file, the hB-tree and a new scheme, called the BUDDY hash tree. We were surprised to see one method to be the clear winner which was the BUDDY hash tree. It exhibits an at least 20 % better average performance than its competitors and is robust under ugly data and queries. In part II we compare spatial access methods for rectangles. After presenting a survey and classification of existing spatial access methods we carefully selected the following four methods for implementation and performance comparison under six different data files (distributions) and various types of queries: the R-tree, the BANG file, PLOP hashing and the BUDDY hash tree. The result presented two winners: the BANG file and the BUDDY hash tree. This comparison is a first step towards a standardized testbed or benchmark. We offer our data and query files to each designer of a new point or spatial access method such that he can run his implementation in our testbed.

Keywords : access methods, performance comparison, spatial database systems

---

* This work was supported by grant no. Kr 670/4-2 from the Deutsche Forschungsgemeinschaft (German Research Society) and by the Ministry of Environmental an Urban Planning of Bremen

1. Introduction

Access methods for secondary storage which allow efficient manipulation of large amounts of records are an essential part of a data base management system (DBMS). In traditional applications, objects are represented by records, which are d-dimensional points, $d \geq 1$, and thus point access methods (PAMs) are required. We distinguish access methods for primary keys (one-dimensional points) and access methods for secondary keys (multidimensional points). A large number of multidimensional PAMs, also called multiattribute index structures, has been suggested in the past few years. Many of these PAMs claim to be "very efficient for arbitrary queries", to be "robust, coping well with arbitrary distributions", to "exhibit almost the same retrieval performance for independent nonuniform data distributions as for uniform distributions", or to "gracefully adapt to the actual data". However, no performance comparison of these structures under strongly correlated nonuniform data distributions and under various types of queries has been performed, simply because for many of these PAMs no implementations are available. In 1984 we have reported on a performance comparison of four PAMs, the grid file, two variants of multidimensional B-trees and the traditional inverted file, see [Kri 84]. However, all of these PAMs are outdated.

In this paper, we will present a performance comparison of the most promising PAMs under skewed data and under various types of queries. Our goal will eventually be to develop a standardized testbed or benchmark such that each designer of a new PAM may implement her or his method and run it against this benchmark. Such a performance comparison of PAMs will be the fundamentals of automatic physical database design tools that would choose a physical schema and then monitor the performance of the schema making changes as necessary.

Now, considering new applications such as Computer Aided Design/Computer Integrated Manufacturing (CAD/CIM), image processing and geographic or environmental information systems, PAMs are not sufficient. In particular, new access methods are necessary for the organization of multidimensional spatial objects, like rectangles, polygons etc. We call these methods spatial access methods (SAMs). Additionally, queries asking for spatial objects seem to be more complex than queries asking for points. For instance a typical spatial query is the point query: Given a point, find all spatial objects that contain the point.

The significance of efficient PAMs is underligned by the following facts. In [SK 88] we have shown that known SAMs for simple spatial objects (rectangles, intervals, etc.) are based on an underlying PAM using one of the following three techniques: clipping, overlapping regions and transformation. The better the underlying PAM, the better will be the performance of the resulting SAM. The distribution of objects which the underlying PAM handles is in almost all spatial applications nonuniform and strongly correlated; extremely correlated if the technique of transformation is used. As an underlying PAM we used in [SK 88] the most efficient multidimensional dynamic hashing scheme (MDH) without directory which is PLOP-Hashing [KS 88], mainly because it supports a nice adaption of the three different techniques. In this paper, we will compare in part II the R-Tree, PLOP-Hashing, the BANG file and the BUDDY hash tree, all storing rectangles.

This paper is organized as follows. Part I deals with PAMs and consists of sections 2-5. In section 2 we will give a survey and classification of existing PAMs and we will justify our selection of PAMs for the performance comparison. In the third section we describe how we implemented the selected PAMs and we specify the general experimental setup for our comparisons. The result of the experiments are reported in section 4. In the following section 5 those results are interpreted. Furthermore, from the attempt to explain bad performance of the different PAMs, suggestions for improvements for most PAMs are made. Part II compares SAMs for rectangles and covers sections 6-8. In section 6 a brief survey and classification of existing SAMs for rectangles is presented. In the following section 7, we describe our general experimental setup and the selected SAMs. The results of the experiments are then reported in section 8. Section 9 concludes the paper.

Part I: Performance comparison of multidimensional point access methods (PAMs)

2. Classification and selection of PAMs

Even for someone working in this area, it is difficult to keep track of all multidimensional PAMs suggested until today. Most important for the performance of a multidimensional PAM under arbitrary (nonuniform correlated) data is the partitioning process, how the PAM adapts to the particular data distribution. Therefore, we will present a classification of existing multidimensional PAMs according to the way they partition the d-dimensional data space D. In the following classification we will not consider PAMs based on binary trees, such as kd-trees, since they are not suitable for the organization of data in secondary storage. Furthermore, we will omit variants of multidimensional B-trees [Kri 84] from our classification, because they cluster data according to a lexicographical ordering, instead of according to proximity in data space.

The basic principle of all multidimensional PAMs is to partition the data space into page regions, shortly regions, such that all records in one region are stored in one and the same data page. We will classify according to the following three properties of regions: the regions are pairwise disjoint or not, the regions are rectangular or not and the partition into regions is complete or not, i.e. the union of all regions spans the complete data space or not. Obviously, this classification yields six classes, four of which are filled with known PAMs.

class	property			PAM
	rectangular	complete	disjoint	
(C1)	X	X	X	interpolation hashing [Bur 83], MOLHPE [KS 86], quantile hashing [KS 87], PLOP-hashing [KS 88], k-d-B tree [Rob 81], multidimensional extendible hashing [Tam 82,Oto 84], balanced multidimensional extendible hash tree [Oto 86], grid file [NHS 84], 2-level grid file [Hin 85], interpolation-based grid file [Ouk 85]
(C2)	X	X		twin grid file [HSW 88]
(C3)	X		X	buddy hash tree [SFK 89], multilevel grid file [WK 85]
(C4)		X	X	B$^+$-tree with z-order [OM 84], BANG file [Fre 87], hB-tree [LS 89]

Table 1 : Classification of multidimensional PAMs.

As mentioned before our goal is to find PAMs with a good overall performance under nonuniform correlated data. Since it was not feasible to implement and compare all of the structures in the above classification, we selected the following 4 PAMs for implementation and comparison: the 2-level grid file, the BANG file, the hB-tree and the buddy hash tree. Before describing the selected PAMs in more detail, we will justify why we restricted our comparison to these four structures.

Considering class C 1, the most promising structures definitely are the interpolation-based grid file and the balanced multidimensional extendible hash tree. However, both structures can be obtained as a special case of the buddy hash tree by restricting the properties of the regions. Therefore these two PAMs need not to be implemented. We do not include the best multidimensional dynamic hashing scheme without directory, PLOP hashing, since it is efficient only for weakly correlated data, but not for strongly correlated data. From class C 1 we selected the 2-level grid file because it is generally accepted to be "the measuring stick" and because its efficient Modula-2 implementation by Klaus Hinrichs [Hin 85] was available to us which we thankfully acknowledge.

From class C 4 we omitted the B$^+$-tree storing z-values from our comparison, because both implemented PAMs, the BANG file and the hB-tree are improvements of the basic B$^+$-tree storing z-values. We decided to implement the buddy hash tree (class C 3) due to its non-complete partition of the data space thus avoiding to partition empty data space. Since the concept of the twin grid file (class C 2) of organizing two dependent grid files at the same time is generally applicable to any PAM, we did not include it in our comparison. It might be worth investigating the application of this principle to the winners of our comparison.

In the following, we will present a short description of the selected PAMs. This description is slightly longer in case of the latest PAM, the buddy hash tree, since its paper might not be readily available.

The 2-level grid file was first suggested in the original grid file publication [NHS 84] and then described in detail and implemented in [Hin 85]. The basic idea is to manage the grid directory with another grid file. This 1st level grid directory is a scaled-down version of the original grid directory in which the limit of resolution is significantly coarser. Since the 2nd level grid files are independent from each other, this 2-level approach supports a better adaption to nonuniform distributions than the original 1-level grid file. However, the 1st level grid directory still grows superlinearly, just starting its superlinear growth later. Let us emphasize that the regions in the 2-level grid file are rectangular.

In order to adapt to the clustering of points in the data space, Freeston has suggested the BANG file (Balanced and Nested Grid file) [Fre 87] using the concept of nested regions. As in the 2-level grid file the data space is partitioned by rectangular shaped basic regions. However, contrary to the 2-level grid file, regions may be formed from these basic regions using the difference operation. The difference operation is applied to nondisjoint basic regions where one of them completely contains the others. Thus this operation supports a process of nesting which produces non-rectangular shaped logical regions. This process of nesting is applied to data pages and equivalently to directory pages. Obviously the motivation of the BANG file was a graceful adaption to object distributions where almost all of the data occurs in a few relatively small cluster points.

Conceptually similar to the BANG file, the hB-tree (holey brick tree) [LS 89] allows non-rectangular shaped regions on the level of data pages and more important on the level of directory pages. Contrary to the BANG file, such a region is generated by union of rectangular shaped basic regions. This potentially more efficient constructive method (versus the descriptive method in the BANG file), however, trades in again one of the basic disadvantages of the 2-level grid file: a logical region may need more than one directory entry.

Both, the BANG file and the hB-tree use a balanced search tree structure for the directory. The BANG file directory organizes a hash-based partition of the data space, whereas the hB-tree uses a kd-tree-type node organization in the directory, to reflect a median-based partitioning. Thus the BANG file is a hashing scheme with a tree-structured directory, hash tree for short, organizing the embedding data space, whereas the hB-tree is a search tree, organizing the specific set of data. To be precise, the hB-tree is actually a search graph due to its duplicate directory entries.

For none of the two structures a deletion algorithm has been specified. From our experience having implemented both of them, we believe that an efficient deletion algorithm will be especially hard to design for the hB-tree.

All existing PAMs including the 2-level grid file, the BANG file and the hB-tree have the following property in common: they partition the complete data space. More exactly, the union of all partitioning blocks spans the complete data space. Consequently empty data space is partitioned, even if it is partitioned efficiently as in the case of the BANG file.

The goal of the buddy hash tree [SFK 89] is not to partition empty data space at all, even more, to partition the data space into nearly minimal bounding rectangles of objects. As the name says, it is, similar to the BANG file, a dynamic hashing scheme with a tree-structured directory where the leaves of the directory point to the data pages. A (page) node of the directory contains a list of entries (R, P) where $R \subseteq D$ is a d-dimensional rectangle in the data space D and P is a pointer to a subtree containing all points (records) in R. R is the minimal bounding rectangle of the points and subrectangles obtained by recursive halfing of the data space. The partitioning hyperplanes are parallel to the axis of the data space.

Consider an entry (R, P) in a directory node where P refers to a son $((S_1, P_1), ..., (S_k, P_k))$, $k \geq 1$. Then the following two conditions are fulfilled:

(i) $\qquad S_i \cap S_j = \emptyset \quad \forall_{i,j} \in \{1, ... k\}, i \neq j$

(ii) $\qquad \bigcup_{i=1}^{k} S_i \subseteq R$

Condition (ii) implies the important property of the buddy hash tree that it does not have to partition the complete data space. Together with the concept of minimal bounding rectangles condition (ii) implies that empty data space is not partitioned at all. Conditions (i) and (ii) have already been incorporated in the multilevel grid file [WK 85]. However, additionally to the multilevel grid file the buddy hashtree exhibits the following performance improving properties:

(1)   Each directory node contains at least two entries.

(2)   An overfilled page (data page or directory page) is always split in a minimal way i.e. the "minimal bounding rectangle property" is not destroyed by page splitting.

(3)   Except for the root of the directory, there is exactly one pointer referring to each directory page.

(4)   Let (R, P) be an entry in a leaf of the directory, i.e. P points to a data page. Then there may exist other pointers $P_1, ... P_k$, and accordingly directory entries $(R_1, P_1), ... (R_k, P_k)$, $k \geq 1$, iff

(a) the rectangle R contains less than b/2 records (points), where b is the capacity of a directory page

(b) the entries $(R_i, P_i), 1 \leq i \leq k$, are accomodated in the same leaf of the directory as (R, P).

The balanced multidimensional extendible hash tree and the multilevel grid file are artificially balanced by allowing one entry in a directory page. Due to property (1) the buddy hash tree shortens paths by omitting directory pages with one entry. Thus the buddy hash tree is not balanced, i.e. the leaves of the directory may be on different levels of the tree. We would like to emphasize that this is a performance improvement for all operations (queries and updates) compared to the balanced competitors of the buddy hash tree. An important performance measure for a tree-structured directory is the maximum height of the directory. The maximum height h_{max} of the buddy hash tree is :

$$h_{max} \leq \log_{b/2} \left(\frac{n}{b/2} - w \right) + \frac{w - \log_2 b}{b} \quad , \text{ where : } \quad n \text{ is the number of records}$$

$$b \text{ is the capacity of a directory page}$$

$$|D| = 2^w$$

Obviously , $\left(\frac{n}{b/2} - w \right) \ll n$ and $\frac{(w - \log_2 b)}{b} < 2$ is fulfilled for most applications.

Property (2) guarantees that for answering queries no pages are accessed and searched which do not contain an answer. Properties (1) and (3) imply that the directory grows linearly in the number of records under all circumstances. Property (4) results in a high storage utilization. However, the most important of these properties is property (2), the minimal bounding rectangle property which avoids partitioning empty data space.

Implementation specific details as well as the general experimental setup for our comparisons are described in the next section.

3. Experimental setup

We ran the performance comparisons on SUN workstations (3/50 and 3/60) under UNIX using Modula-2 implementations of the selected PAMs. We will first describe in more detail how we implemented these PAMs.

As mentioned before, there exists an efficient fine-tuned and well-tested Modula-2 implementation of the 2-level grid file [Hin 85], in the following tables and figures abbreviated by GRID. We are thankful to Klaus Hinrichs for making this implementation available to us. Since we use GRID as a measuring stick for the other PAMs, we will standardize the number of page accesses for range queries and partial match queries of GRID to 100 % for the sake of an easier comparability.

Contrary to the 2-level grid file, the BANG file implementation is not publicly available from the ECRC, Munich, West Germany (European Computer-Industry Research Centre). Thus we had to implement the BANG file, in the following comparisons abbreviated by BANG, on our own. In [Fre 87] the search path in an exact match query may be longer than the height of the tree. This results in a performance penalty particularly for range queries with small volume. This phenomenon is caused by the fact that the original BANG file suggestion does not fulfill the so-called "spanning property" which requires each directory node and thus each region to be completely spanned by its entries. Our implementation is according to the original BANG file concept [Fre 87] and does not yet include the spanning property. We are presently incorporating this spanning property in our implementation and we will investigate the potential improvement. Furthermore, we are presently extending our implementation from fixed-length to variable-length directory entries which is incorporated in BANG*.

When we decided in September 1988 to include the hB-tree in our comparison of PAMs, no implementation was available. Our implementation of the hB-tree, denoted HB in the following figures and tables, gracefully follows the specification in [LS 89]. Additionally, we have implemented an optimized choice of the split axis which minimizes the margins of the regions in order to improve range query performance.

Obviously we had to implement the buddy hash tree [SFK 89] on our own. The implementation of the directory is very general, i.e. it is prepared to support a neighbor system. Since we decided for a special case of the neighbor system, the buddy system, there is room for improvement in the directory implementation which may easily result in an increase of the average branching factor of at least 40 %. To be fully dynamic we have incorporated a deadlock algorithm which contrary to the 2-level grid file is not a "must" in the buddy hash tree. Underfilled regions of highly varying sizes may not be merged in the original buddy hash tree because only rectangular regions are permissible. Thus it is possible to pack (merge) data pages such that the pointers to those data pages originate from one and the same directory page. For the sake of avoiding an unlimited number of indirect splits we have restricted "packing" to data pages. We have implemented the unpacked version, abbreviated by BUDDY in the comparison, and we have generated the packed version, called BUDDY+, by computation and simulation from the BUDDY implementation.

In order to compare the performance of the PAMs, we generated seven 2-dimensional datafiles (F1) - (F7) where (F1) - (F6) consists of 100 000 records without duplicates. (F7) consists of real cartography data and actually contains 81 549 records without duplicates. We consider records whose keys are in the unitcube $[0,1)^d$, since some of the PAMs require this. In the following, N(m,v) denotes a Gaussian distribution with mean value m and variance v. Below we will give a specification of the data files (F1) - (F7) which are additionally depicted in figure 3.1:

(F1) **"Diagonal"** :
The records follow a uniform distribution on the main diagonal.

(F2) **"Sinus Distribution"** :
The records follow a sinus curve, more precisely the x-values are uniformly distributed and the y-values follow a Gaussian distribution with mean value sin(x) and variance 0.1.

(F3) **"Bit Distribution"** :
The records follow a bit distribution bit(z) with parameter z, $0 \leq z \leq 1$. Each key component K can be represented as a bitstring $(b_1, b_2, ...)$, where

$$K = \sum_{j \geq 1} b_j \cdot 2^{-j}$$

The key component K follows a bit distribution bit(z) with parameter z, if for any j, the bit b_j satisfies $Pb(b_j=1) = z$, where $Pb(X)$ denotes the probability that event X is true. For our testfile we have chosen $z = 0.15$.

(F4) **"x-Parallel"** :

the x-values are uniformly distributed and the y-values follow an N(0.5,0.01) distribution.

(F5) **"Cluster Points"** :

The records follow a 2-dimensional independent Gaussian distribution with variance 0.05 (in x- and y-direction) around the centers of the cluster points as mean values and the records are inserted finishing one cluster point before starting the next.

(F6) **"Uniform Distribution"** :

The records follow a 2-dimensional independent uniform distribution. Since there is no need, this distribution is not depicted in figure 3.1.

(F7) **"Real Data"** :

Consists of real cartography data representing the elevation lines in a "rolling-hill-type" area in the Sauerland, West Germany. The points are obtained as interpolation points of the elevation lines. Since the data is originally stored in a quad-tree, it is inserted in a sorted sequence which is due to the partitioning sequence of the quad-tree. We thankfully acknowledge receiving this data from the Landesvermessungsamt NRW, Bonn, West Germany.

For each of the files (F1) - (F7) we generated the following five query files for comparing the selected PAMs:

(RQ1) 20 quadratic range queries with volume 0.1 %, where the center of the square follows a uniform distribution.

(RQ2) 20 quadratic range queries with volume 1 %, where the center of the square follows a uniform distribution.

(RQ3) 20 quadratic range queries with volume 10 %, where the center of the square follows a uniform distribution.

(PMQ1) 20 partial match queries where the specified x-value is uniformly distributed and the y-value is unspecified.

(PMQ2) 20 partial match queries where the specified y-value is uniformly distributed and the x-value is unspecified.

Here the volume of a range query is the volume of the specified range divided by the volume of the data space. For these queries we have computed the average number of disk accesses per query where the average is taken over 20 queries.

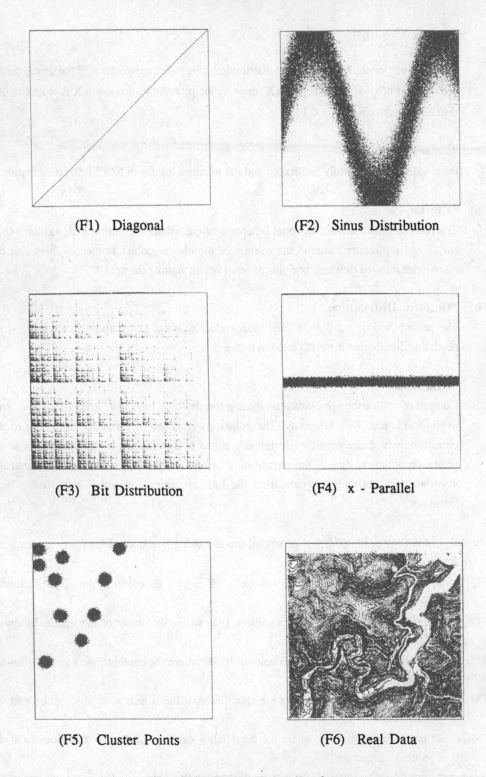

(F1) Diagonal

(F2) Sinus Distribution

(F3) Bit Distribution

(F4) x - Parallel

(F5) Cluster Points

(F6) Real Data

Fig. 3.1 : Data - Distributions

As mentioned before, for the BANG-file and the hB-tree no deletion algorithms have been specified. Therefore, for our comparison we only consider the case of the growing file.

In order to keep the performance comparison manageable (we already had more than 2.7 billion insertions), we have chosen the page size for data pages and directory pages to be 512 bytes which is at the lower end of realistic page sizes. Using small page sizes, we obtain similar performance results as for much larger file sizes, e.g. a doubling of the page size can accomodate an eight times higher file size within the same directory height for tree-based directories (BANG, HB, BUDDY). We want to emphasize that for the 2-level grid file the 1st level grid directory is always kept in main memory whereas for the other methods with their tree-based directories only the root page is main memory resident. Since the 1st level grid directory grows superlinearly, this may become infeasible (e.g. we had to keep up to 45 directory pages in main memory for only 100 000 records). Furthermore, in order to support update operations, in tree-based directories we additionally store the last accessed search path in a buffer and analogously for the 2-level grid file the last two accessed pages. Naturally this buffer for the search path is dynamically growing and shrinking according to the height of the tree.

Summarizing we can state that the performance results in the next section of BANG, HB and BUDDY hold as well for much larger file sizes whereas GRID will perform worse for larger file sizes due to its superlinear growth of the 1st level directory for nonuniform distributions.

4. Results of the experiments

As mentioned before, for the query types (RQ1) - (RQ3) and (PMQ1), (PMQ2) we will report the average number of disk accesses per query in the following tables. For the sake of an easier comparability, we have standardized the average number of page accesses for these queries in GRID to 100 %. Under the considerations of real-life applications and robustness, we have further visualized our results for the datafiles "Real Data", "Cluster" and "Diagonal".

During and after building up each datafile from empty, the following parameters were measured:

1. the storage utilization, denoted by stor.
2. the ratio of directory pages to data pages, denoted by dir/data.
3. the average number of disk accesses for an insertion (read and write) averaged over all 100000 or 81 549 insertions, denoted by insert.
4. the height of the directory after completely building up the file, denoted by h.

The results of the experiments are reported in the following figures and tables:

Real Data

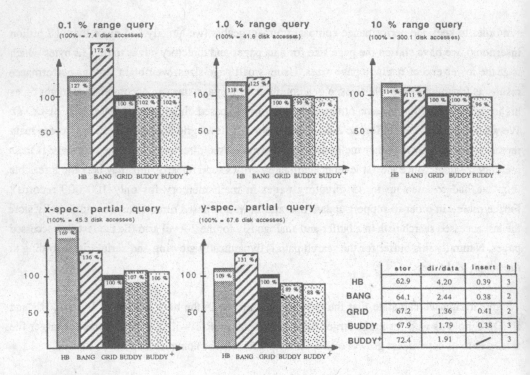

0.1 % range query
(100% = 7.4 disk accesses)

1.0 % range query
(100% = 41.6 disk accesses)

10 % range query
(100% = 300.1 disk accesses)

x-spec. partial query
(100% = 45.3 disk accesses)

y-spec. partial query
(100% = 67.6 disk accesses)

	stor	dir/data	insert	h
HB	62.9	4.20	0.39	3
BANG	64.1	2.44	0.38	2
GRID	67.2	1.36	0.41	2
BUDDY	67.9	1.79	0.38	3
BUDDY+	72.4	1.91	/	3

Diagonal

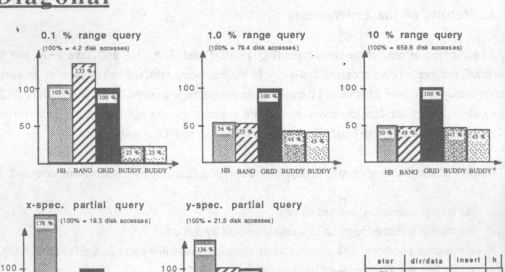

0.1 % range query
(100% = 4.2 disk accesses)

1.0 % range query
(100% = 79.4 disk accesses)

10 % range query
(100% = 659.6 disk accesses)

x-spec. partial query
(100% = 19.3 disk accesses)

y-spec. partial query
(100% = 21.5 disk accesses)

	stor	dir/data	insert	h
HB	70.1	3.61	3.29	3
BANG	69.9	2.34	3.03	3
GRID	35.4	8.98	3.13	2
BUDDY	69.9	2.27	3.19	2
BUDDY+	74.1	2.41	/	2

Cluster Points

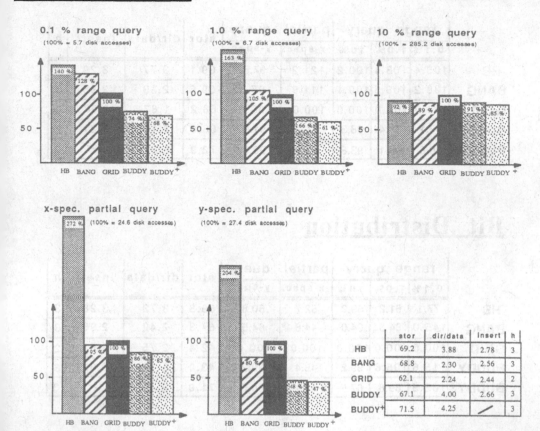

0.1 % range query
(100% = 5.7 disk accesses)

HB 140 %, BANG 128 %, GRID 100 %, BUDDY 74 %, BUDDY+ 68 %

1.0 % range query
(100% = 6.7 disk accesses)

HB 163 %, BANG 105 %, GRID 100 %, BUDDY 66 %, BUDDY+ 61 %

10 % range query
(100% = 285.2 disk accesses)

HB 92 %, BANG 89 %, GRID 100 %, BUDDY 91 %, BUDDY+ 85 %

x-spec. partial query
(100% = 24.6 disk accesses)

HB 272 %, BANG 95 %, GRID 100 %, BUDDY 86 %, BUDDY+ 85 %

y-spec. partial query
(100% = 27.4 disk accesses)

HB 204 %, BANG 80 %, GRID 100 %, BUDDY 48 %, BUDDY+ 47 %

	stor	dir/data	insert	h
HB	69.2	3.88	2.78	3
BANG	68.8	2.30	2.56	3
GRID	62.1	2.24	2.44	2
BUDDY	67.1	4.00	2.66	3
BUDDY+	71.5	4.25	/	3

Uniform Distribution

	range query			partial query		stor	dir/data	insert	h
	0.1%	1.0%	10%	x-spec	y-spec				
HB	113.3	104.3	103.9	137.3	92.7	69.9	3.53	3.29	3
BANG	113.9	105.8	101.9	110.6	103.5	70.1	2.35	3.06	3
GRID	100.0	100.0	100.0	100.0	100.0	70.2	1.12	2.90	2
BUDDY	101.7	102.7	101.2	108.3	100.0	70.2	2.28	3.19	2
BUDDY+	101.2	100.5	96.8	107.4	99.6	74.5	2.42	/	2

Sinus Distribution

	range query			partial query		stor	dir/data	insert	h
	0.1%	1.0%	10%	x-spec.	y-spec.				
HB	105.4	103.4	100.2	121.2	97.5	69.1	3.77	3.29	3
BANG	139.2	109.5	100.1	111.9	107.3	69.6	2.33	2.95	3
GRID	100.0	100.0	100.0	100.0	100.0	68.2	1.67	2.97	2
BUDDY	97.1	98.4	98.3	92.2	91.9	68.8	2.10	3.21	2
BUDDY+	96.6	95.1	93.8	89.8	90.3	72.9	2.22	/	2

Bit Distribution

	range query			partial query		stor	dir/data	insert	h
	0.1%	1.0%	10%	x-spec.	y-spec.				
HB	77.1	61.2	59.2	52.7	50.8	69.5	3.72	3.28	3
BANG	145.0	84.3	64.0	44.8	64.5	67.3	2.42	2.96	3
GRID	100.0	100.0	100.0	100.0	100.0	42.4	2.75	3.03	2
BUDDY	115.6	105.6	99.2	48.4	69.7	43.0	5.10	3.62	3
BUDDY+	105.5	89.6	67.5	46.1	66.5	71.0	8.42	/	3

x-Parallel

	range query			partial query		stor	dir/data	insert	h
	0.1%	1.0%	10%	x-spec.	y-spec.				
HB	94.9	89.2	91.1	132.4	59.6	69.6	3.62	3.29	3
BANG	126.5	100.1	95.8	83.6	114.7	65.4	2.19	3.03	3
GRID	100.0	100.0	100.0	100.0	100.0	62.9	3.77	3.01	2
BUDDY	74.5	83.1	92.3	72.8	50.4	67.2	2.45	3.21	2
BUDDY+	72.4	78.5	87.3	72.6	50.0	71.1	2.60	/	2

5. Interpretation of the results

Obviously, a physical database designer or a user of a database system can select from the above distribution mix those distributions which are typical and representative in his application. He will then choose the winner in those typical distributions. As a decision support for someone aiming for robustness and good average performance we present the following table 5.1. As mentioned before, our BANG file implementation incorporates fixed-length directory entries. For curiosity and as originally intended, we have generated a variable-length version, called BANG*, by simulation from the BANG implementation. We will only present the averaged results of BANG* in the following two tables 5.1 and 5.2.

In table 5.1 for the parameters stor and insert we computed the unweighted average over all seven distributions (datafiles). As an indicator for the average query performance we present the parameter query average which is averaged (unweighted) over all five query types for each distribution and then averaged over all seven distributions. The goal of this indicator is to help make things more clear, at first glance; however, we are aware that such an average implies a loss of information. The loss of information is considerably less in table 5.2 where the parameter query is displayed for each distribution as an average over all five types of queries.

	query average	stor	Insert
HB	110.9	68.6	2.80
BANG	102.6	67.9	2.43
BANG*	95.8	67.9	2.49
GRID	100.0	58.3	2.56
BUDDY	80.2	64.9	2.78
BUDDY+	76.6	72.5	

Table 5.1: unweighted average over all 7 distributions

	uniform	sinus	bit	x-par.	real data	diagonal	cluster
HB	110.3	105.5	60.2	93.4	127.4	105.0	174.2
BANG	107.1	113.6	80.5	104.1	135.0	78.4	99.4
BANG*	100.2	108.0	72.8	99.8	131.8	68.2	90.1
GRID	100.0	100.0	100.0	100.0	100.0	100.0	100.0
BUDDY	102.8	95.6	87.7	74.6	99.4	28.4	73.0
BUDDY+	101.1	93.1	75.0	72.2	97.6	27.8	69.2

Table 5.2 : unweighted average over all 5 types of queries depending on the distribution

In the following, we will discuss the performance of each PAM in the sequence in which they appear in the tables focussing on the average over the 5 types of queries.

Considering the indicator query average, HB would be the looser. However, this simple approach is not fair. For the bit distribution HB clearly outperforms its competitors and for the x-parallel HB closely follows BUDDY and BUDDY+. This good performance for the bit distribution is a consequence of the median-based partitioning, whereas the performance for the x-parallel profits from the additional feature of the minimized margins of the regions which was not an ingredient in the original specification [LS 89], but was incorporated in our implementation. For all other distributions (Real Data, Diagonal, Cluster, Sinus Distribution and Uniform Distribution) the average over all 5 types of queries is clearly worse than the 100 % value of GRID. More specifically, for Cluster, Diagonal and Uniform Distribution HB is the extreme looser in average query performance with values up to 272 %. Thus HB does not guarantee robustness. Although HB is the only PAM incorporating the efficient median-partitioning, it suffers from the following severe disadvantages:

(i) the height of the directory is in most experiments one more than in the other PAMs.
(ii) considering the partitions of HB for all distributions we observe that HB often partitions empty data space with unnecessarily fine granularity.
(iii) the directory may contain duplicate entries in two respects:
    (a) the father of a directory node may contain subtrees of its sons
    (b) different directory entries may point to one and the same page (directory or data pages).

From the above it follows that the hB-tree is actually a graph. We believe that the only way to improve HB is to incorporate the concept of not partitioning empty data space. With this and the median partition it might become very competitive.

As mentioned before, the GRID implementation [Hin 85] always keeps the 1st level grid directory in main memory whereas for the other PAMs only the root page of the directory is main memory resident. Since it was crucial to change the GRID implementation to allowing only one root page of the directory in main memory, we accepted that the relative ranking of GRID, our 100 % measuring stick, is too good in comparison to the other structures. To clarify this: for the Diagonal Distribution the 1st level grid directory needed 45 directory pages in main memory, which is sufficient for BANG, BANG*, BUDDY and BUDDY+ to keep the complete directory in main memory. Thus the rating of GRID in a comparable environment would be considerably worse. With the available implementation, GRID outperforms its competitors for uniform distribution as expected. If we exclude HB from our considerations it performs considerably worse than BANG and BUDDY for Diagonal, Bit Distribution and Cluster. Our comparisons show that GRID is not robust against arbitrary data.

Considering BANG and BANG* for the indicator query average, the concept of nested regions seems not to imply any improvement over GRID. However, BANG and BANG* turn out to be more robust towards ugly distributions than HB and especially GRID are. Looking more closely at the different queries, we realize that BANG performs very poorly for small range queries. This is a direct consequence of the not incorporated "spanning property" and will be improved by its implementation. A further disadvantage in robustness of BANG is the fact that different sequences of insertions imply different partitions. In particular sorted insertions seem to result in low storage utilization and poor retrieval performance.

For distributions where large portions of empty data space occur, i.e. x-Parallel, Diagonal, Sinus Distribution and Cluster Points, BANG and BANG* perform considerably worse than BUDDY. Looking at the ingredients of both PAMs it follows that incorporating an adapted concept of minimizing regions into BANG will improve the retrieval performance to some extent.

However, a consequent minimization of regions will lead to an incomplete partition of the dataspace, i.e. not partitioning empty data space, and thus to the most performance-important ingredient of BUDDY.

Considering the indicator query average, BUDDY and BUDDY⁺ offer themselves to be the winners of our comparison. It is interesting to observe that BUDDY does not fulfill the often cited rule "best storage utilization - best query performance". Even the improvement in storage utilization of BUDDY⁺ over BUDDY is not adequately reflected in the improvement of the retrieval performance. As mentioned before, we have to take a closer look at the different distributions. The only distributions where BUDDY and BUDDY⁺ are not the winners are the Uniform and the Bit Distributions, see table 5.2. According to [SFK 89], the Bit Distribution $bit(z)$, $0 \leq z \leq 1$, is the worst case distribution for BUDDY and BUDDY⁺ when z approaches 0. Even for its worst case distribution BUDDY⁺ is 3rd winner for the average query performance. This underlines the robustness of the structure. By the way, the motivation for the design of BUDDY⁺ to improve the storage utilization stems from exactly this pathological distribution. For Uniform Distribution BUDDY and BUDDY⁺ are within a 3 % margin of GRID, the winner. This is surprising for a scheme designed for nonuniform data incorporating the complex structural concept of not partitioning empty data space.

In all distributions, with the exeption of the Uniform and Bit Distribution, BUDDY and BUDDY⁺ are the clear winners in the average query performance and BUDDY⁺ wins in the storage utilization with more than 71 %. BUDDY and BUDDY⁺ clearly outperform their competitors if at least one of the following two data characteristics occur:

(C1) densely populated and unpopulated areas vary over the data space,

(C2) sorted data is inserted.

Sorted insertions frequently occur in real-life applications, either sorted by some local ordering such as clusters or quadrants or by lexicographical ordering.

Whereas other PAMs suffer from characteristics (C1) and/or (C2), BUDDY and BUDDY+ behave robust, see distributions "Diagonal" and "Cluster Points".

Part II: Performance comparison of spatial access methods (SAMs)

6. Classification and selection of SAMs

Even for someone working in this area, it is difficult to keep track of all SAMs suggested until today, because every multidimensional PAM can easily be extended to a SAM using the techniques of clipping, overlapping regions and transformation.

In this section we will provide an overview of spatial access methods which are based on the approximation of a complex spatial object by the minimal bounding rectangle (MBR) with the sides of the rectangle parallel to the axes of the data space. The most important property of this simple approximation is that a complex object is represented by a limited number of bytes. Although a lot of information is lost, MBRs of spatial objects preserve the most essential geometric properties of the object, i.e. the location of the object and the extension of the object in each axis. We do not consider more complex approximations of spatial objects such as the cell-tree [Gün 89] in this paper.

SAMs organizing minimal bounding rectangles of objects can be classified into three groups. Each of these groups is characterized by a special technique that allows an extension of a multidimensional point access method (PAM) to a multidimensional SAM. Thus the performance of such SAMs depends on the underlying PAM and depends on the applied technique.

In the following we give a short describtion of the several techniques of extending PAMs to SAMs. The interest reader can find these techniques explained in more detail in [SK 88]

Clipping

Clipping can easily be explained by describing the insertion of a new rectangle. Assuming a partition of the data space into disjoint regions, an insertion of a rectangle will be performed like an insertion of a point. Problems will only occur, if a rectangle R intersects with more than one disjoint region. Clipping of a rectangle means that R is partitioned into a minimal set of rectangles $\{R^1, ..., R^q\}$, where

$$R = \bigcup_{i=1}^{q} R^i, q > 1$$

Every rectangle R^i, $1 \leq i \leq q$, intersects with exactly one disjoint region. Now we can insert these q rectangles $R^1, ..., R^q$ into the file.

Overlapping regions

Such as clipping, overlapping region schemes (OR-schemes) organize d-dimensional rectangles using a d-dimensional PAM. For the following considerations we define the region of a bucket as the minimal bounding box of the rectangles belonging to the bucket. Contrary to clipping, OR-schemes allow data buckets where the corresponding regions have a common overlap. We will discuss the principle of OR-schemes by a brief summmary of the concepts of the R-tree [Gut 84], one of the most popular SAMs.

The R-tree is a balanced tree generalizing the B^+-tree concept [Com 79] to spatial objects. Storage utilization is guaranteed to be above 50 %. Minimal bounding rectangles of spatial objects are stored in the leaves of the tree, where each of the leaves corresponds to a data bucket. In an inner node of the tree there are tuples (R, p), where p is a pointer referring to a son and R is the minimal bounding rectangle of all rectangles in the corresponding son. Since clipping of rectangles is avoided, a rectangle is stored in exactly one of the data blocks. Thus overlapping regions of different data blocks are allowed for the organization of spatial objects.

The advantage of OR-schemes is that storage utilization depends only on the underlying PAM, since every rectangle is uniquely represented in the file. Thus the B^+-tree inherits the guarantee of at least 50 % storage utilization to the R-tree. Another nice property is that, in analogy to clipping methods, d-dim. points and d-dim. rectangles can be organized together in one file. However, retrieval performance heavily depends on the amount of overlap, as shown in [SFR 87].

Transformation

The basic idea of transformation-schemes (T-schemes) is to represent minimal bounding rectangles of multidimensional spatial objects by higher dimensional points. For instance, a 2-dimensional rectangle R with sides parallel to the axis is represented by a 4-dimensional point (center representation)

$$(c_1, c_2, e_1, e_2)$$

where $c = (c_1, c_2) \in [0,1)^2$ is the center of the rectangle and $e = (e_1, e_2) \in [0,0.5)^2$ is the distance of the center to the sides of the rectangle. As proposed by Nievergelt and Hinrichs [NH 85], these 4-dimensional points can be organized by the grid file [NHS 84] , generally speaking by a multidimensional PAM.

Another choice of parameters is the corner representation, where a 2-dim. rectangle can be represented by its lower left corner $(l_1, l_2) \in [0,1)^2$ and its upper right corner $u_j \in [1_j,1)^2$, $l_j=1,2$.

However, the choice of the parameters can influence performance and characteristics of the SAM.

7. Experimental setup

We ran the performance comparisons on SUN workstations (3/50 and 3/60) under UNIX using Modula-2 implementations of the selected SAMs.

Not much has to be said with respect to the selection and the implementation of the SAMs. The measuring stick in our comparison is the R-tree. Our implementation of the R-tree gracefully follows the specification of the R-tree in [Gut 84]. According to Diane Greene´s [Gre 89] implementation we chose at first a minimum storage utilaization of 50%, but our tests showed that the R-tree exhibits best retrieval performance for a minimum storage utilization of 30%. The "measuring stick role" of the R-tree is particulary justified because it basically wins the performance comparison by Diane Greene [Gre 89]. The obvious competitors are the two best PAMs in our comparison of PAMs, BUDDY and BANG.

Using the technique of transformation with corner representation we extended both our BANG and our BUDDY implementation to SAMs. To be precise, we used the BANG* implementation for rectangles, but for the sake of simplicity we will denote it by BANG. Which is the more efficient representation to use with transformation, the corner or the center representation? In order to answer this question Bernhard Seeger experimentally compared both representaions for BUDDY in his PhD thesis [See 89] for different types of queries and different distributions of rectangles. Simply speaking the corner representation yields approximately half the number of page accesses of the center representation. The basic reason is that for the corner representation the limits of the query ranges (areas) are parallel to the partitioning lines of BUDDY (and BANG) and thus the margin of the query range intersects fewer partitioning blocks than for the center representation. Now we have to make a statement with respect to the PAM versions of BUDDY and BANG on which we applied the corner representation. The BANG version was more refined than in our PAM comparison, already incorporating the spanning algorithm, whereas the BUDDY version was the first version, even without packing. Thus the results of BUDDY can easily be improved by incorporating packing and other refinements whereas BANG leaves practically no more room for improvement. In the final version of the paper we will have a refined version of BUDDY ready for our experiments.

The last SAM is based on PLOP-Hashing and uses the technique of overlapping regions as described in [SK 88] in detail.

In order to compare the performance of the SAMs, we generated five 2-dimensional datafiles (F1) - (F5) consisting of 100 000 rectangles without duplicates. A rectangle is characterized by its center and its x- and y-extension from the center. We consider rectangles which are in the unitcube $[0,1)^2$, since some of the SAMs require this. In the following, N(m,v) denotes a Gaussian distribution with mean value m and variance v. Below we will give a specification of the data files (F1) - (F5).

(F1) **"Uniformsmall-Distribution"** :
The centers of the rectangles follow a 2-dimensional independent uniform distribution within $[0.1)^2$. The extensions in x- and y- direction follow a uniform distribution in [0,0.005].

(F2) **" Uniformlarge-Distribution" :**

The centers of the rectangles follow a 2-dimensional independent uniform distribution within $[0.1)^2$. The extensions in x- and y- direction follow a uniform distribution in $[0,0.5]$.

(F3) **"Gaussiansquare-Distribution" :**

The centers of the rectangles follow a 2-dimensional independent Gaussian distribution $N(0.5,0.25)$ in x- and y- direction. The extensions in x- and y- direction follow a uniform distribution in $[0,0.05]$.

(F4) **" Gaussianslim-Distribution" :**

The centers of the rectangles follow a 2-dimensional independent Gaussian distribution $N(0.5,0.25)$ in x- and y-direction. The extension in x-direction follows a uniform distribution in $[0,0.05]$ and the extension in y-direction follows a uniform distribution in $[0,0.25]$.

(F5) **"Diagonal-Distribution" :**

First we generated two dimensional points which follow a uniform distribution on the main diagonal. Then the x- and y-coordinate of these points follow a Gaussian distribution $N(0,0.5)$ .The two dimensional points generated in this way are the centers of the rectangles. The extensions in x- and y- direction follow a uniform distribution in $[0,0.2]$.

For each of the files (F1) - (F5) we generated queries of the following four types:

"rectangle containment":
Given a d-dim. rectangle $S \subseteq E^d$, find all d-dim. rectangles R in the file with $R \subseteq S$.

"rectangle enclosure":
Given a d-dim. rectangle $S \subseteq E^d$, find all d-dim. rectangles R in the file with $R \supseteq S$.

"rectangle intersection":
Given a d-dim. rectangle $S \subseteq E^d$, find all d-dim. rectangles R in the file with $S \cap R \neq \emptyset$.

"point query":
Given a d-dim. point $P \in E^d$, find all d-dim. rectangles R in the file with $P \in R$.

For each of the files (F1) - (F5) we performed 500 queries for each SAM. By definition, each of the query types rectangle intersection, rectangle enclosure and rectangle containment uses a query rectangle. Therefore we generated 160 query rectangles with uniformly distributed centers for each of the three query types. In order to analyze the influence of the query rectangles on the performance, we are varying their size and shape. We generate 20 "square shaped" rectangles of sizes 0.1% 0.5%, 1% and 5% where the length of the rectangles is uniformly distributed between

1/2 squareroot(size) and 3/2 squareroot(size). Analogously, we generate 20 "slim" rectangles of sizes 0.1%, 0.5%, 1% and 5% where the length of the rectangles is uniformly distributed between 1/10 squareroot(size) and 19/10 squareroot(size). With these 160 query rectangles we perform the three query types rectangle intersection, rectangle enclosure and rectangle containment, thus yielding 480 queries. The remaining 20 queries are point queries, where the points follow a two dimensional independent uniform distribution.

8. Results of the experiments

As mentioned before, we will report in the following five tables the average number of disk accesses per query for each of the five files (F1) - (F5) and the four different query types.

Gaussianslim-Distribution

	point query	intersection	enclosure	containment
R-Tree	189.4	472.0	34.8	472.0
BANG	167.7	401.4	41.7	37.1
BUDDY	159.8	394.9	30.4	34.5
PLOP	273.6	637.3	55.5	637.3

Uniformsmall-Distribution

	point query	intersection	enclosure	containment
R-Tree	55.9	195.8	15.0	195.8
BANG	52.5	177.1	17.4	61.1
BUDDY	37.0	162.8	7.2	58.5
PLOP	41.4	172.9	6.1	172.9

Gaussiansquare-Distribution

	point query	intersection	enclosure	containment
R-Tree	86.5	266.7	14.0	266.7
BANG	68.8	236.3	16.0	68,2
BUDDY	57.6	232.6	6.4	65.7
PLOP	97.2	299.2	6.8	299.2

Uniformlarge-Distribution

	point query	intersection	enclosure	containment
R-Tree	742.8	988.2	518.7	988.2
BANG	388.6	603.8	239.4	20.2
BUDDY	380.2	593.3	231.2	18.0
PLOP	783.6	965.4	613.0	965.4

Diagonal-Distribution

	point query	intersection	enclosure	containment
R-Tree	283.4	568.2	163.7	568.2
BANG	187.8	413.3	97.2	25.6
BUDDY	187.5	421.0	92.9	22.9
PLOP	435.2	748.1	245.5	748.1

Similar as in our PAM comparison we computed the unweighted average over all five files and depict in the following table. In order to prevent overweighting of distributions with high number of page accesses, such as the Uniformlarge Distribution, we normalized the distributions by replacing the absolute values by percentage values where we use the R-tree as a 100% measuring stick. Additionally the average storage utilization denoted by stor and the average number of disk accesses for an insertion (read and write), averaged over all 100000 insertions when building up the file are presented in the following table.

	point query	intersection	enclosure	containment	stor	insert
R-Tree	100.0	100.0	100.0	100.0	67.6	110.3
BANG	76.1	79.5	91.2	14.3	68.5	2.88
BUDDY	66.9	77.6	56.5	13.5	65.5	2.92
PLOP	98.1	113.0	103.4	113.0	61.0	2.74

After running the experiments for the five files (F1) - (F5) and the four different query types we became aware that the performance comparison for rectangles is far more complex than the comparison for points for the following reasons:

1. The objects, here rectangles, are more complex than points. Whereas points as zero-size objects are determined by their position in dataspace, rectangles are determined by the following parameters: position, size, shape (square or long and slim) and degree of overlap. Obviously all of these parameters have to be extensively varied in a comparison.

2. The queries are more complex. One reason is that already the query object which is a rectangle in rectangle containment, rectangle enclosure and rectangle intersection is more complex. Furthermore, there are additional important operations and queries such as spatial join ("overlay two maps") and near neighbor-type queries.

3. The access methods are more complex. A SAM for rectangles is based on a PAM and uses one of the techniques clipping, overlapping regions and transformation. As shown in [SK 88] a hybrid method combining two techniques and avoiding their weak points improves performance over just using one of the techniques. Questions arise like which technique is best for which query type? For example, in our experiments it turned out that the technique of transformation was always best for the rectangle containment query. An additional example for the higher complexity of the access methods is the R-tree. Guttman's original design of the R-tree [Gut 84] can easily be improved by improving its split condition, e.g. by using Diane Greene's split condition [Gre 89]. Even this split condition can still considerably be improved as our implementations of Guttman's, Greene's and our own split conditions show.

From the above reasons it is obvious, that a considerably more extensive comparison for SAMs storing rectangles has to be performed. The presently available results indicate that BANG and particularly BUDDY are first choices.

9. Conclusions

In our performance comparison of point access methods, we were surprised to see one point method to be the clear winner. We had expected a much more complex result depending on the particular data distribution and on the particular query type. Summarizing the outcome of our comparisons we can state that the BUDDY hash tree exhibits an at least 20 % better average query performance than its competitors and, even more important, is more robust under ugly data and queries. Looking at the results of the experiments and at the partitions of the data space more closely, it turns out that the good performance of the BUDDY hash tree is not by chance, but is due to the concept of not partitioning the complete data space. Thus it might be worthwhile to incorporate this performance improving concept into other methods, in particular into the BANG file.

From our comparison of spatial access methods for rectangles it follows that this comparison has to be performed with a considerably higher variation of object parameters (position, size, shape and degree of overlap), query parameters and techniques (clipping, overlapping regions and transformation). The presently available results indicate that BANG and particularly BUDDY both using transformation are first choices for spatial access methods storing rectangles.

Further work in this area should deal with performance comparisons of access methods for more complex spatial objects, such as polygons, where only very few access methods are known. Therefore access methods for complex spatial objects have to be designed and compared with the most promising candidate, the cell-tree [Gün 89].

As mentioned before this comparison is a first step towards a standardized testbed or benchmark. We offer our data and query files to everybody who wants to run his implementation in our testbed. At the same time, we are thankful for "hard" datafiles, in particular for "hard" real data.

Acknowledgement:

First of all, we would like to thank our colleagues Peter Heep and Stephan Heep for their valuable advice and support. Bernhard Seeger implemented the buddy hash tree, the implementation of the hB-tree is due to Michael Schiwietz and the BANG file was partially implemented by a group of computer science students and partially by Michael Schiwietz. Furthermore we are thankful to the Landesvermessungsamt NRW, Bonn West Germany, for making real cartography data available to us. Last, not least, we thank Ursula Behrend for professionally writing this manuscript.

References:

[Com 79]   D. Comer: 'The Ubiquitous B-tree', Computing Surveys, Vol.11, No.2, 121-137, 1979

[Bur 83]   W.A. Burkhard: 'Interpolation-based index maintenance', BIT 23, 274-294, 1983

[Fre 87]   M. Freeston: 'The BANG file: a new kind of grid file', Proc. ACM SIGMOD Int. Conf. on Management of Data, 260-269, 1987

[Gre 89]   D. Greene: 'An Implementation and Performance Analysis of Spatial Data Access Methods', Proc. 5th Int. Conf. on Data Engineering, 606-615, 1989

[Gün 89]   O. Günther: The design of the cell tree: An object-oriented index structure for geometric databases, in Proc. Fifth Intl. Conf. on Data Engineering, Feb. 6-10, 1989, Los Angeles

[Gut 84]   A. Guttman: 'R-trees: a dynamic index structure for spatial searching', Proc. ACM SIGMOD Int. Conf. on Management of Data, 47-57, 1984

[Hin 85]   K. Hinrichs: 'The grid file system: implementation and case studies for applications', Dissertation No. 7734, Eidgenössische Technische Hochschule (ETH), Zuerich, 1985

[HSW 88]   A. Hutflesz, H.-W. Six, P. Widmayer: 'Twin grid files : space optimizing access schemes', Proc. ACM SIGMOD Int. Conf. on Management of Data, 183-190, 1988

[Kri 84]   H.P. Kriegel: 'Performance comparison of index structures for multikey retrieval', Proc. ACM SIGMOD Int. Conf. on Management of Data, 186-196, 1984

[KS 86]   H.P. Kriegel, B. Seeger: 'Multidimensional order preserving linear hashing with partial expansions', Proc. Int. Conf. on Database Theory, Lecture Notes in Computer Science 243, 203-220, 1986

[KS 87]   H.P. Kriegel, B. Seeger: 'Multidimensional quantile hashing is very efficient for non-uniform distributions', Proc. 3rd Int. Conf. on Data Engineering, 10-17, 1987, extended version will appear in Information Science

[KS 88]   H.P. Kriegel, B. Seeger: 'PLOP-Hashing: a grid file without directory', Proc. 4th Int. Conf. on Data Engineering, 369-376, 1988

[LS 89]   D.B. Lomet, B. Salzberg: The hB-tree: A robust multiattribute search structure, in Proc. of the Fifth Int. Conf. on Data Engineering, Feb. 6-10, 1989, Los Angeles, also available as Technical Report TR-87-05, School of Information Technology, Wang Institute of Graduate Studies.

[NHS 84]   J. Nievergelt, H. Hinterberger, K.C. Sevcik: 'The grid file: an adaptable, symmetric multikey file structure', ACM Trans. on Database Systems, Vol. 9, 1, 38-71, 1984

[NH 85]   J. Nievergelt, K. Hinrichs: 'Storage and access structures for geometric data bases', Proc. Int. Conf. on Foundsations of Data Organization, 335-345, 1985

[OM 84]   J.A. Orenstein, T.H. Merrett: 'A class of data structures for associative searching', Proc 3rd ACM SIGACT-SIGMOD Symposium on Principles of Database Systems, 181-190, 1984

[Oto 84]   E. J. Otoo: 'A mapping function for the directory of a multidimensional extendible hashing', Proc. 10th Int. Conf. on Very Large Databases, 491-506, 1984

[Oto 86]   E. J. Otoo, : 'Balanced multidimensional extendible hash tree', Proc. 5th ACM SIGACT-SIGMOD Symposium on Principles of Database Systems, 110-113, 1986

[Ouk 85]   M. Ouksel: 'The interpolation based grid file', Proc. 4th ACM SIGACT-SIGMOD Symposium on Principles of Database Systems, 1985

[Rob 81]   J. T. Robinson: 'The K-D-B-tree: a search structure for large multidimensional dynamic indexes', Proc. ACM SIGMOD Int. Conf. on Management of Data, 10-18, 1981

[See 89]   Seeger, B.: 'Design and implementation of multidimensional access methods' in German), PhD thesis, Department of Computer Science, University of Bremen.

[SFK 89]   B. Seeger, S. Frank, H.P. Kriegel: The buddy hash tree, English version in preparation, German version available as a Technical Report

[SFR 87]   Sellis, T., Roussopoulos, N., Faloutsos, C.: 'The R+ -tree: a dynamic index for multi-dimensional objects', Proc. 13th Int. Conf. on Engeneering, 1988.

[SK 88]   B. Seeger, H. P. Kriegel: 'Design and implementation of spatial access methods', Proc. 14th Int. Conf. on Very Large Databases, 360-371, 1988

[Tam 82]   M. Tamminen: 'The extendible cell method for closest point problems', BIT 22, 27-41, 1982

[WK 85]   K.-Y. Whang, R. Krishnamurthy: 'Multilevel grid files', Technical Report, IBM Research Lab., Yorktown Heights, 1985

Strategies for Optimizing the Use of
Redundancy in Spatial Databases

Jack A. Orenstein
Object Design, Inc.*
One New England Executive Park
Burlington, MA 01803

odi!jack@talcott.harvard.edu

Abstract

Several spatial access methods can handle non-point data by placing each data object in a container, e.g. a box, and storing the collection of containers. As complexity of the spatial objects increases, the effectiveness of this strategy decreases, due to the inaccuracy of the approximation. Some access methods store objects redundantly to compensate. Each copy represents some portion of the object. The method by which redundancy is obtained is crucial in determining the degree of success that can be achieved. Two strategies for obtaining redundancy are compared, one based on recursive partitioning of the space containing the data objects, and the other based on type-specific object partitionings. Experimental results using a data set containing line segments suggest that the former approach is more effective in improving performance.

Introduction

A spatial database system must be able to store spatial objects and efficiently retrieve those objects in response to queries involving spatial predicates such as overlap, containment and proximity. Many useful queries are special cases of the *overlap query*. This query takes as input two sets of spatial objects, R and S, and returns a set of pairs (r, s) such that r is a member of R, s is a member of S, and r and s overlap spatially [OREN86, OREN88]. Many queries involving spatial predicates can be easily mapped into overlap queries.

The *range query* is a special case of the overlap query in which one set contains n data points, and the other set contains a single query box. (Here, and in the rest of this paper, boxes are oriented so that each edge is parallel to one axis of the space.) Many solutions to the range query problem have been described. Algorithms for main memory [BENT75, SAME84] and secondary storage [LOME87, LOME89, MERR78, MERR82, NIEV84, OREN84, ROBI81, SELL87] are known. All of these algorithms work in spaces of any dimensionality.

Spatial database systems require the ability to deal with data objects other than points and query

---

* The work reported here was performed on equipment owned by the author, and does not relate to anticipated Object Design products.

objects other than boxes. It is well-known that any spatial access method capable of supporting range queries can handle more complicated data and query objects through the use of approximation and parameterization. Approximation involves placing complicated spatial objects inside containers with simpler shapes, e.g. boxes or circles. Parameterization involves describing these containers by points in higher-dimension spaces (e.g., see [FALO87, HINR85]). The alternative is to store these containers directly. The R-tree [GUTT84], the R+-tree [SELL87], the cell tree [GUNT89], and z-order based structures [OREN86, OREN88] are designed to do this. However, it will be shown that many access methods for point data can be adapted to do the same thing.

Because approximation is so commonly used, query processing strategies based on spatial access methods must process spatial queries in two steps. First there is a *filter step* in which the spatial access method is used to rapidly eliminate objects that could not possibly satisfy the query. The result of this step is a set of *candidate* objects which includes all the objects satisfying the query, and possibly some that do not. These are called *false hits*. The second step is the *refinement step* in which each candidate is examined. False hits are detected and eliminated.

Parameterization is an appealing solution because of its simplicity. However, it is not yet known how performance is affected by the transformation to a space with more dimensions. Very little work has been done in this area. I am currently working on this problem and expect to report results in future papers. Parameterization will not be considered further in this paper.

The use of approximation by containing objects is not entirely satisfactory. For a disjoint object or an object with holes or concavities, the volume of the container may far exceed that of the object. As a result, the object will be involved in many false hits. A poor approximation can also occur when the object is continuous and has no holes, but because of its shape, is not capable of filling the container selected by the spatial access method, e.g., a line segment inside a containing circle. This can be dealt with by using containers with more parameters, (e.g., an ellipse instead of a circle), but this increases the number of parameters which tends to decrease performance.

These problems suggest that spatial searches based on the approximation by containers will yield increasingly inaccurate answers as the complexity of the data objects increases. In the extreme case, the filter step would return the entire set of data objects, all of which would then have to be examined during the refinement step.

Complexity of data objects need not destroy the accuracy of the filter step. An alternative is to introduce redundancy into the spatial access method. The goal is to retain the speed and accuracy of the filter step in exchange for a larger space requirement. While several spatial access methods use edundancy in this way, there has been very little discussion of redundancy itself. There are many questions to answer: How can redundancy be introduced? Should the redundancy of an object, (the number of copies of an object in a spatial access method) depend only on properties of the object, or should other factors such as distribution be considered? What other factors? How are performance and accuracy of the filter step affected by the amount of redundancy and by the method in which it was achieved? I have started investigating these questions. Preliminary results were reported in [OREN89] which examined one technique for introducing redundancy that is applicable in the context of z-order based spatial access methods. The results will be summarized below. This paper extends the earlier work by examining an alternative technique for introducing redundancy, that has broader applicability, as it is applicable to any spatial access method, including those that are not based on z-order.

Performance of the two techniques - one specific to z order, and one which is more general - are compared. Section 2 reviews z-order based spatial access methods. Section 3 describes different strategies for obtaining redundancy and indicates where they have been used in spatial access methods that appear in the literature. Section 4 summarizes results on the effect of redundancy on performance. Section 5 analyzes one technique for obtaining redundancy, "type-specific redundancy", and compares it to a previously-analyzed technique. Conclusions are in section 6.

2 Overview of z order-based access methods

In [OREN84] a solution to the range query problem is given. The technique used is to transform the problem of finding all the points in a k-dimensional (k-d) box into an equivalent search problem in 1-d. Each data point is transformed into a 1-d interval of size 1, and the query box is transformed into a set of intervals of varying size. A data point is contained by the box iff the corresponding interval falls in one of the query's intervals. This approach yields a *family* of data structures for evaluating range queries. A member of this family is derived by providing a data structure that supports random and sequential access, e.g. a sorted array, an AVL tree, or a b-tree. The search algorithm is expressed in terms of random and sequential accesses to the underlying data structure. In spite of the generality of this approach, performance is comparable to that of more specialized structures. Furthermore, this approach permits all the theory, techniques, and even *software*, that has been developed for ordinary (one dimensional) searching problems, to be applied to spatial searching. For example, the experiments reported in section 5 were carried out using the *zkd b-tree*, an ordinary b-tree loaded with 2-d line segments transformed to 1-d intervals.

This approach can be generalized to deal with arbitrary spatial objects involved in overlap queries

[OREN86]. Each spatial object in each input set is transformed to a set of 1-d intervals. An algorithm called *spatial join* implements the filter step. Each resulting candidate is a pair of objects, one from each input set, that are likely to overlap. The output from spatial join has to go through a refinement step as described above. Spatial join and filtering algorithms for other spatial problems appear in [OREN88]. These algorithms comprise the *geometry filter* (GF).

2.1 Decomposition: generating the geometry filter's representation

As discussed above, the geometry filter works by transforming a k-d spatial object into a set of 1-d intervals. There are many ways to do this. Many of the modularity and performance benefits of the geometry filter derive from the particular way in which the geometry filter does this transformation.

The "conceptual" representation used by the geometry filter is a grid of fixed resolution. The representation for an object is obtained by noting which cells are completely or partially occupied by the object. This representation is a conservative approximation. Partially occupied cells are included so that the filtering property is retained. If such cells were omitted, then the approximation would not be conservative, and some positive results would be lost in the output of the filter step.

The grid representation can easily be transformed to 1-d, e.g., by listing the occupied cells in row-major order. However, the number of occupied cells depends on the volume of the object. As a result, the space and time requirements for algorithms based on this representation will be very high. Instead, an encoding of the grid is used. The space is recursively partitioned until the resolution of the grid is reached. Regions that are entirely contained in the object do not have to be split further. The space requirement for this encoding is proportional to the surface area of the object, not the volume, so the space and time requirements are much better. However, further improvements can be obtained, as described below.

By constraining the partitioning process as in [OREN84, OREN88], a highly compact representation of the spatial object can be obtained. A region created by partitioning under these constraints is called an *element*. Together, these constraints lead to a very concise description. Typically, each element can be described by one 32-bit word. Each partition is represented by one bit, and the relationship of the element to the partition is described by the value of the bit. (In 2-d space, a 0 means to the left of or below. A 1 bit means to the right of or above.) The bit-sequence corresponding to an element is called a *z value*. Given a z value, the size, shape and position of an element can be reconstructed.

Figure 1 shows the encoding of a spatial object achieved by elements. This is a more compact epresentation than the explicit listing of each grid cell, since the space requirement for each element is ne same, regardless of its size.

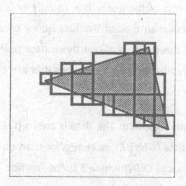

Figure 1. Decomposition of a spatial object

The *decompose* algorithm is responsible for generating the elements corresponding to a spatial bject. In spite of the constraints on the partitioning process, there are actually a variety of ecomposition strategies. The algorithm presented in [OREN88] yields the most accurate decomposition ossible, given the resolution of the space. [OREN89] describes two generalizations of the algorithm nat are less accurate but use less space and permit the filter step to execute more quickly, (see section .2).

The geometry filter's representation for a set of spatial objects is obtained by decomposing each bject, associating each z value with the object, and then merging all the (z value, object) pairs into a ingle 1-d search structure, keyed by z value. Redundancy occurs when the same object is associated ⁻ith multiple z values. This structure will be referred to as the GF representation, GF file, or GF equence.

The geometry filter algorithms operate by generating random and sequential accesses against GF equences.

.2 Spatial join: generating candidates

The spatial join algorithm performs a merge of two GF sequences, searching for situations where n element in one sequence, as represented by its z value, contains an element from the other input. his can be determined by checking whether one z value is a prefix of the other.) When such a pair is ound, a candidate, comprising the objects associated with the elements, is generated. If the sizes of the nput sequences are n and m, then the time for the merge is O(n + m). However, it is often possible to do much better. For example, consider a range query. The n data points yield a GF sequence of size n. The other input set will contain some small number of elements for the query box. The merge can be optimized by taking advantage of the fact that the elements of the query box usually occur in clusters. For example, all the data points whose z values are less than that of the first query element can be skipped. Similarly, the data points between elements of the query box and those data points following the last element of the query can be skipped. The ability to "skip over" elements that are clearly not of interest is the source of the random access requirement.

This optimization has been built into the spatial join algorithm. The details are in [OREN88]. With this optimization, and assuming a certain distribution of data (which is more regular than uniform), it can be shown that the expected performance for range queries is O(fN) where f is the fraction of the space covered by the query, and N is the number of data objects [OREN83].

3 Techniques for obtaining redundancy in spatial access methods

Redundancy can be introduced by decomposing a spatial object into smaller, simpler objects. The spatial access method contains an entry for each component of each decomposed object. This section describes different ways to obtain redundancy, and how they are used by various spatial access methods.

3.1 Density-dependent redundancy (DDR)

Many spatial access methods designed for point data can be easily adapted for non-point data. Virtually all point access methods partition space either by placing creating a grid in the space containing the data objects [MERR78, MERR82, NIEV84] or by recursive splitting of the space [BENT75, LOME87, LOME89, ROBI81, SAME84, TAMM82]. In either case, each data point always falls in exactly one of the partitions. For non-point data, another possible outcome is that an object spans partitions. In this case, the object is replicated, appearing once in each partition [SELL87, MANT83]. In [HORN87] each partition stores the portion of the object that falls in the partition. (R-trees [GUTT84] deal with this situation by introducing "ambiguity" into the search path, avoiding redundancy - see section 4.2) This technique will be referred to as *density-dependent redundancy* because the redundancy for a collection of objects will be determined by the size and shape of the objects, (as for all other techniques to be described), but also by the local density of objects. Insertions into densely-filled regions of space drive up the replication of *other* objects nearby, (see figure 2.)

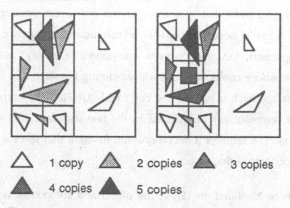

△ 1 copy   ▲ 2 copies   ▲ 3 copies

▲ 4 copies   ▲ 5 copies

Figure 2

Grid file, before and after insertion of an object
(the square). Page capacity is two objects. The
insertion causes six data pages to be added, which
in turn, increases the replication of several
objects in the vicinity.

Two spatial access methods for non-point data derive from point access methods in this way. In
[MANT83], EXCELL, a point access method [TAMM82] is used to store 3-d objects. Also, the R+-tree
[SELL87], although it is described as a variation of the R-tree [GUTT84], is in some respects closer to
the KDB-tree [ROBI81]. By using DDR in conjunction with the KDB-tree an R+-tree is obtained.

3.2 Density-independent redundancy, (DIR)

Another technique for obtaining redundancy is to decide on the number of copies of an object
based solely on the object itself, without considering any spatial context, e.g. density as in DDR. This
approach was taken in [OREN89], in conjunction with z-order based spatial access methods. A similar
approach has been taken by D. Abel, in the context of quadtrees. Each element resulting from the
decomposition of an object represents a copy of that object. The decompose algorithm can place a
bound on the number of intervals generated, or on the accuracy of the representation. In [OREN89]
these alternative strategies were referred to as SIZE-BOUND and ERROR-BOUND respectively. Each
strategy has a parameter controlling output size or accuracy. Through this parameter, the redundancy
of a collection of objects can be controlled. These strategies will be called *density-independent*, due to
the fact that redundancy depends on object size and shape, and not on local density.

3.3 Type-specific redundancy, (TSR)

A third way to obtain redundancy is to take advantage of type-specific properties of spatial objects. For example, any polygon, even if it is disjoint or has holes, can be decomposed into a collection of convex polygons. A spatial access method for a collection of polygons can be created by indexing on the convex components. I.e., each convex component is a "key" associated with its containing object. Any polygon whose component is retrieved during the filter step is then examined during the refinement step. This approach is used in the cell tree [GUNT89]. Similarly, linear features, approximated by chains of line segments, can be indexed by the line segments. This technique will be called *type-specific redundancy*. TSR requires a decomposition function that takes a spatial object as input and returns a set of components of that object.

Two varieties of TSR can be identified. In TSR-2, the object and component types are different. The component type is simpler, as with the polygon and linear feature examples above. The number of components usually does not have a fixed bound. In TSR-1, the object and component types are the same. For example, a linear feature can be decomposed into smaller linear features using TSR-1, but there is no guarantee that these components are line segments. The purpose of TSR-1 is to allow an upper bound to be placed on the number of objects returned by the decomposition. This technique seems applicable to a wide variety of representations. (About the names: TSR-1 deals with one type of object, TSR-2 deals with two types.)

Polygons can also be handled by TSR-1 or TSR-2. For an n-vertex polygon, TSR-2 returns $O(n)$ convex components. TSR-1 can return any number of polygons, but their convexity cannot be guaranteed.

4 How redundancy affects performance

The traditional goal of clustering in a database system is to place objects that will be retrieved together, near one another on disk (i.e., the same page). For spatial search predicates, objects that are retrieved together are usually near one another in the space being modeled. That is, proximity in space must translate into proximity in secondary storage in order to obtain the best possible performance for spatial queries. Redundancy within a spatial index can be used to obtain good clustering when the topology, shape, or size of a spatial object are such that no single placement within the file makes sense.

In measuring the performance effects of redundancy, there are two characteristics of the filter step that are of concern, speed and accuracy. Because the query is being evaluated in the context of a database system, the appropriate criterion for speed is the number of data page faults required by the filter step. Accuracy is a concern because the time required for the refinement step is directly related to the amount of output from the filter step.

A balance must be struck between the goals of optimizing speed and accuracy. 100% accuracy can be achieved, but the speed benefit of filtering would then be lost. The results of [OREN89] and section 5 indicate that accuracy initially increases rapidly with redundancy, and then the rate of growth slows down. Fortunately, the most rapid increase occurs while page faults decrease with redundancy. If this turns out to be true in general, then it suggests that the primary goal should be to minimize page faults.

.1 Summary of earlier results

This section summarizes [OREN89]. One contribution was the identification of a "strategy space" for the processing of overlap queries. These strategies differ in their use of redundancy and parameterization as follows:

1   **No redundancy**: Each spatial object is placed in a container which is then represented by a point in a parameter space.

2   **Redundancy induced by object structure**: The spatial objects are partitioned into natural components. Each component is placed in a container and represented by a point in a parameter space.

3   **Redundancy induced by region boundaries**: The spatial objects are partitioned along region boundaries. The resulting partitions, which describe pieces of the object in the original space, are placed into a spatial index.

4   **Redundancy induced by object structure, then by region boundaries**: Partition the spatial objects into their natural components and then partition each component along region boundaries. Each piece resulting from this two-step partitioning is placed into an index which describes the original space.

This description is from [OREN89].) "Redundancy induced by object structure" is TSR, and "redundancy induced by region boundaries" covers both DDR and DIR.

The paper then examined strategy 3 in the context of z-order based spatial access methods. The approach was experimental. Speed of the filter step, measured by data page faults, and accuracy of the filter step were measured against redundancy. As redundancy increases (starting at 1 - no redundancy) the time required by the filter step first decreases rapidly until an optimal amount of redundancy, R_{opt}, is reached, typically 1.3 - 1.7 (30% - 70% redundancy). Then, as redundancy is increased further, time requirements increase. The rate of increase is slower than the rate of decrease.

Accuracy is defined as the ratio of the number of objects satisfying the query to the number of objects retrieved in the filter step. Accuracy of 1.0 indicates that the filter step produces perfect results. Accuracy increases monotonically with redundancy, with the rate of increase slowing as redundancy is increased. By the time R_{opt} is reached, the rate of increase of accuracy is close to zero. Figures 3 and 4 show the page fault and accuracy result for the ERROR-BOUND strategy applied to data squares of size 30 x 30.

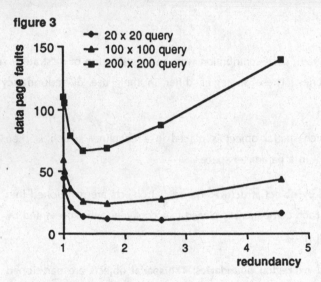

figure 3

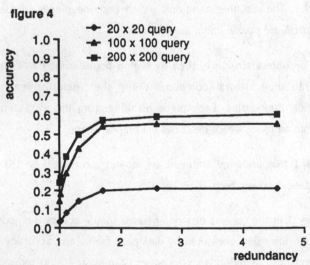

figure 4

The experiments examined both the ERROR-BOUND and SIZE-BOUND strategy. ERROR-BOUND was almost always superior on both criteria, although the difference was often very small.

One important feature of ERROR-BOUND is that it provides finer control over redundancy where it is most important, near R_{opt}.

The data sets used in the experiments consisted of 5000 small square boxes. Box size was fixed in each experiment, ranging from 5x5 to 30x30 in a 1000x1000 space. The graphs shown in [OREN89] were obtained from 20x20 boxes. Box positions were selected with a uniform random number generator.

The experiments were also run against a VLSI data sample. Qualitative results were the same as for the generated data. Page faults were higher than for generated data objects of the same average volume. Accuracy was better for the VLSI data, (this was surprising).

.2 The R-tree

The framework described above does not accomodate the R-tree, which avoids redundancy, but does not rely on parameterization. Instead, an "ambiguity" is introduced into the search path. The R-tree works approximately like a b-tree. Leaf nodes contain spatial objects (approximated by boxes). An index page entry comprises a box and a pointer to a child page. All data objects in a sub-tree are contained in the box of the corresponding index node. An R-tree is always balanced because it grows at the root. When a leaf page containing data objects overflows, it is split, and the index term that represented the leaf is replaced by two index terms, each consisting of a box and a pointer.

During a search, boxes in index nodes are compared with the search argument, (another box), and if there is overlap, the child node associated with index node box is retrieved and searched recursively. The ambiguity occurs because boxes in index nodes may not be disjoint, (see figure 5).

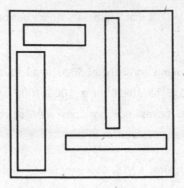

Figure 5. There is no way to split this R-tree leaf node evenly (two objects per sub-region) and avoid overlapping index terms.

There is sometimes no way to split a leaf so that the index terms of the newly-created leaves will be evenly distributed and disjoint. Instead, the goal of the splitting algorithm is to minimize the amount of overlap of the index terms. If a search region intersects the region of overlap of two index node boxes, then both sub-trees have to be searched. The R+-tree avoids this ambiguity by splitting offending data objects. This introduces redundancy but avoids overlapping index terms.

The zkd b-tree is the z-order based spatial access method derived from the b-tree [OREN84, OREN89]. It is interesting to compare the zkd b-tree and the R-tree because of their common ancestor. When the zkd b-tree is used with zero redundancy (by the ERROR-BOUND(0) or SIZE-BOUND(1) decomposition strategy), a similar "ambiguity" can be observed. This is the "backup" phenomenon discussed in [OREN89]. For both structures, the net result is an increase in the number of pages to be searched (relative to the number that would be predicted based on query size), and an associated drop in accuracy, i.e. more spatial objects passed to the refinement step than would otherwise be necessary.

The R+-tree uses DDR to introduce redundancy and avoid the ambiguity. Z-order structures use DIR.

5 Analysis of TSR

For z-order based spatial access methods, redundancy obtained by the DIR strategy is very effective in reducing the page faults required by the filter step and improving accuracy. In the experiments described earlier, the difference in performance between $R = 1$ and $R = R_{opt}$ was dramatic. In the graphs shown above, page faults were lowered by a factors of 3.8 (query size 20 x 20), 2.4

query size 100 x 100), and 1.6 (query size 200 x 200). Accuracy increased by factors of 7.0, 3.9, and 2.1, respectively.

The use of DIR alone corresponds to strategy 3 (from section 4.1). Using TSR prior to DIR - strategy 4 - is the alternative considered in this section. The other strategies, which involve parameterization, will be examined in future research.

Strategy 4 is really a generalization of strategy 3. DIR is a special case of the combined TSR+DIR strategy, since a TSR-1 algorithm can simply return its input. In general, a file of spatial objects, loaded using TSR+DIR has two sources of redundancy. R_T is the amount of redundancy due to TSR. R_D is the amount of redundancy due to DIR. R_T is determined by the nature of the objects being decomposed, and whether the decomposition algorithm is TSR-1 or TSR-2, (see section 3.3). R_D is determined by the objects and by the decomposition algorithm (ERROR-BOUND or SIZE-BOUND) and the value of the parameter to the decomposition algorithm. The total redundancy is $R = R_T R_D$. The question considered here is what value of R_T optimizes performance of the filter step.

The motivation for TSR is that certain spatial objects are difficult to approximate by the z-order encoding because of their size, shape or topology. Examples were given in section 1. By carving up such objects in type-specific ways, smaller and simpler objects are obtained, which can be encoded more compactly or more accurately.

In the discussion that follows, let the value of R_T (respectively, R_D) minimizing page faults in the filter step be denoted by R_T^* (R_D^*). Note that R_D^* is dependent on R_T^*, as it depends on the shape and size of objects emerging from the TSR decomposition. The optimal redundancy for the DIR strategy, called R_{opt} in section 4.1, will be denoted $R_{opt}(DIR)$. The optimal redundancy for the TSR+DIR strategy will be denoted $R_{opt}(TSR+DIR)$, and is equal to $R_T^* R_D^*$.

The approach taken here is experimental. The data set to be queried contains line segments of arbitrary orientation, instead of (oriented) boxes, as in the earlier experiments. This creates an opportunity to check on the robustness of the earlier results. Second, for the spatial access methods that have been developed, boxes are the simplest non-point objects. This is why boxes are so often used as bounding containers when approximation is called for. For any other shape it should be more difficult to retain the accuracy of the filter step without sacrificing speed.

The analysis will proceed as follows:

1. Run experiments on the line-segment data, measuring the effect of redundancy on

data page faults and accuracy. If the general trends described in section 4.1 are seen, then this will establish R_{opt} for this data set.

2. Decompose the line segments of the data set "artificially", to simulate the TSR strategy, and run the experiments again.

3. Compare the results from steps 1 and 2 by plotting data page faults against redundancy, and accuracy against redundancy.

The design of the experiments is as follows:

- The space contains 1000 x 1000 pixels.

- The data set consists of 5000 line segments, each of length 100 pixels. The position and orientation of each line segment is selected randomly, using a uniform random number generator. The data objects were decomposed using the ERROR-BOUND(g) strategy, for g = 0, 2, 4, 6, 8, 10.

- Queries of size 20 x 20 and 200 x 200 were generated randomly. There were five trials for each query size. Query objects were decomposed using ERROR-BOUND(8).

- The data and query objects were loaded into zkd b+-trees with leaf capacity of 20 objects.

- Buffer management was LRU. Separate buffer pools were used for the data and query trees, and each pool had 15 buffers.

The software for the experiments was developed and run on a Commodore Amiga 2000. The language of implementation is C.

5.1 Verification of earlier results for the new data set

The reasons behind the qualitative observations of section 4.1 have nothing to do with the shape of the data objects, so it would be very surprising if the same general trends did not hold for other data sets. Figures 6 and 7 show the results for the original (undivided) line segments. It is clear that the trends described in section 4.1 hold for this data set. As in the earlier study, page faults drop rapidly as redundancy is increased from 1, and then increase more slowly. Accuracy is considerably better at R_{opt} than at 1, although the rate of increase at R_{opt} isn't quite as low as in the previous experiments.

As in earlier experiments, ERROR-BOUND provides more control over redundancy at low values where it is particularly important). Otherwise, the results for ERROR-BOUND and SIZE-BOUND are almost indistinguishable. Only ERROR-BOUND will be used in the remaining experiments.

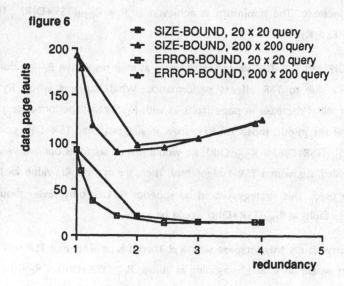

figure 6

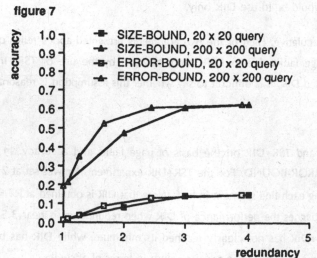

figure 7

$R_{opt}(DIR)$ is larger than in the earlier study - 1.7 for the larger query, 2.4 for the smaller one - compared with values from 1.3 to 1.7 previously.

5.2 The prospects for TSR

Suppose that the qualitative results of [OREN89] apply to the objects resulting from the TSR decomposition. This is a reasonable supposition as pointed out in section 5.1. This means that as redundancy, R, is increased from R_T, as a result of increasing R_D, (by raising the ERROR-BOUND or SIZE-BOUND parameter), it is reasonable to expect that the data page faults required by the filter step will decrease initially, and then increase. The minimum is achieved at $R = R_{opt}(TSR+DIR)$. The conclusion here is that $R_{opt}(TSR+DIR) > R_T$.

How do page faults for the DIR and TSR+DIR strategies compare at their respective R_{opt} values? This depends on how redundancy due to TSR affects performance. What happens when R_T is increased from 1? Will there be an initial decrease in page faults as with R_D, or will performance just decrease monotonically? If the results mimic those of R_D, then it suggests that TSR+DIR could outperform DIR at some value of $R_{opt}(TSR+DIR) > R_{opt}(DIR)$. R_T would first be set to its optimal value, R_T^*, (assuming that it can be controlled, e.g. with a TSR-1 algorithm). Then, the optimal R_D value for the output of the TSR step would be used. This strategy would be superior to DIR only. Even though $R_{opt}(TSR+DIR) > R_{opt}(DIR)$, the page faults at $R_{opt}(TSR+DIR)$ would be lower.

On the other hand, what if page faults only increase with R_T? Then it is unlikely that TSR will be of any use. The optimal value of R_T would be 1, and, reasoning as above, $R_{opt}(TSR+DIR) = R_{opt}(DIR)$. In other words, the optimal strategy would be to use DIR only.

The reasoning here is highly speculative. Each of the two arguments presented above relies on an assumption: that the decrease in page faults due to DIR is not affected by the use of TSR. In the absence of analytical models of TSR and DIR, it is difficult to say whether this assumption is reasonable.

5.3 Experimental results for $R_T > 1$

Figures 8 and 9 compare DIR and TSR+DIR on the basis of page faults and accuracy. In both cases, the DIR decomposition was ERROR-BOUND. For the TSR+DIR experiment, R_T was set at 2 - the minimum non-trivial value - by splitting each line segment in half. (Note that DIR is obtained at RT = 1.)[1] For the smaller query, TSR+DIR approaches the performance of DIR when redundancy is near 3.5. The curves might cross further up as TSR+DIR has not clearly reached its minimum, while DIR has begun increasing very slowly. At this point, the two strategies are very close in terms of accuracy.

---

[1] The results are somewhat incomplete due to limitations of the software used in the experiments. The results for ERROR-BOUND(10) are missing. The software has been improved, and the graphs will be completed in the final version of this paper.

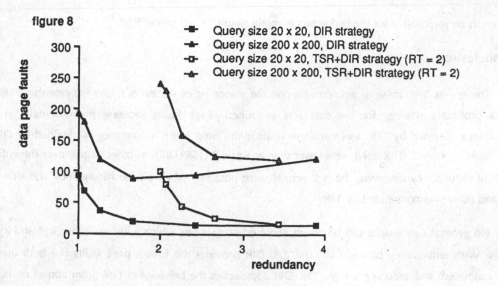

figure 8

- ■ Query size 20 x 20, DIR strategy
- ▲ Query size 200 x 200, DIR strategy
- □ Query size 20 x 20, TSR+DIR strategy (RT = 2)
- △ Query size 200 x 200, TSR+DIR strategy (RT = 2)

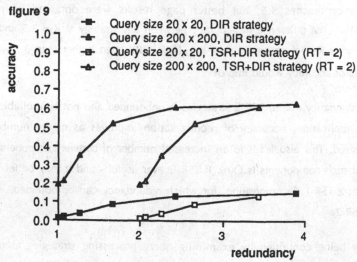

figure 9

- ■ Query size 20 x 20, DIR strategy
- ▲ Query size 200 x 200, DIR strategy
- □ Query size 20 x 20, TSR+DIR strategy (RT = 2)
- △ Query size 200 x 200, TSR+DIR strategy (RT = 2)

For the larger query, the situation is different. It appears that TSR will not beat DIR in page faults. Accuracy of the two strategies is again close when redundancy reaches the 3.0 - 3.5 range.

There is evidence to suggest that there is *no* initial drop in page faults as redundancy due to TSR increases. The TSR+DIR curve, representing $R_T = 2$, can be compared to the DIR curve, representing $R_T = 1$ (no redundancy due to TSR). In all cases, better results are obtained at $R_T = 1$.

At $R_{opt}(DIR)$, (2.4 for the smaller query, 1.7 for the larger one), TSR does not perform well, because at this point, most of the redundancy is accounted for by R_T. The R_D contribution, which appears to be responsible for the performance improvement, is still below R_D^*.

6 Conclusion

The results from these experiments support the reasoning of section 5.2, and indicate that TSR is *not* a profitable strategy for the data sets examined. Page faults increase monotonically with redundancy obtained by TSR, whereas there is an initial drop when redundancy is obtained by DIR. Page faults at $R_T = 1$ (DIR only) were lower than at $R_T = 2$ (TSR+DIR). In other words, over the entire range of redundancy observed, the best results were obtained when all the redundancy was due to DIR and none was contributed by TSR.

No general conclusions can be drawn about other data sets which will have other R_T^* and R_D^* values. With redundancy between 1.7 and 2.5, DIR provides the lowest page faults (for both query sizes examined) and accuracy is high. TSR+DIR approaches the behavior of DIR (from above) on both criteria only when redundancy reaches 3.5, but better page results were obtained with less redundancy by DIR at R_{opt}(DIR). The difference in accuracy between any strategy at $R = 3.5$ and DIR at R_{opt}(DIR) is negligible. Higher R_T values would shift R_{opt}(TSR+DIR) even higher than 3.5, and it seems unlikely that page faults or accuracy would improve.

As discussed earlier, redundancy due to TSR-2 strategies is unbounded and not controllable. For example, in a cartographic application, accuracy of representation improves as n, the number of vertices per polygon is increased. This also leads to an increased number of convex components per polygon, since the number of such components is $O(n)$. If TSR is ever useful - and it may be for other data sets - it seems likely that a TSR-1 decomposition, for which redundancy can be bounded, would provide better results than TSR-2.

This work is currently being continued by examining query processing strategies involving parameterization, and by developing analytical models that describe how the DIR and TSR strategies affect performance.

References

BENT75   J. L. Bentley.
          Multidimensional binary search trees used for associative searching.
          Comm. ACM 18, 9 (1975), 509-517.

FALO87   C. Faloutsos, W. Rego.
          A grid file for spatial objects.

Technical report CS-TR-1829, Department of Computer Science, University of Maryland, College Park, (1987).

GUTT84   A. Guttman.
R-trees: a dynamic index structure for spatial searching.
Proc. ACM SIGMOD, (1984).

GUNT89   O. Gunther.
The design of the cell tree: an object-oriented index structure for geometric databases.
Proc. Data Engineering Conference, (1989), 598-605.

HINR85   K. H. Hinrichs.
The grid file system: implementation and case studies of applications.
Doctoral dissertation, ETH Nr. 7734, Swiss Federal Institute of Technology, Zurich, Switzerland, (1985).

HORN87   D. Horn, H.-J. Schek, W. Waterfeld, A. Wolf.
Spatial access paths and physical clustering in a low-level geo-database system.
Technical report, Technical University of Darmstadt, West Germany (1987).

LOME87   D. B. Lomet, B. Salzberg.
The hB-tree: a robust multi-attribute indexing method.
Technical report TR-87-05, Wang Institute of Graduate Studies, (1987). (The Wang Institute is defunct. Contact Lomet at DEC, Nashua NH, or Salzberg at Northeastern University.)

LOME89   D. B. Lomet, B. Salzberg.
A robust multi-attribute search structure.
Proc. Data Engineering, (1989), 296-304.

MANT83   M. Mantyla, M. Tamminen.
Localized set operations for solid modeling.
ACM Computer Graphics, 17, 3 (1983) 279-288.

MERR78   T. H. Merrett.
Multidimensional paging for efficient database querying.
Proc. Int'l Conference on Management of Data, Milan (1978), 277-290.

MERR82   T. H. Merrett, E. J. Otoo.
Dynamic multipaging: a storage structure for large shared databases.
Proc. 2nd Int'l Conference on Databases: Improving usability and responsiveness, Jerusalem (1982).

NIEV84   J. Nievergelt, H. Hinterberger, K. C. Sevcik.
The grid file: an adaptable, symmetric multi-key file structure.
ACM TODS 9, 1 (1984), 38-71.

OREN83   J. A. Orenstein.
Algorithms and data structures for the implementation of a relational database system.
Ph.D. Thesis, McGill University, (1982). Also available as Technical Report SOCS 82-17.

OREN84   J. A. Orenstein, T. H. Merrett.
A class of data structures for associative searching.
Proc. 3rd ACM SIGACT-SIGMOD Symposium on Principles of Database Systems (1984), 181-190.

OREN86   J. A. Orenstein, F. A. Manola.
          Spatial data modeling and query processing in PROBE.
          Technical report CCA-86-05, Xerox Advanced Information Technology Division
          (formerly Computer Corporation of America).

OREN88   J. A. Orenstein, F. A. Manola.
          PROBE spatial data modeling and query processing in an image database application.
          IEEE Trans. on Software Eng. 14, 5 (May, 1988) 611-629.

OREN89   J. A. Orenstein.
          Redundancy in Spatial Databases. Proc. ACM SIGMOD (1989).

ROBI81   J. T. Robinson.
          The K-D-B tree: a search structure for large multidimensional dynamic indexes. Proc.
          ACM SIGMOD (1981).

SAME84   H. Samet.
          The quadtree and related hierarchical data structures.
          ACM Comp. Surv. 16, 2 (1984).

SELL87   T. Sellis, N. Roussopoulos, C. Faloutsos.
          The R+-tree: a dynamic index for multi-dimensional objects.
          Proc. VLDB, (1987).

TAMM82   M. Tamminen, R. Sulonen.
          The EXCELL method for efficient geometric access to data.
          Proc. 19th ACM Design Automation Conf. (1982), 345-351.

Geographic Applications

TILING LARGE GEOGRAPHICAL DATABASES

Michael F. Goodchild

National Center for Geographic Information and Analysis
University of California
Santa Barbara, CA 93106, USA

ABSTRACT

Geographical variation is infinitely complex, so the information coded in a spatial database can only approximate reality. The information will always be inadequate, in spatial resolution, thematic or geographical coverage. "Large" can be usefully defined as exceeding our current capacity to deliver. We provide examples of large geographical databases. Traditional stores partition geographical data by theme and geographically. We assume that digital geographical databases will be largely archival, and will be similarly partitioned. A general model of a large archival store is presented. We analyze the properties of a generalized Morton key as a means of indexing tiles, and illustrate its role in traditional systems of tile indexing. For global databases, we propose a tiling based on recursive subdivisions of the triangular faces of an octahedron using a rule of four.

1. INTRODUCTION

The theme of this conference on Large Spatial Databases raises a host of complex issues. The term "spatial" includes both two and three dimensions, and covers applications as diverse as medical imaging, CAD and remote sensing. The purpose of this paper is to provide a geographical perspective, and to enquire into the handling of large geographical databases, while noting that the geographical case is a somewhat limited subset of the larger set of spatial database problems. Although geographical data are complex, we propose in this paper to make and justify certain assumptions which may in fact simplify the issues. However it is clear that these assumptions do not apply to the more general spatial case.

The first part of the paper discusses the meaning of "large" in the context of geographical data, and provides a number of examples of current and planned databases. The next section looks at traditional methods which have evolved for handling large geographical datasets in the absence of digital technology. Section Four presents a simple model of access within a large geographical data store, and analyzes the model using a generalization of the Morton key. We illustrate the consistency of the model with traditional methods of map indexing using a simple example. Finally, Section Six looks at the extension of the technique to the global case of data for the sphere or spheroid.

2. THE NATURE OF GEOGRAPHICAL DATA

The spatial variation of many properties of the earth's surface is continuous and almost infinitely complex. The simple question "How long is a shoreline?" raises difficult issues as it is clear that the length of a simple cartographic object like a shoreline depends on the spatial resolution of the measuring device, or the scale of the map. Mandelbrot (1965) showed that the increase in length of a shoreline with increasing scale is often systematic, and continues without limit at least until the definition of shoreline breaks down. In general, the process by which increasing spatial resolution reveals more detail continues without limit for most forms of geographical data. Geographical surfaces and curves lack well-defined derivatives in many cases, and are better analyzed within the framework of fractals than with continuous functions.

There are some exceptions to this generalization, particularly when geographical objects have mathematical definitions. For example there is no difficulty in defining the length of a surveyed parcel boundary, or the area enclosed. Other cases are more marginal: the attribute "in the World Trade Center" is well-defined if the relevant object is taken to be the surveyed parcel boundary on which the World Trade Center is built, but not if it is taken to be the building itself. However many objects in spatial databases are generalizations of continuously varying fields (e.g. shoreline, contour, woodlot), and the precise form of the object is therefore sensitive to the approximation inherent in the generalization.

The relationship between a geographical database and the reality which it approximates is complex. Unfortunately the user of such databases is concerned with learning about reality, and often sees the approximation inherent in the database as an unwanted and often poorly understood filter. In a typical application of a geographical database, such as a resource management study, it is almost certain that the user will find the database inadequate in some respect - in its level of spatial detail, currency, geographical coverage, or in the range of geographical variables available. In essence, users have expectations which will almost always exceed the contents of the database, and an effectively infinite appetite for knowledge about geographical reality. With this assumption, we define "large" as beyond the current capacity of systems to deliver with reasonable efficiency. In this sense, large geographical databases provide an unsolved, but well-motivated set of problems.

2.1 Examples

The global context provides the best-known set of large geographical database problems. Current remote sensing instrument systems, such as Landsat and SPOT, generate data at the rate of 10^7 bytes/scene for 10^3 scenes every few days, producing around 10^9 bytes of data per day. The systems being planned for the 1990s, such as EOS, have much higher data rates to accommodate higher spatial and spectral resolution, and figures of 10^{12} bytes/day are anticipated.

At the national level, we find similar data volumes in the systems being developed to build and maintain digital versions of national topographic map series. The typical topographic map sheet requires on the order of 25 Mbytes of digital storage, so a full digital cartographic database of the order of 10^5 sheets covering the US will require on the order of 10^{12} bytes. Similar capacity will be needed to store the digitized versions of the 250,000 sheets of the UK 1:1250 base mapping series. At the county level, the parcel database currently being built by the County of Los Angeles is expected to reach 300 Gbytes. The fact that such large data volumes are anticipated even at the county level seems to reinforce the point made earlier: reduced geographical coverage is offset by increased geographical resolution, so that expectations are comparable at all levels.

Demands for very large volumes of geographical data are driven by a need for high levels of spatial resolution, which is costly to deliver: a doubling of spatial resolution produces at least a fourfold increase in data volume in many cases. Yet high spatial resolution is inescapable if analysis is to be useful. For example, effective forest management requires a resolution sufficient to see individual trees if harvest estimates are to be reasonably accurate; land ownership records must be as accurate as the survey data on which they were based; many military applications require resolutions of better than 1m; and management of elections in Los Angeles County requires resolution finer than the parcel level because of complex and detailed precinct definitions.

3. TRADITIONAL METHODS

Geographical information has been available in map form for a long time, and in many ways the digital problem of handling large amounts of geographical data is a simple extension of more traditional issues. The methods used to compile, reproduce, distribute, store and access maps have evolved through time as a compromise of conflicting objectives under a set of technological constraints. Although the constraints are different, it may nevertheless be useful to begin by looking at traditional methods.

Geographical information is traditionally partitioned thematically across different map series. The topographic map groups together elevation, roads, railways and a variety of cultural features. A soil map is created by overprinting a single variable, represented by a tesselation of irregular area objects with associated soil class attributes, on a base map. Since the topographic map already exploits the limits of the technology fully by showing as many themes as possible, the base map is usually generated by dropping one or more themes from a topographic map, often the contours or a green "wooded" tint. Land use maps are similarly produced by adding a single variable to a base map. Information must also be dropped if the scale is reduced, because of the limitations imposed by the technology on the size of lettering and density of information. Thus to make a road map by reducing the scale of a base map it is also necessary to drop certain themes or classes of features.

Geographical information is also partitioned geographically into map sheets or "tiles". Printing, distribution and storage all place technological limits on the sizes of map sheets, and these constraints have led to the familiar series of rectangular, equal-size sheets. Tilings at different scales often nest within eachother, which is another advantage of choosing a rectangular system of tiles.

This system of thematic and geographical partitioning seems to have arisen as a result of at least four issues: the next four subsections discuss these in turn.

3.1 The storage volume

The individual volume in the traditional map store is the map sheet. The physical size of map sheets is limited to approximately 2m by 1m by the printing process, handling and storage: the user would also find larger sheets difficult to handle. Cartography imposes a resolution limit of about 0.5mm for several reasons: pen construction, human vision and instability of the base medium, among others.

3.2 Storage devices

Consider the map library as an example of a traditional geographical data store. We consider the time required for the user to move from one object to another in the store. Clearly it is least when the two objects are shown on the same map sheet or volume, higher when the objects are on different sheets within the same drawer, and highest when the sheets are in different drawers.

3.3 Use patterns

Queries in a map library database often require access to more than one volume, within the same or different themes, and the grouping of themes onto volumes reflects these complex patterns of use. For example, roads are shown on soil maps because queries frequently involve both themes. Queries often involve access to adjacent map sheets, so it is common to group sheets according to some geographical hierarchy. The fact that most map libraries sort maps first by theme, and then geographically, suggests that transitions between adjacent sheets of the same theme are more common than transitions between different themes for the same tile or geographical area. Thus we can interpret the organization of data in a traditional store as the outcome of an informal analysis of transition probabilities between tiles and themes.

3.4 Data collection

The traditional system of data collection and map compilation divides responsibilities between agencies on thematic lines: in the US, for example, the Geological Survey produces the topographic series, while the Bureau of the Census produces much of the demographic mapping. This reflects the importance of interpretation in the mapping process, and the role played by discipline specialists, for example soil scientists, in the production of soil maps. It would be much less efficient to organize data collection geographically, by assigning agencies responsibility for all themes in one area.

. A MODEL OF TILING

n this section we present a simple model of tiling for large geographical databases. We ssume that data will continue to be partitioned by theme and geographically, based on he previous discussion. First, division of responsibility between data collection agencies vill continue to lead to thematic partitioning. Second, geographical partitioning is dministratively convenient in a system of varying currency and regular updating. Jpdating requires long transactions and is best handled by checking out partitions. 'hird, partitioning is essential as long as expectations over volume exceed capacity, and s long as fast access is desirable. However partitioning may be at least partially hidden rom the user, who may value the ability to browse the database in an apparently eamless fashion.

Ve assume that geographical partitioning will be rectangular, as modified if necessary to ake account of the earth's curvature in specific projections. We further assume that hemes will therefore be grouped within tiles, and that transitions between groups of hemes will be rare, as in the traditional organization.

Ve further assume that the predominant role of geographical data stores will be archival. Geographical data is inherently static, as evidenced by the long update cycles of most nap series. Databases which provide access to administrative records are often ransactional, but their geographical content is not - customer accounts change frequently ut their locations do not. However we should clarify that archival as used here does ot necessarily mean static, but refers to the comparative absence of updates. Landsat cenes are recollected every 19 days, which makes them much less static than topographic naps, but it is rare for transactions with a specific Landsat scene to include updates. VORM devices are eminently suitable for geographical data because of the overwhelming lominance of read access over write. Where update is required, we assume that the user vill check out a section of the database for intensive transactions.

'he model which follows is intended to apply to a variety of storage media, including ptical WORM, optical jukeboxes, cassette tape, and other devices in the terabyte range, s well as the traditional map library store.

.1 Notation

.et the generalized device be positioned at tile i, and assume that we wish to access tile . The probability of this transition from i to j will be written as p_{ji}. The "cost" or delay n accessing tile j from i is c_{ij}.

'o organize the tiles on the device in the most efficient manner we should minimize the xpected cost. The expected delay in accessing j from i is given by:

$$\vdots \quad = \quad E(c_{ij}) \quad = \quad \sum_i p_i \sum_j c_{ij} p_{ji} \tag{1}$$

vhere p_i is the marginal probability that the previous access was to tile i.

Unfortunately almost nothing is known about the marginal or transition probabilities for tile access. They clearly depend heavily on the nature of the application: the oil and gas industry, for example, would have very different patterns of map use from recreational hikers. In some fields surrogate information might be useful. For example, where street network databases have been used to support vehicle navigation systems the transition probabilities between tiles have been determined at least in part by the presence of major traffic arteries.

In the temporary absence of better information we make simplifying assumptions. We assume that the p_i are constant, and that the p_{ij} are equal to 1/4 when j is a 4-neighbor of i, and 0 otherwise. We thus restrict transitions to the set of four adjacent tiles, and assume equiprobability. The optimization model (1) has the general form of a quadratic assignment problem (Koopmans and Beckmann, 1957).

Let x_i represent the location of tile i on the device. If tiles are of equal size and stored sequentially then x_i will be proportional to the ranked position of the tile, which we can equate to a key. Note that this assumption will be reasonably robust since transitions will be evaluated only between 4-neighbors. Thus in the first instance we look at the case where c_{ij} is proportional to the absolute difference in positions:

$$c_{ij} = k \, |x_j - x_i| \qquad (2)$$

Thus our problem is to minimize the expected difference in keys between a tile and its 4-neighbors.

Different devices have different versions of (2). Our work on optical WORMs has shown that seek time c_{ij} is effectively zero within volume, in relation to transfer time, but is directly proportional to difference in position between volumes in a jukebox device. Tape has highly asymmetrical characteristics within volume, where (2) holds for $j>i$, but for $i>j$ c_{ij} is approximated by $k_1 x_i + k_2 x_j$: k_1 is the rate of rewind and k_2 the rate of forward motion of the tape device.

4.2 Generalized digit-interleaved keys

Goodchild and Grandfield (1983) computed the expected difference between neighboring keys in certain orderings of rectangular tiles. For an n by n square matrix, the expected difference is $(n+1)/2$ for the Morton order (note that Morton is well-defined only for $n=2^m$ where m is integer), and also for row by row order, and a modification of row by row order with every other row reversed. This last order, which Goodchild and Grandfield termed "row-prime" and is also known as "boustrophedon", allows every pair of tiles which are adjacent in the key to be adjacent in space. They also analyzed the expected squared difference between neighboring keys, and more recently Mark (1989) has looked at this statistic over a large number of alternative orderings of a 2^m by 2^m matrix.

The Morton key can be generated by numbering rows and columns from 0 to $n-1$, and interleaving the bits of the binary representations of the row and column numbers. For example, row 2 (10) column 3 (11) has Morton key 13 (1101). Now consider a generalization of this concept to digit interleaving. Suppose row and column numbers are represented to any collection of bases, and interleaved. Morton is a digit-interleaved key, as is row order (row and column as single digits to base n). Row-prime can be generated by applying an operator which complements the column digit if the preceding row digit is even.

Theorem: *For any digit-interleaved key of an n by n matrix, the expected difference of 4-neighbor keys is $(n+1)/2$.*

Proof: See Goodchild and Yang (1989a), who obtain general expressions for expected differences in rectangular arrays.

Although there have been frequent references in the literature to the efficiency of the Morton key at preserving adjacencies between tiles, it appears that no digit-interleaved key has advantages over any other, at least under the assumptions made here.

. TRADITIONAL MAP INDEXES

In this section we compare the concept of generalized digit interleaving with the structure of traditional map indexes. The GEOLOC grid (Whitson and Sety, 1987) is typical of many such systems in its use of rectangular tiles at each level of a hierarchical structure, and the nesting which it imposes between levels. We summarize the system below:

Level 0: The continental US is divided into 2 rows and 3 columns of tiles, each 25 degrees of longitude by 13 degrees of latitude, numbered row by row from the top left using the digits 1 to 6.

Level 1: Each level 0 tile is divided into 25 columns of 1 degree each and 26 rows of 0.5 degrees each. The rows are lettered from the left from A to Y, the columns from the top from A to Z. These tiles are the 1:100,000 quadrangles used by the USGS topographic series.

Level 2: Each level 1 tile is divided into 8 columns and 4 rows, to form 32 tiles numbered row by row from the top left from 1 to 32. Each tile is 7.5 minutes square, and corresponds to the 1:24,000 quadrangles of the USGS topographic series.

Level 3: Each level 2 tile is divided into 2 columns and 4 rows, lettered A through H row by row from the top left.

Level 4: Each level 3 tile is divided into 5 rows, lettered A through E, and 10 columns, numbered 0 through 9.

The row and column references of the system use 5 bases each, {2,26,4,4,5} and

{3,25,8,2,10} respectively. Interleaving produces a 10-digit reference with bases {2,3,26,25,4,8,4,2,5,10}. However the system combines row and column bases in some cases, so the full reference contains only 7 digits: {6,26,25,32,8,5,10}. Of these, the first and fourth are expressed using decimal notation starting with 1, the last using decimal notation starting with 0, and the remainder using the alphabet. Note that to avoid ambiguity, the fourth digit which uses decimal notation for a base greater than 10 (the only case where the base of the digit exceeds the base of the notation) is positioned between two alphabetic digits. At level 4, the GEOLOC reference is unique to an area about 200m square on the earth's surface. For example the reference 4FG19DC6 identifies an area just north of Los Angeles.

As an example of digit interleaving, the GEOLOC system is relatively complex, due to the desirability of nesting the system within the 1:100,000 and 1:24,000 quadrangles, and the unequal sizes of latitude and longitude divisions.

6. TILING THE GLOBE

Rectangular tilings are difficult to apply at global scales without significant distortion. For example if a rectangular tiling is superimposed on a simple cylindrical projection such as the Mercator or Cylindrical Equidistant, three problems arise: the tiles are unequal in area and shape, adjacencies are missing at the 180th meridian, and adjacencies at the poles are severely distorted. Analyses based on such tilings may be severely biassed. Instead, it is desirable to find a tiling which is hierarchically nested, preserves adjacencies, and in which tiles are roughly equal in area and shape at a given level. It is clearly impossible to satisfy all of these requirements perfectly and simultaneously, so the optimum tiling must be some form of compromise, as in map projections themselves.

Dutton (1984; 1988; 1989) has proposed a tiling called Quaternary Triangular Mesh or QTM. The sphere or spheroid is first projected onto an octahedron aligned so that two vertices coincide with the poles, and the remaining four occur on the equator at longitudes 0, 180, 90 West and 90 East. Each triangular facet is then recursively subdivided by connecting the midpoints of its sides. Goodchild and Yang (1989b) have implemented this scheme and provide algorithms for conversion between latitude and longitude and tile address at any level. A tile address at level k consists of a base 8 digit followed by k base 4 digits. At each level of Goodchild and Yang's scheme the central triangle is assigned digit 0, the triangle vertically above (or below) is assigned 1, and the triangles diagonally below (above) to the left and right are 2 and 3 respectively. The system provides a single address in place of latitude and longitude, and the length of the address determines its precision, or the size of the tile. For example, the US has address {null} because it spans more than one level 0 tile, while the block bounded by 3rd and 4th Streets, Fulton and Broadway in the city of Troy, New York has the level 13 address {102230221113013} (the Broadway and Fulton faces are entirely within level 16 tiles, but the block as a whole spans two level 14 tiles).

7. CONCLUSIONS

Because much geographical data is comparatively stable over time, we have argued that the normal case is archival. While short transactions may predominate in many administrative records, the basis of their geographical access is stable and is likely to be updated by long transactions carried out after checkout. The problems of large geographical databases are therefore issues of data gathering, compilation, assembly in archives, and distribution. We assume that analysis and query will be carried out on extracts which are moved from the archival store in blocks or tiles.

We have argued in the paper that much can be learned about the optimal ways of organizing large geographical archives by looking at traditional methods of geographical data handling. Traditional cartography partitions databases along thematic and geographical lines, grouping themes in ways which have been found to satisfy the user community. It uses rectangular tiles and concepts of digit interleaving to index map sheets, in order to provide hierarchical nesting and to ensure rapid access to adjacent tiles. However, we have seen that under certain assumptions the entire class of digit interleaved indexes, which include both Morton and row order, yields the same expected access time. Further research is clearly needed to determine the robustness of this result under different sets of assumptions.

Many of the assumptions made in this paper concern the ways in which users access large geographical databases. In order to optimize the organization of the database, we need to know much more about applications, about the types of access required to satisfy queries and support analysis, and about the geographical distribution of accesses in specific applications. The information available on these questions at this time is virtually nil.

In general, we have suggested that the best strategy for organizing large geographical databases at this time may be to emulate traditional practice, which has arisen as an optimum response to traditional constraints, and to consider carefully the impacts of new sets of technological constraints on traditional methods. Thus far, digital technology has been adopted with little change in traditional practice in such areas as data collection, map compilation, cartographic design, map distribution, thematic grouping and geographical partitioning. In the long run, the new technologies available in each of these areas may lead to radical changes in methodology, but such changes should be incremental; in the absence of evidence to the contrary, it seems better to assume that traditional methods are the best guide.

8. ACKNOWLEDGMENTS

The research on which this paper is based has been supported by the US Geological Survey, Digital Equipment Corporation and the National Science Foundation, Grant SES 88-10917.

9. REFERENCES

Dutton, G., 1984. Geodesic modeling of planetary relief. <u>Cartographica</u> 21:188-207.

Dutton, G., 1988. Computational aspects of quaternary triangular meshes. Unpublished.

Dutton, G., 1989. Modeling locational uncertainty via hierarchical tesselation. In M.F. Goodchild and S. Gopal, editors, <u>The Accuracy of Spatial Databases</u>. Taylor and Francis, Basingstoke.

Goodchild, M.F. and A.W. Grandfield, 1983. Optimizing raster storage: an examination of four alternatives. <u>Proceedings, AutoCarto 6</u>. Ottawa, 1:400-7.

Goodchild, M.F. and S. Yang, 1989a. On average distance in Morton and generalized digit interleave tiling. Unpublished.

Goodchild, M.F. and S. Yang, 1989b. A hierarchical spatial data structure for global geographic information systems. Technical Paper 89-5, National Center for Geographic Information and Analysis, University of California, Santa Barbara.

Koopmans, T.C. and M. Beckmann, 1957. Assignment problems and the location of economic activity. <u>Econometrica</u> 25:53-76.

Mandelbrot, B.B., 1965. How long is the coast of Britain? Statistical self-similarity and fractional dimension. <u>Science</u> 156:636-8.

Mark, D.M., 1989. Neighbor-based properties of some orderings of two-dimensional space. <u>Geographical Analysis</u> (in press).

Whitson, J. and M. Sety, 1987. GEOLOC geographic location system. <u>Fire Management Notes</u> 46:30-2.

Extending a Database to Support the Handling of Environmental Measurement Data

Leonore Neugebauer [*)]
IPVR, University of Stuttgart

Abstract

This paper presents an approach to handle environmental measurement data within a relational database. The approach has been developed within a cooperative environmental research project exploring the contamination of groundwater and soil. Considering the special properties of measurement data we suggest an extension to data retrieval that allows the user to query measurement attributes without knowing the exact spatial and temporal measurement points. Further on, the interaction of this extension with the relational operations is outlined and a system design for an implementation is sketched.

1. Introduction

Environmental research has seen a tremendous increase in recent years, and new measuring devices have been installed at many places, delivering a large amount of data. So the demand for DBMSs to support environmental research in terms of administrating, analysing, and interpreting this data is growing rapidly.

The enhancements to overcome the shortcomings of commercial DBMSs include modifications of data modelling and data definition as well as support for new user-defined predicate functions during query evaluation that allow the user to compare (spatially or temporally) parallel measurement series even if the single recording points are not identical. The extensions introduced in this paper include the embedding of procedures or stored sequences of DML commands.

Various approaches to extend conventional DBMSs to overcome shortcomings in handling spatial and temporal data have been made and were included into new DBMS designs and implementations: The EXODUS system [CDFG86] offers an open architecture that may be adapted to the special needs of various applications. DBMSs that are designed to be used within non-standard applications are Starburst [SCLF86], POSTGRES [Sell87], PANDA [EgFr89] for spatial data, and the proposal of [AMKP85] for VLSI/CAD support. Further approaches are discussed by [CaDe85], [LiMP87], [StAH87], and [WSSH88]. Our approach mainly deals with extensions denoted as 'data extensions' by [LiMP87].

[*)] The work of the author is supported by the PWAB Project of Baden-Württemberg under grant no. PW 87 045

This paper is organized as follows: Section two describes the environmental research project for which this data system is designed, while section three derives general properties of environmental measuring systems and requirements for the support of environmental data administration. Section four outlines the innovative part of our data system. In section five, these extensions are integrated into an overall system design. Appendix A describes the schema of a part of the project database where most of the examples in this paper are taken from. Appendix B shows the application of the proposed extensions to SQL syntax by means of examples.

2. The Environmental Research Project

As a motivation for the DBMS extensions proposed in the remainder of this paper, the properties of our environmental research project are described. This project is an example of similar interdisciplinary applications.

2.1 Overall Project Goals

The research project "Experimental Field Site 'Horkheimer Insel' for Environmental Research" ('Horkheimer Insel' is the name of an island in the Neckar river) is split into four sub-projects, three application projects (from the computer scientist's point of view) and a database project of which an important part is described in this paper. The application projects are concerned with geohydrology, chemical and biological properties of soil, agriculture and water chemistry.

The main objectives of the project as a whole are to explore soil and groundwater pollution. This requires investigations of the groundwater flow and the impact of fertilizers, plant protecting agents, etc. on soil and groundwater. To this end, different measuring methods and devices are tested, compared, and calibrated.

One of the long-term goals is to determine agricultural techniques with minimum impact on the environment. A more detailed description of the environmental research goals is given in [Kobu88] and [Teut89].

The demands on the database project are to relieve environmental researchers from data structuring and administration tasks. The use of a DBMS will facilitate communication, interaction and data exchange between application project partners, and will help them to prepare data for application programs such as simulation and graphical representation programs. Since this is a long-term project, new sub-projects, new measuring devices, and new test field locations will be added. As a consequence, new sites, new data, new applications, etc. will have to be integrated along the way.

The comfortable handling of measurement data is one of the most interesting parts in the support of environmental research by means of DBMSs, but there are other demands that should not be entirely neglected. An important point is the design of a user interface adapted to environmental researchers' demands. Moreover, software that has been used by the environmental researchers up to now has to be incorporated or suitable interfaces to the DBMS must be made available. The modules that are required to fulfill these demands could be built on top of a standard commercial DBMS. But this would mean to write or rewrite another application program for every distinctive situation (relation(s), 'old' application program). Therefore, we suggest a more general approach that allows to easily incorporate new relations and formats and, in addition, will make interpolation interactively available to the end user.

2.2 Hardware and Software Equipment

The present equipment for each sub-project consists of the relational DBMS Ingres[1] running on a UNIX[2] workstation. Three of the project workstations are connected by 10 Mbit/s fiber optic links, one can only be reached via BITNET. The experimental field site is run completely off-line for the forseeable future. The number of workstations per sub-project is likely to grow during project life time.

As earlier results and programs will be re-used in the application projects, several heterogenous hardware and software components have to be incorporated into the project environment. The project hardware environment is illustrated in Fig. 2.1.

The experimental field site (Horkheimer Insel) is located at a distance of about 60 km from the University institutes doing the research projects, therefore no link to the measuring devices has been established. Later on a wireless transmission facility may be installed.

The measuring values are recorded on diskettes, data loggers or just written on paper. These storage media are periodically collected by the colleages who supervise the sub-projects the data belongs to. Within adapted bulk load routines it is normalized to fit into flat relations and loaded into the database. Data generated by laboratory experiments is processed in a similar way.

3. Properties of Measurement Data

The main purpose of the computer science part within the environmental project is to hold and to process measurement data, which is distinguished by the following properties (partly enumerated in [LSBM83] as well):

- Any single instance of measurement data is assigned to a specified location and a specified time. E.g., a soil specimen was taken at exactly one three dimensional location at an exact time. For some purposes time or location may be irrelevant; weather data is the same at any surface location of the experimental field, and geological formations do not change during project life time (hopefully).

---

[1] Ingres is a trademark of RTI   [2] Unix is a trademark of AT&T

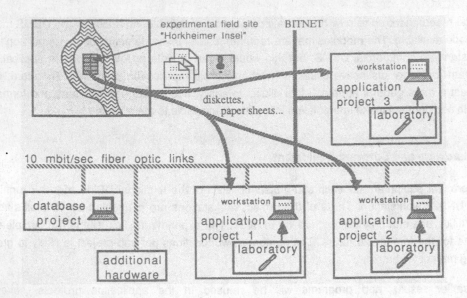

<u>Fig. 2.1</u>: The Environmental Research Project

- Measured values never change. They do not become obsolete. Sometimes their importance grows, if they are considered emdedded into a long-range series of measuring values. E.g., weather data only becomes a representative average over a period of about ten years.

- Relationships between different measuring series are usually not complex or varied. Sometimes, these relationships are object of research. But if two different measuring series are compared, there are always some instances related by location and time.

- To record a natural phenomenon completely and exactly a number of devices performing different measurings that issue data of many various formats are necessary. The number of instances of most measuring attributes is rather small, but there are some measurements e.g., weather data, generating fairly high amounts of data.

Geographical data will be stored within the project database as well. Sometimes, e.g., when recording surface altitudes, the distinction of measurement and geographical data is arbitrary. With the exception that geographical data is nearly independent of time, its properties are comparable to those of the measurement data and it may be treated in a very similar way.

3.1 Spatial and Temporal Aspects of Measurement Data

In [LSBM83] it was first recognized that the space and time attributes related to measurement values are different from space and time in commercial databases where only discrete points and time stamps or surfaces, solids and time intervals related to a constant attribute value or steady event can be modelled. With regard to temporal aspects the power and handling of these conventional attributes were comprehensively described by [JaMa86], [SnAh85] and [Gadi88]. A special treatment of spatial data (CAD data) is offered within the PROBE project [Oren86] and within the 'Geo-Kernel-System' designed by [ScWa86]. Several structures for geometric, i.e. spatial data management are discussed in [Guen88]. In connection with geographical databases and a geo-object data model [LiNe86] the requirement for a special treatment of space and time attributes appeared again.

In our project the handling of measurement data is the main objective. There are two properties distinguishing measurement data from commercial data:

- Measured values are just samples of a continuously running natural process. The related space coordinates and time identify the sampling point with respect to the graph or function describing this process. (If there are any undefined values this means that an inappropriate domain was chosen.) But measurement attributes do not hold a constant value during a space or time interval.

- For any possible space/time coordinate there exists exactly one value (in the domain of the measurement). In many cases, rules or algorithms are known to compute these values based on a number of samples.

The second property implies that there are only slight changes of the measurement value (within a small interval) and that the function mapping the space/time values into the measurement domain is continuous. This is similar to the continuity demanded for the representation scheme of spatial objects by [Guen88]. Therefore, measurement attributes are referred to as "continuous attributes" in the remainder of this paper while the space/time attributes are called "base attributes" in the following. (Of course, the space and time domains have the properties of continuity and slight changes as well.)

An example is the groundwater level that is recorded at a number of measuring wells (in weekly intervals) located in our experimental field site. The groundwater level between the measuring points is similar to the surrounding measured values but not equal to them. It is not exactly known but can be estimated by interpolation using the surrounding values and, if available, soil quality and granularity. Other examples are surface altitude or, for temporal attributes, outside temperature that is recorded in discrete time intervals.

3.2 Applications on Measurement Data

The applications usually performed on measurement data consider its special properties. Typical applications are

- statistics and graphical output charts (here, statistics to evaluate measurement series are meant, statistics to speed up performance are automatically collected by the DBMS);
- visualization within thematic maps, combining geograhical, cartographic and measurement data;

- simulation programs to verify environmental models e.g., groundwater flow models or models of the dissemination of contaminating agents in soil, air or groundwater;
- research on how the different parameters are connected and dependent on each other.

These applications do not change data. They produce further data that is not stored in most cases, because it is reproducible as long as the orignal data is available. These applications have in common that they need for input - in most cases equidistant - series of (measurement) values of predefined domains.

4. Continuous Attributes

During subsequent treatment of measurement values the environmental researchers know about the special properties (enumerated in section three) and exploit this knowledge within the further evaluation. But a conventional DBMS does not know (and cannot be told) of the existence of any measurement data owning special properties and therefore, it cannot offer a special treatment. In the following the main problems are captured and a solution is proposed.

4.1 Problems of Handling Measurement Data

In a conventional database it is not possible to query interactively a measurement value, if it was not recorded exactly at this point e.g., the soil temperature at arbitrary depth or the groundwater level at any specified location. Rather, the user has to supply an interval query which will only deliver results if there is at least one sample in the specified interval. In the groundwater level example this may deliver very misleading results, if the interval was chosen inappropriately.

In a conventional relational DBMS the comparison of two continuous attributes via natural join of their base attributes that belong to (or have been transformed to) identical space and time domains issues an empty and impracticable result, if the spatial or temporal sampling points are not the same which in practice they never are.
For instance, if an environmental researcher wants to compare results from soil specimens (e.g. permeability) and groundwater levels (recorded at the same time), he cannot do this via natural join because the locations are not identical. Soil specimens cannot be taken at (or close to) the locations of measuring wells.

It is impossible to select data directly from a conventional relational database for a simulation program which needs equidistant values, if any values are missing, or the measuring (time) intervals or distances were not equidistant, or have a different interval length.
An application program simulating the transport of contaminating agents within the groundwater flow requires groundwater levels spatially and temporally equidistant, geological formation, and soil quality at the same points.

In conventional DBMS it is not possible to distinguish between "normal" (e.g. commercial), continuous and base attributes to determine which attributes are just samples, and which attributes contain all existing values.

A (political) border line surrounding an homogenous area is treated in the same way as contour lines that are samples of the surface altitude.

4.2 Approach of Solution: Exploiting the Properties of Measurement Data

The project database has to hold both, conventional data and measurement data. In the conventional part of the environmental database crop yield is recorded and economy computations are carried out.

As the distinguishing properties of measurement data can be utilized throughout its existence in the database, it seems appropriate to mark them at conceptual or logical level during database design. Hence, the data model, the relational model has to distinguish two classes of relations:

1) Conventional relations R_i, formally defined as sets of (ordered) value combinations, the tuples. The domain function D issues the domain of an attribute A:

$$R_i (A_{i1}, ... A_{in}) \subseteq D (A_{i1}) \times ... \times D (A_{in}), \ i \in IN$$

where the A_{ij} are the attributes of relation R_i. The key attribute(s) of relation R_i are arbitrary.

2) Measurement relations that are extended by several properties and operations outlined in the following.

As pointed out in section 3.1, an essential property of environmental measuring values and also of the attribute values representing them in relational databases is that they are just samples from a continuous natural process. Therefore we will refer to them as "continuous attributes" in the remainder of this paper. In the groundwater level example (see appendix A) the attribute 'meas_value' is a continuous attribute.

Since continuity can be both spatial and temporal, one or more attributes describing location and time belong to each continuous attribute. In the ground-water level relation the attributes 'x_coord', 'y_coord', and 'measurement_date' form the base attributes. The domains of base attributes imply the property of continuity as well.

Hence, formally described a measurement relation MR $_i$ looks like:

$$MR_i (A_{ib1}, ... , A_{ibk}, A_{ic1}, .. , A_{icj}, A_{i1}, ..., A_{in}) \subseteq$$
$$D (A_{ib1}) \times ... \times D (A_{ibk}) \times D (A_{ic1}) \times ... \times D (A_{icj}) \times D (A_{i1}) \times ... \times D (A_{in}), \ i \in IN, \ k, j \ \geq 1;$$

where the A_{ib} denote base attributes and the A_{ic} denote continuous attributes. A measurement relation must have at least one base attribute and one continuous attribute.

An important property of the base attributes is that they form the key or at least a part of the key of the relation.

The implementation approach is to use additional system relations that contain information on continuous attributes and corresponding base attributes.

For the applications of our system, a continuous attribute and its related base attributes represent a continuous mathematical function $f \in F$ that maps value combinations of the base attributes domain i.e., the inverse image domain, upon the continuous attribute domain i.e., the image domain.

$$f_i: A_{b1} \times A_{b2} \times \ldots \times A_{bk} \rightarrow A_{ci}, \quad i = 1, \ldots, j.$$

A continuous attribute holds some value at any location (in the experimental site) during the whole time the test is running. To any combination of the base attribute values a value out of the measurement domain can be computed. This allows to recognize and to take advantage of the properties of measurement data.

Syntactically, some minor extensions to the data definition are nessessary to tell the DBMS which attributes are continuous attributes and which attributes are their related base attributes. A relation definition containing base and continuous attributes is recognized as a measurement relation. (The DDL syntax follows the syntax in [RTI86].)

```
CREATE TABLE <relation name >
  (<attr.name>   <data format> BASE ATTRIBUTE
  {, <attr.name> <data format> BASE ATTRIBUTE}
  , <attr.name> <data format> CONTINUOUS ATTRIBUTE
  {, <attr.name> <data format> CONTINUOUS ATTRIBUTE}
  {, <attr.name> <data format>} )
```

The groundwater level relation (see appendix A) will be defined as follows by this syntax:

```
CREATE TABLE groundwater_levels
  (x_coord              float4 BASE ATTRIBUTE,
  y_coord               float4 BASE ATTRIBUTE,
  measurement_date date  BASE ATTRIBUTE,
  meas_value            float4 CONTINUOUS ATTRIBUTE,
  well_id               vchar(8))
```

For implementing it, we need procedures for interpolating all possible values between the sampling points. Such procedures can be either general-purpose (e.g., spline, mean values) or domain-specific.

As a prerequisite for the following, we assume that a library containing appropriate, correctly working interpolation functions exists and is available to the database.

4.3 Additional Operations

In this section two important additional operations on measurement relations are introduced, formally described by means of abstract data types (ADTs) and illustrated within examples.

The extensions introduced are proposed by means of ADTs which was shown to be an adequate mechanism by [Gutt77] and [LMWW79]. Of course, the definitions should be embedded into a complete database specification similar to that one given in [Maib85]. The syntax is similar to the syntax used in [LMWW79]. In contrast to other approaches [WSSH88], [StRG83] we do not offer the ADT mechanism to the user, because (s)he should be offered a system that is exactly tailored to her/his specific needs i.e., the processing of measurement values. But we use this notation to describe the class of operations we included.

Let R_i be the sort of all possible relations and A_i the attributes derived of the possible domains. The new sort measurement relation MR is derived from R as follows:

type: MR from R, A, f

operations: new: $R \times (A_{b1}, ..., A_{bk}) \times (A_{c1}, ..., A_{cj}) \rightarrow MR$

$...$

interpolation$_1$: $MR \times f_1 \times (A_{b1}, ..., A_{bk}) \rightarrow A_{c1}$

$...$

interpolation$_j$: $MR \times f_j \times (A_{b1}, ..., A_{bk}) \rightarrow A_{cj}$

equations: $D (\Pi_{Ab1 ... Abk} (MR)) \subseteq D (A_{b1}, ..., A_{bk})$

$D (\Pi_{Aci} (MR)) \subseteq D (A_{ci})$

This interpolation operation may be applied in the first example of section 4.1 to compute groundwater levels at any given location.

To solve the problem of joining two continuous attributes i.e., joining their base attributes, and to construct appropriate data for application programs a more complex operation is needed. Hence, the next step is the computation of an equidistant series of (continuous attribute) values. In addition to the interpolation operation proposed above a second operation is required that issues series of values:

operations: interpol_series $_1$: $MR \times f_1 \times (A_{b1}, ..., A_{bk}) \times A_{step} \rightarrow R (A_{b1}, ..., A_{bk}, A_{c1})$

$. . .$

interpol_series $_j$: $MR \times f_j \times (A_{b1}, ..., A_{bk}) \times A_{step} \rightarrow R (A_{b1}, ..., A_{bk}, A_{cj})$

equations: $D (\Pi_{Abj} (MR)) \subseteq D (A_{step})$

$R \subseteq D (A_{b1}) \times ... \times D (A_{bk}) \times D (A_{ci})$

where A_{step} may be one or more dimensional i.e., an interpolation along a straight line in an n-dimensional space. For a later version, interpolation along a two- or n-dimensional plane will be a useful extension. But here performance problems are likely to occur.

This solves the second and third problem presented in section 4.1. The solutions are given in appendix B by means of examples.

The base attributes that do not appear in the step specification will be evaluated to the measuring points held in the database.

The syntax to declare an interpolation method to the DBMS is the following:

```
DECLARE METHOD <interpol.meth.>
  ON TABLE <rel.name>
  CONTINUOUS ATTRIBUTE <attr.name>
  VARYING BASE ATTRIBUTES <attr.name> {, <attr.name>}
```

The declaration of the groundwater level interpolation is the following:

```
DECLARE METHOD gw_levels
  ON TABLE groundwater_levels
  CONTINUOUS ATTRIBUTE meas_value
  VARYING BASE ATTRIBUTES x_coord, y_coord
```

Of course, this approach does not actually solve the problem of how to find the most adjacent samples (and further surrounding samples) to the points queried. But it hides these problems from the end user and leaves the syntax of the query language straightforward and easily understandable. The problem is shifted to the implementation of the interpolation procedures. The interpolation procedures will use a version of the query language (SQL) that is embedded in a high level programming language.

The retrieval of surrounding samples within the interpolation functions may be performed best by spatial search operators as looking for points in surfaces or solids. The spatial retrieval may be supported by a library of predefined SQL queries. This could be helpful to find hints how to improve performance (e.g., by means of spatial indexes, see [Oren86]) that is known to be rather poor in large spatial applications.

It should be possible to specify more than one function to interpolate the same continuous attribute (with identical varying base attributes) for two reasons: First, there might exist several distinct methods, and secondly, this allows to implement different versions of a method that issue the results either more quickly or more exactly.

4.4 Interaction with Relational Operations

First, it must be pointed out that measurement relations may be considered as 'conventional' relations as well and any relational operation is applicable. For instance, surface altitude is used as a continuous attribute during processing of a groundwater flow model, but it will be considered as a conventional attribute in cartographic applications where contour lines are to be drawn.

If interpolation is involved, data manipulation is not possible any longer, because it does not make sense to update or delete data which is not materialized but just temporarily computed. Insertion of interpolated values into measurement relations should be strictly forbidden, because it is undesirable to mix up original measurement data and computed values.

In any other case the results of interpolation routines may be inserted in all constructions where single continuous attribute values or projections of measurement relations to their base attributes and one continuous attribute can be used.

More interesting is the evaluation time in connection with other relational operations. Do restrictions work before or after interpolation ?

4.4.1 Qualifications (Restrictions)

(This applies to the restrictions that are specified in the SQL WHERE-clause: Existence, universality, interval and other horizontal restrictions.)

Three cases are to be considered separately:

- Restrictions to base attributes.
  For the results it makes no difference whether these restrictions are applied to original or computed values becaused they are not changed during interpolation. With a look at system performance they should be evaluated as early as possible.

- Restrictions to continuous attributes.
  This applies to the computed values. During interpolation values outside interval limitations may be used but the user should only see values within the specified limitations.

- Restrictions to further attributes in measurement relations.
  The application of interpolation involves a projection to base attributes and one continuous attribute. Therefore restrictions to other attributes must be evaluated before interpolation.

4.4.2 Joins

The main purpose of the interpolation of a series of equidistant values is to find a common base for two or more measurement relations to be compared by a natural join. Considering the second and third example in appendix B, we note that the base attributes are joined, not the continuous attributes. The continuous attributes are objects of the query. Their values are not known ahead and therefore cannot be used for a join that is likely to issue a useful result.

4.4.3 Projection

The computation of interpolation values includes the projection to a continuous attribute and the base attributes. Further projections (base attributes) after interpolation are possible.

4.4.4 Grouping, Built-In Aggregation Functions, and Ordering

These operations are applied to the results of the base relational operations like selection, projection, and join, therefore they have to be applied after computation of the new values.

4.4.5 Error Handling

No additional error handling is required. If an interpolation function delivers an empty result due to inappropriate interval specification (or missing additional informations), this will be treated exactly the same way as if any other qualification evaluates to an empty set.

4.5 Difficulties Arising During Interpolation

An interesting problem appears if the user specifies a value to be computed that is actually available as an exact measuring point. There are two possible solutions:

1) no invoking of an interpolation and delivering of the exact value;

2) invoking of the interpolation function (and pushing the problem down to the implementation of the functions).

The first possibility has the advantage that it issues the exact value, but requires additional effort for checking each value whether it is a measuring point. The second possibility may be utilized to detect errors in measurement by comparing the measured value to the computed value. If the interpolated values will be used for graphical output charts, values computed according to the second method will deliver smoother graphs.

The most reasonable solution to this problem is to include an interpolation function whenever it is specified within the query. The exact values can always be retrieved by standard SQL queries. The interpolation functions themselves may treat exact values exceptionally.

Another problem arises, if the interpolation function selects and includes additional information from other (measurement) relations within the database. (E.g., a groundwater flow model to compute arbitrary groundwater levels that requires soil granularity and permeability.) If this information is not available, the interpolation function delivers an empty result not easily understandable to the user. Detailed error messages delivered by the interpolation function itself may solve this problem.

A closer look to the syntax presented in appendix B shows that interval specification for base attributes is optional. If extrapolation methods are to be incorporated, the implementation of each procedure that issues a set-valued result must guarantee a limited set of result tuples.
In our project the prediction of high water and especially flood for the next week in advance derived from actual weather data and groundwater levels is a useful application of extrapolation.

4.6 Demands on Language Extensions

A syntax proposal is given in appendix A. The syntax extensions include both data definition and querying. During data definition the following should be additionally specifyable:

- the declaration of measuring relations i.e., continuous and base attributes in some relations and

- the declaration of (names of) interpolation methods.

The extensions to enable the inclusion interpolation into data querying should have the power to express the following details seperately and in combination. Here, the main requirements are enumerated:

- The continuous attribute value of any possible coordinate of the base attributes can be referenced within the valid domain of the interpolation function.

- The user can address equidistant sequences of values in one or more dimensions.

- If there are several interpolation techniques, the user may choose one.

- Joining two base attributes or a normal and a base attribute is allowed.

- Continuous attributes and base attributes may occur in different relations related by foreign keys.

- The interpolation algorithm may refer to information stored in other relations. This should be fully transparent to the user.

Inventing extensions of SQL that allow the user to handle continuous attributes is a straightforward method that is likely to be accepted by future users. (The extended version of SQL is referred to as Continuous SQL or "CSQL" in the following.)

A CSQL syntax allowing the specification of interpolation methods, arbitrary 'measuring points' (entry points) and step widths for equidistant series of values will look like the following (similar to the syntax given in [RTI86]:

```
SELECT [ALL | DISTINCT] "*" |  [<result_column> =] <expression>
                              {, [<result_column> =] <expression>}
FROM   <table> [<corr_name>] |   <table>  [<corr_name>]
                          BY METHOD <method> { (cont.attr.>) }
                    ENTRY <base_attr.> = <value> {, <base_attr.> = <value> }
                    STEP  <distance> {, <distance>}
                        { BY METHOD <method> { (<cont.attr.> }
                    ENTRY <base_attr.> = <value > {, <base_attr.> = <value> }
                    STEP <distance> {, <distance>} }
            {, <table> [<corr_name>] | ...}
[WHERE  <search_condition> ]
[GROUP BY <attr.> {, <attr.>}
[HAVING <search_condition>] ]
[ORDER BY <result-attr.> [ASC | DESC] {<result_attr.> [ASC | DESC] ]
```

Similar extensions of QUEL, called POSTQUEL where proposed by [StRo86] to handle aggregate functions, complex objects, and geometrical operations. They consider procedure calls and sequences of DML-operations as data types that are attributes of (complex) objects. So the extensions are part of the data definition but not of the query language.

If interpolation is to be done in more than one dimension and more than one interpolation method is involved, the result values may vary considerably depending on the order the functions are involved. Fortunately, within our project mainly smooth processes are involved. Hence, this problem may be neglected in our first approach.

5. Integration of Interpolation Functions into the DBMS

To make the interpolation functions available to the database users, they should be fully integrated into the DBMS. Generally, this may be done in two different ways:

- ○ modifying the SQL interpreter itself or

- ○ the installation of an SQL preprocessor that scans the queries and data definition statements where procedure calls are to be included (which is recognized easily because of the modified syntax).

Since we installed the environmental research database distributed on workstations from different manufacturers, we used a commercially available DBMS, Ingres, where the SQL interpreter cannot be modified directly. Hence, we decided to build a preprocessor which will be integrated in a way that the interface visible to the user is not changed.

This is possible because the environment of the Ingres DBMS has a modular structure that allows the application programmer to call Ingres tools through application programs and to rewrite the surfaces of Ingres tools or complete Ingres tools without interferences with the DBMS itself. This has the additional advantage that it will be more easily portable.

5.1 New System Components

The main system components required to process CSQL statements are (see fig. 5.1)

- ○ a CSQL preprocessor that parses the statements and invokes the required interpolation functions,

- ○ the functions themselves that include the search for the surrounding samples using 'standard' SQL and the storing of the results in temporal relations,

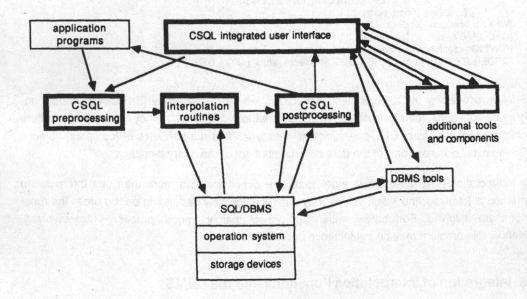

Fig. 5.1: The integration of interpolation functions into query evaluation

° a CSQL postprocessor that reduces the selected and computed values to the required intervals and, if necessary invokes 'standard SQL' to evaluate the standard parts of the query, drops temporal relations and the like.

The CSQL preprocessor will include an optimizer that decides about evaluation plans if two or more dimensions of the base attribute are missing and two or more calculation methods are involved. In a later version, this optimizer will have to cope with the problems arising due to the order in which the interpolation functions are to be invoked.

For instance, if a method is known how to interpolate groundwater levels in observation wells on dates when they were not measured, and another method is known to compute groundwater levels at coordinates between the wells, the two methods have to be combined to compute groundwater levels at any coordinate at any time.

5.2 Additional System Information

Additional system information is required to mark attributes containing measurement data and the corresponding space and time attributes they are recorded against. If the locations are not stored in a common base e.g., world coordinates, the DBMS must store how to compute a location in the common base unit from the available values. This knowledge should be used when queries including spatial and temporal relationships are evaluated:

- additional descriptions of relations containing measurement values: continuous attributes and related base attributes.
  (It might be helpful to keep upper and lower bounds of the base attributes which are actually present within the database to optimize the computation of step widths. Otherwise minimum and maximum values have to be computed each time interpolation is invoked.)

- the interpolation procedures that calculate intermediate values: the relation, the varying base attributes, and the affected base attribute.

The CSQL interpreter has to scan the data definition statements to recognize, which relations are measurement relations, and to store this additional information within the system relations.

6. Conclusions

The approach to integrate interpolation into database querying outlined in this paper forms the basis for efficient database support of environmental research projects. It relieves the researchers from writing long and troublesome transformation procedures for various applications. As this feature will be available interactively, the environmental researchers may form complex queries in an ad hoc manner that would require long evaluation programs otherwise. This will be very useful, for instance, while seeking explanations of natural phenomena.

The extensions are designed to be integrated into a general framework allowing for addition of further tools or system components which may become necessary during future development of the project. This guarantees a successful employment of the approach presented and the integrated data system on a long-term basis.

Moreover, if this approach proves to be useful in supporting the environmental researchers, there are many other areas where it may be applied, for instance database support for applications involving geological or geographical data, or measurement data within chemical or engineering applications.

Acknowledgements

I would like to thank Prof. Andreas Reuter for encouraging me to work on this topic and to write about it. Thanks to my colleages Franz Haberhauer and Andreas Zell for helpful discussions and reviewing this paper. Finally, thanks to the referees for their detailed and helpful comments on an earlier version of this paper.

References

[AMKP85] Hamideh Afsarmanesh, Dennis McLeod, David Knapp, Alice Parker: "An Extensible Object-Oriented Approach to Databases for VLSI/CAD"; in: Proc. of the 11th Conf. on VLDB, Stockholm, Sweden 1985, pp. 13-24

[CaDe85] Michael J. Carey, David J. DeWitt: "Extensible Database Systems"; in: Proc. of the Islamorada Workshop on Large Scale Knowledge Bases and Reasoning Systems, Feb., 1985, Islamorada, Florida, pp. 335-352

[CDFG86] Michael J. Carey, David J. DeWitt, Daniel Frank, Goetz Graefe, Joel E. Richardson, Eugenie J. Shekita, M. Muralikrishna: "The Architecture of the EXODUS Extensible DBMS: A Preliminary Report"; Computer Science Technical Report #644, May 1986, University of Wisconsin-Madison

[EgFr89] Max J. Egenhofer, Andrew U. Frank: "PANDA: An Extensible DBMS Supporting Object-Oriented Software Techniques"; in: Datenbanksysteme in Büro, Technik und Wissenschaft, Proc. BTW'89; GI/SI-Fachtagung, Zürich, March 1989, pp. 74-79

[Gadi88] Shashi K. Gadia: "A Homogeneous Relational Model and Query Language for Temporal Databases"; in: ACM ToDS, Vol. 13, No. 4, Dec. 1988, pp. 418-448

[Guen88] Oliver Günther: "Efficient Structures for Geometric Data Management"; Lecture Notes in Computer Science, No. 337, Springer Verlag, Berlin 1988

[Gutt77] John Guttag: "Abstract Data Types and the Development of Data Structures"; in: CACM, Vol. 20, No. 6, June 1977, pp. 396-404

[JaMa86] Donald A. Jardine, Aviram Matzov: "Ontology and Properties of Time in Information Systems"; in: Proc. IFIP Working Conf. Knowledge & Data (DS-2), Algarve, Portugal 1986, pp. F1-F16

[Kobu88] H. Kobus: "Das PWAB-Testfeld Wasser und Boden" ("The PWAB Experimental Field Site 'Water and Soil'"); in: Bericht über das 1. Statuskolloquium, February 23, Karlsruhe, Projekt Wasser-Abfall-Boden (Project Water-Waste-Soil), KfK-PWAB 1, 1988, pp. 96-116

[LiMP87] Bruce Lindsay, John McPherson, Hamid Pirahesh: "A Data Management Extension Architecture"; in: ACM SIGMOD Record, Vol. 16, No. 3, Dec 1987, pp. 220-226

[LiNe86] Udo W. Lipeck, Karl Neumann: "Modelling and Manipulating Objects in Geoscientific Databases"; in: Proc. of 5th Int. Conf. on ER-Approach, Dijon, France, 1986, pp. 105-124

[LSBM83] Guy M. Lohmann, Joseph C. Stoltzfus, Anita N. Benson, Michael D. Martin, Alfonso F. Cardenas: "Remotely-Sensed Geophysical Databases: Experience and Implications for Generalized DBMS"; in: ACM Sigmod'83 Proceedings of Annual Meeting, San Jose, 1983 (SIGMOD Record Vol. 13, No. 4), pp. 146-160

[LMWW79] Peter C. Lockemann, Heinrich C. Mayr, Wolfgang H. Weil, Wolfgang H. Wohllieber: "Data Abstractions for Database Systems"; in: ACM ToDS, Vol. 4, No. 1, March 1979, pp. 60-75

[Maib85] T. S. E. Maibaum: "Database Instances, Abstract Data Types, and Database Specification"; in: The Computer Journal, Vol. 28, No. 2, 1985, pp. 154-161

[Oren86] Jack A. Orenstein: "Spatial Query Processing in an Object-Oriented Database System"; in: ACM SIGMOD Record, Vol. 15, No. 2, June 1986, pp. 326-336

[RTI86] Relational Technology Inc.: "INGRES/SQL Reference Manual"; Release 5.0, UNIX, 1986

[SCFL86] P. Schwarz, W. Chang, J. C. Freytag, G. Lohman, J. McPherson, C. Mohan, H. Pirahesh: "Extensibility in the Starburst Database System"; in: Proc. of 1986 Int. Workshop on Object-Oriented Database Systems, Asilomar, Pacific Glore, Cal., pp. 85-92

[ScWa86] H.-J. Schek, W. Waterfeld: "A Database Kernel System for Geoscientific Applications"; in: Proc. of the 2nd Int. Symp. on Spatial Data Handling, Seattle, Washington, July 1986, pp. 273-288

[Sell87] Timos K. Sellis: "Efficiently Supporting Procedures in Relational Database Systems"; in SIGMOD Record, Vol. 16, No. 3, Dec. 1987, pp. 220-226

[SnAh85] Richard Snodgrass, Ilsoo Ahn: "A Taxonomy of Time in Databases"; in: Proc. of ACM-SIGMOD'85 Int. Conf. on Management of Data, Austin, Texas, 1985, pp. 236-246

[StAH87] Michael Stonebraker, Jeff Anton, Eric Hanson: "Extending a Database System with Procedures"; in: ACM ToDS, Vol. 12, No. 3, September 1987, pp. 350-376

[StRG83] Michael Stonebraker, Brad Rubenstein, Antonin Guttman; "Application of Abstract Data Types and Abstract Indices to CAD Data Bases"; in: ACM SIGMOD/SIGDBP Proc. of Annual Meeting, Engineering Design Applications, San Jose, May 1983, pp. 107-113

[StRo86] Michael Stonebraker, Lawrence A. Rowe: "The Design of POSTGRES"; in: Proc. of ACM SIGMOD'86 Int. Conf. on Management of Data, Washington D.C., 1986, pp. 340-355

[Teut89] G. Teutsch et.al.: "The Experimental Field Site 'Horkheimer Insel': Research Program, Instrumentation and First Results"; submitted to: IAHR Journal of Hydrolic Research, 1989

[WSSH88] P. F. Wilms, P. M. Schwarz, H.-J. Schek, L. M. Haas: "Incorporating Data Types in an Extensible Database Architecture"; in: Proc. of 3rd Int. Conf. on Data and Knowledge Bases, Jerusalem, Israel, June 1988, pp. 180-192

Appendix A: Schema of an Example Database

The given database schema is a small but representative part of the database currently being implemented in our project. Most of the special properties and problems of measurement data occur within this part of the research database.

More conventional information is held in the relations about measuring devices, wells and the description of the weather parameters; typical measurement data will be stored in the relations weather, groundwater_levels and soil_specimens. Weather data is recorded in 10-minute intervals while groundwater levels and soil specimens are collected weekly. (Soil temperatures are recorded by a different measuring device than the rest of the weather data.) Groundwater levels are collected by the geohydrology site while weather data and soil specimens are recorded at the soil science site. The database schema looks as follows:

```
measuring_devices (x_coord, y_coord, date_installed, name, measurement);
wells (drill_date, well_id, depth);
weather_params (parameter, dimension, measuring_channel, remarks);
groundwater_levels (x_coord, y_coord, measurement_date, meas_value, well_id);
soil_specimens (x_coord, y_coord, depth_top, depth_bottom, measurement_date, permeability, ...);
weather (measurement_date, rainfall, outside_temperature, global_radiation, wind_velocity, wind_direction);
soil_temperatures (measurement_date, depth, s_temp);
```

Appendix B: Example Queries

The following examples will show how the syntax proposals given throughout the paper are to be applied:

1) In the first example a single interpolated value is selected, the groundwater level at an arbitrary location:

```
SELECT x_coord, y_coord, meas_value
FROM   groundwater_levels BY METHOD gw_level
       ENTRY x_coord = 50.0, y_coord = 225.0
WHERE  meas_date = '29/03/88'
```

If the measurement date was not given in the WHERE-clause, the interpolation function would interpolate a value at any date the groundwater levels of the surrounding wells were recorded.

If the groundwater_level table holds the following samples:

```
|x_coord    |y_coord    |meas_date                   |meas_value |well_id |
|-----------------------------------------------------------------------|
|    35.000|   260.000|26/03/88             |      158.689|p10      |
|    50.000|   212.500|26/03/88             |      158.694|p11      |
|    62.500|   215.000|26/03/88             |      158.687|p12      |
|    75.000|   217.500|26/03/88             |      158.674|p13      |
|    42.500|   235.000|26/03/88             |      158.687|p14      |
|    25.000|   257.500|26/03/88             |      158.680|p9       |
|    35.000|   260.000|29/03/88             |      157.119|p10      |
|    50.000|   212.500|29/03/88             |      157.144|p11      |
|    62.500|   215.000|29/03/88             |      157.137|p12      |
|    75.000|   217.500|29/03/88             |      157.124|p13      |
|    42.500|   235.000|29/03/88             |      157.127|p14      |
|    25.000|   257.500|29/03/88             |      157.110|p9       |
|-----------------------------------------------------------------------|
```

and the gw_level function computes the groundwater level as the weighted mean value of the groundwater levels of the three less distant wells, the result would be:

50.0, 225.0, 157.136 [m]

2) The second example shows the join of computed and measurement values. The groundwater levels are computed at locations where soil specimens were collected:

```
SELECT x_coord, y_coord, meas_value, permeability
FROM   soil_specimens sp,
       groundwater_levels gw BY METHOD gw_level
       ENTRY x_coord = 12.56, y_coord = 165.8
       STEP 2, 5
WHERE meas_date = '03/05/88' AND
       sp.x_coord = gw.x_coord AND
       sp.y_coord = gw.y_coord
```

Here, the user knows the distances of the locations where the specimens have been collected.

3) To explore dependencies between air and soil temperature, the measured values collected during 1988 are joined. This example shows the comparison of continuous attributes selected from two different relations (outside temperatures and soil temperatures) by means of joining their related base attributes. This is a typical query used to get a first idea of the relationships that exist between different measurement attributes:

```
SELECT w.outside_temperature, s.depth
FROM   weather w BY METHOD weather_time_int
           ENTRY meas_date = '01/01/88
           STEP 12h,
       soil_temperatures s BY METHOD soil_time_int
           ENTRY meas_date = '01/01/88'
           STEP 12h
WHERE w.meas_date > '01/01/88'     AND  w.meas_date < '01/01/89'
   AND s.meas_date > '01.'01/88'   AND  s.meas_date < '01/01/89'
   AND w.meas_date = s.meas_date
ORDER BY w.meas_date;
```

Thematic Map Modeling[1]

Michel Scholl and Agnès Voisard
I.N.R.I.A., 78153 Le Chesnay, France
(scholl, voisard)@bdblues.altair.fr

Abstract

We study here how to provide the designer of geographic databases with a database query language extensible and customizable. The model presented here is a first step toward a high level spatial query language adapted to the manipulation of thematic maps.

For this, we take as an example a toy application on thematic maps, and show by using a complex objects algebra that application dependent geometric operations can be expressed through an extension of the *replace* operator of [AB88].

---

[1]This work was partially supported by a grant from the french PRC BD_3, and by the BRA ESPRIT W.G. Basic GOODS.

1   Introduction

The representation and manipulation of geometric information require the use of two technologies: database systems and computational geometry. Several recent proposals have been made for the modeling and design of Geographic Information Systems (GIS) (see for example [LM84], [OM86], [SW86], [MOD87], [Dav88], [RFS88]). For a comprehensive study on the requirements for the design and implementation of large-scale GIS, see [Fra84], [SMSE87]. Several spatial query languages have recently been proposed in [CF80], [CK81], [BB81], [Fra82], [SMO87], [CJ88], [Gut88]. A survey on data structures for spatial databases can be found in [Sam84].

One characteristics of GIS is that they cover an extremely wide range of applications for which, neither a common definition of objects, nor a common set of functions on these objects exist. Designing a close general information system for geographic applications therefore becomes an ambitious and somewhat hazardous task.

It is our belief that there might exist a set of *application dependent* basic objects and operations on these objects, and that the database system should permit an easy extension of this set or an easy change to another set more adapted to a particular application. Examples of applications we consider are cartography and urban planning which both manipulate thematic maps.

In order to validate the concepts presented in the paper, we consider a restricted application with limited functionalities since it manipulates only regions, i.e. subsets of R^2 (and neither lines nor points).

This application is described in Section 2. Basically, one would like to answer queries such as:

- *"Display the districts of the province of Toulouse"*,

- *"From the map of the districts of France, zoom to the map of provinces"*,

- *"Overlay the map of crops with the map of the province of Rennes"*,

- *"Create the map of districts from the map of provinces belonging to the North of France" (district boundaries as well as data associated to districts must be entered)*,

- *"Display districts with more than 20% of the people voting for the communist party in the district of Lille"*.

For designing such an application, the following are required:

- some high level query and manipulation language with the confidence that, when the application changes (and therefore the query language changes), there are only minimal incremental changes to bring to the system in order to provide new functionalities,

- a powerful manipulation of a large amount of data.

A candidate approach is to take an "extended" relational system where we model geometric information by means of specific attributes with the two-dimension space for domain. By *extended* we mean that the database system is augmented with capabilities such as defining and running specific functions associated with a given domain (see for example [SR86,GCK*89]). Then by attaching application dependent functions to geometric objects, one may hope to design specific GIS.

Augmenting the relational query language by specific geometric operators was, to our knowledge, first proposed in [CF80]. In [SRG83], abstract data types are proposed for geometric objects and their operations. A similar approach to [SRG83] is described in [Ore86]. But the most significant integration of geometric data type and operators into a relational algebra is due to [Gut88].

However such approaches suffer from the following drawbacks:

1. Data structures represented by relational systems are very poor. More recent database approaches such as complex object models [HY84], [KV85], [BK86], [Hul87], [AG87], [AB88]), or object oriented systems (see for example [K*88], [K*89], [BBB*88], [LRV88], [LR89]) are more powerful for representing complex data structures.

2. User defined operations are not part of the relational model. This is why extended relational systems are currently designed. The disadvantage of such an approach is its lack of flexibility: once the extended relational system has been designed, it becomes cumbersome to adapt it to new functionalities required by other applications and users.

Although object oriented systems provide the representation of complex structures and a flexible definition of user defined operations, they do not yet provide query languages. Their interface can still be considered as a low level approach not adapted to unsophisticated users who require a high level language for spatial queries.

The purpose of this paper is to show that user defined geometric operations can be embedded into a very general database query language, in a simple and flexible way.

In some sense, our model can be seen as continuing the work reported in [Gut88]: we believe that an algebraic approach is a powerful tool for efficiently manipulating large sets of data. However, our approach differs from the above work in two aspects:

1. To relational algebra, we prefer a complex object algebra because of its expressive power.

2. Such a complex object model is still unsufficient for representing user defined geometric operations. This is why we suggest not to embed the geometric operations into the data model, but rather to associate them to the data model through simple and general constructs.

As far as implementation of the spatial query language is concerned, object-oriented systems are good candidates. But object-oriented features such as object identity or inheritance are not necessary at the language level.

The paper is organized as follows: Section 2 describes the application chosen for illustrating our approach. The model presented in Sections 3 and 4 is a first step towards the definition of a high level spatial query language adapted to the manipulation of thematic maps. Recall that the objective is to associate a powerful database modeling tool independent of the (geometric) application, to an adaptative manipulation of geometric objects. It is our belief that the same methodology can be applied for the design of GIS manipulating lines.

In Section 3, we define what is a map and which are the operations on maps, i.e. we define a query language on maps. We also define regions as well as a set of operations on regions. We show that these operations on maps are sufficient to implement primitives such as those described in Section 2.

In Section 4, we show that these operations on maps apparently closely related to the application can be expressed by means of very general constructs: the approach followed for modeling maps is basically a *complex objects* approach. Among all existing models we chose the model of [AB88]. Such a model is adequate for representing and manipulating databases whose objects have various complex structures. Besides it includes a powerful operator called *replace*. This operator applies a function to each element of a set of objects. This operation is necessary for expressing elaborate operations on complex structures. But classical operations such as selection and projection can be expressed by a *replace* as well.

The function specification in *replace* is not user defined in [AB88]. We extend this specification to express various user defined (geometric) functions, and call it *apply*. This provides independence between (i) an algebraic language for general (non geometric) data manipulations on maps independently of the application and (ii) the operations on basic geometric objects specific to a given application.

Section 4 defines the *apply* construct and shows how the operations on maps described in Section 2 are expressed through the *apply* construct. The map representation chosen may imply certain redundancies. They are discussed in Section 5.

2   A toy application

In this Section, we informally describe a few primitives for thematic maps manipulation. A more formal presentation will be given in Section 3. We just assume here that a map has two kinds of components: non-spatial and spatial components. The former take alphanumerical values, while the latter represent geometric regions.

The operations described here are the following: projection, fusion, cover, map overlay, superimposition, selection, windowing, and finally clipping.

● **Projection:**

This operation corresponds to the relational projection. As an example, take map m of figure 2.1. The attributes "crop" and "district" whose domains are respectively "string" and "integer" represent its non-spatial components. Assume that we want to get the map of districts, without mention of the crops of each district: we have to project out attribute "crop".

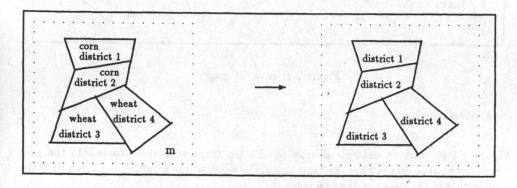

Figure 2.1: projection on attribute "district"

Assume now that instead of projecting the previous map on districts, we want to get the map of crops (without mention of the districts). After having applied the projection operation, two neighbour regions may have the same crop value. Then we may want to replace such neighbour regions by a single region, i.e. erase their common boundary. The **fusion** operation realizes the geometric union of the regions of a map which have the same value for a given component. Figure 2.2.a represents the map m of crops and districts. Figure 2.2.b represents the map of crops after projecting out the district name and realizing the fusion of regions with common crop value: we do not distinguish anymore districts boundaries.

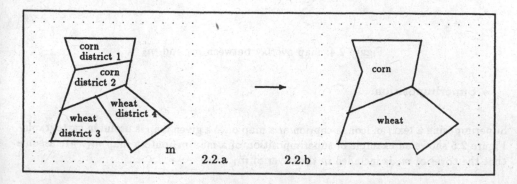

Figure 2.2: projection and fusion of map m on attribute "crop"

If we further fusion the two regions of Figure 2.2.b, after projecting out attribute "crop", we obtain the **cover** of m, i.e. the (geometric) union of the regions of m (Fig 2.3).

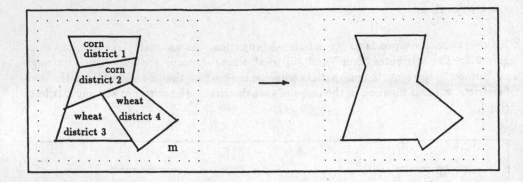

Figure 2.3: cover of map m

• **Map overlay:**

Figure 2.4 exhibits an example of map overlay on maps with same cover. In the case where both maps do not have the same cover, the cover of the resulting map would be the intersection of the covers of the two maps.

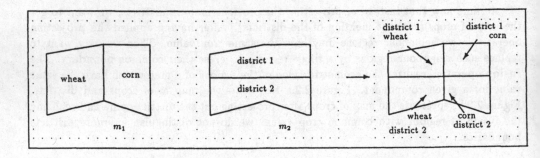

Figure 2.4: map overlay between m_1 and m_2

• **Superimposition:**

Superimposing a text, an icon, a caption or a map onto a given map is useful in cartography. Figure 2.5 shows an example of superimposition of a map m_2 onto a map m_1. We assume that the cover of m_2 is included in the cover of m_1.

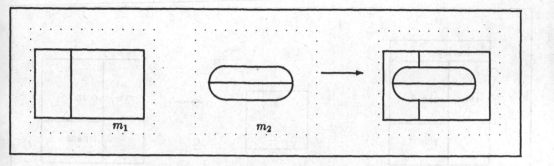

Figure 2.5: superimposition of m_2 onto m_1

- **Selection:**

Consider again the example of Figure 2.1. Getting the map of districts producing "wheat" corresponds to the relational selection (Figure 2.6).

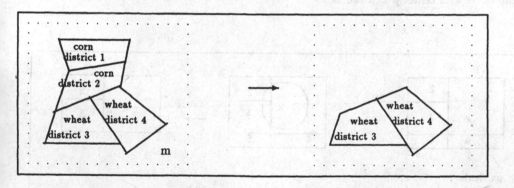

Figure 2.6: example of relational selection

The following operations are examples of *geometric* selections:

- **Windowing:**

Windowing (Figure 2.7) allows to get the regions of a map whose intersection with a given window is not empty.

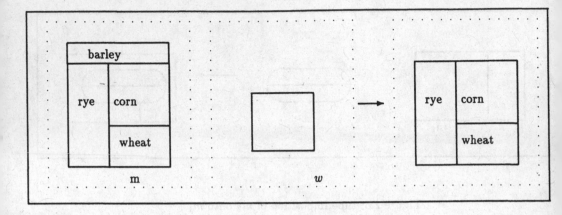

Figure 2.7: windowing of map m with window w

As another example, consider the query "what are the communes whose distance to a given point p is less than r=twenty kilometers". Windowing is applied where the window is the circle with center p and radius r:

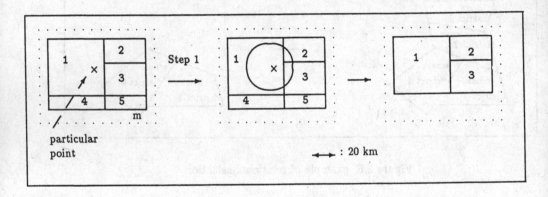

Figure 2.8: "communes whose distance to a given point is less than 20 kilometers"

• **Clipping:**

This operation allows to select the part of a map which is inside a window.

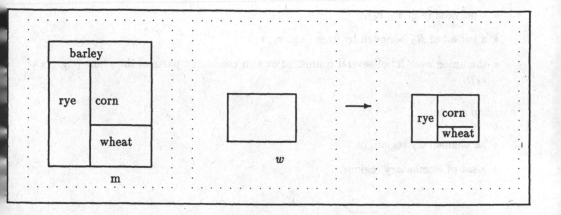

Figure 2.9: clipping of a map m with a window w

3   The model

We are interested in querying a set of thematic maps in two distinct ways: (i) issuing queries with respect to the alphanumeric information associated to maps (e.g. relational selection), and (ii) asking information related to the geometric component of the map (e.g. geometric selection, map overlay). Database systems efficiently manipulate sets of objects. This is why it sounds natural to represent a thematic maps database by a set of *maps*, where a map is a set of *tuples*. A tuple basically represents a geometric region to which is usually associated non geometric information.

In this section, we introduce a data model on maps. Operations on maps are database operations extended with geometric operations on regions.

We first introduce regions and operations on regions (Section 3.1). The data model on maps is then defined (Section 3.2). Finally, Section 3.3 illustrates this map data model on the application described in Section 2.

Notations

In the sequel, we adopt the following conventions: we use greak letters, γ for a geometric type, and τ, μ,... for a non geometric type.

Capital letters such as A, B, ... are used for alphanumeric attribute names, and R, S, ... for geometric ones. Values are denoted by lower case letters.

3.1   Regions

3.1.1   Definition of a region

An *elementary region* is a subset of the two-dimension space R^2 (figure 3.1). It can be :

- a polygon (e.g. r_3, r_4),

- a subset of R_2 bounded by lines (e.g. r_1, r_2),

- the union over R^2 of several connected or non connected parts of the plane (e.g. $r_3 \cup r_4$).

A *region* can be:

- an elementary region, or

- a set of elementary regions.

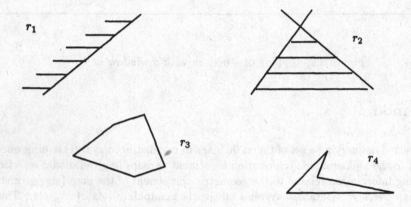

Figure 3.1: a few examples of elementary regions

Let us consider now the following example:

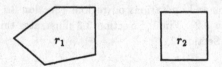

Figure 3.2: elementary regions or set of regions

Looking at Figure 3.2, we may choose between the three following interpretations: (i) r_1 and r_2 are two distinct elementary regions, (ii) the geometric union of r_1 and r_2 is an elementary region, and (iii) the set of elementary regions $\{r_1, r_2\}$ is a region.

More precisely, let γ be a given subset of R^2.

- γ is a region type, called atomic type: an elementary region is a region of type (domain) γ.

- $\{\gamma\}$ is a region type: a set of elementary regions is a region of type $\{\gamma\}$.

3.1.2 Operations on regions

We introduce now a set of operations on regions which is sufficient to implement the application of Section 2, and which will be useful to describe operations on maps:

1. we first use a boolean algebra over R^2, where the operators $+$, $\bullet$ and $-$ are interpreted by the corresponding set operations: union, intersection and difference:

   (a) $+$ (union) :
   r_1, r_2, $r_1 + r_2$ of type γ.

   (b) $\bullet$ (intersection):
   r_1, r_2, $r_1 \bullet r_2$ of type γ.

   (c) $-$ (difference):
   r_1, r_2, $r_1 - r_2$ of type γ.

We then extend this algebra with the following operations:

2. we introduce the "non-empty" unary predicate over γ, denoted $\neq \emptyset$.
   $r \neq \emptyset$ is true if r is not the empty subset of R^2, where r is of type γ.

   Similarly, if r is of type $\{\gamma\}$, $r = \{s_1, ... s_n\} \neq \{\emptyset\}$ if there is at least one s_i such that $s_i \neq \emptyset$.

3. $\oplus : \{\gamma\} \to \gamma$.
   $\oplus\{r_1, ..., r_n\} \stackrel{\text{def}}{=} r_1 + ... + r_n$.
   This operator performs the union over R_2 of the elementary regions elements of a set and gives as an output a single elementary region.

4. $\sqcap$ (set from singleton): $\gamma \to \{\gamma\}$.
   $\sqcap r \stackrel{\text{def}}{=} \{r\}$.
   This operator transforms an elementary region r into a set with unique region r.

5. intersection is extended by:

   (a) $\{\gamma\} \times \gamma \to \{\gamma\} : \{r_1, ..., r_n\} \bullet r \stackrel{\text{def}}{=} \{r_1 \bullet r, ..., r_n \bullet r\}$.

   (b) $\gamma \times \{\gamma\} \to \{\gamma\} : r \bullet \{r_1, ..., r_n\} \stackrel{\text{def}}{=} \{r \bullet r_1, ..., r \bullet r_n\}$.

   (c) $\{\gamma\} \times \{\gamma\} \to \{\gamma\} : r \bullet s \stackrel{\text{def}}{=} \{t \bullet u \mid t \in r, u \in s\}$, where r, s are of type $\{\gamma\}$ and t, u are of type γ.

3.2 Maps

3.2.1 Definition

A map is a set of tuples. As an example of tuple, $[A : a, B : b, R : r]$ will designate a region with geometric attribute R with value r and with two non geometric attributes A and B with respective values a and b.

We do not require the existence of non geometric attributes (e.g. $\{[R : r]\}$ represents a map including a single region). However a map must have at least one geometric attribute.

We accept maps with several geometric attributes. This is explained in Section 5.

To define more formally a map, we follow the *complex objects* approach of [AB88]. Maps are typed objects defined as follows.

Types and objects

We assume an infinite set of attribute names (geometric or not), a given set of non-geometric domains $\{D_1, ..., D_n\}$ and a given set of geometric domains $\{\triangle_1, ..., \triangle_m\}$, where $\triangle_i \subseteq R^2$.

Types are constructed from domains, attribute names, and the set $\{\}$ and tuple $[\ ]$ constructors. Each object is an instance of a type which is defined as follows:

1. if D $(\triangle)$ is a domain, then D $(\triangle)$ is a type (geometric or not).

2. if τ_1, ..., τ_n are types and L_1, ..., L_n are attributes names not used in any of them, then $[L_1 : \tau_1, ..., L_n : \tau_n]$ is a tuple type.

3. if τ is a type and L an attribute name not used in it, then $\{L : \tau\}$ is a set type.

4. if τ is a type and L a name not used in it, then $L : \tau$ is a named type.

We illustrate this definition by examples of maps and associated types:
$\{R : r, R : s\}$ of type $\{R : \gamma\}$
$\{[A : a, B : b, R : r, S : s]\}$ of type $\{[A : string, B : string, R : \gamma, S : \gamma]\}$
$S : \{[A : a, B : \{C : 1, C : 2\}, R : r]\}$ of type
$S : \{[A : string, B : \{C : integer\}, R : \gamma]\}$

3.2.2   Operations on maps

To define operations on maps, the algebra of [AB88] is extended with "geometric" operations. Let us consider first the standard database operations. Among the useful operations are the following ones: projection, selection, cartesian product, nest and set operations. We recall the usual notations for the four first operations:

1. **Relational algebra operations:**

   (a) *Projection* is denoted by $\pi_{list\ of\ attribute\ names}$. The value of the component A of tuple t of map m is denoted: $t.A$.

   (b) *Selection* is denoted by $\sigma_{condition}$. For example, "all the regions of a map m whose altitude is more than 1000 meters" where m is of type: $\{[Height : integer, Crop : string, R : \gamma]\}$ is expressed by:

   $$\text{``}\pi_R(\sigma_{Height>1000}(m))\text{''}.$$

   (c) *Cartesian product* is denoted by $\times$. For example, $m_1 \times m_2$ where m_1 is of type[2] $\{[A, R_1]\}$ and m_2 is of type $\{[B, R_2]\}$ will generate a map m of type $\{[A, B, R_1, R_2]\}$.

---

[2]From now on, when there is no ambiguity, we omit in a tuple type, the type of each component; for example, $\{[A, R]\}$ denotes type $\{[A : String, R : \gamma]\}$.

2. **Nesting** map m on attribute A is denoted $Nest_A(m)$. As an example, if m is of type $\{[A : String, \ R : \gamma]\}$ nesting m on attribute A will group in a single tuple all regions having the same value for attribute A. $Nest_A(m)$ is of type $\{[A : String, S : \{R : \gamma\}]\}$.

"Geometric" operations on maps are now introduced:

1. **Fusion** ⊎:
   without loss of generality, consider a map m of type $\{[A : \tau, R : \{\gamma\}]\}$. The fusion operation replaces in each tuple of m the set of regions by its geometric union $\oplus$. Let $m' = \uplus(m)$. m' is of type $\{[A : \tau, R' : \gamma]\}$ and has the following value:

$$m' = \{t'|t \in m, t'.A = t.A \wedge t'.R' = \oplus t.R\}$$

2. **Geometric selection** denoted by σ_G, where G stands for geometric condition. G is one of the following predicates[3]:
$$t.R \bullet k \neq \emptyset,$$
$$t.R \bullet t.S \neq \emptyset,$$
   where k is a constant of type γ, (or $\{\gamma\}$), $t.R$ and $t.S$ are component regions of type γ, (or $\{\gamma\}$).

   $\sigma_G(m)$ keeps the tuples of m for which condition G is true.

3. **Geometric product** ⊙:
   $\odot_{T \leftarrow R,S}(m)$ is only defined if m has at least two geometric attributes R and S. Its type is that of m except that attributes R and S are replaced by a single geometric attribute T. The value of $\odot_{T \leftarrow R,S}(m)$ is defined as follows:

$$m' = \{t'|t \in m, \ t'.T = t.R \bullet t.S \wedge t'.A = t.A \text{ for each non geometric attr. A in m }\}.$$

   As an example, consider m of type :$\{[A, B, R, S]\}$, the product m' is of type $\{[A, B, T]\}$, and is defined as:
   To each tuple t of m corresponds a tuple t' in $m' = \odot_{T \leftarrow R,S}(m)$ such that:
$$t'.A = t.A$$
$$t'.B = t.B$$
$$t'.T = t.R \bullet t.S.$$

We next illustrate these definitions with more involved operations that are expressible in the algebra just described:

1. **Geometric join** $\bowtie_G$:
   Given two maps m_1 and m_2 with respective geometric attributes R_1 and R_2, we have:

$$m_1 \bowtie_G m_2 \stackrel{\text{def}}{=} \odot(\sigma_{R_1 \bullet R_2 \neq \emptyset}(m_1 \times m_2))$$

   Consider for example m_1 of type $\{[A, R_1]\}$, and m_2 of type $\{[B, R_2]\}$.
   $m = m_1 \bowtie_G m_2$ is of type $\{[A, B, R]\}$ and has for value:
   $m = \{t \mid t_1 \in m_1, \ t_2 \in m_2, \ t.A = t_1.A, \ t.B = t_2.B, \ t.R = t_1.R_1 \bullet t_2.R_2 \neq \emptyset\}.$

---

[3]One could also choose as built-in predicate $t \bullet R \neq \emptyset$.

2. **Cover** C:

As an example, consider the map representing the partition of France into districts. The cover of this map would include a single region (without alphanumeric data) representing the whole country without the inner borders between districts.

Assume first each tuple of map m, whose cover we are looking for, has a single geometric attribute R of type γ. Then $C(m)$ is defined as follows:

$$C(m) = \sqcap \oplus \pi_R(m).$$

Observe $\pi_R(m)$ is a projection of m on the geometric attribute R. It is a map including a set of regions: by definition of the projection, it is of type $\{R : \gamma\}$. Obviously $\pi_R(m)$ represents a geometric object (region) as well, closed under the operations defined in Section 3.1.2. Applying to this region, the fusion operator $\oplus$, we get a single region. Applying to this region the singleton operator $\sqcap$, we indeed get a map which represents the cover of m. (More formally, to be consistent with the type of regions defined in Section 3.1.1, there should be a mapping between regions and named geometric components of a map).

Let us now relax the assumption that R should be of type γ. Assume indeed, that R is of type $\{\gamma\}$. Then $\pi_R(m)$ would be of type $\{R : \{\gamma\}\}$. Then, $\sqcup_{\{\}}(\pi_R(m))$, where $\sqcup_{\{\}}$ is the set-collapse operator of the algebra of complex objects [AB88], represents indeed a region of type $\{\gamma\}$ and the cover is expressed as:

$$C(m) = \sqcap \oplus \sqcup_{\{\}}(\pi_R(m)).$$

We shall see below that cover is useful for expressing the "superimposition" primitive of Section 2.

3.3 Back to the application of Section 2

We show in this section how the various user primitives of Section 2 can be expressed by means of the above operations on maps:

- **Projection** and **fusion** (Figure 2.2).

    Extracting the map of cereals, given the map m of districts and cereals of type $\{[crops, districts, R]\}$ (Figure 2.2), is expressed by the following expression:

$$\uplus Nest_{crops} \, \pi_{crops,R} \, (m).$$

We first project out the district attribute, then we gather in a same tuple the regions having same crop value ($Nest$), and finally we apply the fusion operation.

- **Map overlay** (Figure 2.4) is trivially expressed through geometric join $\bowtie_G$.

- Similarly, **windowing** (Figure 2.7), i.e. selecting the set of regions intersecting with a given window w is expressed by a geometric selection:

$$\sigma_{t.R \bullet w \neq \emptyset}(m),$$

where $t.R$ is the region value of tuple t in map m. Observe that if w is small enough, this allows to select a region (or a set of regions, if a map is not a partition of its cover) by windowing inside the region.

- **Clipping** (Figure 2.9), which consists in keeping from map m, only what is inside a given window w is expressed by:

$$m \bowtie_G \sqcap w,$$

where $\sqcap w$ is the map with type $\{[R : \gamma]\}$ and with single tuple $[R : w]$.

- We end up with a more complicate operation: **superimposition** (Figure 2.5). This may be seen as:

  1. taking the cover of the map (m_2) that we want to superimpose onto a map (m_1).
  2. before superimposing m_2, we have to erase the location corresponding to the cover of m_2. In other words we have to make a "geometric difference" denoted $\ominus$ between m_1 and m_2 (we assume that $\mathcal{C}(m_1) \supset \mathcal{C}(m_2)$). We get map m_3.
  3. we finally superimpose m_2, i.e. take the (relational) union of m_3 and m_2

In summary, superimposition is expressed as:

$$(m_1 \ominus m_2) \cup m_2$$

- Geometric difference can be expressed as (i) taking the difference of covers as a window, and (ii) clipping:

$$m_1 \ominus m_2 = m_1 \bowtie_G \sqcap(\mathcal{C}(m_1) - \mathcal{C}(m_2)).$$

4 The *apply* operator

To express the geometric operations on maps (Section 3.2), we only need (i) operations on regions, and (ii) a constructor called *apply*. It is denoted by: "*apply* $< f > (m)$". It takes as an input a map m and gives as an output a map m' obtained from m by applying f to each tuple of m.

The *apply* operator is not new. It is similar to the Lisp "Mapcar", and is an extension of the *replace* operator of the algebra of [AB88][4].

Let m be a map of type $\{\tau\}$ and f a partial function of τ to τ'. f denotes a transformation to "apply" to each member of a set of a given type.
apply $< f > (m)$ is of type $\{\tau'\}$ and is defined as:

---

[4] The original name *replace* has been changed into *apply* because it sounded closer to the intuitive meaning of this constructor.

$$apply < f > (m) = \{f(t)|t \in m \land f(t) \text{ is defined}\}.$$

Informally speaking, if f is applied on a map m, f can have other input parameters than m, for example $m_1, ..., m_n$, and is constructed from other apply functions and/or algebraic operations on $m, m_1, ..., m_n$. This operator is extremely powerful. In particular, it can express a variety of algebraic operations such as selection, projection, nest, unnest.

apply is just an extension of *replace* to take as specifications for the function f, *the operations of the algebra of regions*: f is not only constructed from other apply specifications or algebraic operations on maps, but also from operations of the algebra of regions (Section 3.1.2). We show below that operations on maps such as geometric selection, fusion, join, can be expressed by an *apply* operation.

Let us first define more formally the construction of an *apply* specification. For a more complete definition, see [AB88].

1. **Basis for an apply specification:**
   if B is an attribute name in τ, then B is an apply specification, and $B(t) \stackrel{\text{def}}{=} t.B$.

2. **Tuple construction:**
   if $AS_1, ..., AS_m$ are apply specifications from τ to $\tau_1, ..., \tau_m$, and $B_1, ..., B_m$ are attribute names, then $[B_1 : AS_1, ..., B_m : AS_m]$ is an apply specification from τ to $[B_1 : \tau_1, ..., B_n : \tau_n]$. Its effect is defined by:
   $[B_1 : AS_1, ..., B_m : AS_m](t) = [B_1 : AS_1(t), ..., B_m : AS_m(t)]$.

3. **Application of an operation:** although not necessary, we give separate constructions for operations of the algebra of maps and for operations of the algebra of regions.

   (a) if $op(M_1, ..., M_n)$ is an *algebraic operation* from $\tau_1, ..., \tau_n$ to τ' and $AS_1, ..., AS_n$ are apply specifications from τ to $\tau_1, ... \tau_n$ then $op(AS_1, ..., AS_n)$ is an apply specification from τ to τ'. Note that τ_i, τ' are types of any attribute (geometric or not).

   (b) if $op(r_1, ..., r_m)$ is an *operation on regions* from $\gamma_1, ..., \gamma_m$ to γ' (where γ_i, γ' are geometric types) and $AS_1, ..., AS_m$ are apply specifications from τ to $\gamma_1, ..., \gamma_m$ then $op(AS_1, ..., AS_m)$ is àn apply specification from τ to γ'.

   In both cases, the effect of $op(AS_1, ..., AS_m)$ is defined by:
   $op(AS_1, ..., AS_m)(t) = op(AS_1(t), ..., AS_m(t))$.

4. **Expression of conditional:**
   The effect is that of a selection. Again, we separate the case of regular selection from that of geometric selection.

   (a) if AS_1, AS_2, AS_3 are apply specifications from τ to τ_1, τ_2, τ_3, then "if $AS_1\theta AS_2$ then AS_3" is an apply specification from τ to τ_3. It defines a partial function:

$$f(t) = \begin{cases} AS_3(t) & \text{if } AS_1(t)\theta AS_2(t) \\ undefined & \text{otherwise} \end{cases}$$

θ is one of the built-in predicates of the algebra on complex objects.

(b) if AS_1, AS_2 are apply specifications from τ to γ, τ', then "if $AS_1 \neq \emptyset$ then AS_2" is an apply specification from τ to τ'. It defines a partial function:

$$f(t) = \begin{cases} AS_2(t) & \text{if } AS_1(t) \neq \emptyset \\ undefined & \text{otherwise} \end{cases}$$

Proposition [AB88]: the set of apply specifications is closed under composition. $\square$

We end up this section in expressing the three main "geometric" operations on maps which have been described above (Section 3.2), through the following apply specifications:

- **Geometric product $\odot$:**

  Let m be a map of type $\{\tau\}$, where, without loss of generality, assume $\tau = [B_1 : \mu, \ B_2 : \mu, \ R_1 : \gamma, \ R_2 : \gamma]$. Then the geometric product $\odot_{T \leftarrow R_1, R_2}$ is expressed as:

  $$apply < [B_1 : B_1, \ B_2 : B_2, \ R : R_1 \bullet R_2] > (m).$$

  Indeed, it is an apply specification from τ to $\tau' = [B_1 : \mu, \ B_2 : \mu, \ R : \gamma]$, and can be seen as the tuple construction: $[B_1 : AS_1, \ B_2 : AS_2, \ R : AS_3 \bullet AS_4]$, where the AS_i are the following apply specifications:

  $$AS_1 \equiv B_1$$
  $$AS_2 \equiv B_2$$
  $$AS_3 \equiv R_1$$
  $$AS_4 \equiv R_2.$$

  We denote the geometric product by $apply < \bullet > (m)$ (generic notation independent of the type of m).

- Similarly **fusion $\uplus$** is denoted by $apply < \oplus > (m)$, and if m has the above type $\{\tau\}$, it is expressed as: $apply < [B_1 : B_1, \ B_2 : B_2, \ R : R_1 \oplus R_2] > (m)$.

- **Geometrical selection σ_G:**

  consider map m of type τ with two geometric attributes R and S and the selection $\sigma_{t.R \bullet t.S \neq \emptyset}$; it is expressed as the following apply specifications:

  $$AS_1 \equiv R$$
  $$AS_2 \equiv S$$
  $$AS_3 = AS_1 \bullet AS_2$$
  $$if \ AS_3 \neq \emptyset \ then \ I_\tau$$

  where I_τ is the identity specification on τ. Selection can then be specified as a composition of two *apply*'s: $apply < \neq \emptyset < \bullet > >$. If we had chosen $t.R \neq \emptyset$ as a built-in predicate for geometric selection (see footnote 4), selection would be specified as $apply < \neq \emptyset >$.

Likewise, one can define other apply specifications for the other operations of the section above, such as geometric join or cover. Consider the case of join: the **join** of m_1 and m_2 can be expressed as:

$$m_1 \bowtie_G m_2 \equiv apply <\neq \emptyset < \bullet >> (m_1 \times m_2).$$

We first compute the cartesian product of m_1 and m_2, then apply the "$\bullet$" operation, and finally check whether each tuple has a non-empty geometric component.

5 Redundant maps having same cover

A map is said to be in *normal form* if it has a single geometric attribute. Assume we are initially given a set of normal maps. Obviously, normal maps are not closed under the operations of Section 3.2.2: the cartesian product of two normal maps gives a map with two geometric attributes. This is why we did not require in the definition of maps (Section 3.2.1) that the number of geometric attributes in a map be limited to one.

Consider now a map m_1 of type $\{[A, R_1]\}$ and a tuple $t_1 = [A : a, R_1 : r_1]$ of m_1. Tuple t_1 is to be interpreted as follows: to each point p of r_1 is associated the value a for attribute A. Its "semantics" can thus be viewed as:

$$\{[a, p] \mid p \in r_1\}$$

Then, consider a map m_2 of type $\{[B, R_2]\}$ and the cartesian product $m_1 \times m_2$.

Tuple $t = [A : a, B : b, R_1 : r_1, R_2 : r_2]$ of $m_1 \times m_2$ can be interpreted as the set:

$$\{[a, b, p, q] \mid p \in r_1, q \in r_2\}$$

Cartesian products of normal maps are in general of poor interest (e.g. display couples of districts such that *district 1* has a city with more than one million of inhabitants and *corn* is grown in *district 2*).

Usually, given a tuple with two geometric attributes with values r_1 and r_2, one is interested in the geometric intersection $r_1 \bullet r_2$: given a tuple $[Crop : corn, R_1 : r_1]$ of map m_1 and a tuple $[District : d_1, R_2 : r_2]$ of map m_2, the information of interest is $[Crop : corn, District : d_1, R : r_1 \bullet r_2]$ which is one tuple of the *map overlay* $m = m_1 \bowtie_G m_2$.

Cartesian product $[Crop : corn, District : d_1, R_1 : r_1, R_2 : r_2]$ is only an intermediate step in the computation of map overlay:

$$\bowtie_G = \odot(\sigma_{R_1 \bullet R_2 \neq \emptyset}(m_1 \times m_2))$$

Observe that

$$\bowtie_G = \sigma_{R \neq \emptyset}(\odot(m_1 \times m_2)).$$

$\odot(m_1 \times m_2)$ is a normal map. Then, one may wonder whether it is not sufficient to keep all maps in normal form. This is possible if to each non normal map, we apply geometric product $\odot$.

In the above example, the tuple cartesian product $[A : a, B : b, R_1 : r_1, R_2 : r_2]$ would be replaced after having applied $\odot$ by: $[A : a, B : b, R : r_1 \bullet r_2]$ and would be interpreted as the **intersection** of regions r_1, r_2, i.e. as:

$$\{[a, b, p, p] \mid p \in r_1, \ p \in r_2\}$$

But such a "normalization" (applying $\odot$ to a non normal map) should lead to "equivalent" information:

Given $r_1 \bullet r_2$ for all tuples of $\odot(m_1 \times m_2)$, are we able to reconstruct m_1 and m_2, i.e. all values r_1 and r_2? The answer is of course no in the general case.

However, it turns out that for a very useful class of maps, $\odot$ is done *without loss of information*. The theorem below states that if m_1 and m_2 are normal maps with **identical cover**, then $\odot(m_1 \times m_2)$ is equivalent to $m_1 \times m_2$, i.e m_1 and m_2 can be reconstructed from $\odot(m_1 \times m_2)$.

For the sequel of this section, assume all maps m are of type: $\{[R, A]\}$, where A designates any complex object type on the non geometric attributes of m.

We further assume that a map, say with two geometric attributes R_1 and R_2, has been obtained at some point by applying cartesian product to two maps, say m_1 and m_2 in normal form and of types: $\{[R_1, A_1]\}$ and $\{[R_2, A_2]\}$. $m = m_1 \times m_2$ is of type $\{[R_1, R_2, A_1, A_2]\}$.

Theorem 5.1 If m_1 and m_2 are two normal maps with **same cover**, then:
$m_i = \uplus Nest_{A_i}(\pi_{A_i, R}(\odot(m_1 \times m_2))), i \in [1, 2]$,
where $m' = \odot(m_1 \times m_2)$ is a normal map of type $\{[R, A_1, A_2]\}$.

This is illustrated in the following diagram, on the example of m_1.

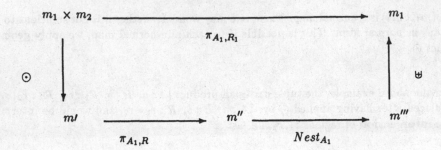

Proof (Sketch):

Each tuple of m' is of type $[R, A_1, A_2]$. By projection on R and A_1 and nest on A_1, we get a map m''' of type $\{[R_1 : \{R\}, A_1]\}$. Let us show that $\uplus m''' = m_1$.

To each tuple t of m''' corresponds a tuple t_1 in m_1 which has the same value for the non geometric attributes:
$$\pi_{A_1}(m''') = \pi_{A_1}(m'') = \pi_{A_1}(m') = \pi_{A_1}(m_1 \times m_2) = \pi_{A_1}(m_1).$$

Let $[a_1, r_1]$ be the value of tuple t_1 in m_1 and $[a_1, \{s_1, ..., s_n\}]$ be the value of tuple t in m'''.

By construction of m', we have for all $i \in [1, n]$,
$$s_i = r_1 \bullet r_{2,i},$$

where $r_{2,i}$ is a region of map m_2 (we have for some tuple t_2 in m_2: $t_2.R_2 = r_{2,i}$). $\{r_{2,1}, ... r_{2,n}\}$ is the set of regions of m_2.

Then applying $\uplus$ to m''' implies applying $\oplus$ to the component R of each tuple t of m''':
$$\oplus t.R = \oplus\{s_1, ..., s_n\}$$
$$= \oplus\{r_1 \bullet r_{2,1}, ..., r_1 \bullet r_{2,n}\}$$
$$= r_1 \bullet \oplus\{r_{2,1}, ..., r_{2,n}\}$$
$$= r_1 \bullet C(m_2)$$
where $C(m_2)$ is the cover of m_2. Since by definition of the cover of a map, $r_1 \subseteq C(m_1)$ and since by assumption, both maps have same cover, then $r_1 \subseteq C(m_2)$, and:

$$\oplus t.R = r_1 \bullet C(m_2) = r_1.$$

Therefore, to each tuple t_1 in m_1 with value $[a_1, r_1]$, it corresponds a tuple t in m''' and a tuple t' in $\uplus m'''$ (of type $\{[R_1, A_1]\}$) such that $t'.R_1 = t_1.R_1 = r_1$.

Besides, by definition of $\uplus$, $t'.A_1 = t.A_1 = t_1.A_1 = a_1$, and there is no other tuple in $\uplus m'''$.

Thus, $\uplus m''' = m_1$.

The same argument holds for m_2.$\square$

In conclusion, if the database includes only maps with same cover, maps with several geometric attributes (one for each component map) have redundant information. Keeping maps in normal form is sufficient for extracting any information about component maps.

6 Conclusion

We studied in this paper how to provide the designer of geographic databases with a database query language extensible and customizable to its own needs. For this, we took as an example a toy application on thematic maps and showed by using a complex objects algebra that application dependent operations could be expressed through a general construct called *apply*, which applies to each element of a set a user defined specific function.

The basic idea behind this construct is that it replaces a set of objects of type τ by a set of objects of type τ' by applying to each object an application dependent (partially) defined function. The database query language itself is in charge of expressing application independent queries appropriate for manipulating a large amount of structured data. Provided the application is data driven and all user needs can be expressed through such a construct, this approach could be used for other applications such as full text systems, form management, etc.

The model we took in this paper was that of a complex object algebra [AB88]. A query language based on this model could be implemented with object oriented database systems such as Orion ([K*88,K*89]) or O_2 ([BBB*88,LRV88,LR89]). The design of database query languages (see for example [BCD89]) for such systems is still a research issue. Since one of the advantages of object oriented systems is customization and extensibility, such query languages should be good candidates for applications such as that investigated in this paper.

Acknowledgments
We are grateful to S. Abiteboul who read earlier drafts of this paper and suggested many improvements. The paper also benefits from discussions with C. Delobel and R. Jeansoulin.

References

[AB88]   S. Abiteboul and C. Beeri. *On the Power of Languages for the Manipulation of Complex Objects.* Technical Report 846, INRIA, May 1988.

[AG87]   S. Abiteboul and S. Grumbach. *COL: A Logic-Based Language for Complex Objects.* Technical Report 714, INRIA, Septembre 1987.

[BB81]   R. Barrera and A. Buchmann. Schema definition and query language for a geographical database system. In Hot Springs, editor, *IEEE Computer Architecture for Pattern Analysis and Image Database Management*, New York, Novembre 1981.

[BBB*88]   F. Bancilhon, G. Barbedette, V. Benzaken, C. Delobel, S. Gamerman, C. Lécluse, P. Pfeffer, P. Richard, and F. Velez. *The Design and Implementation of O_2, an Object-Oriented Database System.* Technical Report 20, GIP Altair, April 1988.

[BCD89]   F. Bancilhon, S. Cluet, and C. Delobel. *Query Languages for Object-Oriented Database Systems: Analysis and a Proposal.* Technical Report, GIP Altair (to appear), 1989.

[BK86]   F. Bancilhon and S. Khoshafian. A calculus for complex objects. In *proc. ACM SIGACT-SIGMOD, Symp. on Principles of Database Systems*, 1986.

[CF80]   N.S. Chang and K.S. Fu. A relational database system for images. In Chang and Fu, editors, *Pictorial Information Systems*, 288-321, Springer Verlag, 1980.

[CJ88]   A.F Cardenas and T. Joseph. Picquery: a high level query language for pictorial database management. *IEEE Transactions on Software Engineering*, 14(5): pages 630–638, May 1988.

[CK81]   S.K. Chang and T.L. Kunii. Pictorial database systems. *IEEE Transactions on Computer*, November 1981.

[Dav88]   B. David. Le modèle Spatiarel. In *Quatrièmes Journées Bases de Données Avancées (BD3)*, pages 73-93, Bénodet, May 1988.

[Fra82]   A. Frank. Map query: data base query language for retrieval of geometric data and their graphical representation. *Computer Graphics*, 16, 1982.

[Fra84]   A. U. Frank. Requirements for database systems suitable to manage large spatial databases. In *First International Symposium on Spatial Data Handling*, pages 38-60, Zurich, 1984.

[GCK*89]   G. Gardarin, J.P. Cheiney, G. Kiernan, D. Pastre, and H. Stora. *Managing complex objects in an extensible relational DBMS.* Technical Report, INRIA, March 1989.

[Gut88]   R.H. Guting. Geo-relational algebra : a model and query language for geometric database systems. In *Conference on Extending Database Technology (EDBT '88)*, pages 506-527, Venice, March 1988.

[Hul87]   R. Hull. A survey of theoretical research on typed complex database objects. In J. Paredaens, editor, *Databases*, pages 193–256, Academic Press (London), 1987.

[HY84]   R. Hull and C.K. Yap. The Format model: a theory of database organization. *ACM*, 31(3), 1984.

[K*88]   W. Kim et al. Integrating an object-oriented programming system with a database system. In *Proc, 2nd Intl. Conf. on Object-Oriented Programming Systems, Languages and Applications*, San Diego, Septembre 1988.

[K*89]   W. Kim et al. Features on the ORION object-oriented database system. In W. Kim and F. Lochovsky, editors, *Object-Oriented Concepts, Applications and Databases*, Addison-Wesley, 1989.

[KV85]   G.M. Kuper and M.Y. Vardi. On the expressive power of the logical data model (extended abstract). In *proc. ACM SIGACT-SIGMOD, Int. Conf. on the Management of Data*, 1985.

[LM84]   R.A. Lorie and A. Meier. Using a relational DBMS for geographical databases. In *Geo-Processing*, pages 243–257, 1984.

[LR89]   C. Lécluse and P. Richard. Modeling complex structures. In *Object Oriented Database Systems, PODS*, Philadelphia, April 1989.

[LRV88]   C. Lécluse, P. Richard, and F. Velez. O_2, an object-oriented data model. In *Conference on Extending Database Technology (EDBT '88)*, pages 556–563, Venice, March 1988.

[MOD87]   F. Manola, J. Orenstein, and U. Dayal. Geographical information processing in Probe database system. In *International Symposium on Computer Assisted Cartography*, Baltimore, 1987.

[OM86]   J. A. Orenstein and F. A. Manola. Toward a general spatial data model for an object-oriented data model. In *VLDB*, 1986.

[Ore86]   J. A. Orenstein. Spatial query processing in an object-oriented database system. In *Proc. of the ACM SIGMOD*, pages 326–336, 1986.

[RFS88]   N. Roussopoulos, C. Faloutsos, and T. Sellis. An efficient pictorial database system for PSQL. *IEEE Transactions on Software Engineering*, 14(5): pages 639–650, May 1988.

[Sam84]   H. Samet. The quadtree and related hierarchical data structures. *Computing Surveys*, 16(2), June 1984.

[SMO87]   R. Sack-Davis, K.J. McDonell, and B.C. Ooi. GEOQL - a query language for geographic information system. In *Australian and New Zeland Association for the Advancement of Science Congress*, Townsville, Australia, August 1987.

[SMSE87]   T. R. Smith, S. Menon, J.L. Star, and J.E. Estes. Requirements and principles for the implementation and construction of large-scale geographic information systems. *International Journal of Geographical Information Systems*, 1(1): pages 13–31, 1987.

[SR86]   M. Stonebraker and L. A. Rowe. The design of POSTGRES. In *proc. ACM SIGACT-SIGMOD*, pages 340–355, 1986.

[SRG83]   M. Stonebraker, B. Rubenstein, and A. Guttman. Application of abstract data types and abstract indices to cad data bases. In *Proc. of the ACM/IEEE Conf. on Engineering Design Applications*, pages 107–113, San Jose, 1983. ·

[SW86]   H. J. Schek and W. Waterfeld. A database kernel system for geoscientific applications. In *Proc. of the Int. Symposium on Spatial Data Handling*, Seattle, Washington, 1986.

Quadtrees

HIERARCHICAL SPATIAL DATA STRUCTURES

Hanan Samet
Computer Science Department,
Center for Automation Research, and
Institute for Advanced Computer Studies
University of Maryland
College Park, Maryland 20742

Abstract

An overview is presented of the use of hierarchical spatial data structures such as the quadtree. They are based on the principle of recursive decomposition. The focus is on the representation of data used in image databases. The emphasis is on two-dimensional regions, points, rectangles, and lines.

1. INTRODUCTION

Hierarchical data structures are important representation techniques in the domains of computer vision, image processing, computer graphics, robotics, and geographic information systems. They are based on the principle of recursive decomposition (similar to *divide and conquer* methods). They are used primarily as devices to sort data of more than one dimension and different spatial types. The term *quadtree* is often used to describe this class of data structures. For a more extensive treatment of this subject, see [Same84a, Same88a, Same88b, Same88c, Same89a, Same89b].

Our presentation is organized as follows. Section 2 describes the region quadtree and presents an application for which it is well-suited. Section 3 briefly reviews the historical background of the origins of hierarchical data structures especially in the context of region data. Section 4 discusses a hierarchical representation of point data. Sections 4, 5, and 6 discuss hierarchical representations for point, rectangle, and line data, respectively, as well as give examples of their utility. Section 7 contains concluding remarks in the context of a geographic information system that makes use of these concepts.

2. REGION DATA

The term *quadtree* is used to describe a class of hierarchical data structures whose common property is that they are based on the principle of recursive decomposition of space. They can be differentiated on the following bases: (1) the type of data that they are used to represent, (2) the principle guiding the decomposition process, and (3) the resolution (variable or not). Currently, they are used for points, rectangles, regions, curves, surfaces, and volumes. The decomposition may be into equal parts on each level (termed a *regular decomposition*), or it may be governed by the input. The resolution of the decomposition (i.e., the number of times that the decomposition process is applied) may be fixed beforehand or it may be governed by properties of the input data.

The most common quadtree representation of data is the *region quadtree*. It is based on the successive subdivision of the image array into four equal-size quadrants. If the array does not consist entirely of 1s or entirely of 0s (i.e., the region does not cover the entire array), it is then subdivided into quadrants, subquadrants, etc., until blocks are obtained (possibly single pixels) that consist entirely of 1s or entirely of 0s. Thus, the region quadtree can be characterized as a variable resolution data structure.

As an example of the region quadtree, consider the region shown in Figure 1a which is represented by the $2^3 \times 2^3$ binary array in Figure 1b. Observe that the 1s correspond to picture elements (termed *pixels*) that are in the region and the 0s correspond to picture elements that are outside the region. The resulting blocks for the array of Figure 1b are shown in Figure 1c. This process is represented by a tree of degree 4.

In the tree representation, the root node corresponds to the entire array. Each son of a node represents a quadrant (labeled in order NW, NE, SW, SE) of the region represented by that node. The leaf nodes of the tree correspond to those blocks for

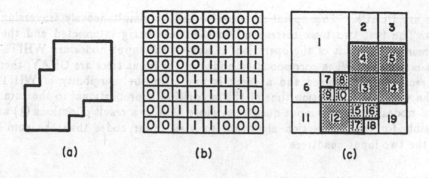

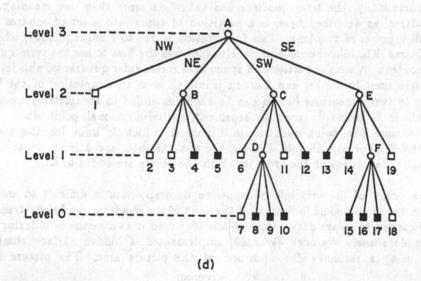

Figure 1. A region, its binary array, its maximal blocks, and the corresponding quadtree. (a) Region. (b) Binary array. (c) Block decomposition of the region in (a). Blocks in the region are shaded. (d) Quadtree representation of the blocks in (c).

which no further subdivision is necessary. A leaf node is said to be BLACK or WHITE, depending on whether its corresponding block is entirely inside or entirely outside of the represented region. All non-leaf nodes are said to be GRAY. The quadtree representation for Figure 1c is shown in Figure 1d. For an efficient algorithm to construct a quadtree from an image represented as a set of rows, see [Shaf87].

Quadtrees can also be used to represent non-binary images. In this case, we apply the same merging criteria to each color. For example, in the case of a landuse map, we simply merge all wheat growing regions, and likewise for corn, rice, etc. This is the approach taken by Samet *et al.* [Same84b].

For a binary image, set-theoretic operations such as union and intersection are quite simple to implement [Hunt78, Hunt79, Shne81a]. For example, the intersection of two region quadtrees yields a BLACK node only when the corresponding regions in both quadtrees are BLACK. This operation is performed by simultaneously traversing three quadtrees. The first two trees correspond to the trees being intersected and the third tree represents the result of the operation. If any of the input nodes are WHITE, then the result is WHITE. When corresponding nodes in the input trees are GRAY, then their sons are recursively processed and a check is made for the mergibility of WHITE leaf nodes. The worst-case execution time of this algorithm is proportional to the sum of the number of nodes in the two input quadtrees. Note that as a result of actions (1) and (3), it is possible for the intersection algorithm to visit fewer nodes than the sum of the nodes in the two input quadtrees.

3. HISTORICAL BACKGROUND

Unfortunately, the term *quadtree* has taken on more than one meaning. The region quadtree, as described here, is a partition of space into a set of squares whose sides are all a power of two long. This formulation is due to Klinger [Klin71] who used the term Q-tree [Klin76], whereas Hunter [Hunt78] was the first to use the term quadtree in such a context. A similar partition of space into rectangular quadrants, also termed a quadtree, was used by Finkel and Bentley [Fink74]. It is an adaptation of the binary search tree to two dimensions (which can be easily extended to an arbitrary number of dimensions). It is primarily used to represent multidimensional point data. As an example, consider the point quadtree in Figure 2, which is built for the sequence Chicago, Mobile, Toronto, Buffalo, Denver, Omaha, Atlanta, and Miami. Note that its shape is highly dependent on the order in which the points are added to it.

The origin of the principle of recursive decomposition is difficult to ascertain. Below, in order to give some indication of the uses of the quadtree, we briefly trace some of its applications to image data. Morton [Mort66] used it as a means of indexing into a geographic database. Warnock [Warn69] implemented a hidden surface elimination algorithm using a recursive decomposition of the picture area. The picture area is

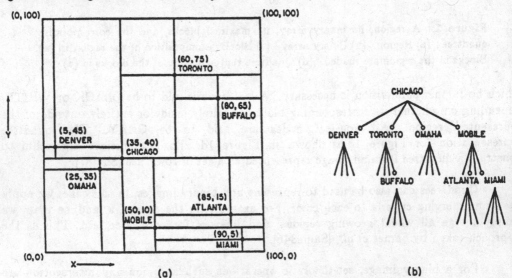

Figure 2. A point quadtree (b) and the records it represents (a).

repeatedly subdivided into successively smaller rectangles while searching for areas sufficiently simple to be displayed. Horowitz and Pavlidis [Horo76] used the quadtree as an initial step in a "split and merge" image segmentation algorithm.

The pyramid of Tanimoto and Pavlidis [Tani75] is a close relative of the region quadtree. It is a multiresolution representation which is is an exponentially tapering stack of arrays, each one-quarter the size of the previous array. It has been applied to the problems of feature detection and segmentation. In contrast, the region quadtree is a variable resolution data structure.

Quadtree-like data structures can also be used to represent images in three dimensions and higher. The octree [Hunt78, Jack80, Meag82, Redd78] data structure is the three-dimensional analog of the quadtree. It is constructed in the following manner. We start with an image in the form of a cubical volume and recursively subdivide it into eight congruent disjoint cubes (called octants) until blocks are obtained of a uniform color or a predetermined level of decomposition is reached. Figure 3a is an example of a simple three-dimensional object whose raster octree block decomposition is given in Figure 3b and whose tree representation is given in Figure 3c.

One of the motivations for the development of hierarchical data structures such as the quadtree is a desire to save space. The original formulation of the quadtree encodes it as a tree structure that uses pointers. This requires additional overhead to encode the internal nodes of the tree. In order to further reduce the space requirements, two other approaches have been proposed. The first treats the image as a collection of leaf nodes where each leaf is encoded by a base 4 number termed a *locational code*, corresponding to a sequence of directional codes that locate the leaf along a path from the root of the quadtree. It is analogous to taking the binary representation of the x and y coordinates of a designated pixel in the block (e.g., the one at the lower left corner) and interleaving them (i.e., alternating the bits for each coordinate). The encoding is also quite similar to a hashing function. It is difficult to determine the origin of this method (e.g., [Abel83, Garg82, Klin79, Mort66]).

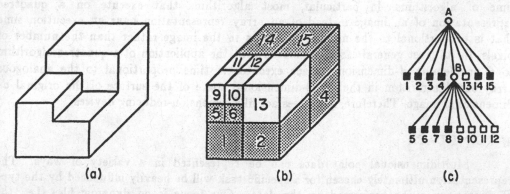

Figure 3. (a) Example three-dimensional object; (b) its octree block decomposition; and (c) its tree representation.

The second, termed a *DF-expression* represents the image in the form of a traversal of the nodes of its quadtree [Kawa80]. It is very compact as each node type can be encoded with two bits. However, it is not easy to use when random access to nodes is desired. Samet and Webber [Same89c] show that for a static collection of nodes, an efficient implementation of the pointer-based representation is often more economical spacewise than a locational code representation. This is especially true for images of higher dimension.

Nevertheless, depending on the particular implementation of the quadtree we may not necessarily save space (e.g., in many cases a binary array representation may still be more economical than a quadtree). However, the effects of the underlying hierarchical aggregation on the execution time of the algorithms are more important. Most quadtree algorithms are simply preorder traversals of the quadtree and, thus, their execution time is generally a linear function of the number of nodes in the quadtree. A key to the analysis of the execution time of quadtree algorithms is the *Quadtree Complexity Theorem* [Hunt78, Hunt79] which states that:

> For a quadtree of depth q representing an image space of $2^q \times 2^q$ pixels where these pixels represent a region whose perimeter measured in pixel-widths is p, then the number of nodes in the quadtree cannot exceed $16 \cdot q - 11 + 16 \cdot p$.

Since under all but the most pathological cases (e.g., a small square of unit width centered in a large image), the region perimeter exceeds the base 2 logarithm of the width of the image containing the region, the Quadtree Complexity Theorem means that the size of the quadtree representation of a region is linear in the perimeter of the region.

The Quadtree Complexity Theorem holds for three-dimensional data [Meag80] where perimeter is replaced by surface area, as well as higher dimensions for which it is stated as follows.

> The size of the k-dimensional quadtree of a set of k-dimensional objects is proportional to the sum of the resolution and the size of the $(k-1)$-dimensional interfaces between these objects.

The Quadtree Complexity Theorem also directly impacts the analysis of the execution time of algorithms. In particular, most algorithms that execute on a quadtree representation of an image instead of an array representation have an execution time that is proportional to the number of blocks in the image rather than the number of pixels. In its most general case, this means that the application of a quadtree algorithm to a problem in d-dimensional space executes in time proportional to the analogous array-based algorithm in the $(d-1)$-dimensional space of the surface of the original d-dimensional image. Therefore, quadtrees act like dimension-reducing devices.

4. POINT DATA

Multidimensional point data can be represented in a variety of ways. The representation ultimately chosen for a specific task will be heavily influenced by the type of operations to be performed on the data. Our focus is on dynamic files (i.e., the number of data can grow and shrink at will) and on applications involving search. In Section 2 we briefly mentioned the point quadtree of Finkel and Bentley [Fink74] and showed its use. In this section we discuss the PR quadtree (P for point and R for region)

[Oren82, Same84a]. It is an adaptation of the region quadtree to point data which associates data points (that need not be discrete) with quadrants. The PR quadtree is organized in the same way as the region quadtree. The difference is that leaf nodes are either empty (i.e., WHITE) or contain a data point (i.e., BLACK) and its coordinates. A quadrant contains at most one data point. For example, Figure 4 is the PR quadtree corresponding to the data of Figure 2.

Data points are inserted into PR quadtrees in a manner analogous to that used to insert in a point quadtree - i.e., a search is made for them. Actually, the search is for the quadrant in which the data point, say A, belongs (i.e., a leaf node). If the quadrant is already occupied by another data point with different x and y coordinates, say B, then the quadrant must repeatedly be subdivided (termed *splitting*) until nodes A and B no longer occupy the same quadrant. This may result in many subdivisions, especially if the Euclidean distance between A and B is very small. The shape of the resulting PR quadtree is independent of the order in which data points are inserted into it. Deletion of nodes is more complex and may require collapsing of nodes - i.e., the direct counterpart of the node splitting process outlined above.

PR quadtrees, as well as other quadtree-like representations for point data, are especially attractive in applications that involve search. A typical query is one that requests the determination of all records within a specified distance of a given record - i.e., all cities within 100 miles of Washington, DC. The efficiency of the PR quadtree lies in its role as a pruning device on the amount of search that is required. Thus many records will not need to be examined. For example, suppose that in the hypothetical database of Figure 2 we wish to find all cities within 8 units of a data point with coordinates (84,10). In such a case, there is no need to search the NW, NE, and SW quadrants of the root (i.e., (50,50)). Thus we can restrict our search to the SE quadrant of the tree rooted at root. Similarly, there is no need to search the NW, NE, and SW

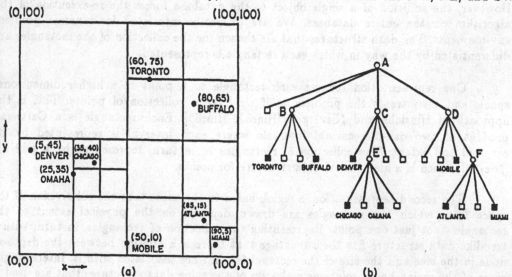

Figure 4. A PR quadtree (b) and the records it represents (a).

quadrants of the tree rooted at the SE quadrant (i.e., (75,25)). Note that the search ranges are usually orthogonally defined regions such as rectangles, boxes, etc. Other shapes are also feasible as the above example demonstrated (i.e., a circle).

5. RECTANGLE DATA

The rectangle data type lies somewhere between the point and region data types. Rectangles are often used to approximate other objects in an image for which they serve as the minimum rectilinear enclosing object. For example, bounding rectangles can be used in cartographic applications to approximate objects such as lakes, forests, hills, etc. [Mats84]. In such a case, the approximation gives an indication of the existence of an object. Of course, the exact boundaries of the object are also stored; but they are only accessed if greater precision is needed. For such applications, the number of elements in the collection is usually small, and most often the sizes of the rectangles are of the same order of magnitude as the space from which they are drawn.

Rectangles are also used in VLSI design rule checking as a model of chip components for the analysis of their proper placement. Again, the rectangles serve as minimum enclosing objects. In this application, the size of the collection is quite large (e.g., millions of components) and the sizes of the rectangles are several orders of magnitude smaller than the space from which they are drawn. Regardless of the application, the representation of rectangles involves two principal issues [Same88a]. The first is how to represent the individual rectangles and the second is how to organize the collection of the rectangles.

The representation that is used depends heavily on the problem environment. If the environment is static, then frequently the solutions are based on the use of the plane-sweep paradigm [Prep85], which usually yields optimal solutions in time and space. However, the addition of a single object to the database forces the re-execution of the algorithm on the entire database. We are primarily interested in dynamic problem environments. The data structures that are chosen for the collection of the rectangles are differentiated by the way in which each rectangle is represented.

One representation reduces each rectangle to a point in a higher dimensional space, and then treats the problem as if we have a collection of points. This is the approach of Hinrichs and Nievergelt [Hinr83, Hinr85]. Each rectangle is a Cartesian product of two one-dimensional intervals where each interval is represented by its centroid and extent. The collection of rectangles is, in turn, represented by a grid file [Niev84], which is a hierarchical data structure for points.

The second representation is region-based in the sense that the subdivision of the space from which the rectangles are drawn depends on the physical extent of the rectangle - not just one point. Representing the collection of rectangles, in turn, with a tree-like data structure has the advantage that there is a relation between the depth of node in the tree and the size of the rectangle(s) that are associated with it. Interestingly, some of the region-based solutions make use of the same data structures that are used in the solutions based on the plane-sweep paradigm. In the remainder of this section, we give an example of a pair of region-based representations.

The *MX-CIF quadtree* of Kedem [Kede81] (see also Abel and Smith [Abel83]) is a region-based representation where each rectangle is associated with the quadtree node corresponding to the smallest block which contains it in its entirety. Subdivision ceases whenever a node's block contains no rectangles. Alternatively, subdivision can also cease once a quadtree block is smaller than a predetermined threshold size. This threshold is often chosen to be equal to the expected size of the rectangle [Kede81]. For example, Figure 5 is the MX-CIF quadtree for a collection of rectangles. Note that rectangle F occupies an entire block and hence it is associated with the block's father. Also rectangles can be associated with both terminal and non-terminal nodes.

It should be clear that more than one rectangle can be associated with a given enclosing block and, thus, often we find it useful to be able to differentiate between them. Kedem proposes to do so in the following manner. Let P be a quadtree node with centroid (CX, CY), and let S be the set of rectangles that are associated with P. Members of S are organized into two sets according to their intersection (or collinearity of their sides) with the lines passing through the centroid of P's block - i.e., all members of S that intersect the line $x = CX$ form one set and all members of S that intersect the line $y = CY$ form the other set.

If a rectangle intersects both lines (i.e., it contains the centroid of P's block), then we adopt the convention that it is stored with the set associated with the line through $x = CX$. These subsets are implemented as binary trees (really tries), which in actuality are one-dimensional analogs of the MX-CIF quadtree. For example, Figure 6 illustrates the binary tree associated with the y axes passing through the root and the NE son of the root of the MX-CIF quadtree of Figure 5. Interestingly, the MX-CIF quadtree is a two-dimensional analog of the interval tree [Edel80, McCr80], which is a data structure that is used to support optimal solutions based on the plane-sweep paradigm to some rectangle problems.

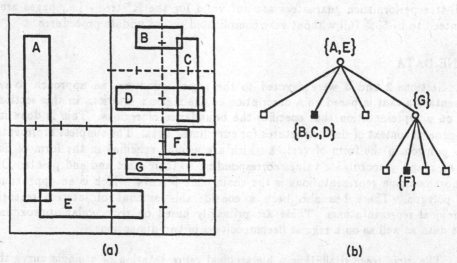

Figure 5. MX-CIF quadtree. (a) Collection of rectangles and the block decomposition induced by the MX-CIF quadtree. (b) The tree representation of (a).

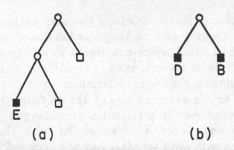

Figure 6. Binary trees for the y axes passing through (a) the root of the MX-CIF quadtree in Figure 6 and (b) the NE son of the root of the MX-CIF quadtree in Figure 6.

The R-tree [Gutt84] is a hierarchical data structure that is derived from the B-tree [Come79]. Each node in the tree is a d-dimensional rectangle corresponding to the smallest rectangle that encloses its son nodes which are also d-dimensional rectangles. The leaf nodes are the actual rectangles in the database. Often, the nodes correspond to disk pages and, thus, the parameters defining the tree are chosen so that a small number of nodes is visited during a spatial query. Note that rectangles corresponding to different nodes may overlap.

Also, a rectangle may be spatially contained in several nodes, yet it can only be associated with one node. This means that a spatial query may often require several nodes to be visited before ascertaining the presence or absence of a particular rectangle. This problem can be alleviated by using the R$^+$-tree [Falo87, Sell87] for which all bounding rectangles (i.e., at levels other than the leaf) are non-overlapping. This means that a given rectangle will often be associated with several bounding rectangles. In this case, retrieval time is sped up at the cost of an increase in the height of the tree. Note that B-tree performance guarantees are not valid for the R$^+$-tree - i.e., pages are not guaranteed to be 50% full without very complicated record update procedures.

6. LINE DATA

Sections 2 and 3 were devoted to the region quadtree, an approach to region representation that is based on a description of the region's interior. In this section, we focus on a representation that specifies the boundaries of regions. This is done in the more general context of data structures for curvilinear data. The simplest representation is the polygon in the form of vectors which are usually specified in the form of lists of pairs of x and y coordinate values corresponding to their start and end points. One of the most common representations is the chain code [Free74] which is an approximation of a polygon. There has also been a considerable amount of interest recently in hierarchical representations. These are primarily based on rectangular approximations to the data as well as on a regular decomposition in two dimensions.

The *strip tree* [Ball81] is a hierarchical representation of a single curve that is obtained by successively approximating segments of it by enclosing rectangles. The data structure consists of a binary tree whose root represents the bounding rectangle of the entire curve. For example, consider Figure 7a where the curve between points P and Q, at locations (x_P, y_P) and (x_Q, y_Q) respectively, is modeled by a strip tree. The rectangle

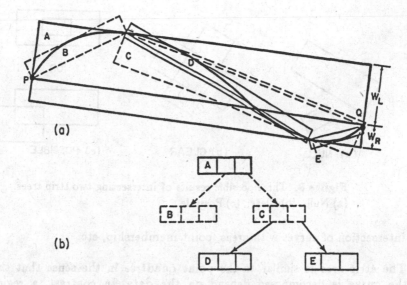

Figure 7. A curve between points P and Q. (a) Its decomposition into strips; and (b) the corresponding strip tree.

associated with the root, A in this example, corresponds to a rectangular strip, that encloses the curve, whose sides are parallel to the line joining the endpoints of the curve (i.e., P and Q). The curve is then partitioned in two at one of the locations where it touches the bounding rectangle. Each subcurve is then surrounded by a bounding rectangle and the partitioning process is applied recursively. This process stops when the width of each strip is less than a predetermined value. The strip tree is implemented as a binary tree (Figure 7b) where each node contains eight fields. Four fields contain the x and y coordinates of the endpoints, two fields contain pointers to the two sons of the node, and two fields contain information about the width of the strip (i.e., W_L and W_R in Figure 7a).

Figure 7 is a relatively simple example. In order to be able to cope with more complex curves, the notion of a strip tree must be extended. In particular, closed curves and curves that extend past their endpoints require some special treatment. The general idea is that these curves are enclosed by rectangles which are split into two rectangular strips and from now on the strip tree is used as before. For a related approach that does not require these extensions, see the arc tree of Günther [Günt87]. Its subdivision rule consists of a regular decomposition of a curve based on its length.

Like point and region quadtrees, strip trees are useful in applications that involve search and set operations. For example, suppose we wish to determine whether a road crosses a river. Using a strip tree representation for these features, answering this query means basically performing an intersection of the corresponding strip trees. Three cases are possible as is shown in Figure 8. Figures 8a and 8b correspond to the answers NO and YES respectively while Figure 8c requires us to descend further down the strip tree. Notice the distinction between the task of detecting the possibility of an intersection and the task of computing the actual intersection, if one exists. The strip tree is well suited to the former task. Other operations that can be performed efficiently by using the strip tree data structure include the computation of the length of a curve, areas of closed

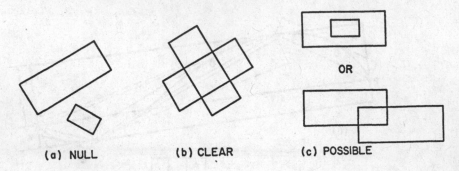

(a) NULL   (b) CLEAR   (c) POSSIBLE

Figure 8. Three possible results of intersecting two strip trees.
(a) Null. (b) Clear. (c) Possible.

curves, intersection of curves with areas, point membership, etc.

The strip tree is similar to the point quadtree in the sense that the points at which the curve is decomposed depend on the data. In contrast, a region quadtree approach has fixed decomposition points. Similarly, strip tree methods approximate curvilinear data with rectangles while methods based on the region-quadtree achieve analogous results by use of a collection of disjoint squares having sides of length power of two. In the following we discuss a number of adaptations of the region quadtree for representing curvilinear data.

The *edge quadtree* [Shne81b, Warn69] is an attempt to store linear feature information (e.g., curves) for an image (binary and gray-scale) in a manner analogous to that used for storing region information. A region containing a linear feature or part thereof is subdivided into four squares repeatedly until a square is obtained that contains a single curve that can be approximated by a single straight line (e.g., Figure 9 where the maximum level of decomposition is 4). Each leaf node contains the following

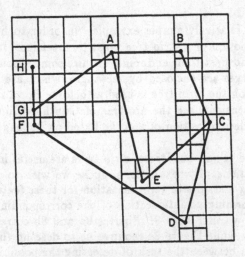

Figure 9. An edge quadtree.

information about the edge passing through it: magnitude (i.e., 1 in the case of a binary image or the intensity in case it is a gray-scale image), direction, intercept, and a directional error term (i.e., the error induced by approximating the curve by a straight line using a measure such as least squares). If an edge terminates within a node, then a special flag is set and the intercept denotes the point at which the edge terminates. Applying this process leads to quadtrees in which long edges are represented by large leaves or a sequence of large leaves. However, small leaves are required in the vicinity of corners or intersecting edges. Of course, many leaves will contain no edge information at all.

The PM quadtree family [Same85, Nels86] (see also edge-EXCELL [Tamm81]) represents an attempt to overcome some of the problems associated with the edge quadtree in the representation of collections of polygons (termed *polygonal maps*). In particular, the edge quadtree is an approximation because vertices are represented by pixels. Moreover, it is difficult to detect the presence of a vertex when more than five line segments meet. There are a number of variants of the PM quadtree. These variants are either vertex-based or edge-based. They are all built by applying the principle of repeatedly breaking up the collection of vertices and edges (forming the polygonal map) until obtaining a subset that is sufficiently simple so that it can be organized by some other data structure.

The PM quadtrees of Samet and Webber [Same85] are vertex-based. We illustrate the PM_1 quadtree. It is based on a decomposition rule stipulating that partitioning occurs as long as a block contains more than one line segment unless the line segments are all incident at the same vertex which is also in the same block (e.g., Figure 10).

Samet, Shaffer, and Webber [Same87] show how to compute the maximum depth of the PM_1 quadtree for a polygonal map in a limited, but typical, environment. They

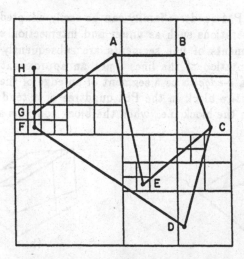

Figure 10. Example PM_1 quadtree.

consider a polygonal map whose vertices are drawn from a grid (say $2^n \times 2^n$), and do not permit edges to intersect at points other than the grid points (i.e., vertices). In such a case, the depth of any leaf node is bounded from above by $4n+1$. This enables a determination of the maximum amount of storage that will be necessary for each node.

A similar representation has been devised for three-dimensional images [Ayal85, Carl85, Fuji85, Hunt81, Nava86, Quin82, Tamm81, Vand84]. The decomposition criteria are such that no node contains more than one face, edge, or vertex unless the faces all meet at the same vertex or are adjacent to the same edge. For example, Figure 11b is a PM_1 octree decomposition of the object in Figure 11a. This representation is quite useful since its space requirements for polyhedral objects are significantly smaller than those of a conventional octree.

The PMR quadtree [Nels86] is an edge-based variant of the PM quadtree (see also edge-EXCELL [Tamm81]). It makes use of a probabilistic splitting rule. A node is permitted to contain a variable number of line segments. A line segment is stored in a PMR quadtree by inserting it into the nodes corresponding to all the blocks that it intersects. During this process, the occupancy of each node that is intersected by the line segment is checked to see if the insertion causes it to exceed a predetermined *splitting threshold*. If the splitting threshold is exceeded, then the node's block is split *once*, and only once, into four equal quadrants.

On the other hand, a line segment is deleted from a PMR quadtree by removing it from the nodes corresponding to all the blocks that it intersects. During this process, the occupancy of the node and its siblings is checked to see if the deletion causes the total number of line segments in them to be less than the predetermined splitting threshold. If the splitting threshold exceeds the occupancy of the node and its siblings, then they are merged and the merging process is reapplied to the resulting node and its siblings. Notice the asymmetry between the splitting and merging rules.

Members of the PM quadtree family can be easily adapted to deal with fragments that result from set operations such as union and intersection so that there is no data degradation when fragments of line segments are subsequently recombined. Their use yields an exact representation of the lines - not an approximation. To see how this is achieved, let us define a *q-edge* to be a segment of an edge of the original polygonal map that either spans an entire block in the PM quadtree or extends from a boundary of a block to a vertex within the block (i.e., when the block contains a vertex).

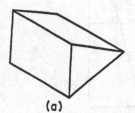   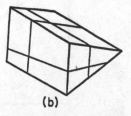

(a)   (b)

Figure 11.   (a) Example three-dimensional object; and (b) its corresponding PM_1 octree.

Each q-edge is represented by a pointer to a record containing the endpoints of the edge of the polygonal map of which the q-edge is a part [Nels86]. The line segment descriptor stored in a node only implies the presence of the corresponding q-edge - it does not mean that the entire line segment is present as a lineal feature. The result is a consistent representation of line fragments since they are stored exactly and, thus, they can be deleted and reinserted without worrying about errors arising from the roundoffs induced by approximating their intersection with the borders of the blocks through which they pass.

7. CONCLUDING REMARKS

The use of hierarchical data structures in image databases enables the focussing of computational resources on the interesting subsets of data. Thus, there is no need to expend work where the payoff is small. Although many of the operations for which they are used can often be performed equally as efficiently, or more so, with other data structures, hierarchical data structures are attractive because of their conceptual clarity and ease of implementation.

When the hierarchical data structures are based on the principle of regular decomposition, we have the added benefit of a spatial index. All features, be they regions, points, rectangles, lines, volumes, etc., can be represented by maps which are in registration. In fact, such a system has been built [Same84b] for representing geographic information. In this case, the quadtree is implemented as a collection of leaf nodes where each leaf node is represented by its locational code. The collection is in turn represented as a B-tree [Come79]. There are leaf nodes corresponding to region, point, and line data.

The disadvantage of quadtree methods is that they are shift sensitive in the sense that their space requirements are dependent on the position of the origin. However, for complicated images the optimal positioning of the origin will usually lead to little improvement in the space requirements. The process of obtaining this optimal positioning is computationally expensive and is usually not worth the effort [Li82].

The fact that we are working in a digitized space may also lead to problems. For example, the rotation operation is not generally invertible. In particular, a rotated square usually cannot be represented accurately by a collection of rectilinear squares. However, when we rotate by 90°, then the rotation is invertible. This problem arises whenever one uses a digitized representation. Thus, it is also common to the array representation.

ACKNOWLEDGMENTS

This work was supported by the National Science Foundation under Grant IRI-8802457. I would like to acknowledge the many valuable discussions that I have had with Michael B. Dillencourt, Randal C. Nelson, Azriel Rosenfeld, Clifford A. Shaffer, Markku Tamminen, and Robert E. Webber.

REFERENCES

1. [Abel83] - D.J. Abel and J.L. Smith, A data structure and algorithm based on a linear key for a rectangle retrieval problem, *Computer Vision, Graphics, and Image Processing* *24*, 1(October 1983), 1-13.

2. [Ayal85] - D. Ayala, P. Brunet, R. Juan, and I. Navazo, Object representation by means of nonminimal division quadtrees and octrees, *ACM Transactions on Graphics 4*, 1(January 1985), 41-59.

3. [Ball81] - D.H. Ballard, Strip trees: A hierarchical representation for curves, *Communications of the ACM 24*, 5(May 1981), 310-321 (see also corrigendum, *Communications of the ACM 25*, 3(March 1982), 213).

4. [Carl85] - I. Carlbom, I. Chakravarty, and D. Vanderschel, A hierarchical data structure for representing the spatial decomposition of 3-D objects, *IEEE Computer Graphics and Applications 5*, 4(April 1985), 24-31.

5. [Come79] - D. Comer, The Ubiquitous B-tree, *ACM Computing Surveys 11*, 2(June 1979), 121-137.

6. [Edel80] - H. Edelsbrunner, Dynamic rectangle intersection searching, Institute for Information Processing Report 47, Technical University of Graz, Graz, Austria, February 1980.

7. [Falo87] - C. Faloutsos, T. Sellis, and N. Roussopoulos, Analysis of object oriented spatial access methods, *Proceedings of the SIGMOD Conference*, San Francisco, May 1987, 426-439.

8. [Fink74] - R.A. Finkel and J.L. Bentley, Quad trees: a data structure for retrieval on composite keys, *Acta Informatica 4*, 1(1974), 1-9.

9. [Free74] - H. Freeman, Computer processing of line-drawing images, *ACM Computing Surveys 6*, 1(March 1974), 57-97.

10. [Fuji85] - K. Fujimura and T.L. Kunii, A hierarchical space indexing method, *Proceedings of Computer Graphics'85*, Tokyo, 1985, T1-4, 1-14.

11. [Garg82] - I. Gargantini, An effective way to represent quadtrees, *Communications of the ACM 25*, 12(December 1982), 905-910.

12. [Günt87] - O. Günther, Efficient structures for geometric data management, Ph.D. dissertation, UCB/ERL M87/77, Electronics Research Laboratory, College of Engineering, University of California at Berkeley, Berkeley, CA, 1987 (Lecture Notes in Computer Science 337, Springer-Verlag, Berlin, 1988).

13. [Gutt84] - A. Guttman, R-trees: a dynamic index structure for spatial searching, *Proceedings of the SIGMOD Conference*, Boston, June 1984, 47-57.

14. [Hinr85] - K. Hinrichs, The grid file system: implementation and case studies of applications, Ph.D. dissertation, Institut fur Informatik, ETH, Zurich, Switzerland, 1985.

15. [Hinr83] - K. Hinrichs and J. Nievergelt, The grid file: a data structure designed to support proximity queries on spatial objects, *Proceedings of the WG'83 (International Workshop on Graphtheoretic Concepts in Computer Science)*, M. Nagl and J. Perl, Eds., Trauner Verlag, Linz, Austria, 1983, 100-113.

16. [Horo76] - S.L. Horowitz and T. Pavlidis, Picture segmentation by a tree traversal algorithm, *Journal of the ACM 23*, 2(April 1976), 368-388.

17. [Hunt78] - G.M. Hunter, Efficient computation and data structures for graphics, Ph.D. dissertation, Department of Electrical Engineering and Computer Science, Princeton University, Princeton, NJ, 1978.

18. [Hunt81] - G.M. Hunter, Geometrees for interactive visualization of geology: an evaluation, System Science Department, Schlumberger-Doll Research, Ridgefield, CT, 1981.

19. [Hunt79] - G.M. Hunter and K. Steiglitz, Operations on images using quad trees, *IEEE Transactions on Pattern Analysis and Machine Intelligence 1*, 2(April 1979), 145-153.

20. [Jack80] - C.L. Jackins and S.L. Tanimoto, Oct-trees and their use in representing three-dimensional objects, *Computer Graphics and Image Processing 14*, 3(November 1980), 249-270.

21. [Kawa80] - E. Kawaguchi and T. Endo, On a method of binary picture representation and its application to data compression, *IEEE Transactions on Pattern Analysis and Machine Intelligence 2*, 1(January 1980), 27-35.

22. [Kede81] - G. Kedem, The Quad-CIF tree: a data structure for hierarchical on-line algorithms, *Proceedings of the Nineteenth Design Automation Conference*, Las Vegas, June 1982, 352-357.

23. [Klin71] - A. Klinger, Patterns and Search Statistics, in *Optimizing Methods in Statistics*, J.S. Rustagi, Ed., Academic Press, New York, 1971, 303-337.

24. [Klin76] - A. Klinger and C.R. Dyer, Experiments in picture representation using regular decomposition, *Computer Graphics and Image Processing 5*, 1(March 1976), 68-105.

25. [Klin79] - A. Klinger and M.L. Rhodes, Organization and access of image data by areas, *IEEE Transactions on Pattern Analysis and Machine Intelligence 1*, 1(January 1979), 50-60.

26. [Li82] - M. Li, W.I. Grosky, and R. Jain, Normalized quadtrees with respect to translations, *Computer Graphics and Image Processing 20*, 1(September 1982), 72-81.

27. [Mats84] - T. Matsuyama, L.V. Hao, and M. Nagao, A file organization for geographic information systems based on spatial proximity, *Computer Vision, Graphics, and Image Processing 26*, 3(June 1984), 303-318.

28. [McCr80] - E.M. McCreight, Efficient algorithms for enumerating intersecting intervals and rectangles, Xerox Palo Alto Research Center Report CSL-80-09, Palo Alto, California, June 1980.

29. [Meag80] - D. Meagher, Octree encoding: a new technique for the representation, The manipulation, and display of arbitrary 3-d objects by computer, Technical Report IPL-TR-80-111, Image Processing Laboratory, Rensselaer Polytechnic Institute, Troy, New York, October 1980.

30. [Meag82] - D. Meagher, Geometric modeling using octree encoding, *Computer Graphics and Image Processing 19*, 2(June 1982), 129-147.

31. [Mort66] - G.M. Morton, A computer oriented geodetic data base and a new technique in file sequencing, IBM Ltd., Ottawa, Canada, 1966.

32. [Nava86] - I. Navazo, Contribució a les tecniques de modelat geòmetric d'objectes polïedrics usant la codificació amb arbres octals, Ph.D. dissertation, Escola Tecnica Superior d'Enginyers Industrials, Department de Metodes Informatics, Universitat Politechnica de Barcelona, Barcelona, Spain, January 1986.

33. [Nels86] - R.C. Nelson and H. Samet, A consistent hierarchical representation for vector data, *Computer Graphics 20*, 4(August 1986), pp. 197-206 (also *Proceedings of the SIGGRAPH'86 Conference*, Dallas, August 1986).

34. [Niev84] - J. Nievergelt, H. Hinterberger, and K.C. Sevcik, The grid file: an adaptable, symmetric multikey file structure, *ACM Transactions on Database Systems 9*, 1(March 1984), 38-71.

35. [Oren82] - J.A. Orenstein, Multidimensional tries used for associative searching, *Information Processing Letters 14*, 4(June 1982), 150-157.

36. [Prep85] - F.P. Preparata and M.I. Shamos, *Computational Geometry: An Introduction*, Springer-Verlag, New York, 1985.

37. [Quin82] - K.M. Quinlan and J.R. Woodwark, A spatially-segmented solids database - justification and design, *Proceedings of CAD 82 Conference*, Butterworth, Guildford, United Kingdom, 1982, 126-132.

38. [Redd78] - D.R. Reddy and S. Rubin, Representation of three-dimensional objects, CMU-CS-78-113, Computer Science Department, Carnegie-Mellon University, Pittsburgh, April 1978.

39. [Same84a] - H. Samet, The quadtree and related hierarchical data structures, *ACM Computing Surveys 16*, 2(June 1984), 187-260.

40. [Same88a] - H. Samet, Hierarchical representations of collections of small rectangles, *ACM Computing Surveys 20*, 4(December 1988), 271-309.

41. [Same89a] - H. Samet, *The Design and Analysis of Spatial Data Structures*, Addison-Wesley, Reading, MA, 1989.

42. [Same89b] - H. Samet, *Applications of Spatial Data Structures: Computer Graphics, Image Processing and GIS*, Addison-Wesley, Reading, MA, 1989.

43. [Same84b] - H. Samet, A. Rosenfeld, C.A. Shaffer, and R.E. Webber, A geographic information system using quadtrees, *Pattern Recognition 17*, 6 (November/December 1984), 647-656.

44. [Same87] - H. Samet, C.A. Shaffer, and R.E. Webber, Digitizing the plane with cells of non-uniform size, *Information Processing Letters 24*, 6(April 1987), 369-375.

45. [Same85] - H. Samet and R.E. Webber, Storing a collection of polygons using quadtrees, *ACM Transactions on Graphics 4*, 3(July 1985), 182-222 (also *Proceedings of Computer Vision and Pattern Recognition 83*, Washington, DC, June 1983, 127-132).

46. [Same89c] - H. Samet and R.E. Webber, A comparison of the space requirements of multi-dimensional quadtree-based file structures, to appear in *The Visual Computer* (also University of Maryland Computer Science TR-1711).

47. [Same88b] - H. Samet and R.E. Webber, Hierarchical data structures and algorithms for computer graphics. Part I. Fundamentals, *IEEE Computer Graphics and Applications 8*, 3(May 1988), 48-68.

48. [Same88c] - H. Samet and R.E. Webber, Hierarchical data structures and algorithms for computer graphics. Part II. Applications, *IEEE Computer Graphics and Applications 8*, 4(July 1988), 59-75.

49. [Sell87] - T. Sellis, N. Roussopoulos, and C. Faloutsos, The R$^+$-tree: a dynamic index for multi-dimensional objects, Computer Science TR-1795, University of Maryland, College Park, MD, February 1987.

50. [Shaf87] - C.A. Shaffer and H. Samet, Optimal quadtree construction algorithms, *Computer Vision, Graphics, and Image Processing 37*, 3(March 1987), 402-419.

51. [Shne81a] - M. Shneier, Calculations of geometric properties using quadtrees, *Computer Graphics and Image Processing 16*, 3(July 1981), 296-302.

52. [Shne81b] - M. Shneier, Two hierarchical linear feature representations: edge pyramids and edge quadtrees, *Computer Graphics and Image Processing 17*, 3(November 1981), 211-224.

53. [Tamm81] - M. Tamminen, The EXCELL method for efficient geometric access to data, *Acta Polytechnica Scandinavica*, Mathematics and Computer Science Series No. 34, Helsinki, 1981.

54. [Tani75] - S. Tanimoto and T. Pavlidis, A hierarchical data structure for picture processing, *Computer Graphics and Image Processing 4*, 2(June 1975), 104-119.

55. [Vand84] - D.J. Vanderschel, Divided leaf octal trees, Research Note, Schlumberger-Doll Research, Ridgefield, CT, March 1984.

56. [Warn69] - J.L. Warnock, A hidden surface algorithm for computer generated half tone pictures, Computer Science Department TR 4-15, University of Utah, Salt Lake City, June 1969.

Distributed Quadtree Processing

C. H. Chien and T. Kanade

School of Computer Science
Carnegie-Mellon University
Pittsburgh, PA 15213

Abstract

Quadtrees have been widely used in computer vision, spatial database, and related area due to their compactness and regularity. It has long been claimed that quadtree related algorithms are suitable for parallel and distributed implementation, but only little work has been done to justify this claim. The simple input partitioning method used in low level image processing could not be equally applied to distributed quadtree processing since it suffers the problem of load imbalance. Load balancing is one of the most crucial issues in distributed processing. In the context of distributed quadtree processing, it appears at various stages of processing in different forms; each requires its own solutions. The diversity in approaches to load balancing is further multiplied by the differences in the characteristics of types of data represented by, and spatial operations performed on quadtrees. In this paper, we propose a new approach to distributed quadtree processing using a task queue mechanism. We discuss dynamic load balancing and related issues in the context of distributed quadtree processing, and provide possible solutions. The proposed algorithms have been implemented on the Nectar system (currently being developed at Carnegie Mellon). Experimental results are also included in the paper.

1. Introduction

Quadtree is a hierarchical data structure used for compact representation of 2D images. The quadtree and its variants (e.g. octree) have been extensively used in such applications as computer vision, computer graphics, robotics, geometric modeling, and geographic information system. A comprehensive survey on quadtrees and related hierarchical data structures can be found in [11]. Conceptually, a quadtree is generated by dividing an image into quadrants and repeatedly subdividing the quadrants into subquadrants until all the pixels in each quadrant have the same value. In the simplest case where the image is a binary image, each quadrant contains only "1" pixels or only "0" pixels.

The advantages of the quadtree structure are due to its regularity and compactness. The regularity ensures that quadtree algorithms are suitable for parallel and distributed implementation, since quadtree nodes can be distributed over multiprocessors and easily integrated

*This research was supported in part by Defense Advanced Research Projects Agency (DOD) monitored by the Space and Naval Warfare Systems Command under Contract N00039-87-C-0251, and in part by the Office of Naval Research under Contracts N00014-87-K-0385 and N00014-87-K-0533.

together as necessary. The compactness makes the quadtree as the natural choice for many applications such as in a geographic information system and allows data (in quadtree forms) to be dynamically redistributed among multiprocessors.

While it has long been claimed that the quadtree and octree structures are suitable for parallel implementation, very little work has been done to justify this claim. Lo et. al. [8] have implemented several octree algorithms on four IBM PCs interconnected by an Ethernet local area network. In their work, a simple approach was taken which partitioned the (3D) image space into 8 octants and mapped two octants onto each IBM PC. This approach suffers load imbalance since data of interest contained in an image are usually not uniformly distributed in the image space. To solve this problem, Wynn [14] proposed an approach which does not assign specific quadrants to processors. Instead, quadrants are dynamically assigned to idle processors after each decomposition. Consequently, this approach can be applied to any number of processors, and nearly all processors are in use until the entire quadtree is generated. However, there are disadvantages of using this approach:

- quadtree nodes are scattered among the processors,
- data transfer is initiated for each decomposition regardless of the amount of data, and
- the approach is not suitable for generating region quadtrees since the distribution pattern of input data is not known *a priori*.

We have also developed parallel algorithms for generating region quadtrees and for generating feature quadtrees. Our algorithms have been designed by taking into consideration the characteristics of each type of data items. The notion of task queue is employed for task allocation, and several data partitioning strategies have been investigated, especially for those cases with spatial proximity constraints (e.g. operations involving neighbor finding). We have simulated these algorithms on a Sun-3, and implemented some algorithms on Nectar, a fiber-optic based network backplane for heterogeneous multicomputers currently being developed at Carnegie Mellon. In this paper, our presentation will focus on the parallel (region) quadtree generation algorithm and related issues on load balancing and data migration. Other parallel algorithms for generating feature quadtrees with or without spatial proximity constraints will be reported in a later paper [3].

Dynamic data migration is required in cases where

- spatial operations change, which in turns changes the distribution pattern of data of interest, and
- binary operations are applied to two quadtrees with different distribution patterns.

It is interested to note that the task queue model once again plays a key role in dynamic data migration as will be discussed in 5.2.

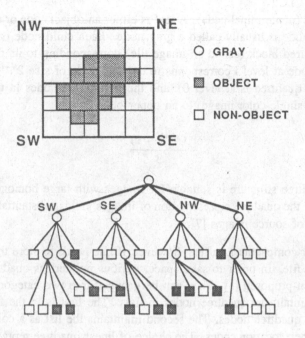

Figure 1: An image and its quadtree representation

The remainder of this paper is organized as follows. Section 2 provides an overview of the quadtree structure and (sequential) quadtree generation algorithms. Section 3 gives a brief description of the Nectar system. A parallel version of the region quadtree generation algorithm is presented in Section 4, followed by a discussion of dynamic data migration in Section 5. Experimental results are also shown after the description of each algorithm. The paper is concluded in Section 6, along with a few word about future work.

2. Quadtrees

In this section we shall give a brief review of the quadtree structure and a quadtree generation algorithm. Parallel algorithms for generating quadtrees will be presented in sections 4.

2.1. The quadtree structure

Shown in Figure 1 is an example of an image and its (region) quadtree. The root of the quadtree corresponds to the entire image. A quadtree node either is a leaf (terminal node) or has four child nodes (nonterminal node). A leaf is either an object node or a non-object node, and a nonterminal node is usually called a gray node. Each child node is associated with a quadrant of the squared block (called an image tile) corresponding to its parent node. For a $2^N \times 2^N$ image, a node at level i corresponds to an image tile of size $2^{N-i} \times 2^{N-i}$ (assuming that the root of the quadtree is at level 0), and the number of nodes in the quadtree could range from 1 (for a single-color image) to an upper bound

$$\frac{(4^{N+1} - 1)}{3}$$

In general, the quadtree structure is suitable for images with large homogeneous regions. It has been shown that the quadtree representation of images yields substantial data compression ratio over a variety of source images [7].

The advantage of compactness suffers, however, if one needs to store the quadtree and its pointers into a disk file. In order to save space, various pointerless quadtrees (called linear quadtrees) have been proposed [5]. They can be grouped into two categories. Both types of linear quadtrees maintain the quadtree nodes in lists. The first is in the form of a preorder tree traversal of the quadtree nodes. The second maintains the list as a collection of the leaf nodes encoded by their location codes. The choice of linear quadtree representations depends on the amount of information stored in each quadtree node. A detailed discussion can be found in [13].

A linear quadtree node is composed of two fields: the *address* filed, and the *value* field. The value field contains either the *color* of the node in a region quadtree or an index to a feature list which stores the properties of the features the quadtree represents. The address field usually contains the node's Morton code address [9]. The Morton code is obtained by bit-interleaving the x and y coordinate of the upper left corner of the tile corresponding to the node. It is also possible to encode the *depth* information, along with the node's Morton code address into the address field [13].

To facilitate the storage and manipulation, linear quadtree nodes are usually packed into blocks (of 1024 bytes, for instance), which are then organized as a B-tree [4]. The block organization of linear quadtrees is especially suitable for moving quadtree nodes over the network (during data migration) since no additional data conversion is required before data transfer as necessary in the pointer-based quadtree case.

2.2. The quadtree generation algorithm

As mentioned in the introduction, a quadtree is usually generated by a recursive dividing and subdividing algorithm [2]. In the case of region quadtree, an underlying assumption of this generation technique is the availability of a 2D (binary) array description of the image. In some cases where images are large, it may be more practical to store the images as disk files, and to generate the quadtree directly from the raster-scan image. This is also true in the case of distributed quadtree generation where image tiles are distributed to each processor in raster order and it may be more efficient for a processor to start processing right after receiving certain amount of image data.

In the past, Samet et. al. [10] proposed an algorithm for converting a raster image to a quadtree by inserting individually each pixel of the image into the quadtree in raster order, and merging those sibling nodes of the same colors. Their experimental results show that the timings are nearly identical for raster images with the same number of pixels (due to the same number of node inserts), regardless of the number of nodes in the quadtree.

More recently, they proposed a more efficient algorithm using the notion of active nodes [12]. A node is *active* if at least one, but not all, pixel covered by the node has been processed. Their algorithm generates a quadtree by

1. processing the image in raster-scan (top to bottom, left to right) order,
2. inserting the largest node for which the current pixel is the first (upper leftmost) pixel, and
3. keeping track of all the active nodes to avoid unnecessary node inserting and thus avoid the necessity of merging.

In this way, the quadtree generation algorithm would at most make a single insertion for each node in the quadtree. The cost of this optimization is the additional storage for maintaining a list of active nodes. It has been shown that given a $2^N \times 2^N$ image, an upper bound on the number of active nodes is $2^N - 1$ [12]. This is negligible, especially when N is large.

Our parallel quadtree generation algorithm is based on this efficient algorithm. Before the description of the parallel algorithm, we shall first give a brief overview of the Nectar system on which the parallel algorithm has been implemented.

3. The Nectar System

The Nectar system is a high speed network backplane for heterogeneous multicomputers. It consists of HUB-net and a set of CABs (Communication Acceleration Boards) as illustrated in Figure 2. The HUB-net connects a number of existing systems called "nodes". It is made of fiber optic lines and one or more HUBs. A HUB is a crossbar switch with a flexible datalink protocol implemented in hardware. A CAB is a RISC-base processor serving three functions: (1) it implements higher-level network protocols, (2) it provides the interface between the HUB-net and the nodes, and (3) it off-loads application tasks from nodes whenever appropriate. Every CAB is connected to a HUB via a pair of fiber optic lines carrying signals in opposite directions. The fiber optic network offers an order of magnitude improvement in bandwidth over commonly available local area network (for the prototype currently in operation, the effective bandwidth per fiber line is 100 Mbits/sec). More importantly, the use of crossbar switches substantially reduces network contention.

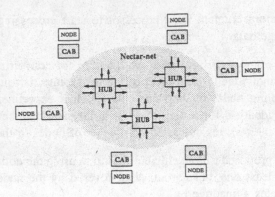

Figure 2: Nectar system overview

The Nectar software architecture targets two areas of inefficiency in current networking implementations: (1) excessive costs due to context switching and data copying, and (2) burden on the node due to interrupt handling, header processing (for each packet) as well as the overhead incurred by higher level protocols. Nectar restructures the way applications communicate. User processes have direct access to a high-level network interface mapped into their address spaces. Communication overhead on the node is substantially reduced for three reasons: (1) no system calls are required during communication, (2) protocol processing is off-loaded to the network interface, and (3) interrupts are required only for high-level events in which the application is interested such as delivery of complete messages.

Nectarine is a low-level programming interface to Nectar that gives the application programmer full access to the Nectar hardware and low-level software. It is implemented as a run-time package that provides a procedure-call interface to the CAB services (including communication); the same interface is available to processes on the node and on the CAB. At the Nectarine level, programmers can specify messages as a series of consecutive byte areas located in any memory in the Nectar system.

A prototype Nectar system has been built and operational at Carnegie Mellon since November 1988. It consists of four CABs (connected to three Suns and one Warp) and two HUBs. Several applications have been implemented on the prototype Nectar system, including

- a general divide and conquer kernel for parallel processing,
- VLSI floor planning using a technique known as simulated annealing [6], and
- a prototype geographics information system based on the QUILT system developed at University of Maryland [13] and parallel algorithms described in this paper.

4. Parallel region quadtree generation

Many naive algorithms for parallel image processing usually partition images into as many subimages (of the same size) as the number of processors. In the context of quadtree generation, an image may only be partitioned into 2^N by 2^N image tiles (given NP processors and assuming that one image tile is processed by each processor), where

$$2^N \times 2^N \leq NP < 2^{N+1} \times 2^{N+1}$$

Given 7 processors, only 4 processors will be used, each of which processes one quarter of the entire image, and the remaining three processors are idle all the time. The problem of load imbalance is further deteriorated by the fact that the data of interset (or the complexity of an image) is in general not uniformly distributed in the image space. In the worst case, if all the data of interest is contained in one quarter of the image, then all but one processor will be idle. Load imbalance has been the known problem for many naive algorithms.

Alternatively, one could dynamically assign specific quadrants to processors as mentioned in the introduction. This approach usually yields very good load balance since all processors are in use most of the time. However, this approach is not practical and is inefficient for generating a quadtree from an images due to the following arguments.

In order to determine if a decomposition of a quadrant is necessary, one needs to check each pixel value in the quadrant. Should a decomposition be necessary, about three subquadrants of the current quadrant need to be transferred to other processors. In this case, all pixel values of these three quadrants will be checked again to see if further decomposition is required. In the worse case, each pixel might be accessed N times, where N is the depth of the quadtree.

A more efficient algorithm could limit the pixel-access to one for each pixel. However, it is still possible that some pixels might be moved among processors for each level of decomposition. Moreover, quadtree nodes are scattered among processors, and thus significant overhead is required for merging partial quadtrees or for data migration. For instance, if an intersection operation is to be applied to two quadtrees which have different distribution patterns, it is necessary to redistribute at least one quadtree such that corresponding subtrees of the two quadtrees are in the same processor before intersection could be performed. If quadtree nodes are scattered among processors, the operation for data migration will be very expensive.

4.1. A task queue algorithm

In this section, we present a parallel algorithm for generating linear quadtrees in a distributed environment which contains a controller and some (logical) processors. In real implementation, the controller and any number of logical processors could be in the same physical processor. The controller assigns tasks to logical processors by distributing image tiles to idle processors, and keeps track of data distribution. Each processor subsequently generates (or modifies) a partial quadtree based on an image tile it received from the controller, and reports back to the controller the completion of current task assignment. In the following, we describe the parallel algorithm for generating region quadtrees.

The heart of the parallel region quadtree generation algorithm is a task queue based on which tasks for generating partial quadtrees for image tiles are distributed to processors. At the outset, the controller divides the image into $B = 2^M \times 2^M$ image tiles; each of which is of size $2^{N-M} \times 2^{N-M}$, where M is a predefined number and is application dependent. In principle, B should be large enough (compared with the number of available processors NP) to warrant good load balance, but not so large as to increase much overhead for keeping track of the locations of partial quadtrees (in terms of both memory requirement and processing time). After the image is divided, each of the first NP image tiles are distributed to one logical processor. The remaining image tiles are put into a task queue, and subsequently distributed to the logical processor which has completed the current assignment. Partial quadtrees generated from image tiles are stored in each processor in linear quadtree forms for further processing. The advantages of this algorithm are

- the task queue algorithm is simple and little overhead is required for keeping track of the locations of tasks processing individual image tiles, and therefore

- good load balancing could be achieved, especially if M is large,

- during the quadtree generation, the data transfer in the network is bounded by the number of pixels in the image, and

- the linear quadtree structure simplifies the transfer of partial quadtrees among processors during quadtree integration or data migration, since no additional data conversion is required before data transfer as necessary in the pointer-based quadtree case.

4.2. Experimental results

We have implemented this algorithm on the prototype Nectar system. Since the prototype system consists of only four (processor) nodes and the Event kernel of the Nectar system has not yet completed at the time of implementation, we also simulated this algorithm on a Sun-3 for performance analysis. We have applied the parallel algorithm to an image of a flood plain shown in Figure 3. The size of the image is 450×400 (1 byte per pixel). Conceptually, the image is extended to 512×512, since a quadtree is corresponding to a $2^N \times 2^N$ images. The extended images is then divided into sixteen 128×128 image tiles that were distributed to four processors for generating partial quadtrees. In order to obtain more reliable estimation of processing time, the quadtree generation program was applied to each image tile ten times, and the average processing time is taken as the estimated time for generating partial quadtree for that image tile. The communication time was estimated based on the following assumptions (that are the (estimated) latency and bandwidth of the prototype Nectar system):

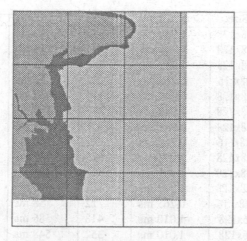

Figure 3: The image of a flood plain

- the overhead for initiating data distribution and for reporting task completion is $15\mu s$,
- the communication bandwidth is about 10^7 bytes per second, and
- the size of each packet is limited to 960 bytes (excluding headers).

For a 128×128 image tile, 7 rows (896 bytes) could be packed into one message, and thus totally 19 messages (one of which is of length 256 bytes) need to be transferred. One additional message is required for reporting the completion of the current task. As a result, the estimated communication time involved in processing one 128×128 image tile is about $1.923ms$, that is much less than the processing time (which is in the order of seconds). Since the size of the original image is 450×400, in some cases only a smaller subimage (e.g. 128×16) needs to be transferred to a processor. The communication time for transferring subimages of smaller sizes can be obtained accordingly and are listed in Table 1.

Also listed in the table are sizes of subimage (before expansion), numbers of nodes in the partial quadtree, time for generating a partial quadtree for each tile, and the processor (in column 'Proc') where the partial quadtree was generated. The load distribution of quadtree generation using the task queue algorithm on four processors is shown in Figure 4. In the figure, each quadrant corresponds to a processor. The image tiles contained in each quadrant were sent to the corresponding processor by the controller. The left bottom quadrant contains only three image tiles since two of the images tiles sent to the corresponding processor are relatively more complex and require more time for processing. The advantage of using the task queue algorithm is clearly demonstrated in Table 2 which shows the comparison of processing time and nodes distribution using the task queue algorithm and a naive algorithm

Tile	Size	Comm. time	#Nodes	Proc. Time	Proc.
0	128x128	1.947 ms	235	442 ms	1
1	128x128	1.947 ms	904	810 ms	2
2	128x128	1.947 ms	373	492 ms	3
3	128x 16	0.265 ms	22	56 ms	4
4	128x128	1.947 ms	1114	936 ms	4
5	128x128	1.947 ms	217	430 ms	1
6	128x128	1.947 ms	1	354 ms	3
7	128x 16	0.265 ms	22	68 ms	2
8	128x128	1.947 ms	973	920 ms	3
9	128x128	1.947 ms	322	486 ms	1
10	128x128	1.947 ms	1	340 ms	2
11	128x 16	0.265 ms	22	58 ms	4
12	66x128	1.010 ms	418	586 ms	4
13	66x128	1.010 ms	352	548 ms	2
14	66x128	1.010 ms	190	464 ms	1
15	66x 16	0.151 ms	40	54 ms	4

Table 1: Statistics of quadtree generation using the task queue algorithm

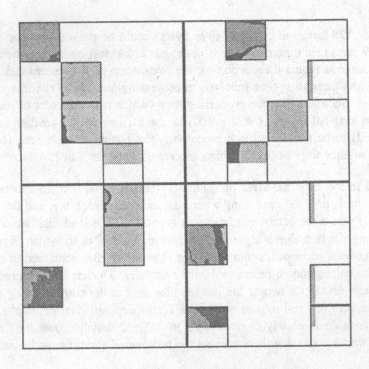

Figure 4: The load distribution of quadtree generation using the task queue algorithm

Proc	Proc. time	#Nodes	Proc	Proc. time	#Nodes
Task queue			Simple Partitioning		
1	1.822 sec	964	1	2.618 sec	2470
2	1.766 sec	1279	2	0.970 sec	418
3	1.766 sec	1347	3	2.540 sec	2065
4	1.609 sec	1616	4	0.916 sec	253

Table 2: Performance comparison of the two algorithms

(that partitions the image into four subimages).

It can be observed from Table 2 that the computation load and data have not been uniformly distributed among processors even with the task queue algorithm. This is due to the fact that there are three image tiles which require much more processing time for processing and generate a lot more quadtree nodes than others. Under this situation, good load balance is difficult to achieve with a small number of image tiles (four in average) distributed to each processor. There are two approaches to obtain better load balance. In one approach, one could arrange the order for processing tiles according to the number of nodes or processing time. This is not possible in generating quadtrees from images since we do not have *a priori* knowledge about the distribution of significant information (i.e. data of interest). Alternatively, one could divide an image into more tiles (e.g. 16 × 16) to smooth out the variation in the amount of significant information contained in each tile.

It is obvious that the larger the size of M (i.e. the level of decomposition) is, the better load balancing could be obtained. However, the improvement in load balancing is achieved not without penalty. First of all, bookkeeping for tracking task/data distribution in the controller will increase with M. Secondly, the communication overhead during task assignment becomes significant as M increases. Lastly, the overhead in determining the data migration pattern (as will be discussed later) will also increase.

It is desirable to find the optimal level for decomposition. It is difficult if not impossible, however, to find the optimal M, since the optimal M depends on the complexity of the image, the quadtree generation algorithm, the underlying data storage format for (partial) quadtrees, the communication overhead (for invoking each communication primitive) and the processing speed of each processor. In order to see the relationship between the decomposition levels and load balancing, we have run some experiments as described below.

In the experiment, we tried different levels of decomposition which divide the 512 × 512 1-byte image into 4×4, 8×8, and 16×16 subimages, respectively. The available processors were varied from 4 to 32. The communication time was estimated based on the same assumptions as described earlier. Under these assumptions, the communication time for transferring one subimage and for reporting task completion is 1.947*ms*, 0.500*ms*, and 0.147*ms* for a 1/16, a 1/64 and a 1/256 subimage, respectively.

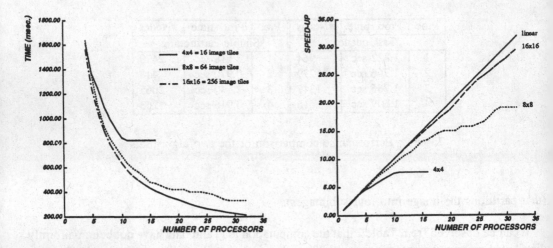

Figure 5: Proc. time/speed-up *v.s.* #processors and decomposition-levels

The plot of processing time *vs* number of processors are illustrated in Figure 5, where solid, dottted, and curved corresponding to 4×4, 8×8, and 16×16 decomposition, respectively. The solid curve is bounded at $820ms$, since one image tile requires $820ms$ for generating the corresponding partial quadtree regardless of the number of available processors. This lower bound shows a necessity for further decomposition, and is relieved at 8×8 decomposition, in which another lower bound at about $330ms$ is observed. A further decomposition into 16×16 image tiles yields a curve in the plot close to a hyperbolic curve. Another lower bound may be observed at about $30ms$. (We didn't pursue this lower bound since the resolution of our software clock on a Sun-3 is $20ms$).

Also shown in Figure 5 is the corresponding speed-up curve. We have also implemented the parallel region quadtree generation algorithm on the hardware prototype of the Nectar [1]. We plan to repeat the same performance analysis discussed in this section on the Nectar.

5. Dynamic load balancing

5.1. Load Balancing

Load balancing is one of the most crucial issues in distributed processing. To achieve load balance, the data should be distributed such that processing time in different processors are almost the same. For a single operation, load balancing may be carried out either by dividing the data items equally among processors, or using a task queue algorithm during data conversion (as in the quadtree generation case). The load balancing problem is more complicated for a sequence of operations. This is due to (1) data distribution pattern usually changes from one operation to another, (2) the data items has been converted to another type, or (3) different operations are applied to various subsets of data items. For example, given an image, we may want to

1. convert the image into a multi-valued image using multi-valued thresholding,

2. generate the quadtree from the thresholded image,

3. compute area of each region, find regions with areas greater than a certain threshold,

4. mark quadtree nodes that are within 5 pixels range of these regions (called a WITHIN operation) [13],

5. display these marked quadtree nodes.

In order to obtain good load balance at each stage, we need to

1. partition the image into subimages of equal size for thresholding,

2. using a task queue algorithm for generating the quadtree,

3. partition the quadtree into subtrees with equal number of nodes for computing area and select those regions of which the areas are greater than the preset threshold,

4. partition the quadtree into subtrees with the same number of nodes associated with regions of interest (or using a task queue algorithm) for the WITHIN operation, and

5. partition the quadtree obtained from the WITHIN operation into subtrees of equal size, or partition the output image into subimage of equal size, or using a task queue algorithm for the quadtree to raster conversion.

It can be seen that no single data distribution pattern is suitable for all operations. In order to achieve the optimal load balancing for each individual operation, the data should be redistributed from one operation to another. However, data migration is not free even with low-latency, high bandwidth communication network such as the Nectar [1]. Furthermore, determining how to redistribute data to obtain optimal load balance is usually an expensive operations. The main purpose of load balancing is to reduce the processing time by keeping all the processors busy most of the time. It would make no sense if determining data redistribution pattern takes a lot of computation time. The implication of this argument is two-fold:

- for simple operations such as area computation, it is not worth redistributing data, and
- for more complicated operations, only simple methods for determining redistribution pattern are acceptable.

However, to determine whether or not data migration is necessary is not an easy task. It deserves a full-length paper's discussion, and is out of the scope of this paper. The basic rule is that the decision should be made based on the current data distribution and the complexity (measured in processing time) of the next operation.

In general, load balancing could be roughly categorized into two types; one with a spatial proximity constraint and the other without the constraint. In the next section, we shall present algorithms for determining data distribution pattern without considering spatial proximity. Other algorithms with the spatial proximity constraint could be found in [3].

5.2. Dynamic Data migration

In this section, we discuss a simple form of dynamic data migration without spatial constraints. The problem is formulated as follows. Assuming that the current data distribution is $\{(V_{i1}, \ldots, V_{in_i}) | 1 \leq i \leq m\}$, where m is the number of processors, n_i the number of data items in processor i, and V_{ij} the value of the jth item in processor i. We wish to have data redistributed such that the sum of the data items in each processor are more or less equal. Solving for the optimal data distribution is out of the question since the number of searches required is

$$\binom{N}{m} \cdot (N - m)^m$$

where N is the total number of data items and $\binom{N}{m}$ indicates the number of different combinations of N different data items, m at a time, without repetition.

We present two algorithms in this section. Note that a data item in the following description refers to a partial quadtree associated with an image tile, and the value of a data item is the number of quadtree nodes in the partial quadtree. The principle of the first algorithm is to move data items to other processors only when necessary. The algorithm as follows:

Controller

1. receive local data distribution pattern (i.e. the sizes of data items and their sum) from each processor, and associate it with one virtual processor,

2. compute the average of the sums obtained in step 1,

3. for those virtual processors with the sum greater than the average value, select a subset of data items such that the sum of data items in this subset is close to the average, and put the remaining data items into a public pool,

4. for those virtual processors with the sum less than the average value, choose some data items from the public pool (and possibly relinquish some of their data items) such that the new sum is close to the average,

5. repeat steps 2 and 3 as necessary, and

Original Distribution				Final Distribution			
P1 235	P1 904	P2 373	P2 22	P4 *	P2 *	P4 *	P2
P1 1114	P1 217	P2 1	P2 22	P1	P1	P2	P2
P3 973	P3 322	P4 1	P4 22	P3	P3	P4	P4
P3 418	P3 352	P4 190	P4 40	P4 *	P2 *	P4	P4

Original Distribution				Final Distribution			
P1 235	P2 904	P3 373	P4 22	P1	P2	P3	P4
P4 1114	P1 217	P3 1	P2 22	P4	P1	P3	P2
P3 973	P1 322	P2 1	P4 22	P3	P1	P2	P4
P4 418	P2 352	P1 190	P4 40	P1 *	P2	P1	P4

Example-1   Example-2

Pn: locations of image tiles   '*' indicates data migration

Table 3: Data distribution patterns before/after data migration using the first algorithm

	Example-1			Example-2	
	Before/After	Sent/Received		Before/After	Sent/Receive
P1	2470/1331	1139/ 0	P1	964/1382	0/418
P2	418/1301	373/1256	P2	1279/1280	0/ 1
P3	2065/1295	770/ 0	P3	1347/1346	1/ 0
P4	253/1279	0/1026	P4	1616/1198	418/ 0

Table 4: Numbers of nodes in each processor before/after data migration, and amounts of related data transfer

6. initiate data migration among processors based on the data redistribution pattern obtained in steps 2 through 4.

Other Processors

1. determine the local data distribution pattern, report it to the controller, and wait for instructions for data migration, and

2. receive instructions for data migration, and send/receive data to other processors as instructed.

For instance, in Example 1 of Table 3, there are four data items in each processor in the original distribution. The average is 1302. The sum of data items in processor 1 is 2470 which is greater than the average. Hence, virtual processor 1 selects data items of size 1114 and of size 217 (of which the sum is 1331) and put the remaining two data items into the public pool. One of these two data items (the one of size 235) in the public pool is later chosen by virtual processor 4, and therefore the controller issue an instruction to processor 1 to send data item of size 235 to processor 4. The results of applying this algorithm to two examples are illustrated in Table 3, which shows the data distribution patterns before and after data migration. 'Pn' in the table indicates the associated tile (and its partial quadtree) is located in processor 'n' and the number below each 'Pn' is the number of nodes in the corresponding partial quadtree. These numbers are removed in the final distribution patterns for clarity. The amount of related data transfer is listed in Table 4.

Let's define the standard deviation of the sums as the quality of data distribution. In theory, several iterations are required before the standard deviation converges. In practice, we can only afford very few iterations to prevent this operation from taking too much computation time. In the cases where the number of data items is large, one iteration usually yields very good load balancing. However, selecting a subset from a large of data items is expensive. It is necessary to pre-specify a threshold value so that the selecting process could be terminated when the difference between the average and the sum of a selected subset is within the pre-specified threshold value. The advantage of this approach is that the amount of data transfer is minimized, and the disadvantage is the time-consuming process in selecting subsets.

The second algorithm is a variation of the task queue algorithm described in the previous section. It is more efficient and usually yields very good load balance. The only disadvantage is that it requires more data transfer among processors, which is not really a problem in the Nectar system. The algorithm is as follows.

Controller:

1. receive local data distribution pattern (size information of data items) from each processor,

2. sort all the sizes of data items in a decreasing order, and

3. subsequently assign the first data item in the sorted data list to the virtual processor that has minimum partial sum,

4. associate each virtual processor with a processor such that the amount of data to be sent or received is as small as possible, and

5. initiate data migration among processors based on the data migration pattern obtained in steps 2 through 4.

Other Processors: the same as in the previous algorithm.

A cost function $C(i,j)$ is defined as amount of data transfer (the number of quadtree nodes to be sent and to be received) if virtual processor i is associated with (logical) processor j. Table 5 shows the assignment of data items to virtual processors along with the cost of

Original Distribution			
P1	P1	P2	P2
235	904	373	22
P1	P1	P2	P2
1114	217	1	22
P3	P3	P4	P4
973	322	1	22
P3	P3	P4	P4
418	352	190	40

Assignment			
VP2	VP3	VP4	VP2
VP1	VP1	VP3	VP3
VP2	VP3	VP2	VP3
VP4	VP4	VP4	VP2

Costs of mapping			
	P1	P2	P3	P4
VP1	1139	1749	3396	1584
VP2	3271	1645	1390	1442
VP3	1933	1643	2692	1480
VP4	3803	1005	1858	1206

Pn: Processor n;
VPn: Virtual Processor n

sub-optimal mapping:
VP4 -> P2
VP1 -> P1
VP2 -> P3
VP3 -> P4

Table 5: Assignment of data to virtual processors and costs of mapping

various association, 'VPn' and 'Pn' indicate virtual processor 'n' and logical processor 'n', respectively. Since Cost(4,2) has the minimum value virtual processor 4 is associated with logical processor 2. Virtual processors 1, 2, 3 are associated with logical processors 1, 3, 4, respectively. Results of applying this algorithm to the two examples are listed in Table 6. The numbers of quadtree nodes in each processor before and after data migration, the number of quadtree nodes to be sent and received are listed in Table 7.

It can be observed from Tables 4 and 7 that

- compared with the previous approach

  - equally good or better load balance is obtained, and
  - the amount of data migration is much larger

- some data migration may be avoided by using a better algorithm; for instances,

  - in Example 1, processor 3 sent 1 quadtree node to processors 1 and 2; this can be avoided by initiating data transfer only when the amount of data to be transferred is greater than some threshold,
  - in Example 2, processor 2 sent 22 nodes to processor 3 and received 22 nodes from processor 4; this case is rare and it is not worth to increase the complexity of the algorithm,

It can also be noted that the amount of data migration among processors in Example 2 is still large even though the initial data distribution is somewhat balanced (e.g. data amount in

Original Distribution				Final Distribution			
P1	P1	P2	P2	P3	P4	P2	P3
235	904	373	22	*	*		*
P1	P1	P2	P2	P1	P1	P4	P4
1114	217	1	22			*	*
P3	P3	P4	P4	P3	P4	P3	P4
973	322	1	22		*	*	
P3	P3	P4	P4	P2	P2	P2	P3
418	352	190	40	*	*	*	*

Example-1

Original Distribution				Final Distribution			
P1	P2	P3	P4	P3	P2	P1	P2
235	904	373	22	*		*	*
P4	P1	P3	P2	P4	P4	P3	P3
1114	217	1	22		*		*
P3	P1	P2	P4	P3	P2	P2	P2
973	322	1	22		*		*
P4	P2	P1	P4	P1	P1	P1	P3
418	352	190	40	*	*		*

Example-2

Pn: locations of image tiles   '*' indicates data migration

Table 6: Data distribution patterns before/after data migration using the task queue algorithm

Example-1			Example-2		
	Before/After	Sent/Received		Before/After	Sent/Receive
P1	2740/1331	1139/ 0	P1	964/1333	774/1143
P2	418/1333	45/ 960	P2	1279/1271	374/ 366
P3	2065/1271	1092/ 298	P3	1347/1271	373/ 297
P4	253/1271	231/1249	P4	1616/1331	502/ 217

Table 7: Numbers of nodes in each processor before and after data migration using task queue, and amounts of related data transfer

Threshold = Average/50			Threshold = Average/25		
	Before/After	Sent/Received		Before/After	Sent/Receive
P1	964/1330	425/791	P1	964/1276	190/502
P2	1279/1279	None	P2	1279/1279	None
P3	1347/1293	373/319	P3	1347/1347	None
P4	1616/1304	502/190	P4	1616/1331	502/190

Table 8: Numbers of nodes in each processor before and after data migration, and amounts of related data migration

processors 2 and 3 are close to the average). While the amount of data to be shuffled certainly depends on the initial data distribution, it is not directly related to the degree of initial load balance using the second data migration algorithm. The algorithm could be modified, however, by taking advantage of initial good load balance to reduce the amount of data migration. This is done by excluding certain processors from data migration if the amount of data in them is close to the average. Table 8 tabulates the experimental results using the modified algorithm. In case 1, processor 2 is not involved in data migration since the amount of data in it is within 2% of the average. In case 2, both processors 2 and 3 are not involved since their data amount are within 4% of the average. It is interesting to note that the amount of data exchange is drastically reduced without degrading load balancing. In addition, the time for determining the data migration pattern is also reduced since few processors (and thus fewer data items) are involved in data migration.

6.   Concluding remarks

We have presented in this paper several algorithms related to distributed quadtree processing, including a parallel algorithm for generating region quadtrees, and algorithms for dynamic load balancing and data migration. These algorithms have been implemented on the prototype Nectar system and laid a foundation for a prototype distributed spatial database system. We are currently designing parallel algorithms for feature quadtree generation.

Load balancing is one of the most crucial issues in distributed processing. It appears at various stages of processing in different forms; each of which requires different solution. In this paper, we discuss load balancing in the context of single operations. Within this context, only tasks of the same type are executed concurrently, and data of the same type are transferred over the network at the same time. In more general cases, such as in a distributed spatial database system or an image understanding system, tasks to be processed and data to be transferred may be of different types at any given time. More complex load balancing mechanisms should be designed to handle these cases.

As evident from experimental results, task queue has played a key role in load balancing, and it will be extensively employed in our proposed distributed spatial database system and image understanding architecture. In a distributed spatial database system, for instance, each task in the task queue is an object in the sense of object-oriented programming. Each task consists of an operation and associated data items. The operation could be a sub-operation derived from a query and data items be subset of a data structure obtained through partitioning. Given a query such as "finding the area within 5 pixels range of a certain area", the query may be divided into a sequence of operations, associated with each a subset of data (a subtree, for instance). These tasks will then be put into a task queue for distributed processing. Most of these issues have been studied in this research work. It is expected that the results obtained from this work will lay a solid foundation for our ongoing project on distributed spatial database and image understanding architecture.

References

[1] E. A. Arnould, F. J. Bitz, E. C. Copper, H. T. Kung, and P. A. Steenkiste. The design of nectar: a network backplane for heterogeneous multicomputers. In *Proc. of Third International Conference on Architectural Support for Programming Languages and Operating Systems*, April 1989.

[2] C. H. Chien and J. K. Aggarwal. A normalized quadtree representation. *Computer, Vision, Graphics and Image Processing*, 26:331–346, 1984.

[3] C. H. Chien and L. J. Lin. Data partitioning and task allocation in parallel vision. in preparation.

[4] D. Comer. The ubiquitous b-tree. *ACM Computing Surveys*, 11(2):121–137, June 1979.

[5] I. Gargantini. An effective way to represent quadtrees. *Communication ACM*, 25(12):905–910, Dec 1982.

[6] R. Jayaraman. *Floorplanning by Annealing on a Hypercube Architecture*. Master's thesis, Carnegie Mellon University, 1987.

[7] A. Klinger and C. R. Dyer. Experiments on picture representation using regular decomoposition. *Computer, Graphics and Image Processing*, 5:68–105, 1976.

[8] D. W. Lo, C. H. Chien, and J. K. Aggarwal. Parallel algorithms for spatial operations on octrees. In *Fifteenth Workshop on Applied Imagery Pattern Recognition*, Washington D. C, October 23-24 1986.

[9] G. M. Morton. A computer oriented geodetic data base and a new technique in file sequencing. *IBM Canada*, 1966.

[10] H. Samet. An algorithm for converting rasters to quadtrees. *IEEE Trans. on Pattern Recognition and Machine Intellegence*, 3(1):93–95, 1981.

[11] H. Samet. The quadtree and related hierarchical data structures. *ACM Computing Surveys*, 16(2):187–260, 1984.

[12] C. A. Shaffer and H. Samet. Optimal quadtree construction algorithms. *Computer, Vision, Graphics and Image Processing*, 37(3):402–419, March 1987.

[13] C. A. Shaffer, H. Samet, and R. C. Nelson. *QUILT: A Geographic Information System Based on Quadtrees*. Technical Report CAR-TR-307, University of Maryland, July 1987.

[14] M. D. Wynn. Computation of exact quadtree and octree representations using parallel processing. unpublished report.

NODE DISTRIBUTION IN A PR QUADTREE[*]

Chuan-Heng Ang
Hanan Samet

Computer Science Department
Institute of Advance Computer Studies and
Center for Automation Research
University of Maryland
College Park, MD 20742

ABSTRACT

A method, termed *approximate splitting*, is proposed to model the node distribution that results when the PR quadtree is used to store point data drawn from a uniform distribution. This method can account for the aging and phasing phenomena which are common in most hierarchical data structures. Approximate splitting is also shown to be capable of being adapted to model the node distribution of the PR quadtree with points drawn from a known non-uniform distribution.

Keywords and phrases: PR quadtrees, population analysis, hierarchical data structures.

---

* The support of the National Science Foundation under Grant IRI-88-02457 is gratefully acknowledged.

1. INTRODUCTION

Geographic information systems store large amount of data including maps of roads and regions, locations of cities, etc. Each of these objects can be described with different data structures. For example, we may store the gray levels of a region map in an array, the locations of cities in lexicographical order of their coordinates, and the roads as a set of line segments which are determined by their end points. Ideally, these objects should be stored using variants of the same underlying data structure so that the effort used to implement and maintain the data structure can be kept to the minimum. This goal has been achieved in the implementation of **QUILT**, a geographic information system [Same84b]. In this system, the underlying data structure is the linear quadtree [Garg82].

The quadtree is a hierarchical data structure used to organize an object space. If the object space is an image plane (e.g., a region map), then the quadtree describing it is called a *region quadtree* as defined by Klinger [Klin71, Same84a]. The region quadtree decomposes an image into homogeneous blocks. If the image is all one color, then it is represented by a single block. If not, then the image is decomposed into quadrants, subquadrants, ..., until each block is homogeneous. If the object space is a set of line segments, then the quadtree that is used is called a *PM quadtree* [Same84a]. If the object space consists of points within a square, e.g., the locations of all the cities in certain region, then the corresponding quadtree is a *PR quadtree* [Same84a]. In this case the square is decomposed into quadrants, subquadrants, ... similarly until the number of points in each block is within a certain limit. This limit is termed the *node capacity* of the PR quadtree.

The quadtree variants that we described enable us to have a unified representation of three different types of objects encountered in a geographic information system, namely regions, points, and lines. The storage requirements of the region quadtree are analyzed in [Dyer82, Shaf88] and those of the PM quadtree are analyzed in [Same85]. In this paper, we focus on the storage requirements of the PR quadtree. Given n points which are to be stored in a PR quadtree, we show how to compute the storage requirements, the node distribution, and the average node occupancy. By learning more about the storage requirements of the PR quadtree, we will be able to predict the storage used by the PR quadtrees in a dynamic environment.

Nelson and Samet [Nels86] use a technique termed *population analysis* to analyze the node distribution in a PR quadtree. A *population* is defined to be the collection of all the nodes of specific occupancy. For example, all empty nodes form one population, nodes containing one point a second, and so forth. A node containing i points is said to be of type n_i. Adding a point to a node containing i points will either convert it to a node with $i+1$ points or cause the node to split and produce four nodes one level deeper with occupancies that vary between 0 and $m+1$ where m is the node capacity. This transformation is described by the corresponding *transformation matrix*. The fraction obtained by dividing the number of nodes in population i by the total number of nodes in the PR quadtree is called the *population frequency* e_i. The vector $\vec{e}$ formed by all the e_i is called the *population frequency distribution*.

Population analysis assumes that the distribution of node occupancies is independent of the geometric size of the corresponding block. In addition, suppose that a steady state can be reached when the points are inserted dynamically, then a set of equations involving the population frequencies can be derived and solved by numerical method. The population frequency distributions calculated using this technique agree fairly well with the experimental results.

Given a population frequency distribution $\vec{e}$, the predicted average node occupancy can be computed by the dot product of $\vec{e}$ and the vector $(0,1,...,m)$. This number is determined solely by the node capacity and is not affected by the size of the PR quadtree. On the other hand, the actual average node occupancies obtained from our experiments show a cyclical variation which is periodic in the logarithm of the total number of points stored in PR quadtree. This is termed the *phasing* phenomenon by Nelson and Samet [Nels86] and it is shown in Figure 1. In addition, the PR quadtree also exhibits what is termed the *aging* phenomenon by Nelson and Samet [Nels86]. In this case, after a node is created, it is filled to its capacity as more and more points are inserted into it. In other words, the node is aging, or getting older. Our experiments also show that bigger blocks fill up faster. This is consistent with an analysis based on geometric probability [Sant76].

The population analysis method only provides us with the population frequency distribution. It does not indicate how many nodes containing i points are at depth j, i.e., the complete *node distribution*. Thus, we can not predict the average node access cost when the PR quadtree is stored in main memory. The population analysis ignores the aging phenomenon. Also, the average node occupancy derived from the population frequency distribution is fixed regardless of the size of the PR quadtree. Therefore, the population analysis falls short in accounting for the phasing phenomenon.

Since the population analysis method fails to reflect the phasing and the aging phenomena, the two important characteristics of the PR quadtree, we must look for an alternative analysis technique. In this paper, we propose a method termed *approximate splitting* to calculate the approximate values of the average node distribution. This enable us to derive an approximation of the population frequency distribution. We will refer to these approximations as the *predicted node distribution* and the *predicted population frequency distribution*, respectively. For a PR quadtree that is built from a set of random points, i.e., points that are generated from a uniform distribution, we can obtain its *actual node distribution* and *actual population frequency distribution*. In order to ease the comparison with [Nels86], we will use the same notation and examples that they used.

The remainder of this paper is organized as follows. Section 2 introduces the approximate splitting method through an example. Section 3 describes the method. Section 4 compares the results obtained using the approximate splitting method with those in [Nels86]. Section 5 generalizes the method so that it can be applied to the PR quadtree with data points drawn from a non-uniform distribution such as a Gaussian distribution. Section 6 discusses the aging and phasing phenomena. Section 7 discusses the discrepancy between the predicted average node occupancy obtained by using the approximate splitting method and the actual average node occupancy. We draw conclusions in Section 8.

2. THE AVERAGE NODE DISTRIBUTION

Let us first consider a PR quadtree with data points drawn independently from a uniform distribution. The probability that a point will fall within a particular region is proportional to the area of that region. Given a region that has been partitioned into four quadrants, the probability that a point falls within a particular quadrant is $\frac{1}{4}$, and the probability that it falls outside the quadrant is $\frac{3}{4}$. Thus the probability for a node that contains two points to have an empty NW quadrant is $\binom{2}{0}(\frac{3}{4})^2$. Since there are four quadrants in a node, the average number of empty quadrants is $4\times\binom{2}{0}(\frac{3}{4})^2=\frac{9}{4}$. Similarly, the average number of quadrants with one point is $4\times\binom{2}{1}(\frac{1}{4})(\frac{3}{4})=\frac{3}{2}$ and the average number of quadrants with two points is $4\times\binom{2}{2}(\frac{1}{4})^2=\frac{1}{4}$.

When a PR quadtree contains only one point, it has only one node and its average node distribution is trivial. When more than one point is being stored in a quadtree that has a node capacity of one, we have to consider the splitting process. Figure 2 shows an example of a PR quadtree with node capacity one that contains two points. Its actual node distribution is 8 empty nodes and 2 full nodes. In general, a PR quadtree with node capacity m and maximum depth n may contain t points that are drawn from a uniform distribution. We adopt the convention that the root node N is at level n (or depth 0) and a pixel-size node is at level 0 (or depth n). In order to understand the problem involved in calculating and approximating the node distribution, let us look at the following example.

Example 1: Find the average node distribution of the PR quadtrees containing 1000 points with node capacity one and of maximum depth 9.

We can compute by brute force the predicted average node distribution for Example 1 as follows. Since the root node contains 1000 points, it is split to produce some nodes at depth 1. In particular, at depth 1, the expected number of empty nodes is $4 \times \begin{bmatrix} 1000 \\ 0 \end{bmatrix} (\frac{3}{4})^{1000}$, the expected number of nodes containing 1 point is $4 \times \begin{bmatrix} 1000 \\ 1 \end{bmatrix} (\frac{1}{4})(\frac{3}{4})^{999}$, the expected number of nodes containing 2 points is $4 \times \begin{bmatrix} 1000 \\ 2 \end{bmatrix} (\frac{1}{4})^2 (\frac{3}{4})^{998}$, ..., and the expected number of nodes containing 1000 points is $4 \times \begin{bmatrix} 1000 \\ 1000 \end{bmatrix} (\frac{1}{4})^{1000}$. All nodes at depth 1 containing more than one point will be split to produce more nodes at depth 2. To calculate the number of empty nodes at depth 2, we need to find out the number of nodes produced from the splitting of nodes at depth 1 of types $n_2, n_3, ..., n_{1000}$. These numbers are summed up to give the number of nodes at depth 2 of type n_0. Similarly, we have to find out the number of nodes of types n_1, ..., n_{1000} at depth 2. This calculation is carried out up to depth 9 which is the maximum resolution. The average node distribution as well as the average population distribution can then be found.

The amount of calculation involved is so huge that it makes the calculation of the average node distribution by this brute force method impractical. It can be used only when t is small. When t is large, we are content if we can find a good approximation of the average node distribution. In the next section, we describe a method which produces an approximate average node distribution.

3. THE APPROXIMATE SPLITTING PROCESS

Suppose that we already know how to calculate the average node distribution for a subtree, say S, of a certain height. For simplicity, assume that the PR quadtree consists of multiple copies of S. Each subtree's corresponding blocks are of the same size and contain the same number of points. Since the points are uniformly distributed over blocks of the same size, each subtree will have the same average node distribution. Using this assumption, we can now approximate the average node distribution of the splitting process originating at the root node of the PR quadtree by combining the average node distributions of all these subtrees. We use the term *approximate splitting* to describe this method. The required calculation can be divided into three steps.

Step 1 : Find the depth s such that the probability of having a leaf node at depth d, $d \le s$, is smaller than a predetermined small value. In other words, we want to determine the depth at which we are quite sure that all nodes will require splitting.

Since a node will be split when it contains more than m points, we first find the largest integer s such that $f = \dfrac{t}{4^s} > m$. That is, we distribute the t points into all the nodes at depth s so that each node contains f points. This value of s may not be the right choice. For instance, in Example 1, since $\dfrac{1000}{4^4} = \dfrac{1000}{256} > 1$ and $\dfrac{1000}{4^5} < 1$, we have $s = 4$.

Next, we want to estimate the average number of leaf nodes at depth s that can possibly be produced during the splitting process. In particular, we want to find the number of full nodes thus produced. At depth $s-1$, there are 4^{s-1} nodes and each of them contains $4f$ points. A node at depth $s-1$ can be split to produce a node with m points at depth s with probability $p_s = \dbinom{4f}{m} (\dfrac{1}{4})^m (\dfrac{3}{4})^{4f-m}$. In other words, it can split and produce $4p_s$ full nodes. There are 4^{s-1} nodes at depth $s-1$ and hence there are $4^s \times p_s$ full nodes which are leaf nodes at depth s. If this number is smaller than a small constant ε, say 0.1, then we know that when the splitting process begins at depth $s-1$, the number of nodes at depth s containing m points will be so small that these full leaf nodes can be ignored. For a binomial expansion $(p+q)^n$ with $p+q=1$ and $p<q$, all the terms in the expansion before the ith term where $i=np$ are monotonically increasing. When $n=4f$ and $p=\dfrac{1}{4}$, $m < f = 4f \times \dfrac{1}{4} = np$. Thus the probability of splitting a node at depth $s-1$ with $4f$ points to produce a node at depth s with j points, $j<m$, is even smaller than that for producing the nodes with m points. We can safely say that splitting a node at depth $s-1$ will not produce any leaf nodes at depth s (i.e., nodes with m or fewer points). In other words, the probability that all the nodes at depth s are GRAY nodes is very high. Thus we can stop moving up the tree and prepare to split the nodes at depth s.

If $4^s \times p_s \geq \varepsilon$, then we can set s to $s-1$, and f to $4f$, and repeat the test to see whether it is necessary to move up the tree again.

For Example 1, $m=1$, $f = \dfrac{1000}{4^4} > 1$, $s=4$, $4f \approx 16$ and $p_s \approx \dbinom{16}{1} (\dfrac{1}{4})(\dfrac{3}{4})^{15} = 0.008634$. Therefore $4^4 \times p_s = 3.4 > 0.1$. This means that we have to move up one level and now we have $f \approx 16$, $s=3$, $p_s \approx \dbinom{64}{1} (\dfrac{1}{4})(\dfrac{3}{4})^{63} < 0.0000001$ and $4^3 \times p_s < 0.1$. Therefore we may decide to split the nodes at depth 3 with $k = 4^3 = 64$ subtrees each containing $f = \dfrac{t}{k} = \dfrac{1000}{64} = 15.625$ points.

Suppose that we would have split the nodes at depth 4 instead of at depth 3. In this case, the nodes produced by this splitting process are at depth 5 or deeper and we have unnecessarily forced the points to be distributed over too many subtrees. On the other hand, if we split the nodes at depth 2 instead of depth 3, we will produce a more accurate result at the expense of more calculation (i.e., the brute force algorithm). This is shown in the empirical results that are tabulated in the next section. In general, to produce a result which is more accurate, we should try to split the nodes as high up the tree as possible as long as this does not cause any computational problems such as arithmetic overflow or underflow, or running out of memory.

Step 2 : Calculation of the initial node distribution.

After we have determined the value of s, we know that all the nodes will appear at depth $s+1$ and deeper. The initial node distribution of the nodes at depth $s+1$ will be $k \times \binom{t/k}{j} \dfrac{3^{t/k-j}}{4^{t/k-1}}$ where $0 \leq j \leq t/k$ and $k=4^s$.

Step 3 : Calculate the approximate average node distribution.

After we have obtained the initial node distribution for those nodes at depth $s+1$, we can repeat the splitting process for those nodes with more than m points until the maximum depth of the tree is reached, at which depth all nodes with more than m points will be treated as nodes with only m points. The approximate average node distribution thus obtained is the *predicted node distribution* .

4. COMPARISON OF THE RESULTS

In this section, we compare the results predicted by using the approximate splitting method and those predicted by Nelson and Samet's method [Nels86]. For comparison, we also show the node distributions and the population frequency distributions obtained from PR quadtrees built by the insertion of 1000 randomly generated points. Table 1 shows the actual and predicted node distribution for Example 1. The predicted node distribution fits very well with the actual node distribution.

Depth	Actual		Approximate Splitting Method	
	n_0	n_1	n_0	n_1
0	0.0	0.0	0.0	0.0
1	0.0	0.0	0.0	0.0
2	0.0	0.0	0.0	0.0
3	0.0	0.0	0.0	0.0
4	6.6	20.1	4.7	19.4
5	300.2	354.2	309.6	361.5
6	533.7	411.6	536.4	405.6
7	225.4	144.9	226.1	155.3
8	71.5	49.6	64.5	43.3
9	16.1	19.5	16.7	14.9

Table 1. Node distribution of PR quadtree containing 1000 points.

In our comparison, we consider PR quadtrees with node capacity ranging from 1 to 8, and each PR quadtree contains 1000 random points. From the predicted node distribution, we can obtain the predicted population frequency distribution by dividing the number of nodes of each population by the total number of nodes in the quadtree. In Table 2, we show the population frequency distribution $\vec{e_i}$ obtained using the different analyses. $\vec{e_1}$ is obtained using the method in [Nels86], $\vec{e_2}$ is obtained by analyzing the set of 64 subtrees at depth 3 with $\dfrac{1000}{64}$ points apiece, $\vec{e_3}$ is obtained by analyzing the set of 16 subtrees at depth 2 with $\dfrac{1000}{16}$ points apiece, and $\vec{e_4}$ is obtained from the PR quadtrees which are built through insertion of 1000 random points. $\vec{e_1}$ and $\vec{e_4}$ are taken from [Nels86].

Table 2. Average population frequency distributions of PR quadtrees.

$m=1$: $\vec{e_1}=(.500,.500)$

$\vec{e_2}=(.538,.462)$

$\vec{e_3}=(.538,.462)$

$\vec{e_4}=(.536,.464)$

$m=2$: $\vec{e_1}=(.278,.418,.304)$

$\vec{e_2}=(.332,.426,.242)$

$\vec{e_3}=(.330,.425,.245)$

$\vec{e_4}=(.326,.427,.247)$

$m=3$: $\vec{e_1}=(.165,.320,.305,.210)$

$\vec{e_2}=(.221,.359,.268,.151)$

$\vec{e_3}=(.216,.358,.273,.153)$

$\vec{e_4}=(.213,.364,.273,.149)$

$m=4$: $\vec{e_1}=(.102,.239,.276,.225,.158)$

$\vec{e_2}=(.141,.279,.263,.187,.130)$

$\vec{e_3}=(.140,.282,.270,.186,.122)$

$\vec{e_4}=(.139,.293,.264,.184,.120)$

$m=5$: $\vec{e_1}=(.065,.179,.238,.220,.172,.126)$

$\vec{e_2}=(.078,.190,.232,.211,.170,.119)$

$\vec{e_3}=(.083,.204,.244,.208,.155,.106)$

$\vec{e_4}=(.084,.217,.241,.204,.151,.104)$

$m=6$: $\vec{e_1}=(.043,.132,.200,.207,.176,.137,.105)$

$\vec{e_2}=(.037,.117,.190,.221,.202,.148,.086)$

$\vec{e_3}=(.046,.139,.208,.216,.181,.130,.080)$

$\vec{e_4}=(.050,.150,.201,.215,.176,.127,.081)$

$m=7$: $\vec{e_1}=(.028,.098,.165,.189,.173,.143,.114,.090)$

$\vec{e_2}=(.019,.077,.160,.219,.219,.166,.097,.044)$

$\vec{e_3}=(.027,.099,.177,.214,.197,.146,.091,.049)$

$\vec{e_4}=(.034,.110,.177,.214,.187,.143,.091,.044)$

$m=8$: $\vec{e_1}=(.019,.073,.135,.168,.166,.145,.119,.097,.078)$

$\vec{e_2}=(.013,.063,.147,.216,.224,.172,.102,.047,.017)$

$\vec{e_3}=(.019,.079,.160,.209,.203,.155,.097,.052,.025)$

$\vec{e_4}=(.024,.086,.151,.206,.194,.156,.100,.049,.034)$

From the above data, we see that splitting the nodes nearer the root produces better results, i.e., $\vec{e_3}$ is more accurate than $\vec{e_2}$. We also notice that $\vec{e_3}$ matches $\vec{e_4}$ quite closely. Table 3 shows the average node occupancies AVG_i for the distributions shown in Table 2. The *average node occupancy* can be found by computing the dot product of $\vec{e_i}$ with the vector $(0,1,2,...,m)$.

The last column AVG_4/m shows the average storage utilization of the PR quad-tree with node capacity m. The average of all the entries in this column is 0.474. It is an approximation of the average storage utilization of all the PR quadtrees of node capacities ranging from 1 to 8.

Table 3. Average node occupancy.				
Node capacity (m)	AVG_1	AVG_2	AVG_3	AVG_4	AVG_4/m
1	0.50	0.46	0.46	0.46	0.460
2	1.03	0.91	0.92	0.92	0.460
3	1.56	1.35	1.36	1.36	0.453
4	2.10	1.89	1.87	1.85	0.463
5	2.63	2.56	2.47	2.44	0.488
6	3.17	3.22	3.06	3.03	0.505
7	3.72	3.65	3.50	3.44	0.491
8	4.25	3.83	3.76	3.79	0.475

5. APPLICATIONS OF APPROXIMATE SPLITTING

Suppose that we are given a PR quadtree with data points drawn from a known non-uniform distribution. If we can partition the quadtree into subtrees such that each of them can be regarded as a PR quadtree with points drawn from a certain uniform distribution, then the complicated splitting process of the original PR quadtree can be modeled by the combination of the splitting processes of all the subtrees in the partition. With such an adaptation, the approximate splitting process can have a wider application. In the following, we will look at two examples.

Example 2: Consider an application where the locations of the houses in a certain area are captured in a PR quadtree. As shown in Figure 2, it is known that the housing density in a particular sector, say A which is 1/16 of the area, is double the housing density in the rest of the area. Can we predict the node distribution if we know that there are 1000 houses in the area given that at most one house is associated with each node?

To solve this problem, we divide the area into 16 squares and regard each of them as a subtree rooted at a quadtree block at depth 2. Sector A contains $\frac{2}{17} \times 1000$ points and each of the other 15 subtrees has $\frac{1}{17} \times 1000$ points. The predicted node distribution of the PR quadtree is the sum of the predicted node distribution of sector A and 15 times the predicted node distribution of any other sector. The result is shown in Table 4. This result matches very well with the actual node distribution that is obtained by generating three PR quadtrees and taking the average of their node distributions.

Table 4. Node distribution of the PR quadtree in example 2.				
Depth	Actual		Predicted	
	n_0	n_1	n_0	n_1
0	0.0	0.0	0.0	0.0
1	0.0	0.0	0.0	0.0
2	0.0	0.0	0.0	0.0
3	0.0	0.0	0.0	0.0
4	5.00	28.33	5.38	21.12
5	296.33	334.66	303.62	350.92
6	522.66	402.33	526.49	401.18
7	246.66	182.00	229.75	158.31
8	57.66	40.00	66.44	44.66
9	12.66	12.66	17.23	13.45

Example 3: Suppose that a PR quadtree has 1000 points in a 512 by 512 square and that the x and y coordinates are independently distributed according to the Gaussian distribution with mean 256 and standard deviation 128.

For this example, the square contains the points that lie within two standard deviations from the mean. Since the points will cluster around the mean value, we would like to divide the square into smaller areas around the center of the square as shown in Figure 3. This partition also reflects the fact that the leaf nodes correspond-ing to the blocks surrounding the center appear at deeper levels of the PR quadtree. Let $a=0.3830$ be the probability for the x (or y) coordinate of a point to fall within 0.5 standard deviation from the mean and let $b=0.6826$ be that for 1 standard deviation. The probability that a point which is generated according to this specific Gaussian dis-tribution will fall into a particular region can be calculated as follows. There are 4 subtrees of type A with total probability $(\frac{a}{2}) \times 4$; 8 subtrees of type B with probability $(\frac{b-a}{2}) \times \frac{a}{2} \times 8$; 4 subtrees of type C with probability $(\frac{b-a}{2})^2 \times 4$; 8 subtrees of type D with probability $(\frac{1-b}{2}) \times \frac{b}{2} \times 8$; and 4 subtrees of type E with probability $(\frac{1-b}{2})^2 \times 4$. The number of points contained in each subtree is just the product of the probability asso-ciated with the subtree and 1000. The node distribution of each subtree can then be calculated. The sum of the node distributions of all the subtrees is the predicted node distribution of the PR quadtree containing 1000 points. Table 5 shows that the predicted node distribution fit well with the actual node distribution that is obtained by taking the average of the node distributions of three PR quadtrees built from 1000 random points generated according to a Gaussian distribution.

Table 5. Node distribution of a PR quadtree with points drawn from a Gaussian distribution.				
Depth	Actual		Predicted	
	n_0	n_1	n_0	n_1
0	0.00	0.00	0.00	0.00
1	0.00	0.00	0.00	0.00
2	0.00	0.00	0.00	0.00
3	0.33	0.00	0.01	0.09
4	28.00	40.00	16.15	35.34
5	236.00	257.33	259.13	296.41
6	502.66	417.00	511.13	406.96
7	291.00	192.33	266.34	185.92
8	98.00	77.00	81.46	54.93
9	18.00	18.00	21.44	16.75

6. AGING AND PHASING

Nelson and Samet's analysis [Nels86] computes the average population frequency distribution for a PR quadtree with a certain node capacity. As long as the node capacity remains the same, no matter how many points the PR quadtree holds, the average population frequency distribution of the PR quadtree remains the same, and so is the predicted average node occupancy. This is obviously not true. Therefore there is a discrepancy between the actual average node occupancy and the average node occupancy predicted by their method. They attribute the discrepancy to two factors termed phasing and aging that could not be explained by population analysis.

On the other hand, phasing can be demonstrated by the approximate splitting method. In Figure 4, the average node occupancies of the PR quadtrees with node capacity 8 as predicted by the approximate splitting method are plotted against the number of points stored in the PR quadtrees. The actual average node occupancies are superimposed in the same graph for easy comparison. Figure 4 shows clearly that the graph does oscillate and is periodic in the logarithm of the total number of data items stored in the trees.

Aging is responsible for the fact that larger nodes have occupancies in excess of the predicted average occupancy of the whole PR quadtree. This is accounted for in the approximate splitting process as can be seen from Table 6 which shows the average node occupancy by node level for Example 1. The predicted node distribution for Example 1 is shown in Table 1 and its average node occupancy is 0.46 which is the first entry of the column with heading AVG_4 in Table 3. Comparing with the number 0.46, we find that larger nodes in the predicted node distribution do have higher occupancies. The data in Table 6 is obtained from Table 1 as follows. For nodes at depth 4, the actual node occupancy is $\dfrac{20.1}{6.6+20.1}=0.75$ and the predicted average node occupancy is $\dfrac{19.4}{4.7+19.4}=0.81$. Similarly, we can compute the rest of the ratios in the table. From the table, we see that the predicted average node occupancy is smaller for smaller nodes. The anomalously high value for the actual average node occupancy at depth 9 is the result of the implementation which truncates the tree at that depth [Nels86].

Table 6. Average node occupancy by node level.		
Depth	Actual	Predicted
0	0.00	0.00
1	0.00	0.00
2	0.00	0.00
3	0.00	0.00
4	0.75	0.81
5	0.54	0.54
6	0.44	0.43
7	0.39	0.41
8	0.41	0.40
9	0.55	0.47

7. DISCREPANCY

In Figure 4 we see that although the curve of the predicted average node occupancy oscillates in step with that of the actual average node occupancy, the predicted values achieve higher peaks and lower valleys. This is the result of the assumption that all subtrees partitioning a PR quadtree contain the same number of points. According to this assumption, when a subtree achieves its maximum of the average node occupancy, so have all other subtrees when the approximate splitting method is used. If this constraint is relaxed by allowing the subtrees to have different number of points as in the real situation, then the values of their average node occupancies will spread so that the average of these values will have less variation and hence the oscillation of the curve is dampened.

The number of points falling into the root nodes of the subtrees at depth s follows the binomial distribution with parameters t and p, where t is the number of points contained in the PR quadtree, and p is the probability that a random point falls into the root node of a particular subtree of the approximate splitting process. For a PR quadtree of maximum depth n, we have $p = 4^{-(n-s)}$. When t is large, the binomial distribution can be approximated by a normal distribution with mean $\mu = tp$ and standard deviation $\sigma = \sqrt{tp(1-p)}$ [Fell57, page 172]. The probability that the number of points in a subtree is within one standard deviation from the mean value is about 0.68. Since we are only interested in the approximation of the average node occupancy, one simple improvement that can be made to reduce the amplitude of the curve of the predicted average node occupancy is to divide the subtrees into three groups containing $\mu - \sigma$ points, μ points, and $\mu + \sigma$ points in the proportion of 20, 60, and 20. This proportion is chosen because about 60 percent of the points fall within one standard deviation from the mean. Figure 5 shows the curves of the actual and modified predicted (labeled Predicted1) average node occupancies. The corresponding data can be found in Table 7. It is clear that the accuracy of the predicted average node occupancy has been improved noticeably after the modification.

Table 7. Variation in the average node occupancy.			
Number of points	Actual	Modified predicted	Predicted
250	3.846	3.773	3.763
300	4.052	4.147	4.343
350	4.204	4.258	4.494
400	3.977	3.951	4.315
500	3.671	3.585	3.668
600	3.426	3.387	3.280
700	3.282	3.364	3.201
800	3.392	3.432	3.317
900	3.558	3.604	3.530
1000	3.762	3.783	3.763
1100	3.904	3.946	4.127
1200	4.081	4.088	4.343
1300	4.146	4.158	4.466
1400	4.154	4.177	4.494
1500	4.135	4.168	4.433
1600	4.025	3.950	4.315
1700	3.919	3.812	4.155
1800	3.825	3.759	3.986
1900	3.708	3.680	3.819
2000	3.618	3.588	3.668
2100	3.540	3.553	3.537
2200	3.462	3.478	3.429
2300	3.427	3.467	3.343
2400	3.380	3.413	3.280
2500	3.355	3.364	3.235
2600	3.322	3.374	3.209
2700	3.332	3.343	3.198
2800	3.334	3.393	3.201
2900	3.349	3.380	3.217
3000	3.366	3.411	3.242
3100	3.397	3.415	3.276
3200	3.428	3.446	3.317
3300	3.462	3.493	3.365
3400	3.488	3.519	3.417
3500	3.537	3.561	3.472
3600	3.587	3.597	3.530
3700	3.630	3.653	3.588
3800	3.674	3.694	3.647
3900	3.714	3.732	3.706
4000	3.754	3.778	3.763

8. CONCLUDING REMARKS

The approximate splitting process is a means to obtain an approximation of the node distribution and the average population frequency distribution of a PR quadtree. It can account for the aging and phasing phenomena and gives a fairly accurate prediction of both distributions. It does not resort to solving the equations using numerical methods as that was done in [Nels86]. The approximate splitting process can also be adapted to PR quadtrees with the points drawn from a known non-uniform distribution. It is useful in estimating the storage requirements as well as the performance of the PR quadtree when it is built in main memory.

The process of partitioning a given PR quadtree with the points drawn from a known non-uniform distribution is similar to the way we construct a step function to approximate an arbitrary function. Since the partitioning greatly depends on the prior knowledge of the non-uniform distribution, it is difficult to design a scheme to automate the partitioning process of any given PR quadtree, although such a scheme is desirable.

9. REFERENCES

[Dyer82] - C.R. Dyer, The space efficiency of quadtrees, *Computer Graphics and Image Processing 19*, 4(August 1982), 335-348.

[Fell57] - W. Feller, *An Introduction to Probability Theory and its Applications*, Volume 1, second edition, John Wiley, New York, 1957.

[Garg82] - I. Gargantini, An effective way to represent quadtrees, *Communications of the ACM 25*, 12(December 1982), 905-910.

[Klin71] - A. Klinger, Patterns and Search Statistics, in *Optimizing Methods in Statistics*, J.S. Rustagi, Ed., Academic Press, New York, 1971, 303-337.

[Nels86] - R.C. Nelson and H. Samet, A population analysis of quadtrees with variable node size, Computer Science TR-1740, University of Maryland, College Park, MD, December 1986.

[Same84a] - H. Samet, The quadtree and related hierarchical data structures, *ACM Computing Surveys 16*, 2(June 1984), 187-260.

[Same84b] - H. Samet, A. Rosenfeld, C.A. Shaffer, and R.E. Webber, A geographic information system using quadtrees, *Pattern Recognition 17*, 6(1984), 647-656.

[Same85] - H. Samet and R.E. Webber, Storing a collection of polygons using quadtrees, *ACM Transactions on Graphics 4*, 3(July 1985), 182-222.

[Sant76] - L.A. Santalo, *Integral Geometry and Geometric Probability,*, Addison-Wesley, Reading, MA, 1976, Chapters 1-3.

[Shaf88] - C.A. Shaffer, A formula for computing the number of quadtree node fragments created by a shift, *Pattern recognition letters 7*, 1(January 1988), 45-49.

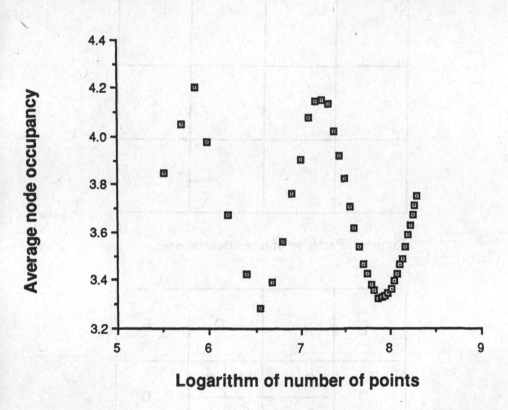

Figure 1 Average node occupancy of a PR quadtree.

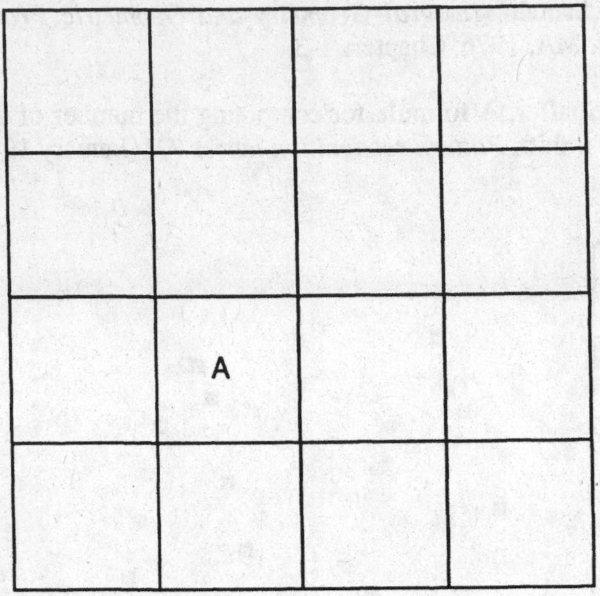

Figure 2 Partition of a residential area.

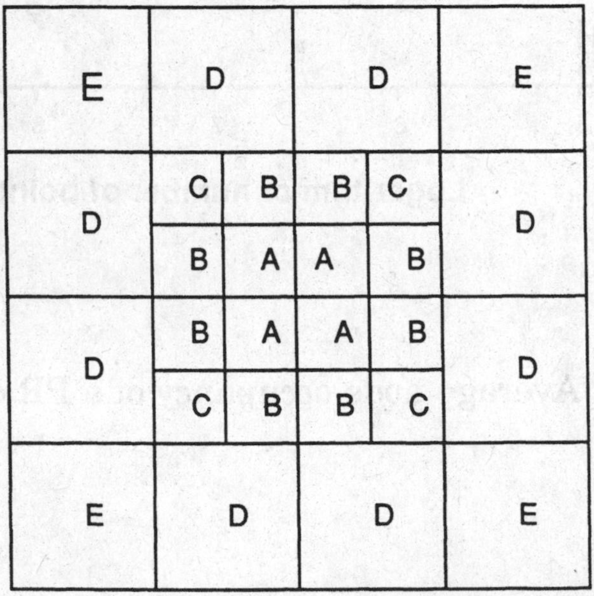

Figure 3 Partition of a square containing the points whose
coordinates follow Gaussian distribution.

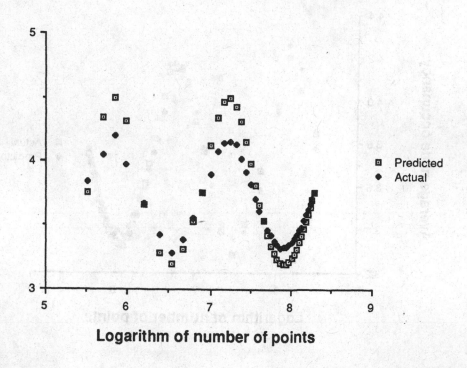

Figure 4 Comparison between the predicted and actual
average node occupancies.

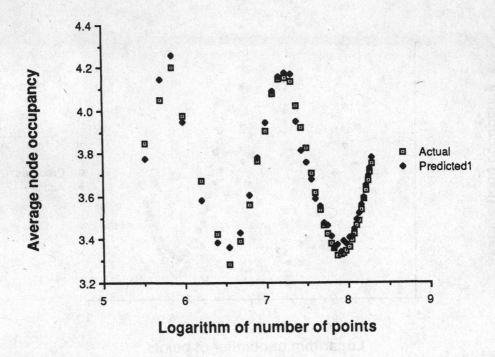

Figure 5 Comparison between the modified predicted and
the actual average node occupancies.

Modeling and Data Structures

An Object-Oriented Approach to the Design of Geographic Information Systems

Peter van Oosterom and Jan van den Bos

Department of Computer Science, University of Leiden
P.O. Box 9512, 2500 RA Leiden, The Netherlands
Email: OOSTEROM@HLERUL5.BITNET

Abstract

The applicability of the Object-Oriented (OO) approach to Geographic Information Systems (GISs) is analyzed. In software engineering, the OO approach as a design model, has been proven to produce quality software. It appears that GISs might also benefit from the OO approach. However, a GIS also imposes special (e.g. spatial) requirements, inclusion of which in the OO model has to be investigated. The proposed solution tries to meet these special requirements by incorporating two data structures: the R-tree and the Binary Line Generalization (BLG) tree. The latter is a novel data structure introduced in this document.

1 Introduction

The Object-Oriented (OO) approach can be useful during several phases of the development of a Geographic Information System (GIS): information and requirements analysis, system design and implementation. The approach also offers good tools for the database and user interface sub-systems of an information system. The interest in object-oriented GISs appears to be growing [15, 8, 6]. The

OO approach has been proven a good method for these purposes in other information and software systems. It leads to quality software which is extendible and reusable [14]. The reuse of software itself tends to improve the quality, because reuse implies testing and, if necessary, debugging. The OO approach also results in good user interfaces, including both visual and non-visual aspects. The explanation for the latter is that if the objects are well chosen, the user can easily form a mental model of the system.

In some sections of this document the OO approach will be illustrated with the case *Presentation of Census Data*. Each of these sections consists of two parts: one with the principles of the OO approach and one with the case. The case will be illustrated with objects described in the language PROCOL, a Protocol-Constrained Concurrent Object-Oriented Language [19]. The next section summarizes the aspects of PROCOL, which are relevant to this document.

In this document the emphasis is on the design of GISs and their databases. However, design must be preceded by information analysis to obtain the requirements. Section 3 contains some notes on object oriented information analysis for a GIS. The design aspects concerning the database and related search problems are discussed in Section 4. Section 5 deals with avoiding data redundancy and also introduces topology. This is accomplished by the *chain* object. Geographic generalization is the topic of the Sections 6 and 7. The term generalization is intended in it's cartographic sense and not in the sense as often used by computer scientists in the inheritance hierarchy of the data/object model The BLG-tree, a data structure for line generalization, is discussed in depth in Section 6. Section 7 is about other generalization techniques in the context of the OO approach.

2 PROCOL

This section gives a short summary of PROCOL, further details can be found in [19]. PROCOL is a simple parallel object-oriented language supporting a distributed, incremental and dynamic object environment. PROCOL does not support inheritance, because this exposes the internals of an object. So in principle, inheritance runs counter to the idea of information hiding. To enable reuse, PROCOL offers delegation, an equally powerful concept. In the remainder of this paper we will neither use inheritance nor delegation.

PROCOL offers two communication primitives: *send* and *request*. A send is based on a one-way message. The request is comparable to the type of communication in ADA: remote procedure call with (possibly) early return. The advantage of send over request is that the objects are only bound during actual message transfer and not during the processing of the message. This short duration object binding promotes parallelism. A PROCOL object definition consists of the following sections:

OBJ	name and attributes
Description	natural language description
Declare	local type defs, data, functions
Init	section executed once at creation

Protocol	(sender-message-action)-expression
Cleanup	section executed once at deletion
Actions	definitions of actions
EndOBJ	name

An object offers a number of services to other objects. In PROCOL the services are specified as *Actions*. The name of an action is known externally. The body of an action may include, besides standard C-code, send-statements and request-statements which have respectively the following syntax:

DestinationObject.ActionName(msg)

DestinationObject.ActionName(msg)→ (mes)

ActionName is the name of the action in *DestinationObject* to which a message *msg* is sent for processing. The message *msg* is comparable to a set of parameters. The values returned by the request are deposited in the variables indicated in the list *mes*. The body of an Action can further contain the PROCOL primitives *new* and *del*, which create a new instance of an object and delete an existing instance of an object, respectively. The latter is only allowed by the creator of the object. The PROCOL primitive *Creator* contains the identification of the creator of the current instance. The bodies of the Init and Cleanup sections have the same form as the bodies of the Actions.

PROCOL constrains possible communications, and thus access to object's actions, by a *Protocol*. The communication leading to access has to obey an explicit protocol in each object. The use of such protocols fosters structured, safer and potentially verifiable communication between objects. The protocol has the form of an expression over *interaction* terms, the counterparts of send-statements and request-statements. During the life of an object this expression is matched over and over again, that is the protocol is repeated. The form of an interaction term is:

SourceObject(msg) → ActionName

The semantics is that upon receipt of message *msg*, from *SourceObject*, *ActionName* will be executed. *SourceObject* can be specified as: object instance, object type (class), and *ANY* object. In the receiving object, the PROCOL primitive *Sender* contains the identification of the communication partner. Expressions over interaction terms are constructed with the following four operators (in this table E and F themselves stand for interaction terms or for expressions):

E + F	*selection:*	E or F is selected
E ; F	*sequence:*	E is followed by F
E *	*repetition:*	Zero of more times E
φ : E	*guard:*	E only if φ is true

3 Finding the objects: information analysis

3.1 Some principles

The problem area must be analyzed, just as in other cases of system development. The application area must be well understood and the task of the new system within it must be clear. This results in a set of requirements for the new system.

The functional requirements and the data affected must be defined in terms of objects types. This means that during the information analysis special attention must be paid to what might possibly be the objects in the target system [14]. There is one golden rule for determining the objects of the functional requirements: *the entities the user is working with and thinking about*. These objects are representations of entities in the real world. After we identify an object, we ask ourselves what do we want this object to do for us (services) in the context of our application. If we can't come up with useful services, this entity is not worthy of being an object in our system.

The resulting object should be reasonable co-

herent and autonomous: strong internal coupling, weak external coupling. An object type (class) is described by a set of attributes and their associated operations (also called actions or methods). The data can only be accessed from the outside by means of the services. In fact this property is called information hiding, and is the basis for the quality of OO software.

In a GIS there must be at least one object type with a geometric attribute. The type of this geometric attribute fixes the basic form of the graphical representation of the object. There are two categories of geometric attributes: raster and vector. The vector type can be subdivided in: point, polyline and polygon.

In an interactive information system the interface must be user-friendly and the required operations must also be performed fast (interactivity). In the case of a GIS this implies that special attention has to be paid to the spatial organization of the objects. Another very important requirement for an interactive GIS is that the user should be able to look at the data (for example thematic maps) at several levels of detail. There are several reasons for this:

- If too much information is presented to the user at one time, it will harm the efficiency in perceiving the relevant information. Old saying: "You can't see the forest for the trees".

- Unnecessary detail will slow down the drawing on the display. This is especially true for sub-pixel sized drawing primitives, because these are hardly visible and thus time is wasted.

The user looking at a small scale (coarse) map, must not be bothered with too much detail. Only if he or she *zooms in* the additional detail should be added. This operation will be called *logical zooming*, in contrast to normal zooming which only enlarges. This must at least have two effects. First, the ob-

Figure 1: Municipalities in The Netherlands

jects which were already visible at the smaller scale map are now to be drawn in finer detail. Second, the objects which were not visible at the smaller scale map, may now become visible. The rule of thumb on *constant pictorial information density*: the total amount of information displayed on one screen is about the same for all scales. A data structure that incorporates both a spatial organization and detail levels is called a *reactive* data structure [21].

3.2 The case

In the case *Presentation of Census Data* the objects typically are the administrative units for which the census data are collected. Figure 1 shows the smallest available administrative units in The Netherlands called municipalities (Dutch: *gemeenten*). So, municipalities are objects in the requirements. The geometric attribute of the object municipality is polygon. This polygon corresponds with the boundary line of the municipality.

In The Netherlands there are five levels of administrative units for which census data are collected. These are called, listed from small to large: municipality, economic geographic region (Dutch: *economisch geografisch gebied*), nodal region (Dutch: *nodale gebied*), corop region (Dutch: *corop gebied*) and province (Dutch: *provincie*). These units are hierarchically organized. The provinces, the largest administrative units, are shown in Figure 2. The different administrative units are natural candidates for the division in detail levels.

The different administrative units form the object types in the functional requirement for this application. Besides the geometric attribute the objects also have attributes describing the relationships with the other administrative units and attributes containing the census data (e.g. the number of inhabitants) and the name of the unit. Note, that this is a very "GISsy" application, because all objects have a geometric attribute. The relationship between the administrative units has a *part-whole* character and not a *class hierarchy* character. In the OO approach one is tempted to use class hierarchy, because this is supported well by the inheritance mechanism. In the case Presentation of Census Data the use of class hierarchy would be a modeling error.

Until now, we have discussed only the data-part of the objects. The operation-part of the objects contains of procedures for:

- Displaying itself in several ways, depending on the selected census data;

- Returning census data. It is possible that the required data are not stored at the current level, but that they are stored in objects lower in the part-whole hierarchy. In that case the census data are collected and aggregated.

- Changing census data. This is only directly possible if the data are actually stored at this level.

Figure 2: Provinces in The Netherlands

These operations are described here in a generalized manner and have to be present for all actual object types, with exception of the "border cases". For instance, it is impossible for a municipality to collect data from objects lower in the hierarchy because it is already the lowest object type in the hierarchy. A part of the PROCOL code describing the object type Economic Geographic Region (EGR) is given below. In this example the object types MUN (municipality) and NODAL, and the data type polygon are already known.

```
/* somewhere:
OBJ NODAL ...
OBJ MUN ...
*/
```

OBJ	EGR (geom, name, nrof..., parent) /* Economic Geographic Region */ polygon geom; string name; int nrof...,;/* census data */ NODAL parent;
Description	Part of the object EGR

Declare	struct list {
	    MUN child;
	    struct list *next;

```
                        } first, curr;
              void Aggregate (...) { ...};
              boolean EGRComplete;
```

Init	parent.AddEGR; first = curr = NULL; EGRComplete = FALSE;
Cleanup	parent.DelEGR;

Protocol	not EGRComplete:
	        MUN() → AddMUN +
	EGRComplete:
	    (MUN() → DelMUN +
	    ANY() → Display +
	    ANY() → RetrieveData +
	    ANY() → ChangeData
	    )

Actions	AddMUN = { ...} DelMUN = { ...} Display = { ...} RetrieveData = { ...} ChangeData = { ...}
EndOBJ	EGR.

The other object types are similar. However, the top level objects (type Province) do not have an attribute parent. The top level objects are created first, then the second level objects, and so on. The Init section of EGR specifies that when a new instance is created, an AddEGR message is send to its parent. This parent, a nodal region, then adds the EGR to its list of EGRs. Note that the parent is not the same object as the PROCOL primitive *Creator*. In a normal situation an object has received all the "Add" messages from its children, before it receives any other message type. This is ensured in the Protocol by the use of the *guard* construction. The variable EGRComplete is set TRUE if all municipalities that belong to the EGR have sent an their registration message, otherwise it has the value FALSE. EGRComplete, which is initially FALSE, is used to control the access to parts of the Protocol. EGRComplete can be set in the body of the AddMUN and DelNUM actions.

4 Object management and search problems

4.1 Some principles

In the previous section we saw that in general an object consists of a data-part and an operation-part. Normally, the object instances are only present when the program is executing. The data must be loaded into the (new) objects when the program is initialized from a file or a database system. Just before the program stops the data must be saved again. This is an inconvenient method, especially in the case of GISs in which there are huge amounts of data that are not all needed in every session. An OO step in the right direction, is to store the objects themselves, including the data (attributes, local variables and protocol status). We will call this operation *save*. After an object is saved, it may be removed with the PROCOL primitive *del* and loaded again with the operation *load*.

The suggestion to store the objects themselves, is not as simple as one might expect. This is because objects usually contain references (in attributes or local variables) to other objects. A reference to an object is an *id* (identification of the right type), which the operating system assigned to that object when it was created with the PROCOL primitive *new*. These id's are stored in attributes and variables of the right type and also in the PROCOL primitives *Creator* and *Sender*. We cannot save an object in a useful manner unless we also save the related objects. This is also true for the load operation.

A better solution to this problem is to have some kind of *Object Management System* (OMS) that takes care of *persistent* objects. If during the execution of a program an object wants to communicate with an object that is not yet present, the OMS tries to find this object and load it. It is the responsibility of the OMS to keep the (references in the) object system consistent. The function of the

PROCOL sections *Init* and *Cleanup* must be reviewed for persistent objects. There should probably be a mechanism to indicate in which persistent objects one is interested. This limits the scope, so the chance that the OMS finds the wrong communication partner decreases. It will be clear that further research is needed in this area.

The objects as specified in the previous section are unsuited for search operations. If we want to solve the query: "How many inhabitants has the municipality with name "Leiden"?", we have to look at all the instances of the MUN object type until we have found the right one. This is an $O(n)$-algorithm. However, this problem can be solved with an $O(log(n))$-algorithm, if a binary search is used. In a relational database efficient search is implemented by a B-tree [2] for the *primary key* and for all other keys on which an *index* is put. The B-tree has many useful properties, such as: it stays balanced under updates, it is adapted to paging (multiway branching instead of binary) and has a high occupancy rate.

The B-tree solution in an OO environment is established by a set of auxiliary objects. These objects do not contain the actual data, but contain references to the objects with the actual data. This must be part of the OMS and, if possible, transparent to the "application" objects. Note that the OMS itself can be implemented in PROCOL as a set of objects.

The searching problem also applies to the geometric data. If no spatial structure is used, then queries such as "Give all municipalities within rectangle X" are hard to answer. A spatial data structure which is suited for the OO environment is the R-tree [11]. This is because the R-tree already deals with objects; it only adds a minimal bounding rectangle (MBR) and then it tries to group the MBRs which lie close to each other. This grouping process is reflected in a tree structure, which in turn may be used for searching. Figure 3

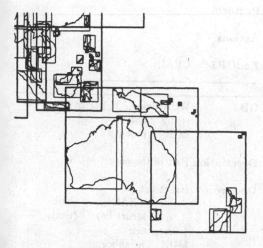

Figure 3: Rectangles in R-tree

shows the rectangles created by the R-tree for a polyline map of the world (zoomed in on Australia). There are two levels of rectangles: the ones drawn with the slightly thinner line width correspond with the leaf nodes. Several test results [7, 9] indicate that the R-tree is a very efficient spatial data structure. Other spatial data structures [20], for example kd-trees, quadtrees, bsp-trees, and gridfiles, are more difficult to integrate in the OO environment, because they cut the geographic objects into pieces. This is against the spirit of the OO approach, which tries to make complete "units", with meaning to the user.

4.2 The case

In PROCOL binary trees can be implemented in two ways. The first method stores the whole tree in one search object. The second stores each node of the tree in a separate instance of the search object. The latter introduces overhead by creating a lot of search objects (nodes). But it has the advantage of being suited for parallel processing in PRO-COL, because the search objects can run on parallel processors. This is useful for range queries: "Give all municipalities with more than 10.000 and less than 20.000 inhabitants".

There must be a separate search tree for each attribute (for which efficient searches are required) on each detail level. This must be made clear to the OMS. So, if we are interested in the number of inhabitants, we have to build search trees on the detail levels of municipalities, economic geographic regions, nodal regions, corop regions and provinces.

In the situation that the value of an attribute changes, after the search tree is created for that attribute, the tree may become incorrect. This is solved if an object sends a message to the search tree object(s) in the OMS, just after the attribute has changed. Upon receipt of this message the search tree adjusts itself.

5 Avoiding redundancy and introducing topology

5.1 Some principles

An additional (implementation) requirement is that redundant data storage is undesirable. This applies to both geometric and non-geometric data. There is one exception to this requirement: attributes which are difficult to aggregate and which are often required, should be stored redundantly. In this situation special protocols and actions must guarantee the consistency of the data.

5.2 The case

In our case the census data are only stored in the administrative units in which the data were collected. The collection and aggregation of census data is very simple. Just retrieve the data from the children and add it.

The type Polygon as used in the attribute *geom* of administrative units is not yet specified. If it is a list of coordinates (x, y), then the attribute geom introduces redundancy in several ways. At a fixed detail level neighbors

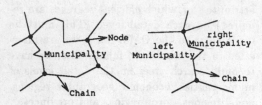

Figure 4: Chains and nodes

have common borders. This implies that all coordinates are stored at least twice. There is also redundancy in the attribute geom between the detail levels. A border of a province is also a border of corop regions, and so on. It is possible that the same coordinate is stored up to ten times.

It is obvious that this is an undesirable situation. We introduce a new object type named *CHAIN*. A chain is a part of the border of a municipality that contains a *node* only at the begin and end point. A node is a point where three or more municipalities meet, see Figure 4. These are the normal definitions in the topological data model [17, 3]. The attributes of the chain object are: a sequence (array) of coordinates and references to a left and a right municipality. A part of the PRO-COL code describing the object type chain is given below.

```
/* somewhere:
typedef struct { float x,y;} Point;
typedef enum { LEFT, RIGHT } Position;
typedef ... BLG;
*/
```

```
OBJ       CHAIN(nop, points, left, right)
          int    nop; /* nr of points */
          Point  *points;
          MUN    left, right;
```

Description Part of the object CHAIN

Declare   BLG tree, Build(...) { ...};

Init   left.AddCHAIN(LEFT,right);
              right.AddCHAIN(RIGHT,left);
              tree = Build(nop, points);

Protocol   ...

Actions   ...

EndOBJ   CHAIN.

```
OBJ       MUN(name,..., parent)
          string  name;
          EGR     parent;
```

Description Part of the object MUN

Declare
```
          struct list {
                  CHAIN      chain;
                  struct list  *next;
          } first, curr;
          MUN     neighbor;
          Position pos;
          boolean BoundaryComplete;
```

Init
```
          parent.AddMUN;
          BoundaryComplete = FALSE;
```

Protocol
```
          /* Lowest object in hierarchy */
          not BoundaryComplete:
                  (CHAIN(pos,neighbor)
                  → AddCHAIN) +
          BoundaryComplete:
                  (ANY() → Display +
                  ANY() → RetrieveData +
                  ANY() → ChangeData
                  )
```

Actions
```
          AddCHAIN = {
          .../* add to list */
          parent.UpCHAIN(Sender,neighbor);
          }
          Display = { ...}
          RetrieveData = { ...}
          ChangeData = { ...}
```

EndOBJ   MUN.

The attribute *geom* is removed from the five administrative units. Instead of this attribute there is a local variable which contains a list of (references to) chains. Initially, the list is empty, because the administrative units are created before the chains. The Display action of an administrative unit should not be called before all chains are created. This can be controlled with a proper Protocol.

The chains are created after the administrative units have been created. In the Init section of the chain object a message is sent to the AddCHAIN action of the municipality left. This message tells that the municipality is to the LEFT of the chain and that its neighbor is the municipality right. A similar message is sent to the municipality right. After these messages have been sent, the BLG-tree (Section 6) of the chain is build and assigned to the local variable tree.

The municipality receiving an AddCHAIN message knows which chain did send the message. This chain is added to the list of chains. Finally the municipality sends a message to the UpCHAIN action of its father (an EGR object), with parameters: the chain (contained in the PROCOL primitive Sender), and the neighbor municipality. The EGR object has also a list of chains. Upon receipt of the message from the municipality, it checks whether the neighbor is also in the list of municipalities. If this is true nothing is done (internal boundary), else the chain is added to the list of chains and again a message is sent to the UpCHAIN action of its father (a NODAL object). This process is repeated on all detail levels if necessary.

Notice that, with the new object chain we have also introduced a topological structure [3]. The chain can be used to determine the neighbors of an administrative units. This is possible at each detail level.

An other interesting issue concerning redundancy is whether the area of an administrative unit is stored. The area can be derived from the polygon (list of chains), but this is a non-trivial operation. The area is not only useful as such, but also in the Display of relative information. For example, the population density is the number of inhabitants divided by the area. Because area is so often needed and difficult to compute, we allow some redundancy here. To guarantee consistency, a border must send a message to the administrative units if it changes. The administrative units then update their area values.

6 Line generalization

When dealing with small scale maps (large regions) only global boundaries will be displayed. But without specific measures the boundary is drawn by the CHAIN object with too much detail, because all points of the chain are used. This detail will be lost on this small scale due to the limited resolution of the display and the drawing will take an unnecessary long period of time. It is better to use fewer points. This can be achieved by the *k-th point algorithm*, which only uses every k-th point of the original chain when drawing it. The first and the last point of a chain are always used. This is to ensure that the chains remain connected to each other in the nodes. This algorithm can be performed "on the fly", because it is very simple. The k can be adjusted to suit the specified scale. However, this method has some disadvantages:

- The shape of the chain is not optimally represented. Some of the line characteristics may be lost if the original chains contains very sharp bends or long straight line segments.

- If two neighboring administrative units are filled, for example in case of a choropleth, and the k-th point algorithm is applied on the contour, then these polygons may not fit. The contour contains the renumbered points of several chains.

Therefore, a better line generalization algorithm has to be used, for instance the *Douglas-Peucker algorithm* [5]. These types of algorithms are more time consuming, so it is wise to compute the generalization information for each chain in a preprocessing step. The result is stored in the CHAIN object in, for instance, a line generalization tree [12]. This tree has the disadvantage that it introduces a discrete number of detail levels, which must be determined in advance. The number of children of a node in a line generalization tree is not fixed. This implies that the tree is not binary, which would be preferable for the implementation.

Strip trees [1] and Arc trees [10] are binary trees that represent curves (in a 2D-plane) in a hierarchical manner with increasing accuracy in the lower levels of the tree. These data structures are designed for arbitrary curves and not for simple polylines (the geometric attribute of a chain). We introduce a data structure that combines the good properties of the mentioned structures. We call this the *Binary Line Generalization Tree* (BLG-tree).

6.1 The BLG-tree

The original polyline consists of the points p_1 trough p_n The most coarse approximation of this polyline is the line segment $[p_1, p_n]$. The point of the original polyline that has the largest distance to this line segment, determines the error for this approximation. Assume that this is point p_k with distance d, see Figure 5a. p_k and d are stored in the root of the BLG-tree, which represents the line segment $[p_1, p_n]$. The next approximation is formed by the two line segments $[p_1, p_k]$ and $[p_k, p_n]$. The root of the BLG-tree contains two pointers to the nodes that correspond with these line segments. In the "normal" situation this is a more accurate representation.

The line segments $[p_1, p_k]$ and $[p_k, p_n]$ can be treated in the same manner with respect to their part of the original polyline as the line segment $[p_1, p_n]$ to the whole polyline. Again, the error of the approximation by a line segment can be determined by the point with the largest distance. And again, this point and distance are stored in a node of the tree which represents a line segment. This process is repeated until the error (distance) is 0. If the original polyline does not contain three consecutive points that lie on a straight line,

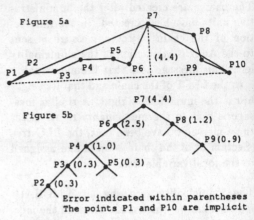

Figure 5a

Figure 5b

Error indicated within parentheses
The points P1 and P10 are implicit

Figure 5: A polyline and its BLG-tree

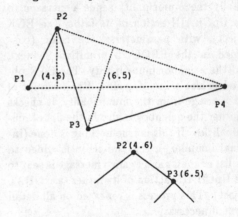

Figure 6: Increasing error in BLG-tree

then the BLG-tree will contain all points of the original polyline. The BLG-tree incorporates an exact representation of the original polyline. The BLG-tree is a static structure with respect to inserting, deleting and changing points that define the original polyline. The BLG-tree of the polyline of Figure 5a is shown in Figure 5b. In most cases the distance values stored in the nodes will become smaller when descending the tree. Unfortunately, this is not always the case as shown in Figure 6. It is not a monotonic decreasing series of values.

The BLG-tree is used during the display of a polyline at a certain scale. One can determine the maximum error that is allowed at this scale. During the traversal of the tree, one does not have to go any deeper in the tree once the required accuracy is met. The BLG-tree can also be used for other purposes, for example:

- Estimating the area of a region enclosed by a number of chains.

- Estimating the intersection(s) of two chains. This is a useful operation during the calculation of a map overlay (polygon overlay).

6.2 Error analysis

As indicated above, the BLG-tree is used for efficiently manipulating digital map data at multiple scales. At smaller scales this will introduce some inaccuracies. During the error analysis it is assumed that the most detailed data, stored in the BLG-tree form, is the exact representation of the mapped phenomenon. Three topics will be discussed in this context: position, circumference and area of a region enclosed by a number of chains. The BLG-tree is traversed until a node is reached with an error below a certain threshold, say E. This is always possible because the error value of a leaf node is 0. This traversal results in an approximation of the region by polygon P, defined by points p_1 through p_n, with coordinates (x_i, y_i) for i from 1 to n and $p_{n+1} = p_1$. The estimated circumference C and area A based on polygon P are [20]:

$$C = \sum_{i=1}^{n} d(p_i, p_{i+1})$$

$$A = \frac{1}{2} \sum_{i=1}^{n} (x_i y_{i+1} - y_i x_{i+1})$$

with d the distance between two points. By definition, the *position* of the region is always within a distance E. If E (in world coordinates) is chosen to correspond with the width of a pixel on the screen, then this will result in a good display function. One can trade efficiency for accuracy and choose E to correspond with the width of three pixels. The

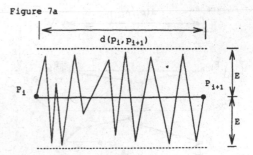

Figure 7a

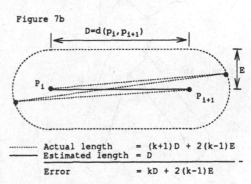

Figure 7b

- - - - - - Actual length   = (k+1)D + 2(k-1)E
————— Estimated length = D

Error   = kD + 2(k-1)E

Figure 7: Error in circumference estimation

accuracy is less, but the display is faster because fewer points are used.

The estimate of the circumference will always be too small. This is because for every skipped point, two line segments are replaced by one line segment, which has a smaller length than the sum of the replaced line segments. It is hard to say something about the accuracy of the estimation of the *circumference C*, because the boundary can be *zig-zag* shaped (Figure 7a). If the total number of points in the exact representation of the region is known, the worst case error can be calculated. On approximation line segment $[p_i, p_{i+1}]$, with k_i points in between in the exact representation, the largest possible error is (Figure 7b):

$$k_i d(p_i, p_{i+1}) + 2(k-1)E$$

Summed over all the approximation line segments this results in: $KC + 2(K-1)E$, with C the estimate of the circumference and $K = \sum_{i=1}^{n} k_i$. This is an inaccurate estimate, because the error can be more than K times

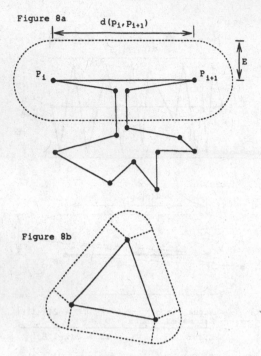

Figure 8a

$d(p_i, p_{i+1})$

E

p_1 p_{i+1}

Figure 8b

Figure 8: Error in area estimation

as large as the estimate itself. The BLG-tree is therefore not suited to make estimates of the circumference. It should be noted that in "normal" cases the estimate may be quite fair in comparison with the worst case.

The estimate of the *area A* can be calculated with reasonable accuracy. The largest error per approximation line segment $[p_i, p_{i+1}]$ is (Figure 8a):

$$2Ed(p_i, p_{i+1}) + \pi E^2$$

Summed over all line segments this gives: $2EC + n\pi E^2$, with n the number of points in the approximation polygon P. A better calculation of the worst case error can be made if one realizes that it is impossible for all approximation line segments to have their worst case situation at the same time. For a convex polygon, see Figure 8b, the largest possible error is: $EC + \pi E^2$, which is about twice as good as the previous one. The same, though less obvious, is valid for a concave polygon.

6.3 Join of BLG-trees

On small scale maps is it possible that a region is represented only by the begin and end points of the corresponding chains. As the chains are defined on the lowest level, see Section 5, this representation can be too detailed. The BLG-tree should be build for the whole polygon of the region instead of a BLG-tree for each part of the boundary. However, if the results are stored on region basis, then this will introduce redundant data storage. Contrary, if the BLG-tree is not stored, then a time consuming line generalization algorithm has to be executed over and over again.

The solution for this dilemma is the dynamic join of BLG-trees, which are stored in the chains. Figure 9 shows how two BLG-trees which belong to consecutive parts of the boundary are joined. The error in the top node of the resulting BLG-tree is not calculated exactly, but estimated on basis of the errors in the two sub-trees:

$$e_t = d(p_2, [p_1, p_3]) + \max(e_1, e_2)$$

with $d(p_2, [p_1, p_3])$ is the distance from point p_2 to the line $[p_1, p_3]$ and e_t, e_1 and e_2 are the error values in the top nodes of the joined and the two sub BLG-trees. The estimate of the error e_t is too large, but this is not a problem. The big advantage is that it can be computed very fast.

The pairwise join of BLG-trees is repeated until the whole region is represented by one BLG-tree. Which pair is selected for a join depends on the sum of the error values in the top nodes of the two BLG-trees. The pair with the lowest sum is joined. The building of a BLG-tree for a region is a simple process, only a few joins are needed; one less than the number of chains by which the region is represented. Therefore, the BLG-tree for the region can be computed each time it is needed. Using this tree an appropriate representation for the region can be made on every scale.

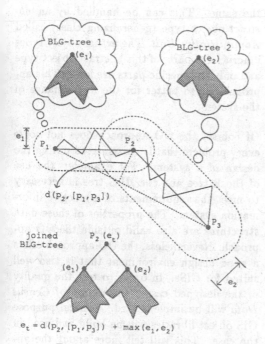

$$e_t = d(P_2, [P_1, P_3]) + \max(e_1, e_2)$$

Figure 9: Join of BLG-trees

7 More on generalization

Geographic generalization, that is, the process of transforming large scale maps (with detailed data) into small scale maps, is supported in several places in the design of a GIS in this document:

- Things can be removed. For example: a border between two municipalities in the same province is not drawn, when displaying a small scale map.

- An object can be drawn with less resolution. For example: A (part of the) border of a country, is drawn with only 5 points on a small scale map. The same part is drawn with 50 points on a large scale map.

Generalization is a complex process, of which some parts (for example line generalization) are suited to be performed by a computer and others not. Nickerson [16] shows that

very good results can be achieved with a rule based system for generalization of maps that consist of linear features. Shea and McMaster [18] give some guidelines when and how to generalize. Brassel and Weibel [4] present a framework for automated map generalization. Mark [13] states that the nature of the phenomenon must be taken into account during the line generalization. This means that it is possible that a different technique is required for a line representing a road than for a line representing a river.

We will shortly examine some generalization techniques, and comment on the fact whether they can be supported by the OO approach to GIS. This does not imply that a certain part of the generalization can be automated, only that the result of the generalization process is reflected (stored) in the system. The major generalization techniques are:

- A *change* of the geometric representation of an object. A city on a small scale map is represented by a point (marker) and on a large scale map by a polygon. Though not described in this document, it is possible to store multiple representations of an entity in one object. At the time this object is displayed, it decides which representation is used on basis of the current scale and resolution of the output device.

- An important object is *exaggerated* on a small scale map. E.g. an important road is drawn wider than the reality. It is not very difficult to implement this type of generalization, if the importance of the object is stored. A simple adaptation of the display action should do the trick (with a procedure call to "set line width").

- An object is slightly *displaced* on a small scale map, because otherwise it would coincide with an other object. For example a city is moved because a road is exaggerated. This could be an annoying thing. The displacement can be stored, but this depends on the scale. A solution might be a procedure which determines the displacement. But this is a very difficult process, which involves the subjective human taste or preferences. These may be simulated to a certain extend by an expert system, but this is not within the scope of this document. An other solution is to store a number of displacements each of which is valid for a certain range of the scale. The number of ranges (and their sizes) varies from object to object.

- Two or more objects are *grouped* and represented by one graphical primitive. E.g. two cities which lie close to each other are drawn on a small scale map as one city. This is the most radical type of generalization, because it involves the creation of a new object, with connections to the contributing objects. Nevertheless, there is no reason why this should not be possible. The resulting GIS will become more complex.

8 Conclusion

Besides an Object-Oriented programming language, PROCOL is also a parallel programming language. It is possible that the objects run in parallel on multiple processors. This can be useful in several operations or actions. The aggregation of census data for different provinces can be done in parallel. The displaying of the administrative units can also be done in parallel.

The design of the case studied in this document is based on the on the principle of data abstraction. Inheritance, a powerful feature in most OO programming languages, is not used in this document. However, there is at least one situation in which it could be very useful. In Section 3, five object types where introduced of which only one, the economic geographic region, was described. The others, province, corop region, nodal region, and municipality, can be described as similar. That is, large parts of the object type are exactly the same. This can be handled by an *abstract* object type (generalizing class) called *Administrative Unit*. The actual object types inherit large parts of this abstract object type and only the specific parts are local. This approach is also better for the maintenance of the system.

Of course, the OO approach does not solve every problem that is encountered during the design of a system. For example: the use of the R-tree and the BLG-tree is necessary to meet the requirements of a reactive information system. The properties of these data structures are also valid outside the OO approach. Nevertheless, the OO approach offers a good design environment that is also well suited for GISs. In order to test the quality of the designed case *Presentation of Census Data* will be implemented. General purpose GIS object libraries will be build and used in the case. This will tell more about the applicability of the OO approach to the whole development process of a GIS.

Acknowledgements

Our thanks go to TNO Physics and Electronics Laboratory[1], the employer of Peter van Oosterom, for giving him the opportunity to perform this research at the Department of Computer Science, University of Leiden. Andre Smits and Peter Essens of TNO made many valuable suggestions in reviewing this document.

References

[1] Dana H. Ballard. Strip trees: A hierarchical representation for curves. *Communications of the ACM*, 24(5):310–321, May 1981.

[1] TNO Physics and Electronics Laboratory, P.O. Box 96864, 2509 JG The Hague, The Netherlands.

[2] R. Bayer and E. McCreight. Organization and maintenance of large ordered indexes. *Acta Informatica*, 1:173–189, 1973.

[3] Gerard Boudriault. Topology in the TIGER file. In *Auto-Carto 8*, pages 258–269, 1987.

[4] Kurt E. Brassel and Robert Weibel. A review and conceptual framework of automated map generalization. *International Journal of Geographical Information Systems*, 2(3):229–244, 1988.

[5] D.H. Douglas and T.K. Peucker. Algorithms for the reduction of points required to represent a digitized line or its caricature. *Canadian Cartographer*, 10:112–122, 1973.

[6] Max J. Egenhofer and Andrew U. Frank. Object-oriented modeling in GIS: Inheritance and Propagation. In *Auto-Carto 9*, pages 588–598, April 1989.

[7] Christos Faloutsos, Timos Sellis, and Nick Roussopoulos. Analysis of object oriented spatial access methods. *ACM SIGMOD (Management of Data)*, 16(3):426–439, December 1987.

[8] Mark N. Gahegan and Stuart A. Roberts. An intelligent, object-oriented geographical information system. *International Journal of Geographical Information Systems*, 2(2):101–110, 1988.

[9] Diane Greene. An implementation and performance analysis of spatial data access methods. In *IEEE Data Engineering Conference*, pages 606–615, 1989.

[10] Oliver Günther. *Efficient Structures for Geometric Data Management*. Number 337 in Lecture Notes in Computer Science. Springer-Verlag, Berlin, 1988. ISBN 3-540-50463-X.

[11] Antonin Guttman. R-trees: A dynamic index structure for spatial searching. *ACM SIGMOD*, 13:47–57, 1984.

[12] Christopher B. Jones and Ian M. Abraham. Line generalisation in a global cartographic database. *Cartographica*, 24(3):32–45, 1987.

[13] David E. Mark. Conceptual basis for geographic line generalization. In *Auto-Carto 9*, pages 68–77, April 1989.

[14] Bertrand Meyer. *Object-oriented Software Construction*. Prentice Hall, London, 1988. ISBN 0-13-629049-3.

[15] L. Mohan and R.L. Kashyap. An object-oriented knowledge representation for spatial information. *IEEE Transactions on Software Engineering*, 14(5):675–681, May 1988.

[16] Bradford G. Nickerson. *Automatic Cartographic Generalization for Linear Features*. PhD thesis, Rutgers – The State University of New Jersy, April 1987.

[17] Thomas K. Peucker and Nicholas Chrisman. Cartographic data structures. *The American Cartographer*, 2(1):55–69, 1975.

[18] K. Stuart Shea and Robert B. McMaster. Cartographic generalization in a digital environment: When and how to generalize. In *Auto-Carto 9*, pages 56–67, April 1989.

[19] Jan van den Bos. PROCOL – A protocol-constrained concurrent object-oriented language. Special Issue on Concurrent Object Languages, Workshop Concurrency, OOPSLA '88, San Diego. *SigPlan Notices*, 24(4), April 1989.

[20] Peter van Oosterom. Spatial data structures in Geographic Information Systems. In *NCGA's Mapping and Geographic Information Systems*, pages 104–118, September 1988. Orlando, Florida.

[21] Peter van Oosterom. A reactive data structure for Geographic Information Systems. In *Auto-Carto 9*, pages 665–674, April 1989.

A Topological Data Model for Spatial Databases*

Max J. Egenhofer

Andrew U. Frank

Jeffrey P. Jackson

National Center for Geographic Information and Analysis

and

Department of Surveying Engineering

University of Maine

Orono, ME 04469, USA

MAX@MECAN1.bitnet

FRANK@MECAN1.bitnet

JACKSON@MECAN1.bitnet

Abstract

There is a growing demand for engineering applications which need a sophisticated treatment of geometric properties. Implementations of Euclidian geometry, commonly used in current commercial Geographic Information Systems and CAD/CAM, are impeded by the finiteness of computers and their numbering systems. To overcome these deficiencies a spatial data model is proposed which is based upon the mathematical theory of simplices and simplicial complexes from combinatorial topology and introduces *completeness of incidence* and *completeness of inclusion* as an extension to the closed world assumption. It guarantees the preservation of topology under affine transformations. This model leads to straightforward algorithms which are described. The implementation as a general spatial framework on top of an object-oriented database management system is discussed.

1 Introduction

Traditionally, applications with spatial data are based upon coordinates and an implementation of Euclidian geometry following the model of analytical geometry. While this method is being taught so convincingly in high school as *the* geometry, its implementation in a finite computer system does not capture regular concepts of analytical geometry. Problems can be observed in many areas and impede

---

*This research was partially funded by grants from NSF under No. IST 86-09123 and Digital Equipment Corporation (Principal Investigator: Andrew U. Frank). Jeffrey P. Jackson was supported by an Undergraduate Research Experience grant from NSF under No. IRI 86-09123. The support from NSF for the NCGIA under grant number SES 88-10917 is gratefully acknowledged.

almost any modern application of CAD, VLSI, common sense physics, spatial information systems, etc. For example, software systems for Geographic Information Systems, such as ARC/INFO, demonstrate the inherent problems of a geometric model based upon Euclidian geometry:

- Scaling of coordinates may change topology, moving points, initially close to a line, from one side to another.

- The intersection of two lines does not necessarily lie on both lines.

- The application of two inverse geometric operations generates a geometry which may differ from the original geometry [Dobkin 1988] [Hoffmann 1989].

- The crucial operation of map overlaying in Geographic Information Systems introduces so-called *gaps and slivers*[Goodchild 1978] which have to be removed with computationally expensive and conceptually dubious methods, introducing errors in the data.

Finite computers cannot provide for infinite precision as is assumed for the Cartesian representation of space used in analytical geometry. The deficiencies of computer number systems and the implementations of their algebras exclude integers and floating point reals as appropriate candidates for coordinate-based geometry [Franklin 1984]. Intersections which do not lie on the intersected lines [Nievergelt 1988] are only one of many undesired outcomes.

A geometry with 'tolerances', that would permit intersections to lie a certain distance off the particular lines and still be considered 'on' the line [Greene 1986], shows strange effects through the necessary transitivity of an equivalence relation. The fact that two points A and B are equal if the distance between them is less than a certain tolerance implies by transitivity that any point in the universe is equal to any other if enough intermediate points are introduced between them—regardless of the distance between them. In actual implementations, points may 'wander' when other points close by are introduced during the computation of map overlays [Guevara 1985].

Another problem with coordinate geometry is the complexity of standard operations and the difficulty of guaranteeing that no geometric inconsistencies are overseen [Frank 1983a]. In particular, objects with holes or objects separated into non-coherent parts causes problems which are difficult to treat.

Obviously, a theory for the representation of spatial data is needed that is compatible with the finiteness of computers. The development of such a coherent, mathematically sound theory—at least for the GIS field—is one of the goals being investigated by the National Center for Geographic Information and Analysis [Abler 1987]. As a contribution to such a theory, the development of a general spatial data model based upon simplicial complexes is presented. This model, using topology rather than coordinates, is better-suited for the implementation in a computer because it does not rely upon the limitation of the applications of number systems in computers. Instead, it records the connection among geometric objects with respect to their neighborhood and allows user queries about neighborhood and inclusion to be processed without the need of numeric calculations.

This spatial data model differs from traditional approaches in solid modeling using constructive solid geometry or boundary representations [Requicha 1980] [Requicha 1983]. The simplicial structure partitions the space and establishes a geometric framework from which meaningful objects can be built. Their geometry is representaed by the aggregate of simplices and complexes, located in the embedding (simplicial) space. Non-spatial properties are added in semantically richer layers built on top of this basis. This separation leads to a two-level model: (1) At a geometric level, all objects are considered *cells* without any meaning about the objects they represent. This level is the geometric framework and deals with all geometric concern. All geometric operations are defined at this level. (2) Any meaningful spatial object is composed as an aggregate of geometric parts and a collection of non-spatial properties. The concept of *inheritance* [Cardelli 1984] is employed to provide geometric operations from the objects in the geometric layer to objects at the semantic level [Frank 1987] [Egenhofer 1988].

This fundamental spatial data model is widely applicable. It is dimension-independent and can be used for 2-D and 3-D. Without the loss of generality, this paper is limited to a two-dimensional model. From the algorithms presented it follows that the same concepts can be applied in any higher-dimensional space as well.

The remainder of this paper is organized as follows: Section 2 presents simplices and simplicial complexes as the spatial objects of concern. *Boundary* and *co-boundary* are introduced as the fundamental operations upon complexes. A set of operations for 2-dimensional geometry inserting nodes, lines, and polygons is introduced in section 3, the algorithms of which are presented in the appendix. Results from the implementation are discussed in section 4.

2 A Model for the Representation of Spatial Data

In the mathematical theory of combinatorial topology, a sophisticated method has been developed to classify and formally describe point sets. Topology has been used for modeling spatial data and their composition for a long time. Recently, combinatorial topology was applied to spatial data models in Geographic Information Systems (GIS) [Corbett 1979], [Frank 1986] [Herring 1987], both for two-dimensional [Egenhofer 1987] and three-dimensional [Carlson 1987] geometry. The simplicity of the implementation demonstrated the simplicity of the coherent mathematical theory [Jackson 1989].

2.1 Simplex

Spatial objects are classified according to their spatial dimension. For each dimension, a minimal object exists, called *simplex*. Examples for minimal spatial objects are 0-simplices representing nodes, 1-simplices which stand for edges, 2-simplices for triangles, 3-simplices for tetrahedrons, etc.

Any n-simplex is composed of (n+1) geometrically independent simplices of dimension (n-1). For example, a triangle, a 2-simplex, is bounded by three 1-simplices (figure 1). These 1-simplices are geometrically independent if no two edges are parallel and no edge is of length 0 [Giblin 1977].

Figure 1: A 2-simplex composed of three 1-simplices.

A face of a simplex is any simplex that contributes to the composition of the simplex. For instance, a node of a bounding edge of a triangle is a face; another face of a triangle is any of its bounding edges. A simplex S of dimension n has $\binom{n+1}{p+1}$ faces of dimension p $(0 \leq m \leq n)$ [Schubert 1968]. For example, a 2-simplex has $\binom{2+1}{1+1} = 3$ 1-simplices as faces. Note that the n-simplex is a face of itself.

An ordered n-simplex s_n may be represented by its vertices in the following form:

$$s_n = \langle x_0, \cdots, x_n \rangle \tag{1}$$

For example, the two ordered 1-simplices in figure 2 can represented as

$$S = \langle A, B \rangle$$
$$T = \langle B, A \rangle$$

An *orientation* of a simplex fixes the vertices to lie in a sequence and is defined through the associated ordered simplices. The orientation of a 0-simplex is unique; the two orientations of a 1-simplex can be interpreted as the direction *from* vertex A *to* vertex B and reverse *from B to A* (figure 2); the orientations of a 2-simplex can be interpreted as *clockwise* or *counterclockwise*.

Figure 2: The two orientations of a 1-simplex.

2.2 Simplicial Complex

A simplicial complex is a (finite) collection of simplices and their faces. If the intersection between two simplices of this collection is not empty, then the intersection is a simplex which is a face of both simplices. The dimension of a complex c is taken to be the largest dimension of the simplices of c.

The configurations in figure 3, for example, are complexes, while figure 4 shows three compositions which are not simplicial complexes. The intersection of some of their simplices is either not a face (figures 4a and b), or not a simplex (figure 4c).

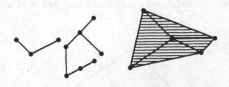

Figure 3: A 1- and a 2-complex.

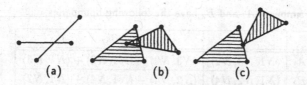

(a)   (b)   (c)

Figure 4: Three compositions which are not simplicial complexes.

2.3 Boundary

An important operation upon an n-simplex s_n is *boundary*, denoted by ∂s_n, which determines all (n-1)-faces of s_n. The property that two successive applications of boundary give the zero homomorphism is in agreement with the geometric notion that the boundary of a simplex is a closed surface.

The algebraic interpretation of the boundary operation is particularly useful for the subsequent formal investigations. Suppose that the representation of the ordered n-simplex s_n is as introduced in equation 1 $s_n = \langle x_0, \cdots, x_n \rangle$, then the boundary of s_n is determined by

$$\partial s_n = \sum_{i=0}^{n}(-1)^i \langle x_0, \cdots, \widehat{x_i}, \cdots, x_n \rangle \tag{2}$$

where $\widehat{x_i}$ denotes that the vertex x_i is to be omitted [Schubert 1968]. The bounding simplices form a chain which is an element of a free Abelian (i.e., additive) group, with $-\langle x_0, \cdots, x_n \rangle = \langle x_n, \cdots, x_o \rangle$ and $\langle x_0, \cdots, x_n \rangle - \langle x_0, \cdots, x_n \rangle = 0$. Hence, the boundary of a simplicial complex c_n can be determined as the sum of the boundaries of all its simplices s_n.

$$\partial c_n = \sum \partial s_n \text{ if } s_n \in c_n \tag{3}$$

Figure 5 illustrates the following example.

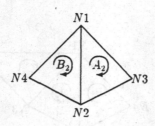

Figure 5: The boundary of the 2-complex c_2, calculated as the sum of the boundaries of the two 2-simplices A_2 and B_2.

The two neighboring 2-simplices A_2 and B_2 have the following boundaries:

	s_2	∂s_2
A_2	$\langle N1, N3, N2 \rangle$	$\langle N3, N2 \rangle - \langle N1, N2 \rangle + \langle N1, N3 \rangle$
B_2	$\langle N1, N2, N4 \rangle$	$\langle N2, N4 \rangle - \langle N1, N4 \rangle + \langle N1, N2 \rangle$

Table 1: Simplices and corresponding boundaries illustrated in figure 5.

Then the complex C_2 formed by A_2 and B_2 has the following boundary:

$$
\begin{aligned}
\partial C_2 &= \partial A_2 + \partial B_2 \\
&= \langle N3, N2 \rangle - \langle N1, N2 \rangle + \langle N1, N3 \rangle + \langle N2, N4 \rangle - \langle N1, N4 \rangle + \langle N1, N2 \rangle \\
&= \langle N3, N2 \rangle + \langle N2, N4 \rangle + \langle N4, N1 \rangle + \langle N1, N3 \rangle
\end{aligned}
$$

2.4 Co-Boundary

The co-boundary of a simplex s_n, denoted by γs_n, is introduced as the set of all $(n+1)$-simplices which are bounded by s_n. The orientation of s_n is not significant.

$$\gamma s_n = \bigcup s_{n+1} \text{ if } s_n \in \partial s_{n+1} \tag{4}$$

For instance, the co-boundary of a 1-simplex is the set of the two bounding 2-simplices. The co-boundary of a complex c_n is then the union of the co-boundaries of the n-simplices of c_n.

$$\gamma c_n = \bigcup \gamma s_n \text{ if } s_n \in c_n \tag{5}$$

Figure 6 illustrates the following example calculating the co-boundary of the 1-simplex $s_1 = \langle N1, N3 \rangle$ in the 2-complex $\langle A_2, B_2, C_2 \rangle$.

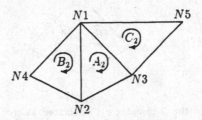

Figure 6: The 2-simplices C_2 and A_2 as the co-boundary of the 1-simplex $\langle N1, N3 \rangle$.

The simplex $\langle N1, N3 \rangle$ (or its inverse $\langle N3, N1 \rangle$) is contained in the boundaries of the two complexes A_2 and C_2:

	s_2	∂s_2	$\partial s_2 \cap s_1$
A_2	$\langle N1, N3, N2 \rangle$	$\langle N3, N2 \rangle + \langle N2, N1 \rangle + \langle N1, N3 \rangle$	$\langle N1, N3 \rangle$
B_2	$\langle N1, N2, N4 \rangle$	$\langle N2, N4 \rangle + \langle N4, N1 \rangle + \langle N1, N2 \rangle$	$\emptyset$
C_2	$\langle N1, N5, N3 \rangle$	$\langle N5, N3 \rangle + \langle N3, N1 \rangle + \langle N1, N5 \rangle$	$\langle N1, N3 \rangle$

Table 2: Simplices and corresponding boundaries illustrated in figure 6.

Then the co-boundary of $\langle N1, N3 \rangle$ is

$$\gamma \langle N1, N3 \rangle = \{A_2, C_2\}$$

2.5 Completeness Axioms

All spatial objects are located in the same world which is represented by the fundamental geometric structure and closed in analogy to the closed world assumption [Reiter 1984] of non-spatial mini-worlds. Within this fundamental level, two completeness principles are guaranteed [Frank 1983a] [Frank 1986]:

- Completeness of incidence: The intersection of two n-simplices is either empty or a face of both simplices. Hence, no two geometric objects must exist at the same location. For example, though an edge may represent both a part of a state boundary and a part of the border of a nation, the geometry of the edge will be recorded only once.

- Completeness of inclusion: Every n-simplex is a face of an (n+1)-simplex. Hence, in a 2-dimensional space every node is either start- or end-node of an edge, and every edge is the boundary of a triangle.

The simplicial structure is a complete partition of the space. In the case of a 2-dimensional world, this structure establishes a triangulated irregular network (TIN) [Peucker 1975]. The characteristics of this space are similar to subdivisions established by regular tilings of space; however, the simplicial structure is more flexible and can represent exact locations and exact topology.

Hierarchical structures can be superimposed [Bruegger 1989], such that a structure like a quadtree [Samet 1984] results in the two-dimensional space. Other possible structures currently investigated at the University of Maine are posets or lattices which are frequently necessary to model geographic data appropriately [Kainz 1988] [Saalfeld 1985]. These non-hierarchical structures permit that the same geometric parts may be components of several objects. For example, the polygon of a state consists of 2-cells which are also part of its counties.

3 Fundamental Operations

A characteristic of the simplicial algebra is its simplicity: only a small set of operations is necessary. The operations are closed within the simplicial structure, i.e., an operation manipulating a simplex can produce only a spatial object that is a simplicial complex. Updates like the insertion of a new node must be consistent, i.e., the structure of the triangulated network and the completeness axioms must be guaranteed after each modifiation. The principle of all operations is that they guarantee consistency, i.e., each successfully completed operation will preserve the simplicial structure. The fundamental operations for inserting new 0-, 1-, and 2-cells in a 2-dimensional simplicial space will be presented and illustrated step by step.

Subsequently, it is assumed that the universe is established by an outer void and no geometry will exist outside of this universe. By this assumption, all operations are reduced to the insertions of geometric objects inside the universe.

The underlying data structure establishes the relationships among 0-, 1-, and 2-cells: each 1-cell is bound by two 0-cells; each 2-cell is bound by three 1-cells; a 0-cell bounds several edges; and each 1-cell bounds two 2-cells. This structure allows for the derivation of adjaceny through the operations boundary and co-boundary. These operations are fundamental for the following algorithms and their implementation is assumed.

3.1 Node Insertion

The addition of a 0-cell c_0 to an existing network may appear as three possible cases: (1) c_0 coincides with an existing 0-cell; (2) c_0 falls on an existing 1-cell; or (3) c_0 falls within an existing 2-cell. Figure 7 shows these three constellations.

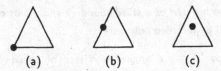

(a)   (b)   (c)

Figure 7: The three cases of node insertion: (a) on a 0-cell, (b) on a 1-cell, and (c) in a 2-cell.

3.1.1 Node Coincidence

The first case is trivial because the object to be added exists already. It is part of the assurance of the completeness of incidence according to which each geometric object cannot exist twice.

3.1.2 Node on Edge

The addition of c_0 which falls on an existing 1-cell c_1 involves in general two 2-cells. The insert operation can be broken down into the following steps:

- Storage of c_0 (figure 8a).

- Connceting c_0 with each 0-cell of the co-boundary of c_1 by storing a new 1-cell (figure 8b).

- Insertion of 2-cells, each made up of two newly inserted 1-cells and one in the boundary of the co-boundary of c_1 (figure 8c).

- Deletion of the 2-cells which formed the co-boundary of c_1 (figure 8d).

- Deletion of the 1-cell c_1 (figure 8e).

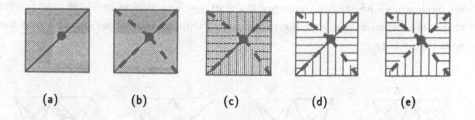

| (a) | (b) | (c) | (d) | (e) |

Figure 8: The insertion of a node on an existing edge.

3.1.3 Node in Polygon

The addition of a 0-cell c_0 which falls within an existing 2-cell c_2 consists of the following operations:

- Storage of the 0-cell c_0 (figure 9a).

- Insertion of the three 1-cells connecting c_0 with the 0-cells in the boundary of c_2 (figure 9b).

- Insertion of three 2-cells, each made up of one bounding 1-cell of c_2 and two newly inserted 1-cells (figure 9c).

- Deletion of c_2 (figure 9d).

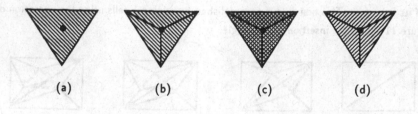

| (a) | (b) | (c) | (d) |

Figure 9: The insertion of a node in an existing triangle.

3.2 Line Insertion

The insertion of a 1-cell is a recursive operation. It can be decomposed into the following steps:

- Insertion of the two bounding 0-cells A_0 and B_0 (figure 10a).

- Retrieval of the smallest 2-complex C_2 inside of which A_0 is completely contained (figure 10b). C_2 is determined with the application of the co-boundary operation, first around A_0 which results in the 1-cells bounded by A_0, and then for the 1-cells yielding the 2-cells.

- Intersection of the boundary of C_2 with the line from A_0 to B_0 (figure 10c) and insertion of the resulting 0-cell D_0 (figure 10d).

- Recursively repeating the retrieval of the boundary of the 2-complex around the node inserted last, the intersection with the line connecting the start and end node of the 1-cell, and the storage of the intersection as new node (figure 10e and f) until the intersection coincides with the end node (figure 10g).

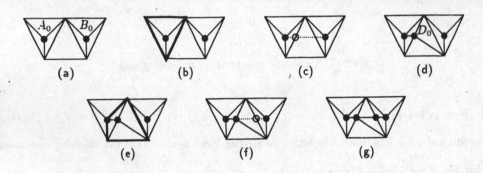

(a)   (b)   (c)   (d)

(e)   (f)   (g)

Figure 10: The insertion of a 1-cell.

3.3 Polygon Insertion

In a two-dimensional model, polygons are described by a sequence of 1-cells which must form one or more closed 1-spheres, representing its boundary. The insertion of a polygon is initially defined by the insertion of its boundary. This first step is accomplished by adding 1-cells using the operation described above. Figure 11 shows the insertion of a triangle.

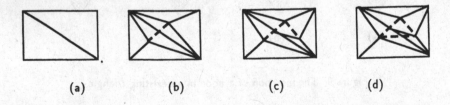

(a)   (b)   (c)   (d)

Figure 11: Part 1 of the insertion of a 2-complex: boundary insertion.

At this stage, the simplicial structure is sound; however, there are no links between the 2-complex and the 2-simplices of which it is comprised. The correct association between the complex and the simplices is accomplished with the following recursive operation:

- Selection of the inner 2-cell of an arbitrary 1-cell in the boundary (figure 12a).

- Reducing the set of bounding 1-cells left by the found one.

- Adding the found 1-cell to the set of visited 1-cells.

- Searching the next 1-cells in the boundary of the current 2-cell without considering already visited and bounding 1-cells.

- Searching the neigboring 2-cells which were not yet visited (figure 12b).

- Adding the found 2-cells to the result.

- Recursively searching for the next neighboring 2-cells through the boundary operator until all 1-cells have been visited (figure 12c).

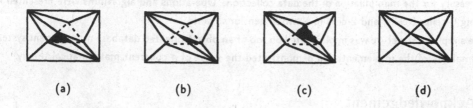

(a)   (b)   (c)   (d)

Figure 12: Part 2 of the insertion of a 2-complex: aggregation of 2-simplices.

The set of bounding 1-cells is not empty if the newly added 2-cell consists of several, non-coherent parts; therefore, the algorithm must loop until the last 1-cell left in the set of bounding cells is processed.

4 Implementation

The simplicial data strucutre was implemented on top of PANDA [Egenhofer 1989], an object-oriented database management system. A particular component of PANDA is the Field Tree [Frank 1983b], a spatial indexing structure organizing spatial data according to their adjacency, and supporting for spatial search techniques and fast retrieval. The spatial search technique was employed for the determination of coincidence of 0-cells.

The implementation gave evidence that a database-like system is necessary for an appropriate and efficient implementation of the operations. In particular, frequent calculations of boundary and co-boundary can be achieved efficiently only if a database-like structure exists.

The transaction concept of database management systems is employed transfering the geometric structure in an atomic operation from one into another consistent state [Härder 1983]. Operations which are—for whatever reason—unsuccessful, are aborted and the simplicial structure will be reset to its initial state before the operation.

The implementation verified the assumption that a large number of small 2-cells is created. From loading one layer of a USGS 7 1/2 minute topographic map, a linear increase of 1-cells by a factor of three was counted compared to the data set.

5   Conclusion

A spatial data model has been presented which is based upon the mathematical theory of simplices and simplicial complexes. These principles of combinatorial topology have been made available to a wide range of applications with spatial data, such as CAD/CAM and Geographic Information Systems. The major contribution of this approach is that inherent problems of implementations of Euclidian geometry are overcome by recording topological properties explicitly.

The simplicial model structures the embedding space in cells, from which meaningful spatial objects can be composed. Completeness of incidence and completeness of inclusion guarantee that the space contains each cell only once and that no isolated cells exist. Only a small set of geometric operations is neccessary for the manipulation of the data collection. Operations and algortihms were presented for inserting 0-cells, 1-cells, and 2-cells in a two-dimensional world.

The simplicial structure was implemented on top of an object-oriented database management system. The simplicity of the implementation demonstrated the value of a coherent mathematical theory.

6   Acknowledgement

Thanks to Werner Kuhn, currently at ETH Zürich, for his valuable contribution in the initial stage of this work. Robert Franzosa improved our mathematical skills in algebraic topology. David Pullar and Eric Carlson helped with the implementation.

Appendix

A   Algorithms for Fundamental Operations

The following operations act upon 0-, 1-, and 2-cells. Chains are a data structure for cells and form an Abelian group with an operation for addition. Sets and its conventional operations are prerequisits. Coercion from set to cell and from chain to set are assumed.

Database operations exist to *store* an n-cell, and *access* its n-simplices, boundary, and co-boundary. *Have* operations store a cell only if it did not exist before. *Make* operations link the a chain of (n-1)-cells and create an n-cell.

A.1   Boundary

```
boundary (c: cell): chain ==
    result := emptyChain;
    FOR EACH simplex IN c DO
      FOR EACH boundingSimplex IN simplex DO
        addCellToChain (result, boundingSimplex, getOrientation (simplex, c));
```

A.2   Co-Boundary

```
coBoundary (c: cell): set of cells ==
```

```
  result := emptySet;
  FOR EACH simplex IN c DO
    FOR EACH boundedSimplex OF simplex DO
      addCellToSet (result, boundedSimplex);
```

A.3 Node Insertion

A.3.1 Node On Node

```
storeC0OncO (c0: 0-cell): boolean ==
    location (retrieveCO (location (c0))) = location (c0);
                          -- True if a 0-cell already exists at the same location.
```

A.3.2 Node On Edge

```
storeC0OnC1 (c0: 0-cell, c1: 1-cell): 1-cell ==
    storeCO (c0);                 -- Storage of c0.
    FOR EACH simplex IN boundary (coBoundary (c1)) DO
      makeC1 (simplex, c0);       -- Connecting c0 with each 0-cell of the
                                  -- co-boundary of c1 by storing a new 1-cell.
    c1Set := coBoundary (c0) + boundary (coBoundary (c1));
    FOR EACH closedChain IN c1Set DO
      makeC2 (closedChain);       -- Insertion of four new 2-cells
    FOR EACH c2 in coBoundary (c1) DO
      deleteC2 (c2);              -- Deletion of the 2-cells which formed the
                                  -- co-boundary of c1.
    deleteC1 (c1);                -- Deletion of the split 1-cell.
```

A.3.3 Node In Polygon

```
storeC0inC2 (c0: 0-cell, c2: 2-cell): 0-cell ==
    storeCO (c0);                 -- Storage of the 0-cell c0.
    FOR EACH simplex IN boundary (c2) DO
      makeC1 (simplex, c0);       -- Insertion of the three 1-cells connecting c0
                                  -- with the 0-cells in the boundary of c2.
    c1Set := coBoundary (c0) + boundary (c2);
    FOR EACH closedChain IN c1Set DO
      makeC2 (closedChain);       -- Insertion of three 2-cells, each madeup of
                                  -- one bounding 1-cell of c2 and two newly
                                  -- inserted 1-cells.
    deleteC2 (c2);                -- Deletion of c2.
```

A.4 Line Insertion

```
inkCO (c0Start, c0End: 0-cell, c1Set: set of 1-cells) ==
    c1 := boundary (coBoundary (coBoundary (c0)));
                                  -- Retrieval of the 2-cell around the first
                                  -- 0-cell stored and calculation of its boundary.
```

```
  s0 := storeC0onC1 (intersection (makeLine (c0Start, c0End), c1), c1);
                              -- Intersection of the boundary with the line
                              -- from c0Start to c0End.
  c1Set := c1Set + getC1Between (s0, c1);
  IF NOT c0Equal (s0, c0End)         -- Recursively repeating the retrieval of the
    THEN linkc0 (s0, c0End, c1Set); --  boundary around the node inserted last,
                              --  the intersection with the line,
                              --  and the storage of the intersection as new node.

toreC1 (c0Start, c0End: 0-cell): set of 1-cells ==
  result := emptySet;
  haveC0 (c0Start);                  -- Insertion of the two bounding 0-cells
  havec0 (c0End);                    --  c0Start and c0End.
  linkc0 (c0Start, c0End, result); -- Connecting c0Start and c0End.
```

A.5 Polygon Insertion

```
mushroom (c1Memory, c11Memory, c1Set: set of 1-cells, c1: 1-cell, c2: 2-cell,
          c2Memory: set of 2-cells) ==
    c11Memory := c11Memory - c1; -- Reducing the set of bounding 1-cells
                              -- left by the found one.
    c1Memory := c1Memory + c1;   -- Adding the found 1-cell
                              -- to the set of visited 1-cells.
    nextC1 := boundary (c2) - c1Set - c1Memory;
                              -- Searching the next 1-cells in the boundary of
                              -- the current 2-cell without considering already
                              -- visited and bounding 1-cells.
    IF nextC1 <> empty THEN
      coB := coBoundary (c1) - c2Memory;
                              -- Searching the neigboring 2-cells which were
                              -- not yet visited.
      c2Memory := c2Memory + coB; -- Adding the found 2-cells to the result.
      mushroom (c1Memory, c11Memory, c1Set, nextC1, coB, c2Memory);
                              -- Continuing recursively.

storeC2 (c1set: set of 1-cells): set of 2-cells ==
    result := emtpySet;
    FOR EACH c1 IN c1set DO      -- Storage of the bounding edges.
      storeC1 (getStart (c1), getEnd (c1));
    c1Memory := c1set;
    c11Memory := c1Set;
    WHILE c11Memeory <> empty DO
      b1 := getFirst (c11Memory); -- Selection of the 1-cell in the boundary.
      c2 := coBoundaryPos (b1, orientation (b1, c11Memory));
                              -- Getting the 'inner' 2-cell.
      mushroom (c1Memory, c11Memory, c1Set, b1, c2, result);
                              -- Mushrooming to collect all 2-cells.
```

References

[Abler 1987] R. Abler. The National Science Foundation National Center for Geographic Information and Analysis. International Journal of Geographical Information Systems, 1(4), 1987.

[Bruegger 1989] B. Bruegger. Hierarchies over Topological Data Structures. In: ASPRS-ACSM Annual Convention, Baltimore, MD, March 1989.

[Cardelli 1984] L. Cardelli. A Semantics of Multiple Inheritance. In: G. Kahn et al., editors, Semantics of Data Types, Lecture Notes in Computer Science, Springer Verlag, New York, NY, 1984.

[Carlson 1987] E. Carlson. Three Dimensional Conceptual Modeling of Subsurface Structures. In: ASPRS-ACSM Annual Convention, Baltimore, MD, 1987.

[Corbett 1979] J.P. Corbett. Topological Principles of Cartography. Technical Report 48, Bureau of the Census, Department of Commerce, 1979.

[Dobkin 1988] D. Dobkin and D. Silver. Recipes for Geometry and Numerical Analysis, Part 1: An Empirical Study. In: Fourth ACM Symposium on Computer Geometry, June 1988.

[Egenhofer 1987] M. Egenhofer. Appropriate Conceptual Database Schema Designs For Two-Dimensional Spatial Structures. In: ASPRS-ACSM Annual Convention, Baltimore, MD, 1987.

[Egenhofer 1988] M. Egenhofer. Graphical Representation of Spatial Objects: An Object-Oriented View. Technical Report 83, Surveying Engineering Program, University of Maine, Orono, ME, July 1988.

[Egenhofer 1989] M. Egenhofer and A. Frank. PANDA: An Extensible DBMS Supporting Object-Oriented Software Techniques. In: Database Systems in Office, Engineering, and Science, Springer-Verlag, New York, NY, March 1989.

[Frank 1983a] A. Frank. Data Structures for Land Information Systems—Semantical, Topological, and Spatial Relations in Data of Geo-Sciences (in German). PhD thesis, Swiss Federal Institute of Technology, Zurich, Switzerland, 1983.

[Frank 1983b] A. Frank. Problems of Realizing LIS: Storage Methods for Space Related Data: The Field Tree. Technical Report 71, Institut for Geodesy and Photogrammetry, Swiss Federal Institute of Technology (ETH), Zurich, Switzerland, 1983.

[Frank 1986] A. Frank and W. Kuhn. Cell Graph: A Provable Correct Method for the Storage of Geometry. In: D. Marble, editor, Second International Symposium on Spatial Data Handling, Seattle, WA, 1986.

[Frank 1987] A. Frank. Overlay Processing in Spatial Informaion Systems. In: N.R. Chrisman, editor, AUTO-CARTO 8, Eighth International Symposium on Computer-Assisted Cartography, Baltimore, MD, March 1987.

[Franklin 1984] W.R. Franklin. Cartographic Errors Symptomatic of Underlying Algebra Problems. In: International Symposium on Spatial Data Handling, Zurich, Switzerland, August 1984.

[Giblin 1977] P.J. Giblin. Graphs, Surfaces, and Homology. Halsted Press, John Wiley and Sons, New York, NY, 1977.

[Goodchild 1978] M. Goodchild. Statistical Aspects of the Polygon Overlay Problem. In: G. Dutton, editor, Harvard Papers on Geographic Information Systems, Addison-Wesley, Reading, MA, 1978.

[Greene 1986] D. Greene and F. Yao. Finite-Resolution Comutational Geometry. 27th IEEE Symposium on the Foundations of Computer Science, November 1986.

[Guevara 1985] J.A. Guevara. A Fuzzy and Heuristic Approach to Segment Intersection Detection and Reporting. In: AUTO-CARTO 7, Washington, D.C., March 1985.

[Härder 1983] T. Härder and A. Reuter. Principles of Transaction-Oriented Database Recovery. ACM Computing Surveys, 15(4), December 1983.

[Herring 1987] J. Herring. TIGRIS: Topologically Integrated Geographic Information Systems. In: N.R. Chrisman, editor, AUTO-CARTO 8, Eighth International Symposium on Computer-Assisted Cartography, Baltimore, MD, March 1987.

[Hoffmann 1989] C. Hoffmann. The Problsma of Accuracy and Robustness in Geometric Computation. IEEE Computer, 22(3), March 1989.

[Jackson 1989] J. Jackson. Algorithms for Triangular Irregular Networks Based on Simplicial Complex Theory. In: ASPRS-ACSM Annual Convention, Baltimore, MD, March 1989.

[Kainz 1988] W. Kainz. Application of Lattice Theory to Geography. In: D. Marble, editor, Third International Symposium on Spatial Data Handling, Sydney, Australia, August 1988.

[Nievergelt 1988] J. Nievergelt and P. Schorn. Line Problems with Supra-Linear Growth (in German). Informatik Spektrum, 11(4), August 1988.

[Peucker 1975] T. Peucker and N. Chrisman. Cartographic Data Structures. The American Cartographer, 55(2), 1975.

[Reiter 1984] R. Reiter. Towards a Logical Reconstruction of Relational Database Theory. In: M.L. Brodie et al., editors, On Conceptual Modelling, Springer Verlag, New York, NY, 1984.

[Requicha 1980] A. Requicha. Representations for Rigid SOlids: Theory, Methods, and Systems. ACM Computing Surveys, 12(4), December 1980.

[Requicha 1983] A. Requicha and H. Voelcker. Solid Modeling: Current Status and Research Directions. IEEE Computer Graphics and Applications, 3(7), October 1983.

[Saalfeld 1985] A. Saalfeld. Lattice Structure in Geography. In: Auto-Carto 7, Washington, D.C., 1985.

[Samet 1984] H. Samet. The Quadtree and Related Hierarchical Data Structures. ACM Computing Surveys, 16(2), June 1984.

[Schubert 1968] H. Schubert. Topology. Allyn and Bacon, Inc., Boston, MA, 1968.

A well-behaved file structure for the storage of spatial objects

M. W. Freeston

ECRC, Arabellastr. 17, D-8000 München 81, West Germany

ABSTRACT A dynamic file structure for spatial object storage and access is described. Based on an extension of the BANG file, it has a self-balancing, tree-structured directory with the following properties:

• no replication of object instances • worst-case search, insertion (excluding overflow) and deletion (excluding underflow) of an individual object requiring no more page accesses than the height of the directory tree • overflow and underflow of data or directory pages propagating only upwards in the tree, and therefore never leading to more page splits or merges than in a B-tree of the same directory depth • fully dynamic - no recombination deadlock condition • compact directory entries, giving a high fan-out ratio • maintenance of spatial relationships between objects

1. Introduction

This paper presents yet another attempt to devise an effective dynamic file structure for the storage of spatial objects. We begin by looking at the merits and failings of the most recent previous efforts, in order to demonstrate the nature and extent of the remaining difficulties. In the light of these, we then give a detailed account of an alternative attack on the problem. A brief but useful discussion and classification of previous methods can be found in [SELL87], based on [SAME86]. We limit ourselves here to consideration of the properties of three of the most recent: the R-tree [GUTT84]; the R^+-tree [SELL87]; and the Cell tree [GÜNT88].

The R-tree and the R^+-tree follow conventional wisdom, representing an n-dimensional object by the smallest n-dimensional *interval* which will enclose or *cover* it. (i.e. a hyper-rectangle with edges parallel to the spatial coordinates). This may of course be a very inaccurate representation of an arbitrarily-shaped object. The Cell tree aims to improve it by using instead a polyhedron as the object cover.

All three structures are based on a balanced, tree-structured directory with properties akin to those of a B-tree. This reflects the requirement for a dynamic, locality-preserving file. Indeed it is almost a prerequisite, since no other kind of file structure has yet demonstrated the same flexibility as the B-tree in these respects. But the similarity extends only as far as the principle of propagating updates upwards from the leaves - thereby maintaining the balanced tree structure. Even this basic principle is sometimes broken in the R^+ and Cell trees, so a casual comparison with the B-tree may be very misleading.

The power of the B-tree rests above all on the fact that its worst-case behaviour for search and update operations is fully predictable and strictly limited. Only one copy of each data item need be stored (apart from the specific representation of duplicates), and the item can be located in a single direct path from root to leaf of the directory tree. An insertion at a leaf node may cause a chain of overflows and insertions at higher directory levels, but never more than the height of the tree. The page occupancy of a B-tree is guaranteed never to sink below 50%, and on average settles at around 67%. How do the R-tree, R^+-tree and Cell tree compare with this performance?

In each case the directory tree represents a recursive partitioning of the data space into sub-regions of the same type as those directly enclosing the objects i.e. cuboids in the case of the R and R^+ trees, polyhedra in the Cell tree. Figure 1 illustrates the way in which this partitioning is performed in each case - for a directory consisting of a single (root) node, containing only two partitions of the data space.

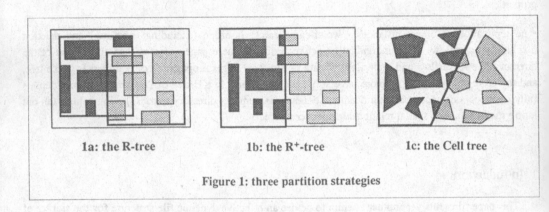

1a: the R-tree   1b: the R^+-tree   1c: the Cell tree

Figure 1: three partition strategies

The example is chosen to illustrate a situation in which there exists no plane which bisects the data space without bisecting one or more of the data object covers. There are two obvious choices: the R-tree (figure 1a) chooses to allow the partitions to overlap by the minimum necessary to enclose each object cover completely within one or other of the partitions; the R^+-tree (figure 1b) and the Cell tree (figure 1c) avoid partition overlap by splitting object covers and lower level directory regions which are bisected by the partition plane. The position of the partition plane is chosen to minimise the number of objects bisected, within a wider set of constraints, such as the maintenance of an acceptable balance between the number of objects in each partition.

The R-tree therefore satisfies the requirement that each object should be uniquely represented, but the partition overlap introduces an ambiguity in its location. Although insertion always takes the shortest path from root to leaf, the search for a single object could, in the worst case, traverse the whole tree. The R^+-tree and Cell tree avoid this at the expense of introducing the possibility of multiple entries for data objects. This guarantees a shortest path search, but introduces traversals of unpredictable length during insertion and deletion. The choice between the two alternatives is invidious, but it is arguable that the R^+-tree and Cell tree pay too high a price for their advantage over the R-tree. The existence of multiple instances of entries introduces a number of disadvantages, apart from the obvious increase in file size, and the loss of a worst-case upper bound on the number of disk accesses required for insertion. Severe additional overheads and complexity are introduced to insertion, deletion, concurrency control and transaction handling, and duplicates (or rather 'system copies') must be removed from the results of range queries.

Apart from the direct additional cost associated with multiple insertions and deletions, there is a less obvious but equally severe overflow problem. When an insertion splits a leaf node, the insertion propagates upward, as in a B-tree, and may split a chain of branch nodes up to and including the root. However, in the R$^+$-tree, as its authors point out, this is by no means the worst case. In general, whenever a branch node splits, the partition boundary will bisect several of the node entries (figure 1b). *Each* of these entries must therefore itself be split along the same partition boundary, and this splitting may continue recursively downward as far as the leaf level. The worst case total number of splits thus depends not only on the tree depth, but also on the number of entries in each node, and the probability that the partition boundary will intersect an entry. The latter depends on both the algorithm by which the partition boundary is chosen, and on the data distribution. So, even if the partitioning algorithm puts the criterion of minimal entry bisections as its highest priority, it is still not possible to quantify the worst case total number of node splits arising from the insertion of a single data object. But it is easy to see that, in a three or four-level directory, it could run into tens or even hundreds. A large number of splits also reduces the average occupancy density of the file.

This problem, which is shared by the Cell-tree, is inherited from the K-D-B tree [ROBI81], an earlier attempt to generalise the B-tree to k dimensions. The K-D-B tree was designed for point data, but the overall structure and partitioning strategy of both the R$^+$-tree and the cell tree retains its fundamental properties. The problem is in fact inherent to any structure which partitions a space by recursive balanced binary division. [N.B. To clarify the subsequent discussion, we distinguish here between *balanced* binary division - meaning that the partition boundary can be positioned anywhere, according to arbitrary balancing criteria - and *strict* binary division, where the partition boundary always lies halfway along the partition interval].

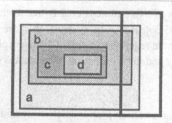

Figure 2a: the problem of partitioning nested object covers

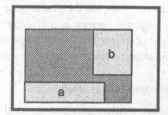

Figure 2b: a measure of the dissimilarity of object covers (dark shaded area)

One aspect of node splitting which is not fully clarified in either the R-tree or R$^+$-tree papers concerns the pathological case when the data object covers within a node are completely nested one within another (figure 2a). The splitting algorithm given for the R-tree would fail in such a case, since it begins by selecting the two entries which are as far apart as possible, as measured by the difference between the minimal area (in two dimensions) of a cover enclosing both entries, and the combined area of the two entries (i.e. maximises the value of the shaded area in figure 2b). Clearly the difference would be zero for all combinations of pairs of nested entries. However, although the R-tree splitting algorithm would need to be modified to detect this condition and apply different splitting criteria, there does not seem to be any fundamental difficulty in including nested objects in the R-tree.

The contrary is the case in the R$^+$-tree. The node splitting algorithm assumes that at least one pair of entries can be found which lies completely on opposite sides of the splitting partition. Otherwise one of the two split nodes must contain the same number of entries as the original overflowing node. Unfortunately, for fully nested entries, this condition cannot be satisfied. Such a configuration of objects is not at all improbable in practice, as the example in figure 2a shows. The problem can be overcome in the same way as that adopted in the Cell tree, which avoids the difficulty entirely by the use of overflow records. The price for this however is the loss of the one remaining worst-case upper bound: the limit on the number of disk accesses required to search for a single data object.

Although all three structures are described as *dynamic*, the R$^+$-tree relies on a periodic re-organisation of the whole tree to deal with the effect of deletions at the leaf nodes. The strategy adopted by the Cell tree appears to be the same as that of the R-tree, namely, that when the contents of a leaf or branch node falls below some threshold value, the node is eliminated and its remaining contents are re-inserted at the same level elsewhere in the tree. Guttman[GUTT84] claims that this strategy has the advantage of algorithmic simplicity, since it re-uses the insertion algorithm. But of course it may trigger a series of node splits, which increases the probability of a large number of disk accesses during deletions. (We recall that the worst-case upper bound to disk accesses during a single deletion in all three structures is in any case the total of file pages).

Apart from deletion, the other potential means of maintaining a high page occupancy in a dynamic environment is re-distribution between sibling nodes. This is possible to a certain extent in structures of the K-D-B type, but is limited by the possibility of recombination deadlock[ROBI81]. In a dynamic environment therefore node occupancies tend to degrade with time. We will show later how a flexible re-distribution capability can improve the performance of certain types of queries, so that inflexibilty in this respect is a significant disadvantage.

To summarise: if we use the performance characteristics of a one-dimensional B-tree as the standard by which to judge the performance of n-dimensional spatial object storage systems, then we must conclude that none of the methods so far proposed or implemented reach that standard. This despite striking apparent similarities between all the structures discussed here and the B-tree itself. The ideal is clear:

- no replication of data objects;
- worst-case single-object search, insertion (excluding overflow) and deletion (excluding underflow) requiring no more disk accesses than the height of the directory tree;
- overflow and underflow propagating only upwards in the tree;
- high average leaf and branch node occupancies (~67%);
- worst-case node occupancy 50%;
- fully dynamic - no recombination deadlock;
- compact branch node entries, giving a high fan-out ratio.
- maintenance of spatial relationships between objects;

Of course, this is not an *absolute* ideal. In fact, it does not seem particularly demanding. But it identifies a clear target for a well-behaved spatial object file structure.

2. An alternative approach

2.1. Design requirements

The author has previously conducted an investigation into the comparative strengths and weaknesses of existing multi-dimensional point data file structures [FREE85]. These included tree structures [BENT79 ROBI81 GARD83 OHSA83], multi-dimensional extendible hashing [FAGI79 OUKS83 OTOO85], and grid files [NIEV81 BURK83 HINR85 OZKA85]. Such a study is the natural starting point for a re-evaluation of spatial object data structures. It was pointed out above that some of the weaknesses in recent designs can be clearly traced back to weaknesses in the point-data structure from which they originated. Conversely, a more robust point data design might form the basis of a better spatial object design.

Although not the original motivation, this study resulted in the development of a new point data file structure. The BANG file [FREE87 89a] meets all the criteria listed above, as far as is applicable to point-data, except that a minimum individual node occupancy of 50% is not guaranteed. This structure therefore offers the possibility of a renewed attack on the spatial object problem. But before attempting to construct a new spatial structure on the principles of this design, we need first to establish precisely:

- what are the characteristics of a point-data file structure that we want to preserve in a spatial object file structure, in order to endow the new structure with the same behaviour characteristics?

- what additional functionality is needed, and can it be imposed without adversely modifying the overall behaviour?

We assume that the representation of a spatial object in the file is a tuple composed of the minimum and maximum bounding coordinates of the object in each dimension, plus either further attributes describing the internal properties of the object, or a link to some other source of descriptive information - probably in a heap file. The most obvious course to take [HINR85] is to transform the n-dimensional bounding coordinates into 2n-dimensional points. A point data structure can then be used unmodified. But, as has often been pointed out, adjacency between objects is not generally preserved in the point transformation, so that the last - but very important - criterion listed above would not be satisfied. We must therefore look for an extension of functionality in n-dimensions.

Nevertheless we note that, if we use the coordinates of the centre of each object cover as the access key of the object, then we can at least use an unmodified point-data file, indexed on this key, to answer exact-match queries on objects. Of course, the centres of several objects of different shapes and sizes may coincide, producing key duplicates, but they could be differentiated by examining the dimensions of each object cover. This representation of objects is also sufficient for certain kinds of range queries on objects:

find the set of objects which are completely enclosed within a specified region of the data space.

We will call queries of this type *full enclosure queries*. The solution set will be a subset of all those objects whose centre points lie within the specified region. But the point representation is not adequate for queries of the form:

find the set of objects which are completely or partially enclosed within a specified region of the data space.

....which we will call *partial enclosure queries*. In the latter case we need additional information on those objects whose covers overlap the search region boundary, but whose centres lie outside it. Unlike the R+-tree and the Cell tree, the partition regions of the point-data representation do not contain this information explicitly. Nor can we directly use the technique of the R-tree, which relies on the principle that every partition region must completely enclose the covers of all the objects contained within it. This rule ensures that all of the object covers which lie wholly or partly within any defined search region must also lie within one of the partition regions intersected by it. In contrast, the boundary of a point-data partition region does not generally completely enclose all the objects whose centre points it contains. It thus seems at first sight that a quite separate partitioning scheme is needed to support such range queries.

2.2. Extension of the BANG file structure

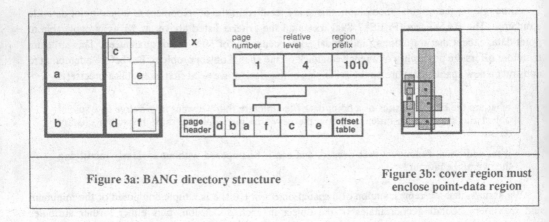

Figure 3a: BANG directory structure

Figure 3b: cover region must enclose point-data region

On further reflection however, the specific partitioning scheme adopted in the BANG file has a useful property in this respect: each partition region is generated by a sequence of strict binary divisions of the partition domain, which is represented as a unique binary string. [In the following examples, binary **1** represents right hand and upper partitions, **0** represents left hand and lower partitions. Partitions are selected in cyclic order through the dimensions, as in the original BANG file design, starting with a vertical partition]. Each entry in the branch nodes of the BANG file directory is composed of such a binary string, together with a *level number* indicating the number of bits in the string (or, equivalently, the relative size of the partition region), and a pointer to the page representing the region in the directory level below (figure 3a).

The particular value of this representation is that any prefix of a binary string represents a partition region which encloses that represented by the whole string. Suppose that a directory entry at the lowest branch node level represents a region **R** immediately enclosing the centre points of a set of spatial objects. Then there must exist some region **R'** in the sequence of strict binary partitions which generated **R** such that **R'** encloses the covers of all the objects in **R**. **R'** is *minimal* if there are no smaller regions in the partition sequence which enclose the covers of all the objects in **R** (figure 3b). **R'** and **R** may of course coincide.

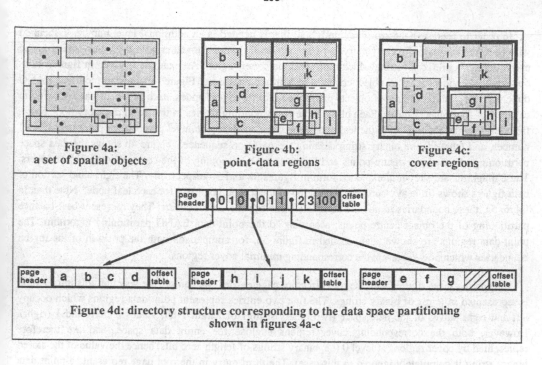

Figure 4a:
a set of spatial objects

Figure 4b:
point-data regions

Figure 4c:
cover regions

Figure 4d: directory structure corresponding to the data space partitioning
shown in figures 4a-c

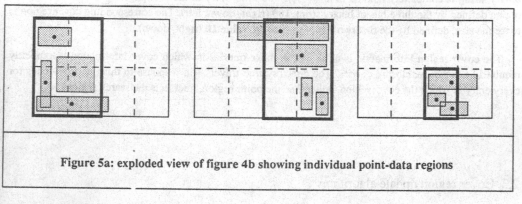

Figure 5a: exploded view of figure 4b showing individual point-data regions

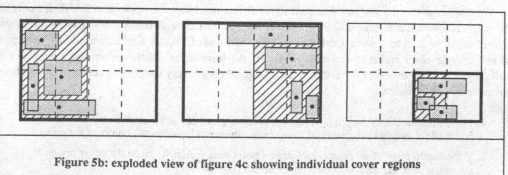

Figure 5b: exploded view of figure 4c showing individual cover regions

In order to represent the *cover region* **R'**, all that is needed is an additional level number associated with each branch node directory entry. This second level number, together with the binary string in the entry, defines a prefix substring which represents the cover region. An example is given in figures 4a to 5b. Figure 4a shows a set of object covers **a** to **k** in a data space. Figure 4d shows a modified BANG directory representing the set of objects partitioned into three leaf nodes, each of which has a maximum capacity of four object entries. Each of the three corresponding entries in the (root) directory node show, from left to right, the pointer to the leaf node below, the cover region level number, the point region level number, and (shaded) the binary string defining the partition sequence. Figure 4b shows the data space partitioning of the object centre points and figure 4c the partitioning of the corresponding object covers. These diagrams are shown in exploded form in figures 5a and 5b respectively. The right-hand section of both figures shows (in heavy outline) the position of the region boundary for each leaf node. Note that, in figure 5a, these boundaries in no case completely enclose the object covers. They represent best-balance partitioning of the object centre points, according to the point-data BANG partitioning algorithm. The point-data regions are shown again shaded in figure 5b, for comparison with the position of the region boundaries which now represent the corresponding minimal cover regions.

Comparing these figures with the root directory page entries, we can see the way that this information is represented in terms of binary strings. The first two entries represent point-data regions which occupy left and right halves of the data space (two binary strings of length 1 bit, values **0** (left) and **1** (right). However, both the corresponding cover regions enclose the entire data space, and are therefore represented by cover regions at level 0 (i.e. binary strings of length zero bits, hence the value of the stored binary string is completely ignored in this case). The third entry in the root page represents a point-data region defined by the three bits of binary string **100** (right, down, left). The corresponding cover region is twice the size, defined by the first two bits of this string, value **10** (right, down).

The cover region information is only used in those queries in which cover information is explicitly required i.e. partial enclosure queries. The directory tree traversal in response to this query searches for every entry in which the cover region, rather than the point region, intersects the search region.

2.3. Cover region update algorithms

We emphasise that the structure described above differs from that of the point data BANG file only in the presence of the cover region level number in each branch node directory entry. Exactly the same algorithm can be used for insertion, deletion, overflow and underflow. We need only to add the operation of updating the cover region level number whenever the insertion or deletion of an object requires the boundary of a cover region to be modified. These algorithms are very simple, but before detailing them we make two observations:

1. The minimum binary partition which will enclose an object cover is given by the common prefix of the binary keys generated from the minimum and maximum vertices of the cover.

2. If the centre point of an object lies within a point-data region R_p, then the cover region R_c associated with R_p must enclose both the object cover and R_p.

• *To compute the minimum binary region which will enclose the covers of all the objects in a leaf node:*

Let this region be represented by the binary key **cover_key** of length **node_cover_level** bits.

    find the minimum bounding value of all the objects in each of the **n** dimensions;

    form the binary key K_{min} from the set of **n** minimum bounding values;

    find the maximum bounding value of all the objects in each of the **n** dimensions;

    form the binary key K_{max} from the set of **n** maximum bounding values;

    cover_key = common_prefix(K_{min}, K_{max});

    node_cover_level = length(cover_key);

• *To compute the level of the minimum binary region which will enclose the covers of all the objects in a branch node:*

If the cover region of any single entry in the node is larger than the point region for the node, then the largest of these cover regions becomes the cover region for the node.

• *To insert an object into the file:*

The object is inserted into the smallest point region which encloses the object's centre point; the point-data BANG file algorithm is used for this, except that the cover key of the object is dynamically generated during descent of the directory tree, in addition to the centre point key. At each directory branch level, both keys are extended only as far as the length of the longest entry key in the node (representing the smallest point region). If the minimal cover key of the object is generated before the leaf node is reached, then its level is compared with the node cover level of each subsequent node visited. If the object cover level is less than the node cover level, then it becomes the new node cover level.

• *To delete an object from the file:*

The object is located in the file as for insertion, except that, instead of updating cover levels during descent of the tree, the cover level of each node visited is simply compared with that of the object. If the object cover level is less than that of the node, then the object cannot exist in the file, and the search can be aborted before the leaf node is reached. If however the object is found, it is deleted from the leaf node, and the cover key for the node is recomputed. If the new cover level is greater than the old, then the old cover key must be replaced by the new on return to the directory level above. This update may in turn trigger a recalculation of the cover key for the updated directory page, and so on up to the root.

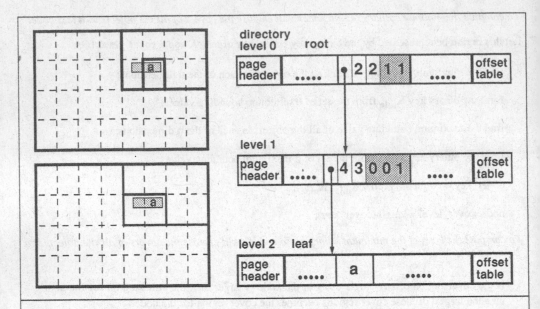

Figure 6a: the point-data regions (upper left) and cover regions (lower left) corresponding to the pages (right) encountered in a directory search for object a

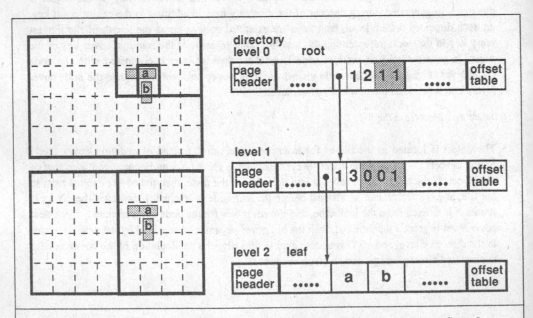

Figure 6b: after the insertion of object b, the point-data regions have not overflowed, but the cover regions have been modified

An example is given in figures 6a and 6b, which show a single path down through a three-level directory, and the corresponding data space partitioned into three regions, one at each directory level. The upper left diagram shows the point-data region partitioning, and the lower left the cover region partitioning.

Notice first that, in practice, the point-data level of an entry is recorded as a level *relative* to the point-data level of the node in which the entry appears. Only the relevant part of the full access key need then be recorded at each level in the directory. In contrast, the cover level is recorded as the *absolute* level, since the cover level can be less than the point-data level of the node in which it appears.

When a second object **b** is added to **a** (figure 6b) the point-data region partitioning is unaffected (i.e. there is no overflow, underflow or redistribution) but the cover level of the leaf node drops from 4 to 1. This value is therefore updated in the corresponding entry in the node (directory level 1) above. This in turn causes the cover level of the node to be recomputed, because an absolute cover level of 1 is less than the *absolute* point-data level of the node, which is 2.

There could not previously have been any entries in this node with cover levels less than 2, otherwise the cover level in the root node entry would have been less than 2. So the updated entry at directory level 1 must now have the largest cover in the node. Thus the recomputed cover level for this node is also 1, which is entered in the root node above.

2.4. Correlation between cover and point-data distributions

The scheme as so far described has the attraction of extreme simplicity in moving from a point-data to a spatial object file structure. But it rests on the implicit assumption that there is a strong correlation between the spatial distribution of the centre points of objects, and the spatial distribution of their maximum and minimum extensions in each dimension. If this is not so then, however small a point-data partition region may be, the corresponding cover region may extend to the whole data space. In figure 5b for example, a partial enclosure range query over a region within the lower right-hand corner of the data space requires the whole tree - albeit three leaf nodes - to be searched. The only way to improve the correlation is to modify the BANG file splitting, recombination and redistribution algorithms to take the consequent change in correlation into account.

Fortunately, the file structure itself provides a clear measure of the degree of correlation: the ratio of the total volume of the point regions to that of the cover regions gives a correlation coefficient, which we will call the *cover coefficient*. Ideally, each cover region should be no larger than its corresponding point region. This will be so, for example, in the (improbable) case that no point data partition boundary intersects an object cover. We also note that there is considerable scope for dynamic redistribution in the BANG file. The contents of any region can be redistributed at any time either with its *buddy* or with its immediately enclosing region (one or the other must exist), or with any enclosed region, of which there may be many. Redistribution means a merge and immediate re-splitting of two regions, with the aim of obtaining a "better" balance. The criteria of best balance can thus be modified to take into account the effect of a particular redistribution on the value of the cover coefficient as well as on the occupancy levels of the resulting regions.

Redistribution following a deletion is equally possible. In addition, the recursive splitting procedure following node overflow may halt at a partition before or after the normal best-balance point, if the resulting cover regions are smaller than they would be at best balance. The sacrifice for this is of course a potential reduction in the average percentage occupancy of file pages. But at least the choice between high correlation and high page occupancy can be made dynamically, and can be preset at preferred levels. A minimum acceptable page occupancy implies a limit to the attempt to achieve a high correlation coefficient.

3. Conclusion

The objective declared in this paper has been the development of a truly <u>dynamic</u> file structure for the storage and retrieval of spatial objects. The resulting design allows strict limits to be placed on worst-case performance for standard operations such as insertion, deletion, or retrieval of a single object so that, particularly in transaction processing environments and real-time systems, the structure can be used with confidence and predictability. The advantages of the point-data BANG file are all carried over to the spatial object extension. The directory, although expanded by an additional field in each branch node entry, remains very compact. The average size of an original directory entry is found in practice to be around 10 bytes (including its entry in the page offset table), so that the additional field increases the average entry length by around 20%. But since, for a file composed of 1 Kbyte pages, the overall directory size in the original BANG file occupies only about 2% of the total file space, the extended version will still only occupy around 2.4%. The average fan-out ratio is reduced in this case from around 67 to 56.

By retaining a dual representation for point and object partition regions, the most effective representation can be selected, according to the type of query. Despite the use of strict binary partitioning, the storage occupancy of the point-data BANG file has shown itself to be extremely insensitive to changes in the data distribution. The main weakness in the design, as originally conceived and as currently implemented, lies in the use of a cyclic partitioning sequence through the dimensions of the data space. Paradoxically this can lead to a considerable difference in the number of effective partitions in each dimension for certain data distributions. Cyclic partitioning is not however a fundamental principle of the BANG file design, and a more flexible partitioning strategy [FREE89b] is being incorporated into a new implementation which will also include the extension in functionality described in this paper.

The abandonment of cyclic partitioning should also give the splitting algorithm more flexibility to adjust the splitting strategy to maximise the cover coefficient. However, a high cover coefficient has not been the primary objective of this design. It is unlikely that range queries which operate on the object cover regions will be more efficient than equivalent queries on the R$^+$-tree or Cell tree, where there is no region overlap. But the comparison is not as simple as might at first seem, because the replication of object instances means that, for a given set of objects and a fixed page size, there will be more node splits in the R$^+$-tree and Cell tree than in the BANG file or the R-tree. Simulation figures for the R$^+$-tree [SELL87] tend to confirm the expectation that the performance of range queries on the R-tree degrades under conditions when the value of the cover coefficient is low e.g. when a few large objects are inserted into a compact cluster of relatively small objects. To what extent the BANG file redistribution algorithms can compensate for this is not yet clear, and must await performance figures of the new implementation.

Acknowledgments

Thanks to all at ECRC, but especially the KB group, for their encouragement and enthusiasm. The author is grateful for the support of Jean-Marie Nicolas throughout this research.

4. References

[BENT79]   J.L Bentley
             Multidimensional binary search trees in database applications
             IEEE Trans. on Soft. Eng., Vol SE-5, No. 4, July 1979.

[BURK83]   W.A. Burkhard
             Interpolation-Based index maintenance
             Proc. ACM SIGMOD-SIGACT Symposium, 1983.

[FAGI79]   R. Fagin, J. Nievergelt, N. Pippenger, H.R. Strong
             Extendible hashing: a fast access method for dynamic files
             ACM-TODS, Vol. 4, No. 3, September 1979.

[FREE87]   M.W. Freeston
             The BANG file: a new kind of grid file
             Proc. ACM SIGMOD Conf., San Francisco, 1987.

[FREE89a]   M.W. Freeston
             Advances in the design of the BANG file
             3rd Int. Conf. on Foundations of Data Organisation and Algorithms,
             Paris, 1989.

[FREE89b]   In preparation

[GARD83]   G. Gardarin, P. Valduriez, Y. Viemont
             Les arbres de predicats
             INRIA, Rapports de Recherche, No. 203, April 1983.

[GÜNT88]   O. Günther
             The Cell Tree: an index for geometric databases
             Internal Report No. TR-88-002, International Computer Science Institute,
             Berkeley, California, 1988.

[GUTT84]   A. Guttman
             R-trees: a dynamic index structure for spatial searching
             Proc. ACM SIGMOD Conf., Boston, 1984.

[HINR85]   K.H. Hinrichs
             The grid file system: implementation and case studies of applications
             Doctoral Thesis Nr. 7734, ETH Zurich, 1985.

[NIEV81]   J. Nievergelt, H. Hintenberger, K.C. Sevcik
             The Grid File: an adaptable, symmetric multikey file structure
             Internal Report No. 46, Institut für Informatik,
             ETH Zürich, 1981.

[OTOO85]   E.J. Otoo
             *A multidimensional digital hashing scheme for files with
             composite keys*
             ACM 1985.

[OUKS83]   M. Ouksel, P. Scheuermann
             Storage mapping for multidimensional linear dynamic hashing
             Proc. of 2nd Symposium on Principles of Database Systems, Atlanta, 1983.

300

[OZKA85]   E.A. Ozkarahan, M. Ouksel
            Dynamic and order preserving data partitioning for database machines
            Proc. of 11th Int. Conf. on Very Large Data Bases, Stockholm, 1985.

[OHSA83]   Y. Ohsawa, M. Sakauchi
            The BD-Tree: a new n-dimensional data structure with highly efficient
            dynamic characteristics
            IFIP 9th World Computer Congress, Paris, 1983.

[ROBI81]   J.T. Robinson
            The k-d-b tree: a search structure for large multidimensional
            dynamic indexes
            Proc. ACM SIGMOD Conf., 1981.

[SAME86]   H. Samet
            Quadtrees and related hierarchical data structures for computer
            graphics and image processing
            1986.

[SELL87]   T. Sellis, N. Roussopoulos, C.Faloutsos
            The R+-tree: a dynamic index for multi-dimensional objects
            Proc. of 13th Int. Conf. on Very Large Data Bases, Brighton, 1987.

Spatial Reasoning

THE DESIGN OF PICTORIAL DATABASES BASED UPON
THE THEORY OF SYMBOLIC PROJECTIONS

Shi-Kuo Chang, Erland Jungert and Y. Li

Department of Computer Science
University of Pittsburgh
Pittsburgh, PA 15260 USA

Abstract

We present a methodology for pictorial database design, based upon a new spatial knowledge structure. This spatial knowledge structure consists of an image database, symbolic projections representing the spatial relations among objects or sub-objects in an image, and rules to derive complex spatial relations from the generalized 2D string representation of the symbolic projections. The most innovative aspect of this spatial knowledge structure is the use of symbolic projections to represent pictorial knowledge as generalized 2D strings. Since spatial knowledge is encoded into strings, inference rules can be applied for spatial reasoning. Finally, we describe a prototype knowledge-based pictorial database system, which supports spatial reasoning, flexible pictorial information retrieval, visualization and manipulation.

1. Introduction

2D string has been proposed as a new way of representing symbolic pictures[2]. It is an effective approach in solving the problem of pictorial information retrieval and in constructing iconic indexes for pictures in an image database. However, if we want to apply the 2D string representation to solving problems of reasoning and planning in many applications, 2D string may be insufficient because it employs only two spatial relational operators '<' and '=' to represent "left-right" (or "below-above") and "at the same location as" relations. By introducing additional spatial operators, the 2D string representation can be extended to represent other types of relations between picture objects[6]. Furthermore, a new representation of multi-resolution symbolic (or binary) pictures, called 2D H-string, is found to combine the advantages of quadtrees with 2D strings[3]. The purpose of this paper is to show that it is possible to consolidate these approaches, by introducing generalized 2D strings. Based upon this spatial knowledge structure, we can develop a new methodology for pictorial database design.

In this paper, we first describe previously proposed spatial operators. Then we define the new representation structure, called *generalized 2D string*. In terms of transformations and levels of representation, the relationships among classes of spatial relational operators are analyzed. It is shown that generalized 2D string subsumes other classes of spatial operators. We also show that spatial reasoning can be carried out effectively on generalized 2D strings using a set of reasoning rules. Finally, we describe a prototype knowledge-based pictorial database system, which supports spatial reasoning, flexible pictorial information retrieval, visualization and manipulation.

2. Spatial Relational Operators

A *symbolic picture* or simply a *picture* is a grid where some of the slots are filled by picture objects[2]. In pictorial information retrieval, we often want to retrieve pictures satisfying certain spatial relations, for example, "find the tree to the left of the house". To specify such spatial relations, two spatial relational operators were proposed[2]. As an example, the picture in Figure 1 can be represented by the 2D string $(u,v) = (a < b = c, a = b < c)$. The symbol '<' denotes the left-right spatial relation in string u, and the below-above spatial relation in string v. The symbol '=' denotes the spatial relation "at approximately the same spatial location as". Therefore, the 2D string representation can be seen to be the *symbolic projections* of a picture along the vertical and horizontal directions.

Figure 1. Symbolic projections of a picture.

In the above representation, the spatial relational operator '=' can be omitted, so that the 2D string is more efficiently represented by $(u,v) = (a < b c, a b < c)$. If the symbolic picture is given, we can take the symbolic projections to obtain the 2D string (u,v). Conversely, if the (u,v) is given, we can reconstruct a picture having symbolic projections (u,v), although the reconstruction may not be unique. Efficient algorithms for picture reconstruction and similarity retrieval have been developed[2].

The two basic spatial relational operators can be augmented by other operators. The edge-to-edge local operator, denoted by the symbol 'l', can be used when two objects are in direct contact either in the left-right or in the below-above direction[6]. Figure 2 illustrates the edge-to-edge relationship and the corresponding string representation.

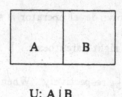

U: A | B

Figure 2. An example of the edge-to-edge operator.

The above three spatial operators, ' < ', '=' and 'l', are the most basic spatial operators. Further refinements are possible. As illustrated in Figure 3, the edge-to-edge operator can be augmented by the following local operators[3].

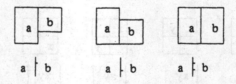

Figure 3. Refined edge-to-edge operators.

Using these operators, the original (u,v) string of a symbolic picture can be extended so that it can represent complex spatial relations among picture objects. For example, the (u,v) string for the picture shown in Figure 1 can be extended to (a < b c , a b | c).

We now show how to define hierarchical spatial operators, so that a symbolic picture can be represented using a hierarchical structure. In a way, this combines the quadtree representation[9] and the 2D string representation[3]. We first define

$$\Downarrow = \{ \downarrow . \downarrow . \downarrow . \updownarrow \}$$

to be the set of *down-level operators*. The down-level operators determine the local spatial relations among picture objects in terms of subdividing picture blocks into quadrants. Similarly, we can define

$$\Uparrow = \{ \uparrow . \uparrow . \uparrow . \updownarrow \}$$

to be the set of *up-level operators*. The up-level operator and the down-level operator must be used as a pair. Therefore, the down-level operator is similar to a left parenthesis, and the up-level operator is similar to a right parenthesis. $\uparrow$. $\uparrow$. $\uparrow$. and $\updownarrow$ have the opposite meanings of $\downarrow$. $\downarrow$. $\downarrow$. and $\updownarrow$. respectively. When subdividing a picture block into its quadrants, we can obtain sixteen different pairs of down-level and up-level operators, as shown in Figure 4.

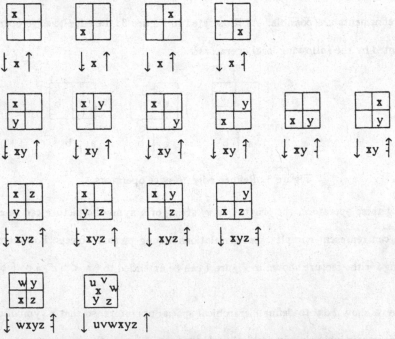

Figure 4. Sixteen pairs of down-level and up-level operators.

The last operator pair in Figure 4 corresponds to the case where no further subdivision can be made. We now give an example on how to use these hierarchical spatial operators to represent a symbolic picture. The resultant representation is called the 2D H-string. The picture P is as shown in Figure 5(a).

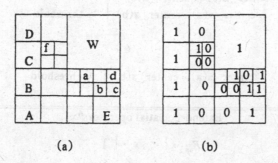

(a)   (b)

Figure 5. Example of 2D H-string representation.

The four quadrants are represented by Q_1 (up-left), Q_2 (down-left), Q_3 (up-right) and Q_4 (down-right). We can then use the operator pairs of Figure 4 to encode a picture recursively. The picture P is first encoded as $\Downarrow Q_1 Q_2 Q_3 Q_4 \Uparrow$, and then each quadrant is encoded in the same manner. The encoded 2D H-string of P is

$$\text{2D-H(P)} = \Updownarrow \updownarrow \text{DC} \updownarrow f \uparrow \Uparrow \updownarrow \text{BA} \uparrow \text{W} \Updownarrow \downarrow a \uparrow \downarrow \text{bdc} \Uparrow \text{E} \Uparrow \Uparrow$$

Similarly, the binary picture P shown in Figure 5(b) can be represented by

$$\text{2D-H(P)} = \Updownarrow \updownarrow 11 \updownarrow 1 \uparrow \Uparrow \updownarrow 11 \uparrow 1 \Updownarrow \downarrow 1 \uparrow \downarrow 111 \Uparrow 1 \Uparrow \Uparrow$$

3. Classes of Spatial Relational Operators

The spatial relational operators described above are used to represent symbolic pictures from different points of view. In fact, different class of operators may be useful for different applications. Table 1 summarizes the three classes of operators introduced in the previous section.

Table 1

Symbol	Definition	Pattern
	Basic spatial operators[2] $B_{op} = \{ < , = \}$	
$a < b$	$center\_x(a) < center\_x(b)$ $\mid center\_x(a) - center\_x(b) \mid > threshold$	a b
$a = b$	$\mid center\_x(a) = center\_x(b) \mid \leqslant threshold$	b a
	Extended spatial operators[6] $E_{op} = \{ < , = , \mid \}$	
$a \mid b$	a is edge to edge with b	a b
	Hierarchical spatial operators[3] $H_{op} = \{ \mid\cdot , \mid\cdot , \mid\cdot , \downarrow , \downarrow , \downarrow , \downarrow , \uparrow , \uparrow , \uparrow , \uparrow \}$	
$a \mid b$	a is edge to edge with b $min\_y(a) = min\_y(b)$	a b
$a \mid b$	a is edge to edge with b $max\_y(a) = max\_y(b)$	a b
$a \mid b$	a is edge to edge with b $min\_y(a) = min\_y(b)$ $max\_y(a) = max\_y(b)$	a b
$a \downarrow b$	$length\_x(a) = 2\ length\_x(b)$ $length\_y(a) = 2\ length\_y(b)$	b a
$a \downarrow b$	$a \downarrow b$, and $max\_x(a) = min\_x(b)$ $max\_y(a) = max\_y(b)$	b a

$$a \downarrow b \text{ , and}$$

$a \downarrow b$
$$\max\_x(a) = \min\_x(b)$$
$$\min\_y(a) = \min\_y(b)$$

$$a \downarrow b \text{ , } a \downarrow c \text{ , and}$$

$a \downdownarrows bc$
$$\max\_x(a) = \min\_x(b)$$
$$\max\_y(a) = \max\_y(b)$$
$$\max\_x(a) = \min\_x(c)$$
$$\min\_y(a) = \min\_y(c)$$

In the above, center_x(a) is the x-coordinate (horizontal direction) of the center of object 'a', and min_y(b) is the minimum y-coordinate (vertical direction) of object 'b'. If the distance between center_x(a) and center_x(b) is within a certain threshold, then the two objects are considered to be at approximately the same horizontal spatial location.

In addition to these three classes of spatial operators, based upon the local operators introduced by Jungert[6], we can define a fourth class of local spatial operators. These operators are defined in Table 2.

Table 2

Symbol	Definition	Pattern
Local spatial operators[6]		
$L_{op} = \{ = , < , \mid , \vdash , \vdash , \dashv , \dashv , \backslash , / , \approx , \simeq \}$		
a $\vdash$ b	$\min\_x(a) = \min\_x(b)$ $\max\_x(a) < \max\_x(b)$ $\max\_y(a) \leqslant \min\_y(b)$	
a $\vdash$ b	$\min\_x(a) = \min\_x(b)$ $\max\_x(a) < \max\_x(b)$ $\min\_y(a) \geqslant \max\_y(b)$	
a $\dashv$ b	$\min\_x(a) < \min\_x(b)$ $\max\_x(a) = \max\_x(b)$ $\min\_y(a) \geqslant \max\_y(b)$	

$a \dashv b$	$\min\_x(a) < \min\_x(b)$ $\max\_x(a) = \max\_x(b)$ $\max\_y(a) \leqslant \min\_y(b)$	
$a \setminus b$	$\min\_x(a) < \min\_x(b)$ $\max\_x(a) < \max\_x(b)$ $\min\_y(a) \geqslant \max\_y(b)$	
a / b	$\min\_x(a) < \min\_x(b)$ $\max\_x(a) < \max\_x(b)$ $\max\_y(a) \leqslant \min\_y(b)$	
$a \approx b$	$\min\_x(a) < \min\_x(b)$ $\max\_x(a) > \max\_x(b)$ $\min\_y(a) \geqslant \max\_y(b)$	
$a \simeq b$	$\min\_x(a) < \min\_x(b)$ $\max\_x(a) > \max\_x(b)$ $\max\_y(a) \leqslant \min\_y(b)$	

4. Generalized 2D Strings

Based upon the previously introduced spatial operators, we want to find a general representation, encompassing the other representations. This consideration leads to the formulation of a generalized 2D string system, which is our proposed knowledge structure for pictorial databases[5].

A *generalized 2D string system* is a five tuple (V, C, E_{op}, e, " $\langle$, $\rangle$ "), where V is the vocabulary; C is the *cutting mechanism*, which consists of cutting lines at the extremal points of objects; $E_{op} = \{ < , = , \;| \}$ is the set of *extended spatial operators*; e is a special symbol which can represent an area of any size and any shape, called *empty-space object*; and " $\langle$, $\rangle$ " is a pair of operators which is used to describe local structure.

The cutting mechanism defines how the objects in an image are to be segmented. It also makes it possible for the local operator " $|$ " to be used as a global operator to be inserted into the original 2D strings. The symbolic picture in Figure 6 has cutting lines as shown by dotted lines. The *generalized 2D string (2D G-string)* representation is as follows:

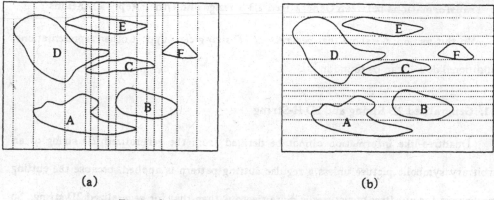

Figure 6. Image segmentation using cutting lines

u: D │ A e D │ A e D e E │ A e C e D e E │ A e A e C e D e E │ A e C e D e E │ A e C e E │

A e B e C e E │ B e C e E │ B e C │ B │ B e F │ F

v: A │ A e B │ B < D │ D e C │ D e F │ D │ D e E

In the above, the symbol 'e' represents "empty space". The term "empty space" was first introduced by Lozano-Perez[8]. Here we use the special symbol , 'e' , to represent empty areas of any size and any shape. Therefore, the expression "A e B" can be rewritten as "A B", and the 2D G-strings can be simplified:

u: D │ A D │ A D E │ A C D E │ A A C D E │ A C D E │ A C E │

A B C E │ B C E │ B C │ B │ B F │ F

v: A │ A B │ B < D │ D C │ D F │ D │ D E

Furthermore, the expression "B < D" in the v-string can also be written as "B │ e │D", indicating objects B and D are not touching.

The special empty-space symbol 'e' and operator-pair " ⟨ , ⟩ " provides the means to use 2D G-strings to substitute for other representations. In other words, we can transform another representation into the 2D G-string and conversely.

5. Transformations between Generalized 2D Strings and Other Representations

In this section, we show that *generalized 2D string* can support other representations. Additional details can be found in [5].

5.1. Generalized 2D String and 2D H-String

Quadtree-like information cannot be derived from the generalized 2D string of an arbitrary symbolic picture unless a regular cutting pattern is applied, because the cutting mechanism for quadtree structures is more rigorous than that for generalized 2D string. So we should first generate 2D G-strings under quadtree cutting mechanism . We will use the operator pair " $\langle \, , \, \rangle$ " to represent the result of each subdivision in the form of $\langle Q_2 Q_1 | Q_4 Q_3 \rangle$ for u-string, and $\langle Q_1 Q_3 | Q_2 Q_4 \rangle$ for v-string. This variation of 2D G-string is called quaternary 2D G-string , denoted as 2D-$G_1(P)$. Here is 2D-$G_1(P)$ for picture P in Figure 5(a).

$$u: \Big\langle\ \big\langle AB \,|\, ee \big\rangle\ \big\langle CD \,|\, \big\langle ef \,|\, ee \big\rangle e \big\rangle\ \big|\ \big\langle e \big\langle ee \,|\, ea \big\rangle\ \big|\ E \big\langle be \,|\, cd \big\rangle \big\rangle \big\rangle W\ \Big\rangle$$

$$v: \Big\langle\ \big\langle Ae \,|\, Be \big\rangle\ \big\langle eE \,|\, \big\langle ee \,|\, ea \big\rangle \big\langle bc \,|\, ed \big\rangle \big\rangle\ \big|\ \big\langle C \big\langle ee \,|\, fe \big\rangle \,|\, De \big\rangle W\ \Big\rangle$$

It is easy to see that the quadtree information is embedded in quaternary 2D G-string by the parentheses. So, the transformation can be carried out easily, which turns $\langle Q_2 Q_1 | Q_4 Q_3 \rangle$ into the corresponding $\Vert Q_1 Q_2 Q_3 Q_4 \Uparrow$ pattern. Of course, the usage of operator " $\langle \, , \, \rangle$ " is not restricted to this purpose. It can be used anywhere in order to define a sub-pattern of interest. We will also show this usage in Section 5.2.

Now let us look at the other side of the problem, i.e., how 2D-G(P) can be obtained from 2D-H(P). In the rest of this subsection, we will present an algorithm for traversing 2D H-strings. Then an algorithm for transforming 2D-H(P) to 2D-$G_1(P)$ is given. Finally, rules for transforming 2D-$G_1(P)$ into 2D-G(P) are presented. First, the down-level operators and up-level operators for 2D H-string are coded as follows.

$$\downarrow \quad \downarrow \quad \downarrow \quad \updownarrow \quad \uparrow \quad \uparrow \quad \uparrow \quad \mathop{\uparrow}\limits$$

| 000 | 001 | 010 | 011 | 100 | 101 | 110 | 111 |

```
Procedure Traverse(q₁q₂...qₖ) /* upon 2D-H(P) */
Begin
    next-symbol = scan(2D-H(P));
    if next-symbol ∈ V ( the vocabulary),
       /* the symbol is at the location indicated by quadcode q₁q₂ ··· qₖ */
       begin
            output (q₁q₂...qₖ , next-symbol);
       end
    else /* must search for the matched operator */
       begin
            left-symbol=next-symbol;
            right-symbol = search(2D-H(P));
            begin
                if left-symbol@1=1 then call procedure Traverse(q₁q₂ ··· qₖ 1);
                else output(q₁q₂ ··· qₖ 1, 0);
                if left-symbol@2=1 then call procedure Traverse(q₁q₂ ··· qₖ 2);
                else output(q₁q₂ ··· qₖ 2, 0);
                if right-symbol@1=1 then call procedure Traverse(q₁q₂ ··· qₖ 3);
                else output(q₁q₂ ··· qₖ 3, 0);
                if right-symbol@2=1 then call procedure Traverse(q₁q₂ ··· qₖ 4);
                else output(q₁q₂ ··· qₖ 4, 0);
            end
       end
End

Procedure Transform(2D-H(P), 2D-G₁(P))
Begin
    next-symbol = scan(2D-H(P));
    if next-symbol ∈ V ( the vocabulary),
        append(2D-G₁(P), next-symbol);
    else /* must search for the matched operator */
       begin
            append(2D-G₁(P), 〈 );
            left-symbol=next-symbol;
            right-symbol = search(2D-H(P));
            begin
                if left-symbol@1=1 then call procedure Transform( 2D-H(P), 2D-G₁(P));
                else append(2D-G₁(P), e);
                if left-symbol@2=1 then call procedure Transform( 2D-H(P), 2D-G₁(P));
                else append(2D-G₁(P), e);
                append(2D-G₁(P), | );
                if right-symbol@1=1 then call procedure Transform( 2D-H(P), 2D-G₁(P));
                else append(2D-G₁(P), e);
                if right-symbol@2=1 then call procedure Transform( 2D-H(P), 2D-G₁(P));
                else append(2D-G₁(P), e);
                append(2D-G₁(P), 〉 );
            end
       end
End
```

The following five transformation rules can then be applied to convert from $2D\text{-}G_1(P)$ expression to $2D\text{-}G(P)$ expression. These transformation rules essentially rearrange the expression so that it becomes consistent with the definition of 2D-G strings.

Rule1: $\left\langle S_1 \,\middle|\, S_3 \right\rangle \left\langle S_2 \,\middle|\, S_4 \right\rangle \;\Rightarrow\; \left\langle S_1 S_2 \,\middle|\, S_3 S_4 \right\rangle$

where S_i is a *proper subsequence* of $2D\text{-}G_1(P)$, i.e., the parenthesis in S_i are balanced, i=1,2,3,4.

Rule2: $A \left\langle S_1 \,\middle|\, S_2 \right\rangle B \;\Rightarrow\; \left\langle A S_1 B \,\middle|\, A S_2 B \right\rangle$

where $A,B \in V \bigcup \{e\}$. S_i is a proper subsequence of $2D\text{-}G_1(P)$,i=1,2.

Rule3: $\Big| \Big\langle \;\Rightarrow\; \Big| \,.\quad \Big\rangle \Big| \;\Rightarrow\; \Big| \,.$

delete $\langle$ and $\rangle$ at the beginning and the end of $2D\text{-}G_1(P)$

Rule4: $a \,\Big|\, e^{n_1} \,\Big|\, e^{n_2} \,\Big|\, ... \,\Big|\, e^{n_k} \,\Big|\, b \;\Rightarrow\; a < b$

where $a,b \in V$.

Rule5: delete e from $2D\text{-}G_1(P)$

If we apply Rule1 to Rule5 to $2D\text{-}G_1(P)$ in that order, $2D\text{-}G(P)$ will be obtained.

5.2. Generalized 2D String and Local Operators

As stated earlier, local operators cannot be used to represent all the spatial relationships in one or two strings, although they are well suited for representing binary spatial relations between two picture objects. On the other hand, we can express the information represented by local operators using generalized 2D strings. That means we can use 2D G-strings to represent any kind of information that can be represented by local operators. We list all the correspondences in the following table. In Table 3, the v string is either "a | b" or "a < b", because the two objects 'a' and 'b' may or may not be touching one another.

Table 3

L_{op}	2D G-String	Pattern
a ⊦ b	u: a = b ∣ b v: a ∣ b ∨ a < b	
a ⊧ b	u: b = a ∣ b v: b ∣ a ∨ b < a	
a ⊣ b	u: a ∣ b = a v: b ∣ a ∨ b < a	
a ⊣ b	u: a ∣ a = b v: a ∣ b ∨ a < b	
a \ b	u: a ∣ b = a ∣ b v: b ∣ a ∨ b < a	
a / b	u: a ∣ a = b ∣ b v: a ∣ b ∨ a < b	
a ≈ b	u: a ∣ b = a ∣ a v: b ∣ a ∨ b < a	
a ≃ b	u: a ∣ a = b ∣ a v: a ∣ b ∨ a < b	

We can use $\langle$ and $\rangle$ to define an area of interest, and describe the hierarchical structure of a picture. An example is illustrated in Figure 7, where the object α is composed from objects 'a' and 'b'.

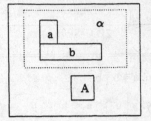

Figure 7. An example of local relations.

u: $\langle\, \alpha\colon \text{ba} \mid \text{b}\,\rangle \mid A\,\langle\, \alpha\colon \text{b}\,\rangle \mid \langle\, \alpha\colon \text{b}\,\rangle$

v: $A < \langle\, \alpha\colon \text{b} \mid \text{a}\,\rangle$

From this generalized G-string, we can derive that

u: $\alpha \mid A\alpha \mid \alpha$

v: $A < \alpha$

where the object α is defined at the next level by

$\alpha.$u: $\text{ba} \mid \text{a}$

$\alpha.$v: $\text{b} \mid \text{a}$

This is equivalent to the representation using the local operators of L_{op}, i.e.

$$\alpha \approx A \text{ where } \alpha\colon \text{a} \models \text{b}$$

6. Spatial Reasoning Using 2D G-Strings

Spatial reasoning is one important application for 2D G-strings, and it was demonstrated[1] that it is possible to use symbolic projection as a knowledge structure. In the following, we will show by examples, how spatial reasoning could be carried out using 2D G-strings. We will use the symbolic picture in Figure 6.

R1 below is an inference rule that describes the 'north of' relationship between two objects.

R1___ IF $\quad u: O_1 = O_2$

$$v: O_1 < O_2 \vee O_1 \mid O_2$$

THEN (north, O_2, O_1)

Query 1 $(?, E, C)$ (What is the relation between picture objects E and C?)

By looking exclusively at objects E and C of the 2D G-string, we have

$$u: C = E$$

$$v: C \mid \ldots \mid \ldots \mid E \Rightarrow C < E$$

The IF part of R1 is hence satisfied, and we can say that E is to the north of C, i.e. (north, E, C).

Query 2 $(\text{north}, ?, B)$ (Which picture objects are to the north of B?)

We can easily detect every object with respect to B. As in Query 1, after stripping off the irrelevant symbols from the 2D G-string, we have

detecting A, u: $B \neq A$, Failure.

detecting C, u: $B = C$, v: $B < C$, then (north, C, B)

detecting D, u: $B \neq D$,   then failure

detecting E, u: $B = E$, v: $B < E$, then (north, E, B)

detecting F, u: $B = F$, v: $B < F$, then (north, F, B)

Obviously, the following query can be processed in the same way.

Query 3 $(\text{north}, D, ?)$ (Which picture objects are to the south of D?)

Similarly. rules for detecting other spatial relations can be written. Since we adopt the cutting mechanism as cutting at every convex and concave points, every relations will be detected regardless of the sizes of the relevant part.

7. An Experimental Intelligent Image Database System

Based upon the theory of symbolic projections described in previous sections, a prototype intelligent image database system (IIDS) was developed at the Visual Computing Laboratory. University of Pittsburgh[4]. A sample session of IIDS will now be described. Initially, the user is presented with a screen that is divided into three major sections. These sections are: the DISPLAY WINDOW, the MESSAGE CENTER, and the MENU WINDOW. The MENU WINDOW presents a series of options at various levels to the user. Selection of one menu item will result in either of the following: an expanded submenu may appear; or a subprocess may be invoked. The MESSAGE CENTER is used for echoing the user's choices, displaying error messages, and for providing special instructions or information. The DISPLAY WINDOW provides an area for printing the results of a user's queries.

At the top level, the user is presented with a set of choices. The user may select: DATABASE MANIPULATION. QUERY. VISUALIZATION. COMMUNICATIONS, and INFORMATION. The DATABASE MANIPULATION choice will allow the user to store and retrieve pictures. QUERY allows the user to ask questions about the pictures stored in the database. VISUALIZATION will allow the display of various queries and COMMUNI-CATIONS will allow for the transfer of information between systems. Finally, INFOR-MATION will provide help and hints about the system.

In the DATABASE MANIPULATION submenu, the user can execute the following: Activate Next Image, which displays the current camera image on the video screen; Write Image, which saves the current image on the video screen to the disk; Load Image, which retrieves images from the disk; and Delete Image which removes a picture from the disk. Before items are written to the disk, the user can give a name to the picture and specify various keywords that denote the picture. The picture is stored on the disk according to its frame number and the frame numbers are automatically updated by the system.

The main focus of the system is in the QUERY submenu. The data that is retrieved is a string representation of the picture along with the name and related keywords. In QUERY BY NAME mode, the user can enter the name of a picture, and the system will retrieve all pictures that have that name (names are not unique). In QUERY BY KEYS mode, the user can enter one or more keywords and the system will retrieve all pictures that contain the user's specified keywords. In QUERY BY FRAME mode, the user can enter a specific frame number. The system will return only one picture since the frame number is the unique key for that picture.

With QUERY BY EXAMPLE, another major submenu is encountered. Here, a series of icons are presented to the user. An example of this is shown in Figure 8(a). This sub-menu allows the user to place the selected icon at any position on the screen. If the icon is placed near a boundary, it is properly clipped. Once the desired icons are placed on the screen, the user can EXECUTE the display window. When such an execution takes place, the icons and their relative positions are converted into their corresponding 2D strings and the query is then made into the database.

Figure 8(a) also shows a sample query. Here the user has posed the query: Find all pictures with a car between two houses. The corresponding 2D string is (house < car < house, house < car < house). Figure 8(b) shows a response to that query. This picture has the 2D string (house car house < car < house car house, house < house < car car < house < house). The system performs 2D string subsequence matching to find the result[2].

By performing QUERY BY 2D STRING, the user can specify the relative positions of various objects. Retrieval will match against those 2D strings which are in the database. The user can then use the DATABASE MANIPULATION submenu to actually retrieve the picture, as shown in Figure 8(c).

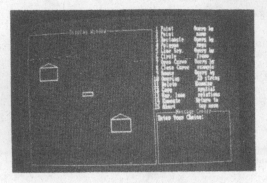

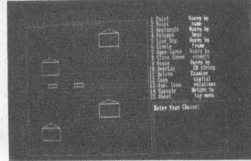

Figure 8(a)   Figure 8(b)

In the EXAMINE SPATIAL RELATIONS mode, the user can then make queries about the retrieved image. Such questions as: EAST OF (X,Y) and SURROUNDED BY (X,Y) can be asked, so that object X which is east of (or surrounded by) object Y can be determined. Our system allows for either or both of the variables to be instantiated so that the query can find everything that is east of something, or confirm that "the church is east of road #2". This is shown in Figure 8(d).

Finally in the VISUALIZATION module, we can get a symbolic interpretation of the response to the query. This is also shown in figure 8(b). Notice that the symbolic interpretation gives us the relative and not absolute positions of the the objects.

8. Conclusions

We have presented a new methodology for pictorial database design. This methodology is based upon 1) A set of three elementary and yet powerful spatial relational operators '<', '=' and '|'; 2) the generalized empty space object 'e'; and 3) means for describing hierarchical and multi-level pictorial data structures using the operator pair $\langle$ and $\rangle$.

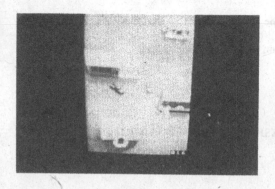 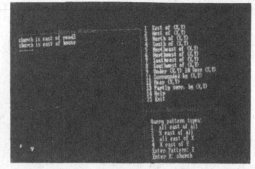

Figure 8(c)   Figure 8(d)

This methodology can be used to develop a knowledge structure for symbolic pictures.

The 2D G-strings can also be used as iconic indexes of a pictorial database. As described in Section 7, the pictorial database can be searched by performing subsequence matching upon 2D G-strings. Furthermore, complicated queries can be answered by combining string matching with spatial reasoning. For example, if we are looking for all picture objects between two given picture objects 'a' and 'b', the 2D G-string is (a < x < b, a x b), where x is a variable. The variable x will match any symbol or any local expression. More complicated queries can be processed in a similar manner.

The image segmentation technique illustrated by Figure 6 (see Section 4), can be applied to automatically construct a 2D G-string, *provided that the objects have already been recognized*. However, the 2D G-string can be used in goal-directed pattern recognition. For example, if the query is (house < tree, house < tree), then we should be looking for a "house" in the lower-left corner, and a "tree" in the upper-right corner. More research along this direction may lead to new techniques in extracting pictorial relations.

Finally, to handle complicated spatial relations, an image algebra is being developed[7]. This image algebra gives the laws for the transformation among generalized 2D strings, as well as the rules for spatial reasoning. The image algebra, once fully developed, can be used for flexible symbolic image manipulation and transformation.

Acknowledgement

This research was supported in part by NSF Grant DMC-8510804, and NSF Grant IRI-8617802.

References

1. S. K. Chang and E. Jungert, "A Spatial Knowledge Structure for Image Information Systems using Symbolic Projections," *Proceedings of FJCC'86*, pp. 79-86, Dallas, Texas, Nov. 2-6, 1986.

2. S. K. Chang, Q. Y. Shi, and C. W. Yan, "Iconic Indexing by 2-D String," *IEEE Trans. on Pattern Analysis and Machine Intelligence*, vol. PAMI-9, no. 3, pp. 413-428, 1987.

3. S. K. Chang and Y. Li, "Representation of Multi-Resolution Symbolic and Binary Pictures Using 2DH Strings," *IEEE Workshop on Language for Automation*, pp. 190-195, 1988.

4. S. K. Chang, C. W. Yan, T. Arndt, and D. Dimitroff, "An Intelligent Image Database System," *IEEE Trans. on Software Engineering, Special Issue on Image Database*, pp. 681-688, May 1988.

5. S. K. Chang, E. Jungert, and Y. Li, "Representation and Retrieval of Symbolic Pictures Using Generalized 2D Strings," *Proc. of SPIE Visual Communications and Image Processing Conference*, November 7-10, 1989.

6. E. Jungert, "Extended Symbolic Projection Used in a Knowledge Structure for Spatial Reasoning," *4th BPRA Conference on Pattern Recognition*, Springer Verlag, Cambridge, March 28-30, 1988.

7. E. Jungert and S. K. Chang, "An Algebra for Symbolic Image Manipulation and Transformation," *Visual Database Systems*, pp. 301-317, North-Holland, 1989.

8. Tomas Lozano-Perez, "Automatic Planning of Manipulator Transfer Movements," *IEEE Trans. on Systems, Man and Cybernetics*, vol. SMC-11, no. 10, pp. 681-698, October 1981.

9. H. Samet, "The Quadtree and Related Hierarchical Data Structures," *ACM Computing Survey*, vol. 16, pp. 187-260, 1984.

REASONING ON SPACE WITH OBJECT-CENTERED KNOWLEDGE REPRESENTATIONS

Laurent BUISSON
Laboratoire ARTEMIS / IMAG
BP 53X - 38041 GRENOBLE Cedex France

Abstract : Spatial knowledge is rarely introduced in knowledge based systems while those systems are able to reason in space. This paper presents a definition of spatial reasoning with a classification of spatial knowledge and describes several properties and needs of spatial reasoning. Two examples of applications concerning symbolic simulation and geographic information data management are surveyed. Object centered representation systems which are well adapted to spatial knowledge are presented.

Keywords : Knowledge based systems, spaces, spatial reasoning, reasoning dynamicity.

INTRODUCTION

Recent developments in knowledge based systems lead to new application domains. Their abilities in evolution and explanation are well-known. Recently they appeared to be well adapted to manage dynamicity and to be complementary to data base systems. They are able to cope with very large knowledge bases.

On an other hand, spatial information has rarely been introduced in such knowledge based systems. As a matter of fact, most symbolic simulations by expert systems do not deal with spatial phenomena, because numerical simulation was so far better adapted. Meanwhile, because most of the relevant spatial information is symbolic spatial expert systems should be more and more used in the future.

In spatial data management, geographic information systems have beeb considered as good tools. Their limitations appeared only recently concerning data dynamicity and deduction mechanisms.

Using knowledge based systems to manipulate spatial knowledge requires knowing exactly what is spatial knowledge. A definition is given which is based on a classification of spatial knowledge : main spatial structures are surveyed. This classification gives a point of view to *present spatial reasoning as an evolution from irrelevant descriptions to more relevant descriptions.*

Several examples come from a system under development : ELSA which is dedicated to avalanche path analysis. ELSA is built with SHIRKA, an object centered representation system. This kind of knowledge management systems appears to be well adapted to spatial representations.

1. KNOWLEDGE BASED SYSTEMS

The knowledge based system concept appeared with expert systems development, but its definition is more precise. As a matter of fact, very often, a computer device is said to be an "expert system" because it contains rules and facts or because it uses experience of specialists.

These ambiguities lead us to choose the knowledge based systems concept instead of the expert systems concept. Meanwhile, knowledge based systems are, probably, the best tools to develop expert systems.

1.1. Definitions

1.1.1. *Knowledge based systems*

We do not intend to define knowledge, but Frost [FROS 86] says that "Knowledge is the symbolic representation of aspects of some named universe of discourse". In other words, this knowledge is understood by a human being as significant.

This definition gives a meaning to a sentence such as "this knowledge is spatial" while "these data are spatial" means nothing. A piece of data cannot be spatial.

What is a knowledge based system ? Most of definitions deal with rule based systems, while PROLOG or object centered representation (ART [WILL84], SRL [WRIG&83], SMECI [ILOG1]) proved that predicate calculus or object representations are good tools to build knowledge based systems.

We define a knowledge based system as a system composed of a *knowledge base* and an *inference engine*. At any time, the base contains units of knowledge which are significant for the user. The inference engine is able to produce new units of knowledge and, as a consequence, to modify the base. In that case there is *inference*.

The inference engine is built by computer specialists but it does not contain any unit of knowledge from the users, i.e. concerning the application domain. On the contrary, the users build the knowledge base in a declarative way and include their own knowledge about the application domain.

1.1.2. *Initial and inferred knowledge*

For an application, the knowledge base contains initial knowledge written by users and knowledge inferred by the inference engine.

In the set of units of knowledge, a function is defined which links a unit to units inferred by using it. This function is called *justification function*.

By definition, the image of this function is the set of *inferred* units of knowledge. The complementary set contains the *initial* units of knowledge. Initial knowledge is written in the base in a *learning* phase. Among initial or learnt units of knowledge, there are units which belong to knowledge based management system, units depending on the application and units of the current session.

These initial units can be implicit or explicit. By definition, implicit knowledge deals with a function graph. This means that if a function exists in the base, its graph must be considered in the base without being explicitly written in it. Other units of knowledge are explicit. Implicit knowledge is important in spatial reasoning. For example if a distance function exists in the knowledge base, its whole graph is implicitly in the base.

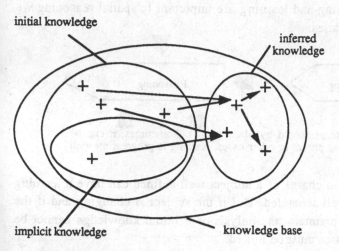

initial knowledge

inferred knowledge

implicit knowledge

knowledge base

Figure 1 : Knowledge in a base. Units of initial knowledge have all been learnt. They are either explicit or implicit. The justification function is described by use of arrows. The image of the function contains inferred knowledge.

1.2. Properties

1.2.1. Evolution of the base

The separation between knowledge base, adapted to users and to the application domain, and the inference engine allows an easy evolution of the base. This property is due to declarative programing. This kind of evolution is difficult to manage in procedural programming and data base management systems for different reasons :

• In procedural programming, application knowledge and exploitation mechanisms are too inter-related to be modified independently. Only input data can be modified.

• On the contrary, in data base management systems, evolution of the base structure is impossible. Here too, only data can be modified.

1.2.2. Explanation

Because all units of knowledge are significant for the users, inference mechanisms are also known. If these inferences are not too complex, the users can retrieve them and understand the reasoning. In other cases, the justification function makes possible the evidence of the reasoning.

Naturally, explanation cannot deal with a function call. Implicit knowledge, as initial knowledge, cannot be proved except by showing the function.

1.2.3. Truth maintenance

The justification function allows the inference engine to maintain truth when initial knowledge is modified.

If a unit K1 justifies a unit K2 and if K1 is modified, K2 must be invalidated. If K2 justifies K3, K3 must also be invalidated. This propagation can be made by a TMS (Truth Maintenance System) [DOYL79].

1.3. Dynamics of learning phases

Because dynamics of reasoning and learning are important in spatial reasoning we must consider several different cases.

Figure 2 : Learning phases are presented by black arrows. Sometimes, it can be separated in time from reasoning phase. In other cases, learning is progressing with reasoning.

A knowledge based system in charge of a subject well defined can have a learning phase and a reasoning phase well separated. But if the subject is changing and if the knowledge based system must maintain its analysis or if initial knowledge cannot be learnt in one time, these two phases must be linked.

> **Example 1** : A diagnosis system is given a set of symptoms in a short learning phase. It produces a diagnosis, then waits for another session which will start with a new learning phase.

> **Example 2** : In a large-scale space [KUIP78], a unique point of view cannot take into account all the space. This means that the learning phase cannot be unique.

> **Example 3** : A knowledge based system contains the description of the spatial environment of a mobile robot. As this robot is moving the knowledge based system is learning new units of spatial knowledge and its reasoning phases on its environment are progressive.

As learning phases are linked with inference phases, initial knowledge can be modified after some inferences. This situation requires a truth maintenance system such as the one presented above.

1.4. Different kinds of representation and inference

We do not intend to present all the knowledge representation tools. There are three main types :
• Rule based systems and predicates calculus systems (e.g. PROLOG)

• Object centered representation.

• Mixed systems with rules and objects. They are the most developed tools (ART, SRL, SMECI).

But a knowledge representation without inference mechanisms is only a structure for data. The main inference mechanisms are pattern matching and procedural inference :

• Mechanism with *pattern matching* is a basic mechanism. In rule based systems, the inference engine uses it to apply a rule. In an object centered representation, matching is able to compute all the objects which are instances of a special class called filter. In mixed systems, matching is used to find objects on which the inference engine must apply a rule.

• *Procedural attachment* allows the user to put a function in the knowledge base. As already explained, the graph of any function in the base is supposed to be known. Procedural attachment are implemented in that way in some object centered representation such as SHIRKA [RECH&89]. Any call to a procedural attachment leads to the creation of an object. This object is an element of the graph.

Any geometric computing will be written in the base by mean of procedural attachments. Efficiency and programming of the functions which are associated to those procedural attachments are not taken into account in this paper.

2. SPATIAL REASONING

2.1. Definitions

2.1.1. Deep and shallow knowledge.

Knowledge based systems may be grouped in two main distinct sets :

First generation knowledge based systems map directly symptoms and observations to conclusions without using the structure of the subject [XIAN&85]. In this case, the knowledge is *shallow*. On the contrary, some systems need a *model* of their subjects to make analysis or synthesis. This is *deep* knowledge.

We cannot talk about *spatial reasoning* without models. For example, if a system maps slope values directly to avalanches potentialities (with a table for example) it uses spatial knowledge (the slope) but we claim that it does not make spatial reasoning. Because there is no model in this example, this system does not reason on the structure of space ; we though that it does not cope with spatial reasoning.

A model is a decomposition of the subject in several components. It is its *structure*. It must also describe these components with their *behaviour* [DAVI84]. The *interactions* between components are also included in a model. All these descriptions can be spatial.

2.1.2. Definition of spatial reasoning

We choose the following definition : A knowledge based system reasons in space when it deals with one or several models of the subject of its reasoning and when this model contains spatial description.

Spatial reasoning is the phase where spatial knowledge is inferred or used to infer new knowledge. Most of the time, knowledge is not only spatial. As a matter of fact, spatial reasoning is always involved in an *application*. The dimension of the space and the nature of spatial knowledge also depend on the application.

2.2. Spatial knowledge

A unit of spatial knowledge is significant only when it is considered in a set provided with a particular mathematical structure. For example, saying that two parts are orthogonal is meaningless except if these parts are included in an euclidean space.

Classifications of spatial knowledge are numerous. A lot of authors in the artifical intelligence field distinguish different kinds of spatial knowledge [KUIP78], [FORB83], [MDER&84], [SRIH87]. In geographic information systems, differences between several kinds of spatial knowledge are used to improve data manipulation.

But, above all, a classification is useful to give an accurate definition of what is a spatial description. As already explained, this discussion is made possible because we deal with units of knowledge.

2.2.1. A classification

In mathematics, "spaces" are numerous (from topology to Hilbert spaces...). But common sense allows us to assume that spatial reasoning deals only with topological, metric, vector and euclidean spaces. Topological spaces are the more relevant spaces. They include only concepts of connectedness and continuity. Metric structures involve notions of distances. Vector spaces are well known; coordinates, directions, dimensions are typically vectorial. The more realistic structures, the euclidean ones, admit notions of scalar products, orthogonality, angle and norm.

In fact, our every day space is euclidean. But in our spatial computations, euclidean information are less relevant than vectorial, metric and specially topological. We see that three buildings are in a line and we do not know their coordinates. We say that building A and building B are adjacent but we cannot describe their shapes. Common sense uses topological properties more often than euclidean properties.

These different structures are not independent. Metric spaces are also topological and euclidean spaces are also vector spaces. We can say that a euclidean space has any kind of properties. Meanwhile, topological properties are more relevant than euclidean ones. This statement can be made either for an expert spatial reasoning or for common sense spatial reasoning as showed [PIAG&47] and [LYNC6O].

topological spaces

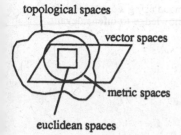

vector spaces

metric spaces

euclidean spaces

Figure 3 : Spaces structures are represented. Metric spaces are included in topological spaces. This means that any metric space can be provided with a topological structure. It is the same for other inclusions. The shape of each set has been chosen according to the structure. Distances, defined in metric spaces, allow definition of bowls ; vector space, directions (thus a parallelogram), euclidean orthogonality (so a rectangle).

Figure 4 : Classification of properties. They are grouped under the structure where they are defined. For example, topological properties exist in euclidean structures but can be defined in topological structures which are, by far, poorer. The figure shows that topological properties are more used than vector and metric ones, and than euclidean.

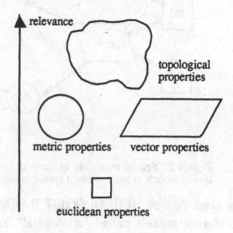

relevance

topological properties

metric properties   vector properties

euclidean properties

2.2.2. *Description and depiction*

A lot of authors make the difference between spatial knowledge based on depiction or description [KOSS83]. This difference comes partly from the computer graphics terminology vectors/rasters.

But in fact, depiction and description are not so different. A depiction contains information about color of a table of pixels. As a result, it appears to be a euclidean spatial description. If no object is defined by using those pixels, it cannot be used by a knowledge based system, except if this system contains knowledge in order to work on pixels.

Most of the time, depiction is used to define objects and description is used to reason on them. Two problems appear : How to generate a good definition ? How to infer a good description ?

2.3. Inferences between different kinds of spatial knowledge

Most application domains of knowledge based systems and especially expert systems allow the user to separate learning and reasoning phases. It is not always possible in spatial reasoning. When it is possible, initial knowledge must be as complete as possible. As a consequence, a lot of new knowledge must be inferred to get knowledge which is relevant in the application domain.

Example : In avalanche path analysis, it is impossible to know, before analysis, what are the terrain features which will be important and relevant. The initial terrain description must be neutral, and as, a result irrelevant. It is made using a digital terrain model. The knowledge based systems will use this initial knowledge to infer relevant information.

Spatial reasoning looks like the net described in figure 5.

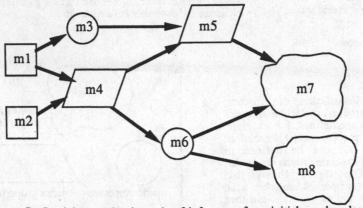

Figure 5 : Spatial reasoning is made of inferences from initial poorly relevant spatial models to more relevant spatial models.

A system such as NEUROLOGIST II [XIAN&85] does the same kind of reasoning with different models called "analogical" and "propositional". The system ELFIN [MCLO85] also builds models that are more and more relevant to find the path of gas through geological layers.

In geographic information systems, spatial objects are defined by digitalisation. Most of the time, they are arcs, points and polygons. In order to improve data management, topological informations are computed :

• for arcs : first and last points, left and right polygons,
• for polygons : boundary arcs.

In this case, the aim is also to compute relevant topological knowledge from a poor, mainly euclidean, description.

In ELSA [BUIS87], passing from an initial model to a more relevant one is also very important. As a matter of fact, most spatial knowledge used in avalanche path analysis is not directly provided by initial models.

Those initial models are a set of triangles and particular lines. The triangles model a surface which fits the natural terrain of avalanche path. The particular lines fit the natural ridges. This knowledge is mainly euclidean and poorly relevant.

On the contrary, the knowledge inferred by the system and used in expert rules or heuristic methods is purely topological, vector or metric as showed on figure 6.

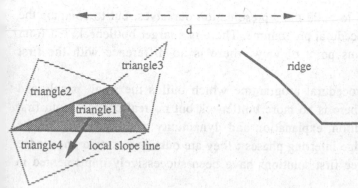

Figure 6 : Triangles and ridges are defined by the coordinates of their vertex. This vector and euclidean knowledge is transformed in topological knowledge (*triangle1 is beside triangle2*), metric knowledge (*distance between triangle1 and the ridge is equal to d*), or vector knowledge (*triangle1 is above triangle4 according to the local slope line*).

2.4. Definition and construction of space

Before inferring a relevant model from the initial model, we have to build this initial model.

2.4.1. Initial knowledge : euclidean knowledge

Most of the time, very initial knowledge is pictorial because common devices give pictures. When digitalising a map, coordinates of points are recorded. They are also mainly euclidean units of knowledge. Moreover they are complete, i.e. all other properties can be obtained from them. As a result, initial knowledge will be euclidean.

Naturally, vectorization or shape extraction is possible from pixels tables. Pattern recognition research developed hardware and software devices, which are very efficient for this kind of work. But from our point of view, using them will forbid any explanation, evolution and management of the dynamicity, because they are not based on architecture of knowledge based systems.

Last, an object is not always defined in an euclidean space. For example, in a synthesis or a shape inference system, the euclidean description is not the initial knowledge but the terminal one. From a functional description, some expert systems infer the euclidean description [INGR85].

2.4.2. An example : natural terrain

In the application of avalanche path analysis, specialists want to work on surface entities called *small-panels*. They are homogeneous from several points of view (vegetation, slope, distance to main ridges, exposure..). Here, we are interested in building these small-panels and inferring their spatial properties.

What is the initial knowledge? Topography is well described by contour lines. Vegetation and ridges are defined by lines.

• The first solution is to build the representation and to infer all the knowledge ourselves, without computer. The initial knowledge will be composed of triangles and ridges completely described as presented in figure 6. But in an operational system this work will be an awful bottleneck because building this representation will be too long!

• The second solution is to build the representation ourselves, but to compute the whole description with a procedural programme. There is a larger bottleneck, but from the knowledge based systems point of view, there is no difference with the first solution.

• We can also use a procedural programme which builds the small panels and computes the description. There is no more bottleneck but no real changes with first and second solution : evolution, explanation and dynamicity are impossible for the building and spatial knowledge inferring phases : they are outside the main knowledge based system S1. These three first solutions have been successively implemented in ELSA project.

• The fourth solution is to create another knowledge based system S2 dedicated to small-panels construction and spatial knowledge inference. In that case, the initial knowledge of S2 can be a map of contour lines, vegetation and ridges. Its terminal knowledge is the initial knowledge of the previous knowledge based systems S1. But there are two knowledge based systems with interface problems. This system is already partially implemented as shown in part 4.

• The last solution should be to build a unique knowledge based system S which should make the jobs of the two previous ones. The properties of evolution, explanation and dynamicity should then be used.

3. APPLICATION DOMAINS

Several features of spatial reasoning have been surveyed in this paper. Most of the examples come from two kinds of application domain : symbolic simulation and geographic information systems.

3.1. Symbolic simulation

More and more symbolic or qualitative simulation appears as a powerful tool to deal with phenomena that physics or mechanics, on one hand, and numerical analysis, on the other hand, cannot cope with. This symbolic simulation can be built by using the specialist's experience but when the phenomenon has a spatial existence, symbolic simulation must take into account spatial description. When the simulation is made by a knowledge based system, this system must manipulate spatial knowledge.

Concerning avalanche path analysis, the system ELSA is able to make a simulation of avalanche starting, according to the experience of snow specialists [BUIS&88]. Those specialists take into account the topography of the natural terrain ; ELSA too.

Initial knowledge is rather relevant here because, as already explained, it describes irregular triangles which fits the natural terrain and particular lines which fit ridges.

Spatial knowledge used by symbolic simulation includes distance to main ridges, incidence of wind on ridges, slopes, boundaries length, and upper relations according to slope lines. This knowledge is inferred by ELSA. It is then used to simulate snow drift, snow cover instability and rupture propagation.

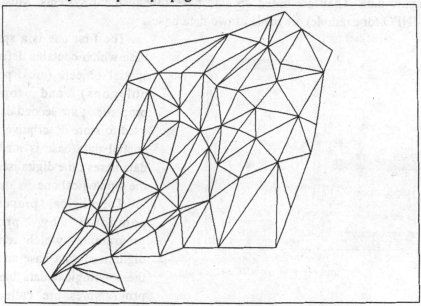

Figure 7 : In this example from ELSA, natural terrain of a starting zone of an avalanche path is described by a surface made of irregular triangles.

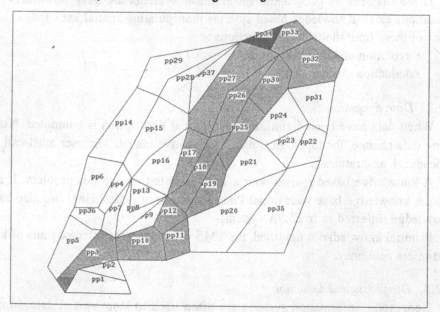

Figure 8 : An analysis of the starting zone. In this meteorological scenario, a strong wind blows from north. It creates large snow accumulations under the main ridge. This part is the trigger. It releases all the grey part of the starting zone.

3.2. Deductive geographic information systems

3.2.1. Architecture

Geographic information systems are well-known. They are used for management of geographic data. They are based on data base management systems. Most of them (ARC-INFO for example) are made of two data bases.

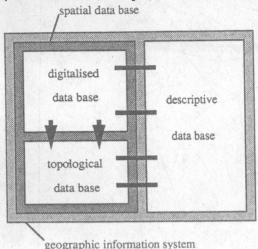

geographic information system

The first one is a spatial data base which contains definitions of spatial objects (arcs, points and polygons) and topological properties ; the second data base is used to store descriptive data. The spatial data base is made of two data bases : the digitalised one and the topological one

Topological properties are computed by procedural programmes which read in the digitalised data base and write in the topological data base. These programmes are called by the user.

These features of geographic information systems are very powerful. But some limitations exist. Knowledge based systems manipulating spatial knowledge could solve some of these limitations in two directions :
- evolution and dynamics of data
- deduction mechanisms.

3.2.2. Data dynamics

When data have been digitalised, topological description is computed. Naturally, if some data change, the topological data base is invalidated. The user must call again the procedural programmes.

A knowledge based system with a TMS is able to solve this problem. It requires a unique knowledge base with initial knowledge (from digitalising) but also topological knowledge (inferred as in ELSA system).

If initial knowledge is modified, the TMS invalidates the affected units of knowledge and infers new ones.

3.2.3. Diagnosis and deduction

Geographic information systems are often used to store spatial data. Most of time some criteria are distributed in space according to some covers. Those representations are used for natural resource or network management. But, as geographic information systems are only data bases, they are only used to help users through maps, graphs or tables. Reasoning and decisions are user's responsability.

Development of expert systems or deductive data bases shows that it should be possible to introduce deduction mechanisms to make diagnosis for example on a defined zone. Geographic information systems become "deductive geographic information systems". Knowledge based systems could be used to reach this aim.

4. KNOWLEDGE REPRESENTATION

Among several knowledge representation systems, we present here object-centered representation. The system chosen is SHIRKA [RECH&89] on which runs the ELSA system.

The main features of SHIRKA are : homogeneity of representation (including *meta-classes*), distinction between *classes* and *instances*, *specialization* and *inheritance* and inference mechanisms of slots values such as *procedural attachment*, *pattern-matching*, *classification* and *default-values*.

SHIRKA inference engine can be used to obtain the values of the slots of an instance by *backward inference*. Slots values are infered using inference *facets*, particularly pattern matching facets and procedural attachment facets which are intensively used to link numerical or qualitative models in the knowledge base. In SHIRKA, classes contain information about inference methods. The inference mechanisms often need the values of other slots of the same instance or slot values of other instances. The inference engine then tries to obtain these values and so on. The inferring mode of SHIRKA appears to be goal-driven reasoning.

SHIRKA is written in Le_Lisp [CHAI86], a Lisp dialect, from which it inherits its high portability, and makes use of the graphic interfaces generator AIDA [ILOG2]. It runs on most of workstations.

4.1. Objects representation

We use the SHIRKA system to describe all the spatial knowledge. Any spatial object is a specialisation of the class `surface`.

For example, here is the spatial definition of the class `small-panel`.

```
{small-panel
  a-kind-of            = surface ;
  area                 $one real;
  c-gravity            $one point
                       $com "centre of gravity" ;
  altitude             $one real
                       $com "mean altitude" ;
  diameter2D           $one real
                       $com "metric horizontal diameter" ;
```

```
diameter3D           $one real
                     $com "metric 3-dimensional diameter" ;
slope-%              $one real
                     $com " slope in percent" ;
is-in                $one avalanche-path ;
contains             $list-of triangle ;
boundary-points      $list-of point
                     $com "list of vertex" ;
beside               $list-of small-panels
                     $com "list of small-panels which are beside the
                           current small-panel" ;
borders              $list-of border
                     $com "list of borders; one border for each
                           small-panel of the previous slot" ;
near-ridges          $list-of ridge
                     $com "list of ridges which are near the current
                           small-panel" ;
above                $one small-panel
                     $com "small-panel which is below the current
                           small-panel according to the local
                           slope line"      }
```

The type of each slot is either simple (real for example) or complex (initial or built objects). The nature is defined using either $one or $list-of which allows *multi-valued* slots. An example of instance of this class is the small-panel pp1.

```
{pp1
  is-a                 = small-panel ;
  area                 = 6850. ;
  c-gravity            = %point-552 ;
  altitude             = 1075. ;
  diameter2D           = 115. ;
  diameter3D           = 138. ;
  slope-%              = 68.     ;
  is-in                = tende ;
  contains             = tr2 tr93 ;
  boundary-points      = po4 po6 po5 po1 ;
  beside               = pp2 pp3 ;
  borders              = %border-589 %border-590 ;
  near-ridges          = ar1 ar3 ar4 ar5 ;
  above                = pp3 }
```

In comparison with PROLOG, we can see that the knowledge about pp1 is grouped in the same object. In PROLOG, the Horn clauses containing the identifier pp1 would have been dispatched throughout the knowledge base.

4.2. A large dynamic knowledge base

Spatial knowledge bases are often very large. The size and the high level of use for some units of knowledge prevent us from inferring them each time they are needed. Recording or *caching* results is necessary to get an efficient knowledge base.

But, as soon as results are cached, incoherence can appear in the base when initial knowledge is modified. As a matter of fact, inferred units of knowledge can become invalidated. SHIRKA is provided with a TMS which is in charge of the dynamicity of knowledge [EUZE&87]. This TMS builds a dependency network which is, in fact, the graph of the justification function.

This caching could be different according to each slot. As already explained, some units of spatial knowledge are more relevant and more useful than others. The values of their slots should be cached. On the contrary, the poorly relevant slots should not be cached because they are rarely used. This system should save time without occupying too much memory.

Many research projects have been concerned with implementing large knowledge bases. SHERPA project at IMAG (Computer Science and Applied Mathematics, Grenoble) is dedicated to the support of large dynamic knowledge bases.

4.3. Spatial inferences

In order to pass from the initial description to a more relevant one, many inferences must be made. They are based on pattern-matching and procedural attachment, but they should also use the regularity properties of some slots.

Here is, for instance, the initial description of the small panel pp1 before inferences.

```
{pp1
   is-a                  = small-panel ;
   contains              = tr2 tr93 }
```

All the other slots are inferred using either pattern-matching (facet $ifn-match$: "if needed match") or procedural attachment (facet $ifn-exec$: "if needed execute") as shown in this partial definition of the class small-panel.

```
{small-panel
   a-kind-of             = surface;
   itself                $var-name p;
   area                  $one real
                         $ifn-exec {m-real-addition
                                 l-sup $var<- sup-tr ;
                                 res   $var-> area } ;
   c-gravity             $one point
                         $ifn-exec {m-pp-c-gravity
                                 l-sup    $var<- sup-tr ;
                                 l-c      $var<- c-tr ;
                                 c-g      $var-> c-gravity }
                         $var-name c-pp;
   altitude              $one real
                         $ifn-exec {m-pp-real-average
                                 l-sup    $var<- sup-tr ;
                                 l-val    $var<- alt-tr ;
                                 res      $var-> altitude } ;
   diameter2D            $one real
                         $ifn-exec {m-pp-diameter2D
                                 l-c      $var<- c-tr ;
                                 c-g      $var<- c-gravity ;
                                 l-d2     $var<- d2-tr ;
                                 d2       $var-> diameter2D } ;
   slope-%               $one real
                         $ifn-exec {m-pp-real-average
                                 l-sup    $var<- sup-tr ;
```

```
                         l-val      $var<- p-tr ;
                         res        $var-> slope-% } ;
contains                 $list-of {triangle
                         c-gravity          $var-name c-tr ;
                         slope-%            $var-name p-tr ;
                         altitude           $var-name alt-tr ;
                         area               $var-name sup-tr ;
                         diameter2D         $var-name d2-tr ;
                         segment1           $var-name s1 ;
                         segment2           $var-name s2 ;
                         segment3           $var-name s3 ;
                         above              $var-name tr-below }
                 $var-name tr-pp;
boundary-points  $list-of point
                 $var-name p-front
                 $ifn-exec {m-pp-boundary-points
                         l-s1       $var<- s1 ;
                         l-s2       $var<- s2 ;
                         l-s3       $var<- s3 ;
                         l-p        $var-> boundary-points };
beside           $list-of small-panel
                 $ifn-match
                    {small-panel
                     itself        $var-> beside ;
                     boundary-points
                         $check {p-pp-beside
                             l-p1 $var-liste<- p-front ;
                             l-p2 $var-liste<- boundary-points }};
borders          $list-of border
                 $ifn-exec {m-pp-frontieres
                             l-pp $var-liste<- beside ;
                             pp   $var<- p ;
                             l-p  $var-liste<- boundary-points ;
                             l-front $var-> borders };
near-ridges      $list-of ridge
                 $ifn-match
                         {ridge
                          itself $var-> near-ridges ;
                          center $check
                                 {p-pp-near-ridges
                                  cpp  $var<- c-pp ;
                                  cridge    $var<- center }} ;
above            $list-of small-panel
                 $ifn-match
                         {small-panel
                          itself     $var-> above ;
                          contains
                          $check
                             {p-pp-above
                              l-tr-sous $var<- tr-below ;
                              l-tr-pp   $var-list<- tr-pp ;
                              l-tr-cont $var-list<- contains }}}
```

4.3.1. Pattern matching

This inference mechanism is used for a lot of slots. For example, the slot beside of class small-panel is valued by pattern matching using the slot boundary-points and a a predicate (introduced by the facet $check) p-pp-beside which checks that the slots boundary-points of the two points have at least a segment in common. The inference engine retrieves all the instances of the class small-panel the slot boundary-points of which verifies this predicate. As a matter of fact, a small-panel p1 is beside a small-panel p2, if their slots boundary-points have at least two points in common which are vertices of one triangle.

Regularity properties of some slots could be dealt with by pattern matching. For example the slot beside is symmetric.

```
{small-panel
   a-kind-of          = surface ;
   itself             $var-name p ;
   beside             $one small-panel
                      $ifn-match    {small-panel
                                     itself     $var-> beside ;
                                     beside     $var<- p}}
```

The pattern-matching mechanism retrieves all the instances of the class small-panel which are beside the current small-panel p ; they become the values of the slot beside of this current small-panel. This pattern-matching mechanism could be used complementary with the one defined above. There still remains a problem which consists of loops.

As it will be explained latter, a special treatment of such properties could be implemented in an object centered representation.

Inferences of near ridges and small-panel which are below are also made by pattern matching. Distance between current small-panel and matched ridge is checked by predicate.

4.3.2. Procedural attachment

This inference mechanism is used to compute metric or vector knowledge. Small-panels areas, slopes, diameters are calculated by call to procedural attachment. Those procedural attachments are written with inference facet $ifn-exec. Beside this facet a class is described. This class is a specialisation of the class method.

The slots of this class are the name of a LISP function, input parameters and output parameters. Here is for example a method which can be associated to a procedural attachment which adds the members of a list of reals l-sup and gives the result res.

```
{m-real-addition
   a-kind-of          = method ;
   function           $value add-list ;
   l-sup              $list-of real ;
   res                $one real }
```

The LISP function add-list is provided with one argument which is an incomplete instance of the method m-real-addition and fills the slot res.

4.3.3. Relations

Pattern matching and procedural attachment are very well adapted to main spatial inference. But they do not take into account regularity or composition of some slots.

Those slots can be seen as relations. Some object centered representations such as SRL [WRIG&83] or ROSACE [HUET&84] implement relations in that way.

The idea should be to define some regularity or composition properties and to use them to infer new knowledge. For example the slot `beside` should be defined as symmetric and the inference engine should infer the corresponding knowledge (i.e. `pp1` is beside `pp2`) as soon as pattern-matching based on the slot boundary-points gives the piece of knowledge (`pp2` is beside `pp1`). Transitivity and inverse slots should be manipulated by the same mean.

CONCLUSION

Knowledge based systems appear to be well adapted to spatial reasoning. Their ability to manage evolution, explanation and dynamicity is higher than for any other kind of computer system.

Spatial reasoning in knowledge based systems can be used to make symbolic simulation of phenomena with spatial properties or to develop deductive and evolving geographic information systems.

Object centered representations are efficient to manage spatial knowledge. Passing from poorly relevant initial knowledge to more relevant knowledge is possible. Large knowledge bases can be used because caching does not handicap the inference engine which infers only new knowledge. Inference mechanisms dedicated to composition and regularity properties of some slots should be very useful.

The largest problem which remains is the construction of space directly from very poor initial knowledge as pictures or contour lines maps. This work requires new capabilities from knowledge based systems especially concerning objects creation.

ACKNOWLEDGEMENTS

This paper has been made possible with the cooperation of the Laboratoire ARTEMIS and the Avalanche Division of CEMAGREF (BP76, 38402 Saint-Martin-d'Hères - France). The author is very grateful to an anonymous reviewer for his helpful comments.

REFERENCES

[BUIS87]   L. Buisson
              "Le raisonnement spatial dans les systèmes à bases de connaissances. Une
              application: l'analyse de sites avalancheux"
              Rapport de DEA Informatique, INPG, june 1987.

[BUIS&88]   L. Buisson, C. Charlier
              "Avalanche starting zone analysis with a knowledge-based system"
              International Glaciological Society, Symposium on snow and glacier
              research relating to human living conditions, Lom, Norway, september
              1988.

[CHAI86]   J. Chailloux
              "Le_Lisp 15.2: Manuel de référence".
              Rapport technique, INRIA, 1986.

[DAVI84]   R. Davis
              "Diagnostic Reasoning Based on Structure and Behavior"
              Artificial Intelligence, 24, pp. 347-410, 1984.

[DOYL 79]   J. Doyle
              "A truth maintenance system"
              Artificial intelligence 12-III, pp. 231-272, 1979

[EUZE&87]   J. Euzenat, F. Rechenmann
              "Maintenance de la vérité dans les systèmes à base de connaissance
              centrée-objet"
              6ème congrès RFIA, Antibes, november 1987.

[FORB83]   K. D. Forbus
              "Qualitative Reasoning About Space and Motion"
              in D.Gentner, A.L.Stevens Eds, "Mental models", Lawrence Erlbaum,
              London, 1983, pp. 53-73.

[FROS86]   R. Frost
              "Introduction to knowledge base systems"
              Collins, London, 1986.

[HUET&84]   G. Huet, D. Vincent
              "ROSACE, un outil de représentation de connaissances sous forme
              d'objets et d'actions; notice de présentation et d'utilisation"
              CNET, october 1984.

[ILOG1]   Société ILOG
              "SMECI ; manuels d'utilisation et de référence"
              Gentilly, 1988.

[ILOG2]   Société ILOG
              "AIDA ; manuels d'utilisation et de référence".
              Gentilly, 1988.

[INGR85]   F. Ingrand
              "Inférence de formes à partir de fonctions. Application à la conception
              de montages d'usinage."
              Thèse de l'Institut National Polytechnique de Grenoble, Grenoble,
              february 1987.

[KOSS83]   S. M. Kosslyn
            "Descriptions and Depictions"
            TR-1275, DCS, University of Maryland, may 1983.
[KUIP78]   B. J. Kuipers
            "Modeling spatial knowledge"
            Cognitive Science, 2, 1978, pp. 129-153.
[LYNC60]   K. Lynch
            "The image of the city".
            Cambridge, Mass. MIT Press 1960.
[MCLO85]   R. Martin-Clouaire
            "Un système expert capable de raisonnement spatial: l'approche ELFIN
            développée pour un problème de géologie pétrolière"
            RFIA, Grenoble, november 1985.
[MDER&84]   D. V. McDermott, E. Davis
            "Planning Routes through Uncertain Territory"
            Artificial Intelligence, 22, n°2, march 1984, pp. 107-156.
[PIAG&47]   J. Piaget, B. Inhelder
            "La représentation de l'espace chez l'enfant"
            Presses Universitaires de France, Paris, 1947.
[RECH&89]   F.Rechenmann, P. Fontanille, P. Uvietta
            "Shirka : manuel d'utilisation"
            Technical report, lab. Artemis, 1989.
[SRIH87]   S. N. Srihari
            "Spatial knowledge representation: a tutorial"
            7th international workshop on Expert Systems and their applications,
            Avignon may 1987.
[WILL84]   C. Williams
            ART: The advanced reasoning tool, conceptual overview
            Inference corporation, Los Angeles, CA, 1984.
[WRIG&83]   J. M. Wright, M. S. Fox
            "SRL/1.5 User manual"
            CMU Robotics Institute, Pittsburgh, december 1983.
[XIAN&85]   Z. Xiang, S. N. Srihari
            "Spatial structure and function representation in diagnostic expert
            systems"
            5th international workshop on Expert Systems and their applications,
            Avignon, may 1985.

Qualitative Spatial Reasoning: A Semi-quantitative Approach Using Fuzzy Logic

Soumitra Dutta

Computer Science Department
University of California
Berkeley, CA 94720

Qualitative reasoning is useful as it facilitates reasoning with incomplete and weak information and aids the subsequent application of more detailed quantitative theories. Adoption of qualitative techniques for spatial reasoning can be very useful in situations where it is difficult to obtain precise information and where there are real constraints of memory, time and hostile threats. This paper formulates a computational model for obtaining all induced spatial constraints on a set of landmarks, given a set of approximate quantitative and qualitative constraints on them, which may be incomplete, and perhaps even conflicting.

1. Introduction

This section provides a general introduction to the fields of spatial reasoning and qualitative reasoning and emphasizes the need for the integration of the two fields. It also describes the focus of the paper and provides an outline of its structure.

1.1. Spatial Reasoning: Definition and Taxonomy

The term **spatial reasoning** refers in general to reasoning about problems dealing with entities occupying space. These entities can be either *physical entities* (e.g., books, chairs, cars, etc.) or *abstract entities* (e.g., enemy territory). Physical entities are tangible and occupy physical space while abstract entities are intangible but nevertheless can be associated with a certain space in some co-ordinate system. It is thus evident that spatial reasoning is a very general problem applicable to many different domains (e.g., human cognition, robot path planning, autonomous vehicle control, battle-field sensor fusion, general purpose planning, etc.). Consequently, it is not surprising to note that it has been an area of active research for researchers from various fields including psychology, linguistics, robotics, vision, artificial intelligence and data-bases. Despite variations in their individual interests and approaches, a broad taxonomy of spatial reasoning problems can be proposed:

- **Representation**: There are two levels of representation of spatial data: *logical* and *physical*. Physical representations are concerned with the actual data-structures and physical storage schemes used for spatial data (as studied extensively by data-base researchers). Logical representations comprise of the logical modeling of spatial information, such as generalized cones, vornoi diagrams, land-marks and topological maps.

This research has been supported by the grants NASA-NSS-2-275 and AFOSR-89-0084.

- **Learning**: There are three distinct activities in this group: *assimilation*, for assimilating new information into an existing core of spatial knowledge, *identification*, for recognizing indentities between known objects and objects in a new scene, and *prediction*, for predicting the nature and behavior of (possibly imprecisely known) objects (usually based on domain knowledge and past experience).

- **Planning**: This refers to the highest level of spatial reasoning, where the core spatial knowledge is used in reasoning and inferencing procedures with some application in mind, e.g., robot path planning or military tactical situation assessment.

The proposed taxonomy of spatial reasoning has some similarities to the four level semantic hierarchy (*sensorimotor, procedural, topological* and *metric*) of spatial information proposed by Kuipers and Levitt[1], but is more general. The learning problem, is ignored in the hierarchy proposed by Kuipers and Levitt. Also, there is no distinction between concepts such as logical vs. physical representations. This paper deals primarily with a subset of the representation problem as defined in section 2.

1.2. Qualitative Reasoning

Qualitative reasoning has been an area of considerable research during the past few years, specially within the artificial intelligence community. Some of the seminal research in this area was done by Hayes[2,3] in the area of *naive physics*, Forbus[4,5] in *qualitative process theory*, deKleer[6,7] in *qualitative physics* and by Kuipers'[8] in *qualitative simulation*. The essential component of all these theories is the provision of a computational framework for the qualitative analysis of both physical and non-physical systems. For example, qualitative process theory is a model building methodology, which recognizes the elements of a model from a physical description of a system, then applies a closed world assumption to create the appropriate set of constraints. Similarly, qualitative simulation starts with a set of qualitative constraints and an initial state, and predicts the set of possible future states for the system. These theories can be used to reason qualitatively about physical systems, e.g., it can be reasoned qualitatively that a ball when thrown upwards shall eventually come to a halt at some height and then fall back to earth.

Classical physics, along with mathematics has been under development for several centuries and has proved to be a very sophisticated and successful tool for analyzing the physical world. The motivation to pursue qualitative modeling and solution techniques may then be a little hard to understand. However, there are certain well accepted reasons for pursuing such a research direction. Kuipers[9] has explained how qualitative reasoning "fills" a gap between conventional model building tools such as difference equations, differential equations and influence diagrams by providing more expressive power for states of incomplete knowledge than differential or difference equations and by providing more inferential power than influence diagrams. Qualitative descriptions are important because they provide the ability to reason with incomplete and weak information. For example, Forbus has demonstrated that qualitative process theory can be used to derive many significant deductions given only weak qualitative descriptions of variable values and relationships. Qualitative analysis can also guide the application of more detailed quantitative theories when additional information is available and reduce the amount of pre-analysis required when such a theory/information is available. This is important as it helps to identify and formalize the *prephysics* knowledge or set of unstated assumptions on which most of modern physics is based (i.e., guide the application of physical laws). Another important reason for the development of qualitative reasoning is that humans often reason qualitatively about their environment. A person totally ignorant about the laws of motion can nevertheless deduce qualitatively that if he/she strikes a ball, it shall roll forward for some time and then eventually come to a halt.

D'Ambrosio[10] has noted that pure qualitative reasoning techniques have certain limitations, e.g., an inability to characterize quantity magnitudes and large ambiguities both in terms of the number of possible situations which may be occurring and the magnitude, time scale, etc. over which they occur. As a possible solution to this, he has suggested the use of linguistic variables (as proposed by Zadeh [11]) as a semi-quantitative extension to the qualitative value and relationship representations in conventional qualitative reasoning. In this paper, we also adopt the position that it is useful and sometimes necessary to augment qualitative spatial reasoning with such a semi-quantitative extension to enable the generation of practically useful conclusions. As a simple example, imagine that an autonomous weapon system knows that an enemy target is about 50 miles north and moving east quite rapidly. Then if it takes 5 minutes to set up the guns, the system must have some quantitative idea of the position of the target after 5 minutes to decide where to aim.

1.3. Qualitative Spatial Reasoning: Motivation

Most research in computer science on spatial reasoning has assumed well defined and certain spatial information, usually expressed in one or more of the following popular representation models: skeletons, generalized cones, convex polygons, vornoi diagrams and configuration space. Within robotics, a large bulk of research has been done on finding paths with optimal values of desired parameters through a known territory, such as the piano movers problem[12]. A number of researchers within robotics have also studied the problem of robot navigation in unknown terrain[13-16]. The usual assumption in these approaches is that while the robot does not know the entire terrain before starting to navigate to its destination, it can determine the locations of obstacles with certainty once it can view them. While such approaches (using either pre-compiled domain maps or assuming perfect sensor data) are applicable in many situations, Elfes [17] has described some of their limitations:

- It is not possible to provide pre-compiled terrain maps for robots to use in new and uncertain environments such as planetary and space exploration.

- Inertial or dead-reckoning navigation schemes may accumulate substantial positional errors over long distances which make it difficult to construct maps precise in cartesian coordinates.

- Multiple sensor views may have to integrated into an consistent, unified world model.

Similar criticisms have also been made by Kuipers and Byun[18] and Brooks[19,20] who observed that:

- Metric consistency is hard to maintain due to noise and inaccuracy of sensory input and slip and miscalibration of motor output.

- It is difficult to achieve man-machine communication naturally as our understanding of the world (e.g., *Move a few meters ahead and take a left turn*) is often drastically different from the underlying representation scheme used.

As a partial response to these limitations, Elfes[17] proposed a probabilistic approach of occupancy grids which used Bayes theorem for updating the probability of determining whether a cell is occupied or not. An alternative approach is adopted by Kuipers and Byun[18] and other researchers who have focussed on qualitative solution techniques for spatial reasoning. In this paper, we explore qualitative solution methods to spatial reasoning problems. By augmenting qualitative reasoning with fuzzy logic, we are able to develop a model that can integrate numerical and quantitative spatial constraints.

Qualitative spatial reasoning can be important for *intelligent autonomous agents* (e.g., robots), especially for those operating in uncertain or unknown or dynamic environments. In such situations, several factors can enhance the benefits of using qualitative reasoning techniques:

- It may be difficult (or often impossible) to collect precise information about the environment.

- There may be real constraints of memory and time which prevent either the collection of large volumes of data or the utilization of a large amount of computation time.

- In hostile environments, quick reactions to sudden stimuli may be facilitated by qualitative reasoning.

- Man-machine interaction can be enhanced (e.g., instructions to robot can be given in natural language).

Qualitative reasoning about space also forms an integral part of our daily lives. Consider the case of crossing a street. We only have approximate, qualitative ideas of the relative locations and velocities of various cars and obstacles, but nevertheless, we manage to cross the road safely and easily. We also reason qualitatively about space while performing other mundane activities such as walking from the kitchen to the bedroom, parking a car, or reaching for a pen to write a letter.

There are several other real world scenarios, e.g., oil spill control, forest fire fighting, unmanned underwater robots, spacecraft robots and battle-field management, where it is useful and often imperative to perform qualitative spatial reasoning.

1.4. Qualitative Spatial Reasoning: Previous Research

There has been some research reported in the literature on qualitative approaches to various aspects of spatial reasoning problems. Forbus[21] developed the FROB program for qualitative reasoning about space and motion in a simplified domain called the *bouncing ball world*. He argued that theorem proving and symbolic manipulation of algebraic expressions cannot account for the incredibly good spatial reasoning capabilities of humans. His approach consisted of constructing a **space graph** (i.e., a graph like structure showing the relative interconnections between various pre-defined regions of space) and describing the motion of balls by a sequence of qualitatively distinct motion states, called an **action sequence**. Kuipers and Byun[18] advocated the use of qualitative spatial reasoning techniques for robot exploration and map learning. Their approach has focussed on learning a topological model of an unknown place by a robot simulator. Levitt *et. al.*[1, 22], developed the Qualnav model that performs qualitative navigation using orientation regions based on a knowledge of landmarks. Some other researchers like McDermott[23, 24], and Davis[25] have attempted to deal with the imprecision in spatial knowledge using range measurements to represent the *fuzziness* in the spatial knowledge, but have not focussed on qualitative solution methods.

1.5. Focus and Structure of This Paper

This paper is also concerned with qualitative spatial reasoning techniques, but the emphasis is different from that in previous research. While other researchers[1, 22] have mainly been concerned with qualitative navigation techniques , i.e., with the planning aspect of the spatial reasoning problem taxonomy (section 1.1), this paper concerns itself with the *logical* representation problem. The logical representation problem considered here roughly corresponds to the *topological* and *metric* levels in the four level semantic hierarchy proposed by Kuipers and Levitt[1].

The focus is on devising a suitable computational framework for correctly representing all induced spatial constraints between a set of objects or landmarks given imprecise, incomplete and possibly conflicting qualitative and quantitative information about the spatial constraints on these objects.

A conceptual description of the problem scenario for which the model developed in this paper is suitable is as follows. Consider a *command center* with a spatial data-base containing all known spatial information. Examples of such command centers in real life include, battle management centers, space station control headquarters, forest fire control centers and planning and control units of robots. There are several sensors or observers feeding spatial data about objects or landmarks of interest to the central command. This data can be either qualitative or quantitative, complete or incomplete and precise or imprecise. The aim of the central command is to fuse all this information into a consistent world model and take decisions about a certain process given all the available spatial information. The spatial reasoning model developed in this paper attempts to provide this fused and consistent world model given spatial information from different sources. This would serve as a useful and necessary basis for the development of solutions regarding other aspects of the learning and planning problems in spatial reasoning. For example, suitable navigation techniques can be devised based on a complete set (qualitative and quantitative) of spatial information available at any moment.

Fuzzy logic is used in this paper as a convenient and useful mathematical tool for representing and manipulating qualitative information. Relevant descriptions of parts of fuzzy logic are included where needed, but the reader is referred to one of the several good references on fuzzy logic[11, 26-28] for additional details.

This paper contains three other sections. The next section presents a formal statement of the problem addressed in this paper. Section 3 describes the representation of the different kind of constraints considered in this paper. The spatial reasoning model is discussed in section 4. Section 5 concludes the paper.

2. Problem Definition

This section presents a formal statement of the problem addressed in this paper. It also describes the different kinds of spatial constraints based on landmarks and relative positions considered in the proposed spatial reasoning model.

2.1. Nature of Spatial Information

Levitt *et. al.*[1] have noted that research by cognitive psychologists[29-31] and zoologists[32] has clearly demonstrated that humans and animals record distinctive visual landmarks and use the structure inherent in local and temporal relationships between landmarks to guide navigation. McDermott and Gelsey[33] have found that military commanders base their judegements regarding terrain analysis on the recognition and analysis of "significant features" or landmarks in the environment. Even preliminary work in the connection between memory structure and neurobiology for spatial reasoning as reported by Foreman and Stevens[34] strongly support landmark based understanding of spatial environments. Levitt *et. al.*[1, 22] have recognized this importance of landmarks while building the Qualnav model for qualitative navigation. In the Qualanav model, navigation is performed by observing the changing position relative to the various landmarks in the environment. Landmarks, as defined by Levitt [22] are uniquely distinguishable points that are visible in the scene. Thus for example, looking at San Francisco Bay from Berkeley, some landmarks are the Golden Gate bridge, the Bay bridge and the San Francisco downtown skyline. On a smaller scale, landmarks can be unique objects in a scene, e.g., the various chairs and tables in a room can be some of the landmarks in a room. Thus the actual defintion of land-marks is domain dependent. In this paper, we shall use the term landmarks to refer to unique, distinct objects in the environment, some or all of which may be visible in any given scene. We shall refer to landmarks as simply objects (in the scene), unless there is some scope for confusion.

Researchers such as Hutchins[35], McReynolds[36], Piaget and Inhelder[37] have emphasized the important role played by information about relative positions of (landmarks) objects in human spatial reasoning. Usually such kind of information about relative positions of objects is known only in approximate or qualitative terms, e.g.,

The chair is near the desk.

The river flows behind the house.

Some researchers such as McDermott[23, 24] and Davis[25] have attempted to deal with this imprecision by using range data on the relative distances between objects, e.g.,

The distance between the desk and the chair is between 2 and 4 feet.

Such an approach can apply in some situations, but suffers from a loss of semantic meaning while replacing the linguistic qualification **near** by the range *between 2 and 4 feet*. This is because it is intuitively clear that not all distances in the range 2 to 4 feet are "near" to the same degree, i.e., the degree to which 2 feet is "near" is different from the degree to which 4 feet is "near" (within the given context). This becomes very important in some situations, e.g., while estimating the location of an enemy target, it is not enough to give the range of its location; it is necessary to be able to specify a specific location for which to aim, i.e., a location where the possibility or probability of the target's existence is highest.

As mentioned in section 1.5, the focus of this paper is to provide a computational framework for reasoning with quantitative and qualitative spatial constraints on the relative positions of objects (landmarks). Some simple examples of the types of problems we would like to be able to solve are:

Example 1:

Given:

> *Object A is far east of object B.*
> *Object C is about 5 miles from object B.*

What can we say about the relative positions of objects A and C?

It is usually impossible to consider spatial reasoning in isolation from temporal reasoning as in any dynamic domain, the positions of many objects change over time. Thus we would also like to deal with problems like:

Example 2:

Given:

> *Object A is to far east of Object B.*
> *Object A is moving south rapidly.*

What can we say about the relative positions of objects A and B after 10 minutes?

2.2. Problem Definition

A more formal statement of the logical representation problem being considered in this paper can be formulated as:

Given:

> *A set of objects (landmarks) and*
> *A set of constraints on these objects.*

To find:

> *The induced spatial constraints.*

There are certain assumptions and limitations in this formulation which need to be clarified. The objects we are considering are simplified point representations of landmarks with possibly an associated set of spatial properties. These properties may include particular physical properties such as color and shape, distinctive features (important for applications such as terrain analysis[18, 33]), contextual information, etc. These properties are important for various aspects of the learning and planning problems, but shall not be discussed in this paper.

There are essentially two different classes of constraints on objects:

[1] **Position constraints:** which constraint the spatial positions of the objects and

[2] **Motion constraints:** which constraint the motion of the objects over time.

Position constraints can be further classified into four different categories:

[1] **Propositional** i.e., qualitative linguistic descriptions of the relative positions of objects (e.g., *the chair is near the desk*).

[2] **Metrical:** i.e., when the positions of objects can be quantitatively specified with accuracy (e.g., *the chair is 2 feet from the desk*).

[3] **Range:** i.e., when relative positions are quantitatively specified by range data (e.g., *the distance between the desk and the chair is between 2 and 4 feet*).

[4] **Visual:** i.e., when it is only possible to graphically depict a fuzzy area in which the object is supposed to exist.

Motion constraints are useful for analyzing dynamic systems and can be classified into three categories analogous to position constraints:

[1] **Propositional:** e.g., *Object A is moving eastwards slowly.*

[2] **Metrical:** e.g., *Object A is moving east at 30 miles/hour.*

[3] **Range:** e.g., *Object A is moving east with a velocity between 25 and 35 miles/hour.*

It is important to note that these constraints are generally incomplete (i.e., not all distances between all objects shall be known accurately) and can potentially be conflicting (e.g., when information from different sources is to be correlated). Thus the developed model should provide the *best* possible answer given the available information and indicate all possible conflicts. More complex propositional constraints are possible (e.g., *If object A is close to object B then object C is quite far from object B*, and *It is quite likely that object B is close to object A*), and details are provided in[38]. It should also be mentioned here that the above classification of constraints is by no means exhaustive; rather they are indicative of the type of constraints considered in this paper.

3. Representation of Constraints

It is necessary to find a suitable computationally tractable representation for the constraints mentioned in the previous section before building a model to reason with them. This section describes how this can be done.

3.1. Position Constraints

The following subsections describe how to represent each of the four different types of position constraints described earlier. The essential idea is to transform the constraint into an equivalent possibility distribution defining the constraint on the objects implicit or explicit in the description of the constraint. Concepts from fuzzy logic such as linguistic variables [11] and test score semantics [28] are used for these transformations.

3.1.1. Propositional Constraints

The central idea of test score semantics is that an proposition p in natural language can be put in the canonical form :

$$p = X \ \ is \ \ F$$

where X is the collection of variables $X_1, X_2, ...,X_n$ either explicit or implicit in p and F is the joint possibility distribution of these n variables. Alternatively, we can say that p translates into a possibility assignment equation:

$$p \rightarrow \Pi_{(X_1, X_2, ...X_n)} = F$$

where F is a fuzzy subset of a universe of discourse U. For example, the proposition

$$p = \text{Bob is short}$$

is translated into the following possibility assignment equation:

$$\Pi_{Height(Bob)} = SHORT$$

where SHORT is a fuzzy subset of the universe of discourse U = [10 inches, 100 inches] (see figure 1) and *Height(Bob)* is a variable implicit in p and $\Pi_{Height(Bob)}$ is the possibility distribution of the variable *Height(Bob)*. The above possibility assignment equation implies that

$$\text{Possibility(Height(Bob)} = u \ ) = \mu_{SHORT}(u)$$

where u is a specified value of the variable *Height(Bob)*, $\mu_{SHORT}(u)$ is the grade of membership of u in the fuzzy set SHORT and the LHS is read as "the possibility that Height(Bob) is u inches". There are several practical methods for obtaining the membership functions of fuzzy sets by adopting principles of psychometry, some of which are reported in [39].

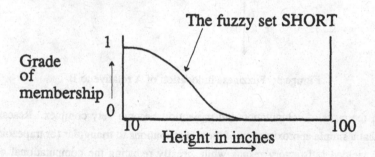

Figure 1: The fuzzy set SHORT

As another example, consider the following propositional constraint:

Object A is about 5 miles away from object B in a north-easterly direction.

The corresponding possibility assignment equation is

$$\Pi_{loc(A), loc(B)} = (about \ \ 5 \ miles , \ north-easterly \ direction)$$

Assume that the fuzzy-sets *about 5 miles* and *north-easterly direction* are defined by the possibility distributions as defined in figure 2. Then the fuzziness in the location of object A relative to object B is as shown in figure 3. We can project this *fuzziness* in the relative positions of A and B onto the X and the Y axes as shown in figure 4. If we assume arbitrary shapes of possibility

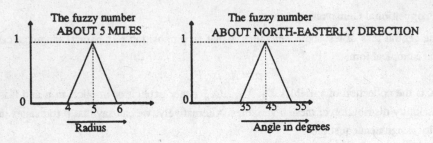

Figure 2: Fuzzy number representations of fuzzy sets

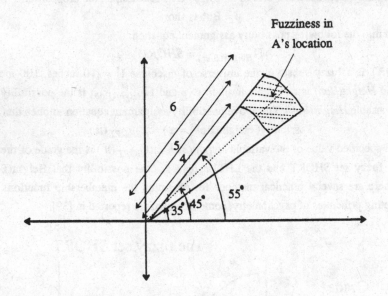

Figure 3: Fuzziness in location of A relative to B

distributions, the tasks of computation and projection become very complex. Researchers [26] have found that a simple approximation of these distributions to triangular (or trapezoidal) shapes have usually yielded satisfactory results while greatly reducing the computational complexity. Once we restrict these distributions to triangular shapes, we can represent them by *fuzzy numbers[26]* where a fuzzy number has the generic format

$$(c, l, r)$$

where c is the mean value, and l and r are the left and right spreads respectively. We assume normal fuzzy numbers, i.e., the membership value at the mean is 1. Thus, referring back to figure 2, the fuzzy sets can be represented by the following two fuzzy numbers:

about 5 miles = (5, 1, 1)

north easterly direction = (45, 10, 10)

The corresponding triangular possibility distributions for the X and the Y axes projections can be found by simple geometry (see figure 4).

Projection along X-axis = (5*cos45 , 4*cos55, 6*cos35)

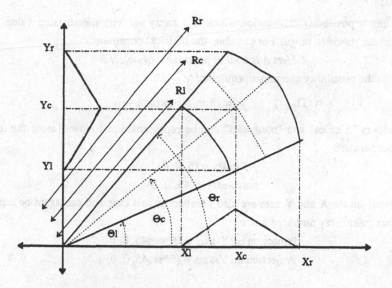

Figure 4: Projections onto the X and the Y axes

Projection along Y-axis = (5*sin45 , 4*sin35, 6*sin55)

Of course here we are making the simplifying assumptions that the mean value of the projections onto the X and the Y axes, X_c and Y_c lie at the point of intersection of the R_c and θ_c, the mean values of the distributions along the radius, R, and the angle, θ.

Thus essentially for the two dimensional case, any linguistic propositional constraint can be transformed into equivalent possibility distributions on the X and Y axes. A similar procedure can be followed for higher dimensions.

Translation procedures for more complex propositional constraints (see section 2.2) are provided in[38].

3.1.2. Metrical and Range Constraints

Let U be a classical set of objects called the universe of discourse and u represent a generic element of U. A fuzzy set F in a universe of discourse U is characterized by a membership function

$$\mu_F : U \rightarrow [0,1]$$

where $\mu_F(u)$ denotes the membership of u in the fuzzy set F. A fuzzy set is a generalization of a classical set as a classical subset A of U can be written as a fuzzy subset with a membership function μ_A taking binary values, i.e.,

$$\mu_A(u) = 1 \text{ if } u \, \epsilon A$$
$$= 0 \text{ if } u \, \epsilon\!\!\!/ A$$

Thus a metrical constraint transforms into a possibility distribution where the distribution is simply a fuzzy set with only one value (with membership value 1) and a range constraint transforms into a possibility distribution which is a fuzzy set with membership value 1 for all values within the specified range. For example, the metrical constraint:

Object A is 5 miles north-east of object B

translates into the possibility assignment equation:

$$\Pi_{loc(A),\,loc(B)} = (5\ miles\ ,\ north-east\,)$$

and the numbers "5 miles" and "north-east" can be represented as follows (using the triangular fuzzy number format):

$$5\ miles = (5, 0, 0)$$
$$north\text{-}east = (45, 0, 0)$$

The projections on the X and Y axes are also numbers in this case and can again be represented using the triangular fuzzy number format:

$$\text{Projection on X-axis} = (5*\cos 45, 0, 0)$$
$$\text{Projection on Y-axis} = (5*\sin 45, 0, 0)$$

3.1.3. Visual Constraints

Figure 5 depicts an example of a visual constraint, in which one can only graphically depict a fuzzy area where object A may be located. For projecting this into equivalent possibility distributions on the X and Y axes, the following simplifying assumption is made: the mean values of the X and Y projections lie at the centroid of the fuzzy area depicting the visual constraint. This shall become clear from figure 5.

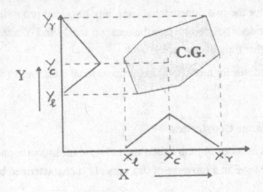

Figure 5: Translation of visual position constraints

3.2. Motion Constraints

The transformation of motion constraints is similar to that for position constraints and we shall not discuss it further here. However, the use of motion constraints in the spatial reasoning model shall be explained with the help of simple examples in the next section.

4. Spatial Reasoning

This section develops the spatial reasoning model based on the representation of constraints (position and motion) as described in the previous section.

4.1. Mathematical Basis

Consider two possibility assignment equations

$$\Pi_{(A_1, A_2, ..., A_l, B_1, B_2, ..., B_m)} = F_1$$
$$\Pi_{(B_1, B_2, ..., B_n, C_1, C_2, ..., C_n)} = F_2$$

where F_1 and F_2 are fuzzy sets defining the joint possibility distributions of the variable pairs (A_i, B_i) and (B_i, C_i) respectively. Now we can derive the joint possibility distribution of $A_1, A_2, ..., A_l$ and $C_1, C_2, ..., C_n$ by applying the compositional rule of inference[26] :

$$\Pi_{(A_1, A_2, ..., A_l, C_1, C_2, ..., C_n)} = F_1 \, o \, F_2$$

where the composition operator "o" can be interpreted by the max-min rule which is defined as:

$$\Pi_{(A_1, A_2, ..., A_l, C_1, C_2, ..., C_n)} =$$
$$\max \ \min_{(b_1, ..., b_m) \, \varepsilon \, (B_1, ..., B_m)} (\Pi_{(A_1, A_2, ..., A_l, b_1, b_2, ..., b_m)}, \Pi_{(b_1, b_2, ..., b_n, C_1, C_2, ..., C_n)})$$

For arbitrary fuzzy sets, F_1 and F_2, the above operation of composition can be computationally expensive. When the fuzzy sets F_1 and F_2 are constrained to triangular possibility distributions, fuzzy numbers can be used to represent them and in such a case, the above composition operation reduces to the addition of two fuzzy numbers[27, 40] :

$$\Pi_{(A_1, A_2, ..., A_l, C_1, C_2, ..., C_n)} = F_1 +_f F_2$$

where $+_f$ refers to the addition of two fuzzy numbers. Assuming the following generic format for F_1 and F_2,

$$F_1 = (c_1, l_1, r_1) \quad \text{and}$$
$$F_2 = (c_2, l_2, r_2)$$

their addition is defined as follows[26, 27] :

$$F_1 +_f F_2 = (c_1 + c_2, l_1 + l_2, r_1 + r_2)$$

where $+_f$ represents fuzzy addition. Similarly, their subtraction and multiplication are defined as:

$$F_1 -_f F_2 = (c_1 - c_2, l_1 + l_2, r_1 + r_2)$$
$$F_1 *_f F_2 = (c_1 * c_2, l_1 c_2 + l_2 c_1, r_1 c_2 + r_2 c_1)$$

where $-_f$ and $*_f$ respectively represent fuzzy subtraction and multiplication.

4.2. Essence of Spatial Reasoning Model

The essence of the spatial reasoning model can be described with the help of a simple example. Consider four distinct objects A, B, C and D as shown in figure 6. Assume that the following pieces of information are available:

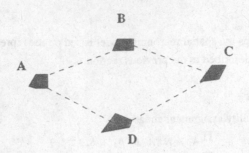

Figure 6: Constraints on relative locations of objects A, B, C and D.

$$\Pi(A,B) = F$$
$$\Pi(B,C) = G$$
$$\Pi(A,D) = H$$
$$\Pi(D,C) = I$$

where F, G, H and I are appropriate possibility distributions expressing the relative position constraints on the objects, A, B, C and D. Now it is evident that there are two distinct methods of computing the relative positions of objects A and C: one using the information about the distance between (A and B) and that between (B and C) and the second method using the information about the relative positions of objects (A and D) and (D and C). Computationally, these two methods can be represented as;

$$\Pi(A,B) \, o \, \Pi(B,C) = F \, o \, G$$
$$\Pi(A,D) \, o \, \Pi(D,C) = H \, o \, I$$

The two different sources for computing the relative positions of objects A and C shall in general yield conflicting results (due to possible uncertainties in the various pieces of information and/or different sources for the information) and it is necessary to maintain consistency between the two answers. This is achieved by taking the fuzzy intersection of the two distributions, i.e.,

$$\min(F \, o \, G, H \, o \, I)$$

Assume that there was another piece of information directly specifying the relative position constraint on objects A and C:

$$\Pi(A,C) = K$$

where K is an appropriate fuzzy set. Then to arrive at the best answer for the relative positions constraint on objects A and C, we would have to take the fuzzy intersection of three distributions:

$$\min(F \, o \, G, H \, o \, I, K)$$

Thus there are two fundamental ideas in the spatial reasoning model:

[1] Compute the spatial constraint on the relative positions of any two objects using all possible routes.

[2] Check all the conflicting answers for consistency.

4.3. Algorithmic Description of Spatial Reasoning Model

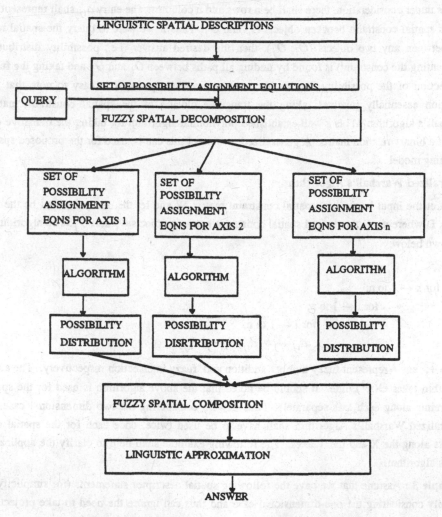

Figure 7: Flow chart of proposed spatial reasoning model

A flow chart describing the proposed spatial reasoning model is described in figure 7. The model relies upon a knowledge-base containing the various constraints expressed in the form of possibility distributions which are then decomposed (projected) onto each axis. Along each axis there is formal algorithm (described informally in the above sub-section) which computes the spatial constraints *induced* by the initial set of constraints. If desired, the constraints along each axis can be composed to give an answer in n-dimensional space. The answer can be expressed in linguistic terms by a process of linguistic approximation [26].

The set of constraints along each axis can be represented in the form of a graph where the nodes represent objects and the arcs between nodes represents the known spatial constraint between the objects representing those nodes. Such a network can also alternatively be represented in the form of a matrix, termed as the **spatial constraint matrix**. If there are n objects under consideration, there shall be n rows and n columns. The entry a_{ij} shall represent the known spatial constraint between objects O_i and O_j. Thus if we were to query the spatial relation between any two objects (O_i, O_j), then the desired answer (i.e., possibility distribution representing the constraint) is found by finding all paths between O_i and O_j and taking the fuzzy intersection of the possibility distributions on these various paths. It is easy to note that this operation essentially involves taking the transitive closure of the spatial constraint matrix. Warshall's algorithm[41] is a well established polynomial algorithm for taking the transitive closure of a binary relation matrix. A generalized version of this can be used for the proposed spatial reasoning model.

Generalized Warshall's Algorithm

Let the input be the nxn spatial constraint matrix W and let the desired output be the nxn matrix D where d_{ij} is the desired spatial constraint between objects O_i and O_j. The algorithm is as shown below:

D ← W

    for k ← 1 to n;

        for i ← 1 to n;

            for j ← 1 to n;

$$d_{ij} \leftarrow \wedge (d_{ij}, d_{ik} +_f d_{kj})$$

where $+_f$ and $\wedge$ represent fuzzy number addition and fuzzy intersection respectively. The above algorithm takes $\Theta(n^3)$ time. It should be noted that the above algorithm is used for the spatial constraints along each axis separately. Thus if were considering the two dimensional case, the Generalized Warshall's Algorithm shall have to be used twice, once each for the spatial constraints along the X and the Y axes. The following example shall help to clarify the application of this algorithm.

Example 3 : Assume that we have the following spatial descriptor statements (for simplicity we are only considering the one-dimensional case and thus can ignore the need to take projections onto different axes):

Object 2 is about 4 miles east of object 1.
Object 3 is more or less 5 miles east of object 2.

and the spatial query:

What is the spatial relation between objects 3 and 1?

Assume that the fuzzy sets ABOUT 4 MILES EAST and MORE OR LESS 5 MILES EAST can be represented by the fuzzy numbers (4,1,1) and (5,1,2) respectively where the left and right spreads of the fuzzy numbers denotes the fuzziness in the spatial constraints between the corresponding objects. Then W, the spatial constraint matrix can be represented as

$$
\begin{matrix}
(0,0,0) & (4,1,1) & (0,\infty,\infty) \\
(-4,1,1) & (0,0,0) & (5,1,2) \\
(0,\infty,\infty) & (-5,2,1) & (0,0,0)
\end{matrix}
$$

where $(0, \infty, \infty)$ is used to represent unknown spatial constraint value. Also note that in the above matrix, while the element $a_{12} = (4,1,1)$ indicates that object 2 is about 4 miles east of object 1, the element $a_{21} = (-4,1,1)$ indicates that object 1 is about 4 miles west (opposite of east) of object 1. After running through the generalized Warshall's algorithm, we get D, the transitive closure of W as shown below:

$$
\begin{array}{ccc}
(0,0,0) & (4,1,1) & (9,2,3) \\
(-4,1,1) & (0,0,0) & (5,1,2) \\
(-9,2,3) & (-5,2,1) & (0,0,0)
\end{array}
$$

Thus the spatial constraint between objects 3 and 1 is represented by the fuzzy number $(9,2,3)$ which is to be interpreted as saying that object 3 is about 9 miles east of object 1 with the fuzziness in the spatial constraint being given by the left and right spreads of 2 and 3 respectively.

4.3.1. Reasoning About Motion

Most real world situations are dynamic and the positions of objects usually change with time. Thus it is important to be able to reason about the changing positions of moving objects.

Suppose the following piece of information is added onto the data given in example 3:

Object 3 is moving east at about 3 miles per hour.

Now if a user queries for the spatial constraint on objects 3 and 1 after about one hour, it can be easily obtained as shown below (assuming that object 1 is stationary):

Assume the following fuzzy set representations:

about 3 miles per hour = (3, 1, 1)
about one hour = (1, 0.2, 0.2)
Distance moved by object 3 in about one hour $= (3, 1, 1) *_f (1, .2, .2)$
$\qquad = (3, 1.6, 1.6)$
Thus spatial constraint between objects 3 and 1 after about one hour =
$\qquad (5, 2, 3) +_f (3, 1.6, 1.6)$
$\qquad = (8, 3.6, 4.6)$

If the description of velocities of objects are given in two (or more) dimensions (e.g., *Object C is moving in north-easterly direction at about 3 miles/hr*), then the fuzzy representations of velocities can be projected onto the X and Y axes (for the two dimensional case) and a similar procedure can be followed to determine the spatial constraint between objects along each axis. It is possible to modify the matrix calculation scheme described in the previous sub-section to account for the motion constraints. The basic idea is

- First, to readjust at any desired time, each entry, a_{ij}, in the spatial constraint matrix along each axis, given the motion constraints on the ith and jth objects along that axis and

- Then to reapply the generalized Warshall's algorithm to determine the new spatial constraints along each axis.

The readjustment of the entries in the spatial constraint matrix is carried out in a manner similar to that shown above. Due to constraints on the length of this paper, we shall not describe it further here.

4.4. Implementation

The above spatial reasoning model has been implemented in F-Prolog[38] which is an extended version of Prolog to support linguistic variables and other approximate reasoning constructs such as semantic unification and temporal unification. Prolog, due to the possible relational interpretation of its data structures, has several similarities to a relational DBMS. The interpreter for F-Prolog is implemented in CommonLISP. While a LISP environment is very useful for development, some researchers [42] have indicated the difficulties faced by LISP based approaches in performing efficient data management. Thus it would be a useful exercise for the future to implement the proposed spatial reasoning model in an extension of a classical query language like QUEL[43].

Such a spatial reasoning model shall find wide applications in a variety of applications including path planning, terrain analysis and general problem solving in the real world. As the algorithm takes polynomial time it is computationally tractable and easily implementable. Details on its use for approximate path planning algorithms and control of dynamic mechanical systems can be found in[38].

5. Conclusion

This paper has described the development of a approximate spatial reasoning model that integrates qualitative and quantitative constraints. Qualitative reasoning techniques are important as most of human reasoning is approximate in nature. Specially in the domain of spatial reasoning, humans consistently reason qualitatively with demonstrably good results. Though the mental processes behind human spatial abilities are not well understood, it is useful to try to install some similar capabilities in machines. The proposed spatial reasoning model is a step in this direction. Only a subset of the representation problem has been addressed in this paper, but it should serve as a useful (and necessary) basis for representing core spatial knowledge on which to build applications involving spatial planning and learning capabilities.

References

1. B. J. Kuipers and T. S. Levitt, "Navigation and Mapping in Large-Scale Space," *AI Magazine*, 1988.

2. P. Hayes, "The Naive Physics Manifesto," *Expert Systems in the Micro-electronic Age*, vol. D. Michie, Ed., Edinburgh University Press, Edinburgh, U.K., 1979.

3. P. Hayes, "Naive Physics 1: Ontology for Liquids," *Formal Theories of the Commonsense World*, vol. J.R. Hobbs and R. Moore, Eds., pp. 71-107, Norwood, NJ, 1985.

4. K. Forbus, "Intelligent Computer-Aided Engineering," *AI Magazine*, vol. 9, pp. 23-26, 1988.

5. K. Forbus, "Qualitative Physics: Past Present and Future," *Exploring Artificial Intelligence*, vol. H. Shrobe, Ed., Morgan Kaufmann, Los Altos, CA, 1989.

6. J. de Kleer, "Qualitative and Quantitative Knowledge in Classical Mechanics," *Tech. Report 352, MIT AI Lab*, 1975.

7. J. de Kleer and J. Brown, "A Qualitative Physics Based on Confluences," *Artificial Intelligence*, vol. 24, pp. 7-84, 1984.

8. B. Kuipers, "Qualitative Simulation," *Artificial Intelligence*, vol. 29, pp. 289-338, 1986.

9. B. J. Kuipers, "Qualitative Reasoning: Modeling and Simulation with Incomplete Knowledge," *Automatica*, July 1989.

10. B. D. D'Ambrosio, "Qualitative Process Theory Using Linguistic Variables," *Ph.D. Dissertation*, University of California-Berkeley, Computer Science Dept., 1984.

11. L. A. Zadeh, "The Concept of a Linguistic Variable and its Application to Approximate Reasoning," *Information Sciences*, vol. Part I, 8, 199-249; Part II, 8, 301-357; Part III, 9, 43-80, 1975.

12. C. K. Yap, "Algorithmic Motion Planning," *Advances in Robotics Vol. I: Algorithmic and Geometric Aspects of Robotics*, (J.T. Schwartz and C.K. Yap, Eds.), pp. 95-144, Lawrence Erlbaum Associated, Hillsdale, N.J., 1987.

13. N. S. V. Rao, "Algorithmic Framework for learned robot navigation in unknown terrains," *Computer*, vol. 22(6), pp. 37-43, June 1989.

14. A. Abelson and A. diSessa, *Turtle Geometry*, pp. 179-199, MIT Press, 1980.

15. V.J. Lumelsky and A. A. Stepanov, "Path planning strategies for a point mobile automaton moving amidst unknown obstacles of arbitrary shape," *Algorithmica*, vol. 2, pp. 403-430, 1987.

16. J. B. Oommen et. al., "Robot navigation in unknown terrains using learned visibility graphs, Part I: The disjoint convex obstacle case," *IEEE Journal of robotics and automation*, vol. RA-12, pp. 672-681, 1987.

17. A. Elfes, "Using Occupancy Grids for mobile robot perception and navigation," *Computer*, vol. 22(6), pp. 46-57, June 1989.

18. B. J. Kuipers and Y. T. Byun, "A Qualitative Approach to Robot Exploration and Map-learning," *Spatial Reasoning and Multi-sensor fusion, Proc. of 1987 workshop*, pp. 390-404, Morgan Kaufmann Publishers Inc., Los Altos, CA, 1987.

19. R. A. Brooks, "Visual Map Making for a Mobile Robot," *Proc. of IEEE Intl. Conf. on Robotics and Automation*, pp. 824-829, 1985.

20. R. A. Brooks, "A Robust Layered Control System for a Mobile Robot," *IEEE Journal of Robotics and Automation*, vol. RA-2, No. 1, pp. 14-23, 1986.

21. K. D. Forbus, "Spatial and Qualitative Aspects of Reasoning About Motion," *Proc. of AAAI*, 1980.

22. T. Levitt, D. Lawton, D. Chelberg, and P. Nelson, "Qualitative Navigation," *Proc. of DARPA Image Understanding Workshop*, pp. 447-465, Morgan Kaufmann, Los Altos, CA, 1987.

23. D. McDermott, "Finding Objects with Given Spatial Properties," *Tech. Report 195*, Yale Univ. Computer Science Dept., 1980.

24. D. McDermott and Ernest Davis, "Planning and Executing Routes through Uncertain Territory," *Artificial Intelligence*, vol. 22, pp. 107-156, 1984.

25. E. Davis, *Representing and Acquiring Geographic Knowledge*, Morgan Kauffman/Pitman, Los Altos, CA/London, U.K., 1986.

26. H. J. Zimmerman, *Fuzzy Set Theory and its Applications*, Kluwer Academic Publishers Group, 1985.

27. A. Kaufmann and M. M. Gupta, *Introduction to Fuzzy Arithmetic: Theory and Applications*, Van Nostrand Reinhold Co., New York, NY, 1985.

28. L. A. Zadeh, "Test Score Semantics for Natural Languages and Meaning Representation via PRUF," *Empirical Semantics (B. Reiger, Ed.)*, pp. 281-349, Bochum:Brockmeyer, 1982.

29. L. T. Kozlowski and K. J. Bryant, "Sense of Direction, Spatial Orientation and Cognitive Maps," *Journal of Experimental Psychology: Human Perception and Performance*, vol. 3, pp. 590-598, 1977.

30. R. N. Shepard and J. Metzler, "Mental Rotation of Three-Dimensional Objects," *Science*, vol. 171, pp. 701-703, 1971.

31. W. Pylyshyn, *Computation and Cognition: Toward a Foundation for Cognitive Science*, MIT Press, Cambridge, MA, 1984.

32. H. Schone, *Spatial Orientation- The Spatial Control of Behavior in Animals and Man*, Princeton University Press, Princeton, NJ, 1984.

33. D. McDermott and A. Gelsey, "Terrain Analysis for Tactical Situation Assessment," *Spatial Reasoning and Multi-sensor Fusion, Proc. of 1987 workshop*, pp. 420-429, Morgan Kaufmann, Los Altos, CA, 1987.

34. N. Foreman and R. Stevens, "Relationships between the Superior Colliculus and Hippocampus: Neural and Behavioral Considerations," *Behavioral and Brain Sciences*, vol. 10 (1), pp. 101-151, 1987.

35. E. Hutchins, "Understaning Micronesian Navigation," *Mental models, D. Gentner and A. L. Stevens, Eds.*, pp. 191-225, Lawrence Erlbaum Associates, 1983.

36. J. McReynolds, "Geographic Orientation of the Blind," *Ph.D. dissertation in U.T.*, 1951.

37. J. Piaget and B. Inhelder, *The Child's Perception of Space*, Norton, New York, 1967.

38. S. Dutta, "Approximate reasoning about time and space in dynamic classification problems," *Ph. D. dissertation*, Dept. of Computer Science, U. C. Berkeley, Berkeley, CA, 1989.

39. D. Dubois and H. Prade, *Possibility Theory: An approach to computerized processing of uncertainty*, Plenum Press, New York, 1988.

40. R. L. Sheng, "A Linguistic Approach to Temporal Information Analysis," *Ph.D. Thesis*, University of California-Berkeley, Computer Science Dept., 1983.

41. S. Baase, *Computer Algorithms: Introduction to Design and Analysis*, Addison-Wesley, Reading, MA, 1978.

42. O. Gunther, "An Expert Data-base System for the Overland Search Problem," *M.S. Report, Dept. of Computer Science, UC Berkeley*, 1985.

43. M. Stonebraker, et. al., "The Design and Implementation of INGRES," *ACM Transactions on Database Systems*, vol. 1, No. 3, pp. 189-222, Sep. 1976.

Vol. 352: J. Díaz, F. Orejas (Eds.), TAPSOFT '89. Volume 2. Proceedings, 1989. X, 389 pages. 1989.

Vol. 353: S. Hölldobler, Foundations of Equational Logic Programming. X, 250 pages. 1989. (Subseries LNAI).

Vol. 354: J.W. de Bakker, W.-P. de Roever, G. Rozenberg (Eds.), Linear Time, Branching Time and Partial Order in Logics and Models for Concurrency. VIII, 713 pages. 1989.

Vol. 355: N. Dershowitz (Ed.), Rewriting Techniques and Applications. Proceedings, 1989. VII, 579 pages. 1989.

Vol. 356: L. Huguet, A. Poli (Eds.), Applied Algebra, Algebraic Algorithms and Error-Correcting Codes. Proceedings, 1987. VI, 417 pages. 1989.

Vol. 357: T. Mora (Ed.), Applied Algebra, Algebraic Algorithms and Error-Correcting Codes. Proceedings, 1988. IX, 481 pages. 1989.

Vol. 358: P. Gianni (Ed.), Symbolic and Algebraic Computation. Proceedings, 1988. XI, 545 pages. 1989.

Vol. 359: D. Gawlick, M. Haynie, A. Reuter (Eds.), High Performance Transaction Systems. Proceedings, 1987. XII, 329 pages. 1989.

Vol. 360: H. Maurer (Ed.), Computer Assisted Learning – ICCAL '89. Proceedings, 1989. VII, 642 pages. 1989.

Vol. 361: S. Abiteboul, P.C. Fischer, H.-J. Schek (Eds.), Nested Relations and Complex Objects in Databases. VI, 323 pages. 1989.

Vol. 362: B. Lisper, Synthesizing Synchronous Systems by Static Scheduling in Space-Time. VI, 263 pages. 1989.

Vol. 363: A.R. Meyer, M.A. Taitslin (Eds.), Logic at Botik '89. Proceedings, 1989. X, 289 pages. 1989.

Vol. 364: J. Demetrovics, B. Thalheim (Eds.), MFDBS 89. Proceedings, 1989. VI, 428 pages. 1989.

Vol. 365: E. Odijk, M. Rem, J.-C. Syre (Eds.), PARLE '89. Parallel Architectures and Languages Europe. Volume I. Proceedings, 1989. XIII, 478 pages. 1989.

Vol. 366: E. Odijk, M. Rem, J.-C. Syre (Eds.), PARLE '89. Parallel Architectures and Languages Europe. Volume II. Proceedings, 1989. XIII, 442 pages. 1989.

Vol. 367: W. Litwin, H.-J. Schek (Eds.), Foundations of Data Organization and Algorithms. Proceedings, 1989. VIII, 531 pages. 1989.

Vol. 368: H. Boral, P. Faudemay (Eds.), IWDM '89, Database Machines. Proceedings, 1989. VI, 387 pages. 1989.

Vol. 369: D. Taubner, Finite Representations of CCS and TCSP Programs by Automata and Petri Nets. X. 168 pages. 1989.

Vol. 370: Ch. Meinel, Modified Branching Programs and Their Computational Power. VI, 132 pages. 1989.

Vol. 371: D. Hammer (Ed.), Compiler Compilers and High Speed Compilation. Proceedings, 1988. VI, 242 pages. 1989.

Vol. 372: G. Ausiello, M. Dezani-Ciancaglini, S. Ronchi Della Rocca (Eds.), Automata, Languages and Programming. Proceedings, 1989. XI, 788 pages. 1989.

Vol. 373: T. Theoharis, Algorithms for Parallel Polygon Rendering. VIII, 147 pages. 1989.

Vol. 374: K.A. Robbins, S. Robbins, The Cray X-MP/Model 24. VI, 165 pages. 1989.

Vol. 375: J.L.A. van de Snepscheut (Ed.), Mathematics of Program Construction. Proceedings, 1989. VI, 421 pages. 1989.

Vol. 376: N.E. Gibbs (Ed.), Software Engineering Education. Proceedings, 1989. VII, 312 pages. 1989.

Vol. 377: M. Gross, D. Perrin (Eds.), Electronic Dictionaries and Automata in Computational Linguistics. Proceedings, 1987. V, 110 pages. 1989.

Vol. 378: J.H. Davenport (Ed.), EUROCAL '87. Proceedings, 1987. VIII, 99 pages. 1989.

Vol. 379: A. Kreczmar, G. Mirkowska (Eds.), Mathematical Foundations of Computer Science 1989. Proceedings, 1989. VIII, 605 pages. 1989.

Vol. 380: J. Csirik, J. Demetrovics, F. Gécseg (Eds.), Fundamentals of Computation Theory. Proceedings, 1989. XI, 493 pages. 1989.

Vol. 381: J. Dassow, J. Kelemen (Eds.), Machines, Languages, and Complexity. Proceedings, 1988. VI, 244 pages. 1989.

Vol. 382: F. Dehne, J.-R. Sack, N. Santoro (Eds.), Algorithms and Data Structures. WADS '89. Proceedings, 1989. IX, 592 pages. 1989.

Vol. 383: K. Furukawa, H. Tanaka, T. Fujisaki (Eds.), Logic Programming '88. Proceedings, 1988. VII, 251 pages. 1989 (Subseries LNAI).

Vol. 384: G.A. van Zee, J.G.G. van de Vorst (Eds.), Parallel Computing 1988. Proceedings, 1988. V, 135 pages. 1989.

Vol. 385: E. Börger, H. Kleine Büning, M.M. Richter (Eds.), CSL '88. Proceedings, 1988. VI, 399 pages. 1989.

Vol. 386: J.E. Pin (Ed.), Formal Properties of Finite Automata and Applications. Proceedings, 1988. VIII, 260 pages. 1989.

Vol. 387: C. Ghezzi, J.A. McDermid (Eds.), ESEC '89. 2nd European Software Engineering Conference. Proceedings, 1989. VI, 496 pages. 1989.

Vol. 388: G. Cohen, J. Wolfmann (Eds.), Coding Theory and Applications. Proceedings, 1988. IX, 329 pages. 1989.

Vol. 389: D.H. Pitt, D.E. Rydeheard, P. Dybjer, A.M. Pitts, A. Poigné (Eds.), Category Theory and Computer Science. Proceedings, 1989. VI, 365 pages. 1989.

Vol. 390: J.P. Martins, E.M. Morgado (Eds.), EPIA 89. Proceedings, 1989. XII, 400 pages. 1989 (Subseries LNAI).

Vol. 391: J.-D. Boissonnat, J.-P. Laumond (Eds.), Geometry and Robotics. Proceedings, 1988. VI, 413 pages. 1989.

Vol. 392: J.-C. Bermond, M. Raynal (Eds.), Distributed Algorithms. Proceedings, 1989. VI, 315 pages. 1989.

Vol. 393: H. Ehrig, H. Herrlich, H.-J. Kreowski, G. Preuß (Eds.), Categorical Methods in Computer Science. VI, 350 pages. 1989.

Vol. 394: M. Wirsing, J.A. Bergstra (Eds.), Algebraic Methods: Theory, Tools and Applications. VI, 558 pages. 1989.

Vol. 395: M. Schmidt-Schauß, Computational Aspects of an Order-Sorted Logic with Term Declarations. VIII, 171 pages. 1989. (Subseries LNAI).

Vol. 396: T.A. Berson, T. Beth (Eds.), Local Area Network Security. Proceedings, 1989. IX, 152 pages. 1989.

Vol. 397: K.P. Jantke (Ed.), Analogical and Inductive Inference. IX, 338 pages. 1989. (Subseries LNAI).

Vol. 398: B. Banieqbal, H. Barringer, A. Pnueli (Eds.), Temporal Logic in Specification. Proceedings, 1987. VI, 448 pages. 1989.

Vol. 399: V. Cantoni, R. Creutzburg, S. Levialdi, G. Wolf (Eds.), Recent Issues in Pattern Analysis and Recognition. VII, 400 pages. 1989.

Vol. 400: R. Klein, Concrete and Abstract Voronoi Diagrams. IV, 167 pages. 1989.

Vol. 401: H. Djidjev (Ed.), Optimal Algorithms. Proceedings, 1989. VI, 308 pages. 1989.

Vol. 402: T.P. Bagchi, V.K. Chaudhri, Interactive Relational Database Design. XI, 186 pages. 1989.

Vol. 403: S. Goldwasser (Ed.), Advances in Cryptology – CRYPTO '88. Proceedings, 1988. XI, 591 pages. 1990.

Vol. 404: J. Beer, Concepts, Design, and Performance Analysis of a Parallel Prolog Machine. VI, 128 pages. 1989.

Vol. 405: C.E. Veni Madhavan (Ed.), Foundations of Software Technology and Theoretical Computer Science. Proceedings, 1989. VIII, 339 pages. 1989.

Vol. 407: J. Sifakis (Ed.), Automatic Verification Methods for Finite State Systems. Proceedings, 1989. VII, 382 pages. 1990.

Vol. 408: M. Leeser, G. Brown (Eds.) Hardware Specification, Verification and Synthesis: Mathematical Aspects. Proceedings, 1989. VI, 402 pages. 1990.

Vol. 409: A. Buchmann, O. Günther, T.R. Smith, Y.-F. Wang (Eds.), Design and Implementation of Large Spatial Databases. Proceedings, 1989. IX, 364 pages. 1990.

This series reports new developments in computer science research and teaching – quickly, informally and at a high level. The type of material considered for publication includes preliminary drafts of original papers and monographs, technical reports of high quality and broad interest, advanced level lectures, reports of meetings, provided they are of exceptional interest and focused on a single topic. The timeliness of a manuscript is more important than its form which may be unfinished or tentative. If possible, a subject index should be included. Publication of Lecture Notes is intended as a service to the international computer science community, in that a commercial publisher, Springer-Verlag, can offer a wide distribution of documents which would otherwise have a restricted readership. Once published and copyrighted, they can be documented in the scientific literature.

Manuscripts

Manuscripts should be no less than 100 and preferably no more than 500 pages in length.
They are reproduced by a photographic process and therefore must be typed with extreme care. Symbols not on the typewriter should be inserted by hand in indelible black ink. Corrections to the typescript should be made by pasting in the new text or painting out errors with white correction fluid. Authors receive 75 free copies and are free to use the material in other publications. The typescript is reduced slightly in size during reproduction; best results will not be obtained unless the text on any one page is kept within the overall limit of 18 x 26.5 cm (7 x 10½ inches). On request, the publisher will supply special paper with the typing area outlined.
Manuscripts should be sent to Prof. G. Goos, GMD Forschungsstelle an der Universität Karlsruhe, Haid- und Neu-Str. 7, 7500 Karlsruhe 1, Germany, Prof. J. Hartmanis, Cornell University, Dept. of Computer Science, Ithaca NY/USA 14850, or directly to Springer-Verlag Heidelberg.

Springer-Verlag, Heidelberger Platz 3, D-1000 Berlin 33
Springer-Verlag, Tiergartenstraße 17, D-6900 Heidelberg 1
Springer-Verlag, 175 Fifth Avenue, New York, NY 10010/USA
Springer-Verlag, 37-3, Hongo 3-chome, Bunkyo-ku, Tokyo 113, Japan

ISBN 3-540-52208-5
ISBN 0-387-52208-5